Notable Scottish Trials

Captain Porteous

NOTABLE
SCOTTISH TRIALS.

Madeleine Smith. Edited by A
Duncan Smith, F S A (Scot.),
Advocate.

City of Glasgow Bank Directors.
Edited by William Wallace,
Sheriff-Substitute, Campbeltown

Dr. Pritchard. Edited by Wm
Roughead, W S, Edinburgh

Eugène Marie Chantrelle. Edited
by A Duncan Smith, F.S A (Scot),
Advocate.

Deacon Brodie. Edited by Wm.
Roughead, W S, Edinburgh

James Stewart (The Appin
Murder). Edited by David N
Mackay, Writer, Glasgow

A. J. Monson. Edited by J W.
More, B A (Oxon.), Advocate

The Douglas Cause. Edited by
A. Francis Steuart, Advocate

Captain Porteous. Edited by Wm
Roughead, W S Edinburgh.

The Porteous Mob.

From the Picture by James Drummond, R.S.A., in the National Gallery of Scotland.

Trial of
Captain Porteous

EDITED BY

William Roughead
Writer to the Signet

GLASGOW AND EDINBURGH

WILLIAM HODGE & COMPANY

PRINTED BY
WILLIAM HODGE AND COMPANY
GLASGOW AND EDINBURGH
1909

P⁻ ̈⸴t

PREFATORY NOTE.

In presenting the following report of the trial of Captain Porteous, the text of which is that of the "Authentic Extract of the Proceedings," printed by order of Parliament on 25th March, 1737, some apology would seem to be due for the modest place occupied in this volume by the actual trial Occasion has, however, been taken to collect all information obtainable regarding the Captain's character and career, the circumstances of the robbery for which Andrew Wilson suffered death, and the fatal and far-reaching events attending his execution; while the amount of unpublished material concerning the riot, which the Editor has been fortunate enough to find, has induced him to deal with that notable affair, and the subsequent proceedings in Parliament, much more fully than he at first intended.

The Editor desires to express his thanks to those who have in various ways facilitated his labours—to Mr. Thomas Hunter, W S , Town-Clerk, for permission to make extracts from the Records of Edinburgh Town Council, and to publish original documents preserved in the City Chambers; to Mr John A Fairley, for the use of valuable unpublished MSS ; to Mr George P. Johnston, Mr. William Cowan, and Mr Henry M Mayhew, for assistance in connection with the Bibliography, and to Miss Margaret Morison, for the care and accuracy of her transcripts made at the British Museum and the Public Record Office He would also acknowledge the courtesy of Mr James L Caw, who has allowed him to reproduce the well-known picture, "The Porteous Mob," by James Drummond, R S A , in the National Gallery of Scotland , and of Mr Charles E Green, who has permitted the reproduction of three plates from the late Mr Grainger Stewart's " Portraits in the Hall of the Parliament House in Edinburgh " (1907)

The Editor would be glad to receive particulars of any publications, other than those included in the Bibliography, relative to the Porteous Riot

Since the Introduction was printed, the Editor has had an

PREFATORY NOTE

opportunity to read a series of articles on the riot, contributed by Mr A. H Millar to *The People's Journal* (11th June to 13th August, 1887), containing excerpts from the papers of Patrick Lindsay, M P., preserved in the charter room at Eaglescairnie, Haddington. The documents quoted by Mr Millar consist of certain letters written by Provost Wilson and others to Mr Lindsay with reference to the scene at Andrew Wilson's execution and the proposed proceedings against Captain Porteous Apart from their intrinsic interest, these add little to our knowledge of the facts. It appears, however, that the Provost was not, as Sheriff, personally desirous to try the Captain; and that, in the opinion of the Lord Advocate, Porteous owed his reprieve to the application of General Wade

W. R

8 OXFORD TERRACE, EDINBURGH,
   November, 1909

CONTENTS

APPENDICES.

LIST OF ILLUSTRATIONS.

CAPTAIN PORTEOUS.

INTRODUCTION.

BETWEEN the eventful years of 1715 and 1745 the affair of the Porteous Mob forms a memorable and striking chapter in the history of Scotland That few incidents of that history are more familiar to modern readers is due to the genius of Sir Walter Scott, who, with an artist's appreciation of its romantic value, has made it tho basis of one of his happiest tales The grim story of popular vengeance, renowned as well for the audacity and skill with which it was conducted as for tho secrecy and success, unparalleled in similar outrages, which attended its execution, has been told once for all with picturesque eloquence in the stirring pages of the *Heart of Midlothian* To the admirable narrative there given it is not proposed, nor is it possible, to add any fresh attraction; albeit the novelist in the exercise of his privilege has elected occasionally to forsake the hard highway of fact for some flowery and fictitious bypath—doubtless to the greater refreshment of his fellow-traveller, which divagations we shall in due course reverently note   Yet avowedly the Porteous affair was to Scott but an episode, though the leading one, in his delightful tale; and there is room for a more particular relation of that strange business and its tragic circumstances than he had need or desire to give.

In the accounts of the Riot by the general historians of Scotland the space allotted to that incident is relatively small, and many remarkable details are of necessity omitted The interest and importance of the matter, however, warrant its treatment upon a larger scale   Mr Hume Brown describes it as "one of the most dramatic incidents in the national history," and remarks, "Though the immediate occasion of this extraordinary manifestation was local and temporary, its causes and results were national and permanent"[1]   Mr Hill Burton

---

[1] *History of Scotland,* III 218

Captain Porteous.

observes, " Acting on none of the minor motives which influence violent mobs, but following the dictates of a sort of political fanaticism, the rioters supported each other with all the firmness and faith of State conspirators; and they were successful in leaving to posterity one of the most profound mysteries which history carries in its bosom '[2] It is improbable that the veil which shrouded that mystery from the penetration of the acutest legal intellects of the day, backed by the resources of a powerful Government, and has baffled the efforts of subsequent inquirers, will ever be raised by modern research But, in the words of Sir Thomas Browne, " What song the Syrens sang, or what name Achilles assumed when he hid himself among women, though puzzling questions, are not beyond all conjecture ", and it has been the Editor's aim to collect from original and authentic sources such material as is now available for the elucidation of the subject It is hoped that the hitherto unpublished documents and other contemporary records not easily accessible, which are printed in the Appendix to the present volume, may prove an interesting contribution to the history of a notable and obscure occurrence

Among the former may be mentioned the Examinations of the witnesses in the Parliamentary inquiry, a Brief Account of the riotous proceedings at Edinburgh, and an Account of previous mobs in that city, from the Newcastle Papers, the Lord Justice-Clerk's letter to Patrick Lindsay, written on the night of the riot, that of General Wade to General Moyle, conveying the orders upon which the latter acted, and other letters of the Justice-Clerk and the Lord Provost of Edinburgh, from the Hardwicke MSS ; a series of important letters, &c, by the Lord Justice-Clerk, the Earl of Ilay, the Lord Advocate (Duncan Forbes of Culloden), the Solicitor-General (Erskine of Tinwald), General Wade, General Moyle, and Lord Provost Wilson, together with the public petition for Porteous's reprieve, from the Scottish State Papers in the Public Record Office, a contemporary account of the murder of Porteous contained in an original letter in the possession of John A Fairley, Esq., also extracts from the Records of Edinburgh Town Council and original documents preserved in the City Chambers, relative to the affair of Captain Porteous and the mob

---

2 *Lives of Forbes and Lovat*, 1847, p 350

Jock Porteous of the Guard.

(1) JOCK PORTEOUS OF THE GUARD.

And thou, great god of *aqua vitæ*,
Wha sways the empire of this city—
When fou we're sometimes capernoity—
Be thou prepar d
To hedge us frae that black banditti,
The City Guard

The Daft Days —Robert Fergusson

Of the career of John Porteous, "a name memorable in the traditions of Edinburgh, as well as in the records of criminal jurisprudence," before the fatal day when he steps into the limelight of the historic stage at the execution of Andrew Wilson, we have but one account, and that so violently partial as to defeat its own design The anonymous author of a curious pamphlet, entitled *The Life and Death of Captain John Porteous, &c* (1737). collected and published, after the murder. the current gossip regarding the character of his unfortunate hero, which he sets forth with a malignant gusto by no means rare in that age of spiteful satire And, indeed, so bitter was then the local feeling and so sore the subject, that any contemporary portrait of Porteous would surely be limned in the blackest colours at the painter's disposal Be that as it may, the statements therein made remained uncontradicted by the friends of the victim of this virulent biography, and that he did not lack such, and those influential, will be manifest in the sequel

Our author, having disclaimed any desire "to disturb the ashes of the dead and to follow him into the other world with insults," prefixes to his narrative certain moral observations, of which the following may serve as a sample —"If the writer of this can represent the Captain as he lived, and make the dead useful to the living in pointing out the life of the man, and in giving by that a seasonable and instructive warning to his readers to shun those rocks upon which he split, he persuades himself he has done him and the world good service. Nothing indeed is more certain than that if the reader can be convinced to shun his vices and to draw insensibly into his mind the practice of the opposite virtues till they turn into habits, he shall live with more satisfaction to himself, and have a fairer character than he could have had without them, and, which is of greater consequence to him, he shall not draw down the vengeance of Heaven upon himself, which such crimes as the Captain's seldom escape We are not to dive into the

3

Captain Porteous.

depths of God's Providence, but there seemed such a concatenation of circumstances in his case that it look'd very like the anger of the Almighty "

John Porteous was the son of one Stephen Porteous, a tailor in the Canongate of Edinburgh, who had, according to this prejudiced authority, " a fair character in his employment, and was esteemed a good honest man in the whole conduct of his life, his greatest misfortune was to have such a son as John was " That he was a burgess and guild-brother of his native burgh appears from the following entry in the burgess roll kept at the Edinburgh City Chambers —" 20th March, 1695 The which day, in presence of Hugh Blair, Dean of Gild and the Gild Council, Stephan Porteous, taillior, Compeirand is made burges and gild brother of this burgh, and gave his oath, &c. And payed p Act of the 13 March instant, in satisfaction of the dues LXlib.' The following is the Act of the Town Council referred to ·—" Edinr , 13th March, 1695. The same day the Counsell appoynts the Dean of Gild and his Counsell to admit and receeve Steven Porteous, taylor in the Cannongaithead, to be burges and gild brother of this burgh for payment of sexty pounds Scots in satisfaction of the dues Whereanent thir presents shall be a wairand And the Counsell declares the same shall be no preparative in tyme coming " No mention is made by the author of the pamphlet of any other children of Stephen Porteous, but we shall afterwards find that John Porteous had at least one brother, who is probably the " Stephan Porteous, Weigmaker," entered as a burgess on 2nd August, 1721

His biographer detects in John from the cradle " a perverseness of nature, and a proneness to commit mischievous, and more than childish, tricks " His mother is said to have hailed his infant peccadilloes as proofs of incipient genius—a not unusual failing For the rest, the story is the common one of a spoiled child and an injudicious father, from whom boyish offences were foolishly concealed by a doting mother The poor woman early appears to have reaped as she had sown, for when, *apropos* of her son's misdoings, she predicted that he would live to be hanged, he returned the unfilial answer, " The devil a one was to blame for it, if it should be so, but the bitch that bare him ' This maternal prophecy is the first of those portents which, according to the writer, attended his hero's darkling path

4

Jock Porteous of the Guard.

Stephen Porteous brought up the lad to his own trade of a tailor, "because it was easiest and cheapest for the father, and sure and good bread for the son", but the latter's vicious propensities increasing, it became apparent that he was unfitted to follow so virtuous a calling His father's belated efforts to correct his wayward offspring met with small success John "advanced from reproaches and curses to blows, and laying violent hands on the parent whenever the misfortunate man would not concur with the folly and madness of the rake" At length the old man, unable to make anything of so unsatisfactory a son, "sent him away to the army, as a recruit in Queen Anne's time, under the command of Brigadier Newton," for the curious reason that thus "his cruelty might be lawfully vented without hazard of the gallows" This was the corps known as the Scots Dutch, long maintained in the service of the States of Holland Our author, who appears to have cherished no illusions on the subject of a military career, significantly adds, ' After he had been some time in the army, he improved in all the arts of mischief and wickedness, of which he showed himself afterwards a great master"

While serving with his regiment in Flanders John Porteous is said to have wantonly shot a hen, the only feat of arms recorded by his biographer When the old woman to whom the bird belonged demanded the price of the slain, "he threatened, if she insisted, to send her after her hen" Whereupon the old lady, incongruously pursuing him with "a whole volley of sincere prayers and curses," expressed her confidence ' that as many might gaze and wonder on him as that hen had feathers on her body" The narrator notes with satisfaction that "Heaven, in its own time, thought fit to answer the voice of the complainer" A similar anecdote is related by Wodrow of Andrew Cant, when preaching at the market-cross of Aberdeen, the ill-omened biped being in his case a dead crow, thrown by an unregenerate boy with consequences equally fatal [3]

The biographer, warming to his work, now flies at higher game than fowls He states that Porteous, while serving in this corps, "was shrewdly suspected, though it was never proven, of having murdered his captain," the alleged motives being robbery and revenge for a beating given him by that officer "It stuck in his stomach, and he vow'd revenge in his

---

[3] *Analecta*, ii 155

Captain Porteous.

heart " The captain, "fast asleep after a bottle," was found in bed with his throat cut. The sole ground of suspicion against Porteous would seem to be his leaving the regiment after the murder, but he had previously mentioned to his comrades his intention of quitting the service, and he appears to have been on excellent terms with his alleged victim 'All this," our historian reluctantly allows, "when examined into, made it so doubtful that it passed at last that the captain had murdered himself, the instrument of the murderer being left in the bed." Campbell, however, writing in 1745,[4] states that Porteous "served some time in Flanders in the last war, and returned to his own country upon the Peace of Utrecht, or shortly after"; while, according to Dr Carlyle, he obtained a subaltern's commission and retired on half-pay [5]

We next hear of John Porteous in London, where, being "hard pinch'd," he followed the trade of his origin, and "wrought as a journeyman-taylor," seemingly without much success, for his biographer gives a list of other occupations, none of them very reputable, whereby he attempted to make a living "He put on, at this time, many shapes, sometimes he appeared in fine clothes, and at other times he was all in rags He was, in one revolution of a moon, a taylor, a bully in a bawdy-house, a street-walker, a gentleman, and a beggar " In one of these divers capacities he was recognised by a man named Baily, a coachman from his native Canongate, through whose good offices he was eventually induced to return to Edinburgh, after an interlude of some months, during which he disappeared with ten pounds sent by his father to bring him home and thirty shillings borrowed from the philanthropic Jehu. On his return the old gentleman "broke out into tears of joy," and, with singular imprudence, evinced his delight at the prodigal's recovery by making over to him his house and business, reserving only one room in the former for his own use This generosity would seem to have been but ill-requited, for it is recorded that John soon began to maltreat his father as of old "first by denying the old man a fire in his room, in the time of frost and snow of the winter, and grudging him even the use of the kitchen fire He added to this a scrimp diet, till the old man was like to be starved with hunger and cold ' The climate of Edinburgh would afford a further aggravation of this cruel treatment

---

4 *Life of Argyll,* p 507   5 *Autobiography,* p 35
5

Jock Porteous of the Guard.

Finally, Stephen Porteous found a refuge from his son's brutality in Trinity Hospital, a charitable institution of greater gentility than the workhouse for the relief of indigent persons, where he may have deduced a belated lesson from the study of *King Lear*

John Porteous had barely time to appreciate this improvement in his temporal concerns when the Jacobite Rising of 1715 took place in the Highlands. The threatened invasion of the Lothians by the Earl of Mar's army created much alarm in Edinburgh, and the authorities trembled for the safety of the capital. The Lord Provost, John Campbell, a capable and energetic official, at once took what steps he could for the protection of the town. The number of the City Guard was increased, and the train-bands and volunteers were provided with arms. The lack of discipline and military training displayed by these new levies necessitated the employment of a drill-master, and John Porteous, on the strength of his Flanders experiences, was selected for the post. He appears to have been thoroughly competent and to have performed his duties to the entire satisfaction of the magistrates—even his biographer allows " he executed his part very well in this office " On the 14th of October Provost Campbell learned that the Highland troops had crossed the Firth of Forth in open boats and concentrated at Haddington With characteristic promptitude he sent a messenger post-haste to the Duke of Argyll, who was in command of the Government forces then guarding the Highland line at Stirling The noble general was equal to the emergency. With three hundred dragoons and two hundred infantry mounted on country horses he galloped to the relief of the capital At ten o'clock that night the Highlanders had advanced as far as Jock's Lodge, within a mile of the Nether Bow Port, the eastern gate of Edinburgh At the same hour Argyll's reinforcements dashed through the West Port, and the city was saved [6]

From this point we are able to supplement our anonymous authority by the original records of Edinburgh Town Council, the following extracts from which are published for the first time [7] The earliest reference is that contained in a minute of date 9th November, 1715, whereby the Council

---

[6] Rae's *History of the Rebellion*, p 261

[7] For other original documents relating to Porteous's connection with the Town Council, see Appendix I

Captain Porteous.

nominated "John Porteous, younger, taylor in Cannongate-head, to be adjutant to the good toun's train-bands during the Council's pleasure." His remuneration was fixed at twenty pounds per annum, under declaration "that what extraordinar trouble he shall be at, they will take the same to their consideration and gratify him accordingly." He continued in office for nearly a year, until, on 7th September, 1716, the Council declared his appointment void and null, but gave no reason for his dismissal. On 28th November, however, "for severall great and weighty considerations them moveing," the Council reinstated him with the usual salary, and also "allowed him to do dutie for any of the officers of the City Guard when valetudinar and absent, the said officer always satisfying him for his said service." It is probable that his dismissal was due to some exhibition of the irascible temper which later led to a similar result, when on apologising he was invested anew. On 9th April, 1718, the Council, "having sufficient knowledge of the fitness and qualifications of John Porteous," appointed him ensign of the City Guard, with "the whole pay and casualties belonging to the said office," on condition of his continuing to discharge gratuitously the duty of adjutant to the train-bands.

On 29th November, 1720, the Town Council passed the following Act.—"The which day the magistrates, taking into consideration the several complaints laid before them by the neighbourhood against the soldiers of the City Guard for their immoral practices of horrid cursing and swearing, thereby profaning the sacred name of God, contrary to His holy laws and precepts, hurtful to their own souls, and offensive to every well-disposed person that hears them, therefore and for remead thereof, we do hereby statute and ordain that the several officers of the said company shall take a close inspection of all under their command, that when they either hear, or it being made appear to them, that any of those aforesaid are guilty of these crimes laid to their charge, that for each oath they stop one penny sterling out of their pay, and put it into the poors' box in the said Guard; certifying such as are oftener than thrice guilty, and so found irreclaimable by this method, that they will be turned out of the city service. We likewise recommend to the officers to give a good example to all inferiors, and that the soldiers may not pretend to be ignorant hereof, we order this Act to be read at the head of the company and afterwards

Jock Porteous of the Guard.

affixed in the Guard-Hall, and also appoint thir presents to be printed, and an printed copy thereof to be delivered to every centinel."[8] It is to be feared that the new officer was little likely to improve his men's manners in this respect, for it is recorded by his biographer that "he was most unaccountable in his expressions "

Porteous's connection with the town's affairs brought him much in contact with Provost Campbell, and, according to his biographer, "this gave him access to make love to a gentlewoman, who had the care of the Lord Provost's house and family, he succeeded in his addresses, and they married " This lady was Isobel Gordon, of whom we shall have more to say hereafter A vacancy occurring at this time in the command of the City Guard, Porteous, by the Provost's influence, was, on 21st January, 1726, elected one of the three captain-lieutenants, the pay being at the rate of four shillings per diem.   Provost Campbell is said by the same authority to have acted in the matter "from a grateful return to the gentlewoman for her care and good management of his family, and from a conviction of Porteous's sufficiency for that office, with a view to make the married couple live the more comfortably together " A different version of the Captain's wooing, however, is given by the compiler of the *Newgate Calendar*,[9] which shows the parties to the transaction in a less agreeable light.   It is there stated that "the Lord Provost of Edinburgh kept a mistress, who was above forty years of age, and whom he was willing to part with, so as he could do it in a genteel manner, that is, by giving her a sum of money, and getting one who was in want of it to take her off his hands.   Porteous, although a very accomplished man, yet was exceeding poor, and therefore the gentleman, who had known him some time, thought he could not embrace a better opportunity of disposing of his kept mistress than by making her his wife   When the proposal was first made to the woman she rejected it with disdain, because Mr Porteous was no more than a journeyman tailor ; but her master having assured her that he would make some provision for her, besides a fortune of five hundred pounds, she readily agreed, and they were married."   It is added that, owing to the solicitation of the lady, the Provost promoted Porteous to his captaincy

---

8 From a broadsheet in the Editor's possession
9 London, 1773, iii 22

Captain Porteous.

"contrary to the opinions of the other magistrates, so that he was provided for in a most genteel manner, while those who had a better right to such a favour were left to starve Many of the citizens complained of such partiality, and it was not long before they found that they had good reason to do so While Porteous was a humble tradesman he was esteemed by all who knew him for his politeness and something agreeable in the whole of his behaviour ; but no sooner was he advanced to honour and entrusted with power than the innate character of the man began to display itself in some very striking instances "

Prior to Porteous's appointment little notice occurs of the City Guard in the local history or traditions of the times , and it is probable that much of the odium which subsequently attached to that corps arose from the association with it of its unpopular Captain   The name of one previous commander, however, is inscribed in lurid characters upon the town's records   In the years 1649-50 a certain Thomas Weir " had the great trust of the Guards of the City of Edinburgh committed unto him under the quality of major, and from that time to the day of his infamous death was always called by the name of *Major Weir* " [10] According to a contemporary account, " his garb was still a cloak, and somewhat dark, and he never went without his staff   He was a tall, black man, and ordinarily looked down to the ground , a grim countenance, and a big nose "   This sinister figure presided over a company of the elect, self-styled the " Bow-Head Saints," and, owing to his superior sanctity and eloquent gift of prayer, rejoiced in the soubriquet of " Angelical Thomas "   " He had acquired a particular gracefulness in whining and sighing above any of the sacred clan, and had learned to deliver himself upon all serious occasions in a far more ravishing accent than any of their ministers could attain unto "   In his official capacity this amiable Presbyterian devoted his energies to the persecution of the Royalists, whom it was his peculiar pleasure to hunt down and bring to the scaffold " This cruel manner after which he used to outrage the poor Royalists passed among the people for extraordinary zeal, and made them consider him as a singular worthy whom God had raised up to support the *cause* "   A " singular worthy "

---

[10] *Satan's Invisible World Discovered*, 1871, Supplement, 1

10

The City Guard.

From a contemporary Print.

Jock Porteous of the Guard.

the major undoubtedly was, for in secret he was on intimate terms with the Prince of Darkness, to whom he was reported to have sold himself, his familiar being a black staff of diabolic properties, without which he was never seen, while the recreations of his private hours will not now bear repetition   He was finally unmasked through the disinterested zeal of a rival preacher, and, having been found guilty of the most atrocious crimes, "that dishonour of mankind" was burned at the Gallow Lee, between Edinburgh and Leith, on 11th April, 1670, his sister—his accomplice or dupe—being hanged the following day   The major was a notable wizard, and for upwards of a century after the world was well rid of his unholy presence memories of the fiery chariot with its six black steeds, used by him upon his Master's errands, haunted the "sanctified bends of the Bow."   "No story of witchcraft and necromancy ever left so general and deep-rooted an impression on the popular mind as that of Major Weir, nor was any spot ever more celebrated in the annals of sorcery than the little court at the head of the Bow, where the wizard and his sister dwelt."[11]

The nucleus of the City Guard of Edinburgh was formed in the year 1513 for the defence of the capital after the national disaster sustained on the fatal field of Flodden, at the time when the second wall was built to protect Edinburgh against "our auld inymis of Ingland", and it was finally established in 1690   The citizens, though by no means attached to this venerable body, had a profound belief in its antiquity, and an ancient legend relates that some of the City Guard were present in Jerusalem at the Crucifixion, and carried off on that occasion from the Temple an original portrait of King Solomon, which used to be shown in support of the tradition [12]   While varying in strength from time to time as occasion required, the corps consisted, in Porteous's day, of about one hundred men, divided into three companies, each commanded by a captain-lieutenant.   Their uniform was a military coat and cocked-hat, and they were armed with firelocks and Lochaber axes—the latter, as defined by Jamieson, being "a sort of halbert of a large size, having a strong hook behind for laying hold of the subject assaulted "

11 Wilson's *Memorials of Edinburgh*, 1848, ii 115
12 *Ibid* i 35.

Captain Porteous.

The service of these civic warriors was limited to the guardianship of the city and the preservation of public order; and, in general, they performed the duties of a body of armed police. Their headquarters were in the City Guard-house, described by Fergusson as a "lumbersome an' stinkin' biggin," a long, low building situated in the middle of the High Street to the west of the Tron Church, till its removal in 1785. While Edinburgh maintained the character of a walled city, certain of the Guard were nightly placed as sentinels at the various ports or gates. Only a small portion of the three companies was regularly on duty, the remainder being allowed to work at their trades till their services were required. The corps was recruited mainly by discharged soldiers from the Highland regiments, and the officers were usually old military men who had sufficient interest with the Town Council to procure their appointment. Some of these combined their warlike duties with more peaceable pursuits; for, when Captain Lind, of the City Guard, was asked in the House of Lords' inquiry, "Whether you and the men of the like rank are of such as live upon the profession of arms in general, or whether, when you are not upon guard, you have any other profession?" he replied, "Sometimes we do; one of the gentlemen has a shop in the town." The Lord Provost for the time being was *ex officio* captain of the City Guard, and no drum but theirs might lawfully be sounded in the High Street between the Luckenbooths and the Nether Bow.

In the command of this ancient and redoubtable band Captain Porteous is said by his biographer to have behaved with unnecessary harshness and cruelty, and to have abused his authority in every conceivable manner. His new position afforded him "great opportunities to lay open and display his nature, and to give full vent to all his ungovernable passions; seldom a day past but some one or other of his squad felt the weight of his stick. He is sadly belied if some of the soldiers went not into the other world by his means." Indeed, the author condescends upon a particular case when the Captain, enraged at one of his sergeants addressing him while covered, gave the man "two severe pushes in the breast," which caused his death. "The public either knew not the facts or winked at them upon the account of discipline." He is said to have regarded the common people with personal animosity, "the mob, on all public occasions, enlarged the sphere of his natural

12

Jock Porteous of the Guard.

temper   You would have seen a plentiful crop of kicks, cuffs,
blows, and strokes, to be reaped from his feet, fists, and cane "
In contrast to all this is the statement later made in his behalf
at his trial—"That as he has been employed for these many
years past as the scourge of the mob, though never once known
to proceed to extremities; yet such station of his may be the
cause of drawing resentment from the lower sort of the people
against him "   That he could ever have been a *persona grata*
to the rabble is obviously impossible, as it was his chief duty
to maintain order and restrain their excesses on occasions of
popular demonstration   The mob of Edinburgh was notoriously
masterful and hard to handle,[13] an annual instance being
the local celebration of the King's Birthday, immor-
talised by Fergusson in his poem of that title, which
presented a time-honoured opportunity for mutual
reprisals between the populace and the Guard   and
the official who firmly quelled the unruly crowd could hardly
be a general favourite   The performance by John Porteous
of his arduous and unpopular functions to the full satisfaction
of his employers, the Town Council, tends to show that he
was at least a trustworthy and efficient officer, and later he
truthfully described himself as one " in whom, he must take
the liberty to say, confidence was generally put upon those
difficult occasions "   The feud between the Guard and the
mob of Edinburgh subsisted both before and after Porteous's
time, and Fergusson, writing a generation later, so often voiced
the common feeling against them that, as Scott says, he may
be termed their poet laureate

The narrator, no less severe upon Porteous in his private
capacity as husband and citizen, accuses him of all kinds of
barbarities practised upon his unhappy helpmate   " The
gentlewoman was a person of virtue and merit, and still has
a good character, whose nature was always as far removed
from the light and wanton as it is from the surly and morose,
earning her bread now partly by the diligent and honest
product of the work of her hands, and belov'd by all who
converse with her, only unlucky in marrying John Porteous,
who was no better husband than he had been a son." Towards
this exemplary female Porteous is said to have behaved with
great cruelty, so much so that his wife, in her turn, predicted

---

13 Appendix VIII

Captain Porteous.

that he would yet be hanged "The whole neighbourhood was frequently alarmed, in the middle of the night, with her shrieks and hideous cries to such a degree that a lady living above them was obliged, in the middle of a term, to take lodgings elsewhere for her own quiet He did things to her which I am ashamed to write and you would blush to read" The lady neighbour was not, as would appear from the context, the subject of these blushful acts The reason alleged by his biographer for this maltreatment was the wife's not unreasonable objection to the husband's attentions to her maid In the end the spouses separated, and Porteous was free to follow his own devices The same authority further charges the Captain with indiscriminate infidelities, and states that he levied blackmail upon the practitioners of vice within the burgh

"He was most unaccountable in his expressions. He used often to say among his comrades *That if his wife was in heaven he would hate to go thither* Playing at goff once, and beat, *He was sure,* he said, *there was no justice in heaven* At another time, being engaged at whisk, and sent for by some of his comrades, he returned for answer, *That if God Almighty would send for him he would not then go.* These expressions are no better proofs of his religion than the treatment of his wife is of his good nature" The golfing example is perhaps not so unaccountable as the narrator believed, and might find a parallel in modern experience The reference reminds us that Captain Porteous was in his day a notable exponent of the royal and ancient game, then generally enjoyed by its devotees in the capital upon the historic Links of Leith Thomas Mathieson, the old Edinburgh writer, in his poem, *The Goff* (1743), thus commemorates this classic ground—

> North from Edina, eight furlongs and more,
> Lies the famed field on Fortha's sounding shore,
> Here Caledonian chiefs for health resort—
> Confirm their sinews by the manly sport

Dr Carlyle records that Porteous, "by his skill in manly exercises, particularly the golf, and by gentlemanly behaviour, was admitted into the company of his superiors, which elated his mind and added insolence to his native roughness, so that he was much hated and feared by the mob of Edinburgh "[14] As an example of this "high company," we read in the

---

[14] *Autobiography,* p 35

Jock Porteous of the Guard.

Caledonian Mercury, under date 6th April, 1724, "On Saturday last there was a solemn match at golf in the Links of Leith for twenty guineas, betwixt Mr Alexander Elphinston, son to the Lord Balmerinoch, and Captain Porteous of the Town Guard; when Mr Elphinston won. His Grace the Duke of Hamilton, the Earl of Morton, and a great many persons of distinction were present, besides a very great mob" Possibly it was on this occasion that the Captain was led to doubt the justice of Heaven. The winner of this important match was the Honourable Alexander Elphinston, then leading a life of pleasure at the family mansion in Coatfield Lane, Leith, a son of that Lord Balmerinoch who was tried for political libel upon the Government of Charles the First in 1634 It is curious to note that this young man's next recorded appearance on Leith Links was in more serious circumstances, when, on 23rd December, 1729, he mortally wounded Lieutenant Swift of Cadogan's Regiment in a duel with swords Elphinston was indicted for this offence; but the case was never brought to trial, and he died in Leith unmolested some three years later [15]

It would thus appear that the Captain's prowess in the national sport enabled him to mix in society much above his position, and this privilege may have aggravated his intolerance of "the rascal multitude" "Jock" Porteous, as he was familiarly called by friend and foe alike, became somewhat of a personage in his bourgeois circle, and the sense of his own importance increased the arrogancy of an overbearing spirit On one occasion, however, we have a glimpse of him meeting his match. At this period that peculiar institution known as the "Scottish Sabbath" was in its highest state of development "The Sunday acquired in Scotland a sanctity which far exceeded that of the Sabbath of the Jews in their most Pharisaical days   .   To attend church was no question of choice, it was a matter of compulsion During services elders went out to 'perlustrate' the streets, to enter change-houses, to look into windows and doors of private dwellings, and to bring deserters to kirk, or report them to the kirk session "[16] It is interesting to note that in those not

---

[15] Chambers's *Domestic Annals of Scotland*, iii pp 566-7
[16] Graham's *Social Life of Scotland in the Eighteenth Century*, 1906, p 315

.

15

Captain Porteous.

otherwise palmy days the ale-houses were open on Sundays to worshippers "between sermons," a merciful exception in view of the length and character of the discourses   One William Braidwood, candlemaker at the head of the West Bow and an eminent Presbyterian of the stricter sort, was, by reason of his physical strength, charged by the kirk with the pleasing duty of conservator of public morals   When on his rounds one Sunday morning to secure the perfect observance of the Lord's Day, as he passed a tavern in James's Court he was shocked to hear jovial and unsabbatarian sounds issuing therefrom   He at once entered and took the landlord severely to task for permitting such scandalous behaviour, but the host, with bated breath, explained that he dared not challenge his customers, as one of them was Captain Porteous of the Guard   Mr Braidwood was no respecter of persons; " armed with a small sword which he usually carried, he rushed into the apartment, denounced the conduct of Porteous to his face, and, seizing the cards with which the party was engaged, threw them into the fire, while the Captain and his associates—astonished and over-awed—retreated with precipitation "[17] On this occasion, at least, Jock Porteous was compelled to forego his " whisk," and that, too, at the bidding of a mere mortal

On 20th November, 1730, the Town Council appointed Captain Porteous to the post of " provisor of coal and candle necessary to the Guard," at an annual stipend of twenty-five pounds.   No doubt there were perquisites incidental to the office.   Notwithstanding his aristocratic acquaintances, the gallant officer's right hand was not allowed to forget its old-time cunning, for we find, on the 25th of the same month the Council directing payment to be made to him of " the sum of nynty three pounds Scots for turning the soldiers' coats in October last "   It does not, however, follow that he personally did the work, as the money may have been paid to him to cover the cost of the repairs

The account of Captain Porteous in the *Newgate Calendar* (1773), before referred to, gives him a very bad character, and, in general, reiterates the charges brought against him by his biographer   The following instance of his alleged brutality, however, must have been obtained from another source —" There happened to be a vacancy in the lectureship

---

[17] *Kay's Portraits*, ii 122-3

Jock Porteous of the Guard.

of a church near Edinburgh, and two young gentlemen were
candidates, who had each an equal number of votes, so that
the dispute was obliged to be referred to the Presbytery The
Presbytery declared the lectureship in favour of Mr Dawson,
but Mr Wotherspoon, the other candidate, brought his appeal
to the Synod, and the order of the Presbytery was reversed.
This greatly exasperated the parishioners, and, as a tumult
was apprehended, Captain Porteous was sent to the church to
keep the peace on the day that Mr Wotherspoon was to preach
his first sermon   When he came there he found that Mr
Dawson had got into the pulpit · and, without the least
ceremony or giving him any notice, he went up the steps, and,
laying hold of him by the collar, dragged him down as if he
had been a thief   Dawson received so many wounds and
bruises that he died within a few weeks after, nor was the
fate of Mr Wotherspoon much better.   While Porteous was
using Dawson in the manner already mentioned, Wotherspoon
came in, and those who had voted against him were so enraged
that they beat him in so terrible a manner that he died a few
weeks after, much about the same time as Mr Dawson   Both
the young gentlemen were much esteemed by all who knew
them, and had Porteous acted with moderation the affair might
have been easily accommodated , but, instead of that, he
ordered his men to knock down all who came in their way,
whether men, women, or children, so that many of them were
dangerously wounded ; and he was never called to any
account " No authority is cited for this sensational statement,
which appears to be a distorted version of an actual occurrence
on 12th March, 1732, in connection with the settlement of the
Rev Patrick Wedderspoon as one of the ministers of the West
Kirk, when the City Guard fired among the people and severely
wounded several persons.   Mr. Wedderspoon died on 12th May
following, his end hastened by the injurious treatment he had
received, but Mr. Dawson survived to become a minister of
St Cuthbert's till his death in 1735 [18]

That the Captain's choleric temper brought him into conflict
with his fellow-officers of the Guard appears from a Council
minute of 23rd July, 1735   Porteous had been for long on
bad terms with his colleague, Captain John Fergusson, and this
quarrel was considered by the authorities as subversive of the

[18] *History of the West Kirk*, 1829, pp 105-109, *Fasti Ecclesia
Scoticanæ*, i 121 ; Information for Captain Porteous

Captain Porteous.

discipline and good order of the corps   The matter was brought to a head when, on 17th July, the two officers actually came to blows within the sacred precincts of the Burgh Room and in the very presence of the Town Council, "whereby they were guilty of an atrocious riot and heinous contempt of the magistrates " Both offenders were immediately ordered under arrest at their own houses, when Captain Porteous further aggravated his offence by breaking the said arrest, notwithstanding there was a sentry placed upon him by order of the magistrates " Accordingly, both combatants were dismissed from their command   On 6th August, however, upon their petitioning the Council to be reinstated on the ground "that these differences are most amicably removed and a good understanding betwixt us," they were "reponed into their offices," after being solemnly warned by the Lord Provost not to offend in like manner again.   This incident tends to show that, in spite of the Captain's fiery disposition, his services were such as to induce the magistrates to overlook so grave a breach of decorum   This is the last glimpse which the Council records afford of John Porteous prior to his dismissal, eight months later, from the office he had held for ten years, following upon the disastrous part played by his Guard at the execution of Wilson

We may close our account of Captain Porteous's career up to this point with his biographer's abstract of the physical and moral attributes of his hero—" He was of a middle size, broadshouldered, strong-limbed, short-necked, his face a little pitted with smallpox, and round , his looks mild and gentle, his features having nothing of the fierce or brutal; his eyes languid, not quick and sprightly, and his complexion upon the brown   His outward appearance answered not his inside   He was insolent to his inferiors, easy and agreeable with his equals, humble and submissive to his superiors , he was cunning, and a great master of the arts of insinuating and gaining upon the young and unwary, and even upon those of better judgment and greater experience   When he had some design on foot, he would then display his wit, and play off the agreeable in conversation.   He was quick in discerning his man and his foible, and knew very well what would take with him and his company   He could cover, upon occasions, an unsupportable pride, a readiness to fly into anger like a sudden fit of madness, with a seeming modesty and command of his

18

Jock Porteous of the Guard.

passions, but when he let himself loose, and threw off the mask, one would have thought he was animated with an infernal demon. Religion and the virtues were as much strangers to his mind as the contempt of it and the opposite vices were familiar. Pride, the passion of anger, cruelty and revenge seemed to have the ascendant over the other vices of his mind. He loved truth so little that he could muster up as many falsehoods to worry and destroy it as he commanded soldiers in his Guard, when it made for his purpose. His courage was often called in question, though his profession was ridiculous without it.

"He was no hypocrite. except on some occasions, he was generally at as much pains among his comrades to lay open his vices as another is to conceal them. He not only was vicious himself, but liked to make others so, since he could not have their friendship by true merit, he endeavoured to have it by that false one of pimping, the innocent as well as the guilty [A cryptic statement.] It was a pleasure to him to observe grudges among people, and, by secret whispers and false suggestions, he was sure to keep them on foot till their hatred was inflamed or they were together by the ears, unless there was some particular friendship he either aimed at keeping up or procuring. In short, he was no better a member of society than he was a dutiful son, a loving husband, and a good officer, without one good quality to balance his many bad ones."

A black enough indictment this, indeed, but one suspects the virtuous author of some "worrying of truth" on his own account. An unpublished letter of much interest and value, in the possession of Mr John A. Fairley, the well-known collector, gives a vivid description, to which we shall later refer, of the slaying of Captain Porteous. The writer, who was probably an officer attached to one of the regiments then quartered in the city, describes the murder of "poor (I say, and most people now say, innocent) Porteous," and alludes to the hatred of him displayed by the Edinburgh rabble, "whose resentments," he writes, "had always run high against him for having, you know, been their standing terror by reason of his courage, strength, and vigilance, which he really possessed in a very eminent degree, though but a mean man."[19] This independent testimony is in striking

---

[19] Appendix IV

Captain Porteous.

contrast to that borne by his biographer The fact, also, that Captain Porteous was employed by the Town Council in divers responsible posts for upwards of twenty-one years, and that their minutes testify to his fitness and qualifications for the various offices he so held, is incompatible with many of the charges brought against him And when, at a later stage, he lay under sentence of death we shall find that over seventy noblemen and gentlemen of Scotland signed the petition for his reprieve That they did so in behalf of a notorious miscreant is hard to believe, and one would fain hope that such a good golfer was not so great a rogue

Through the mists of prejudice which obscure his memory, we may still form some image of the man, and his part in the crowded life of the old city We see his strong, thick-set figure most clearly on duty with his Guard, objects of hatred and derision to the wild mob on the King's birthday,

> By hostile rabble seldom spar'd
> Of clarty unctions,

and vigorously retaliating with firelock and Lochaber-axe, productive of many 'crackit crowns and broken brows" to the obstreperous lieges And again, at the head of his "black squad' and 'canker'd pack," coping with the time-honoured revelries of Hallow Fair or the "daft and gleesome bands" at the races upon the sands of Leith, when

> baxter lads hae seal d a vow
> To skelp and clout the guard,

and those veterans

> .   dearly pay the kane,
> An' get their tails weel sautit
> And sair thin days

Few figures would be more familiar to his fellow-citizens than that of Jock Porteous of the Guard, gossiping with his cronies at the Cross in the open-air club of Auld Reekie, exchanging news and snuff-boxes, and, when the "gill-bells" pealed from St Giles' steeple, adjourning to John's Coffee-house for the invariable "meridian", or swinging his cane as he swaggered down the High Street to the Guard-house, with a keen eye for a comely face in piquant plaid or swaying sedan, proudly indifferent to the menaces of the herd Well seen

20

The Hanging of Andrew Wilson.

in good company, too, upon the Links of Leith, for he was celebrated as a player among famous golfers, of whom Duncan Forbes of Culloden was first, and in an age when golf was essentially the pastime of the Scots gentry, not the popular sport of to-day   Fond of his glass and its proverbial concomitant, ruffling it with the best or worst in that free-living, tavern-haunting society of eighteenth-century Auld Reekie, carrying himself with a high head and a hard hand; equally ready to assert his dignity with oath or cane, arrogant, rash, intemperate, very jealous for his prerogative of office   Not an amiable man, nor a good, yet claiming our respect as one faithful to his masters in the discharge of a difficult and thankless duty, whose faults, however grave and many, were surely expiated by his awful fate

In a rough, rude age, dealing with a mob whose excesses far outvie any performances of our policed proletariat, it may well be that so formidable an officer was a civic necessity, and that his failings in this regard were, to some extent, the result of his environment

(2) THE HANGING OF ANDREW WILSON

O soldiers ! for your ain dear sakes,
For Scotland's, *alias* Land o' Cakes,
Gie not her bairns sic deadly pakes,
    Nor be sae rude
Wi' firelock or Lochaber aix,
    As spill their blude
The King's Birthday in Edinburgh —Robert Fergusson

The general irritation and resentment produced in Scotland by the new system of taxation introduced from England, and administered by English Commissioners of Excise and Customs, had, since the Union of the two countries, added greatly to the difficulties of the Government   The people, to whom fiscal deductions were a disagreeable novelty, eagerly seized every means of evading payment of the obnoxious duties, and the practice of smuggling, even a popular pursuit, achieved the importance of a national art   Notwithstanding the zeal of the imported tax-gatherers, Scotland did not contribute her proper quota to the joint purse, indeed, she had hitherto failed even to maintain her own public institutions or to provide for the upkeep of the military force stationed unwelcomely within her borders   Something had to be done to render the Scottish revenue more productive, and the Government decided

Captain Porteous.

to raise £20,000 per annum by levying a tax of threepence per bushel upon malt   The common beverage of the time was the local ale, obtainable at twopence the pint, and familiarly known and beloved as "tippenny "[20]   To raise the price of this commodity was to wound the consumers' tenderest susceptibilities; and the passing of the Act, which came into force on 23rd June, 1725, provoked on all hands fierce demonstrations of wrath   In Glasgow the rabble, breathing beer and vengeance, wrecked the mansion-house of Mr Campbell of Shawfield, member of Parliament for that city, who was suspected of having furnished the Government with statistics for the imposition of the offensive tax, and this, notwithstanding the presence in the town of a detachment of foot, sent from Edinburgh by General Wade to preserve order   Next day the rioters came into collision with the military, who were driven to fire upon them, killing nine persons and wounding many others   Finally, to prevent a general uprising, the Provost begged Captain Bushell, commander of the company, to withdraw his men to Dumbarton, which he did, pursued part of the way by the victorious mob, who had vindicated their right to drink their "tippenny " free of duty   In response to the public clamour, Bushell was brought to trial for firing on the people without authority from a magistrate   and was found guilty; but, to the disappointment of the populace, he was pardoned by the Crown— a strange anticipation of the case of Captain Porteous in all but its tragic sequel.

The battle of the beer was continued in Edinburgh under the less primitive conditions prescribed by the Court of Session   The brewers there combined in a refusal to brew more ale, but were out-manœuvred by the Earl of Ilay, Lord Justice-General, and Duncan Forbes of Culloden, then Lord Advocate   Ultimately the genial fluid resumed its normal flow

One outcome of all this was an immense stimulus given to the already prevalent evil of smuggling   The "Kingdom" of Fife, from its geographical position, had long been a happy hunting-ground of the contrabandist   Its fringes were studded with petty seaports, each a stronghold of some daring gang, whose encounters with the excisemen often resulted in acts

20 Wi' tippenny, we fear nae evil ,
   Wi' usquabœ we'll face the devil '
                                          Tam o' Shanter

The Hanging of Andrew Wilson.

of violence   The hardy free-trader, having successfully eluded the vigilance of the revenue cutter, was welcomed with open arms by all classes of the community.   Those who lived near the coast were on the best of terms with him, and willingly facilitated the disposal of his run cargo   "To be able to buy brandy at a third of the duty rate and tea and tobacco at half-price meant much to a man convivially inclined   And the liquor primed one the speedier, the tobacco was the more fragrant, the China leaf the more refreshing, that they were found in the outhouse at daybreak, and paid for at the back door on the following night "21

One of the most daring and successful of these illicit traders was a man named Andrew Wilson, originally a baxter (baker) in the village of Pathhead, Fife, between whom and the Custom-house officers a fiscal warfare had long been waged, in which he usually came off the victor   In the end, however, his luck deserted him, and repeated seizures and penalties reduced the once-flourishing practitioner to a state of destitution   The principles of free trade being to him of vital importance, he was prepared to adopt the first means for their vindication which opportunity might offer   He had not long to wait   It happened that Mr James Stark, collector of Excise in Kirkcaldy, "being upon his circuit in collecting that revenue," had put up at an ale-house in Pitten-weem, which also served as the Excise-office, his bags big with public money, the local harvest of an insatiate Govern-ment. The occasion was too tempting to be let slip   Wilson promptly advised with two of his friends, William Hall, "indweller in Edinburgh," and George Robertson, "stabler in Bristo,"22 with the result that these three men, on the morning of the 9th of January, 1736, took ship from Leith to Kinghorn   There they hired horses, and in the course of the evening rode into Anstruther Easter, where they stabled their beasts at an inn   Having supped and arranged their plan of campaign, they set out on foot for Pittenweem, distant "about a little mile," between ten and eleven o'clock   The house in which Collector Stark was lodged was kept by one Widow Fowler, relict of the former Excise-office keeper in that place   Here the three adventurers presented them-

21 *The King's Customs*, 1908, p 184

22 Scott says, "He associated with himself one Robertson and two other idle young men ", which is one idle young man too many

Captain Porteous.

selves, and, having drunk a bowl of punch for the good of the house, Wilson asked the landlady "if she could lodge any casks of brandy for him" The widow, whose sympathies, despite her late husband's occupation and the fiscal character of her abode, appear to have been enlisted on the other side, bade him speak low as the collector was within. Being thus satisfied that their prey was safe, they called for the reckoning, and made as if to leave the house. But when the maid, who had followed them downstairs, proceeded to bar the door for the night, Wilson pushed it open and, accompanied by Hall, remounted the stairs, leaving Robertson, with drawn cutlass, to guard the outer door. The tranquil slumbers of the collector, who had retired betimes, presumably fatigued by his official labours, were rudely broken by the noise of repeated blows upon his chamber door, "which door he had secured before he went to bed by screwing down the sneck" Jumping out of bed, he realised from the violence of the attack that the Philistines of free trade were upon him. He accordingly endeavoured to barricade the door with table and chairs, but, seeing that one of the panels was already yielding, he began to fear for his life, and decided to make good his escape by the window while there was yet time. The Government property reposed in two bags under his pillow, along with "his breeches, which he had put below his head when he went to bed," containing "a purse with 52½ guineas, betwixt six and seven pounds in silver, and a pocket-book with 140 pound in bank notes" In the confusion of the moment the flurried collector could only lay hands on one of the bags, with which, abandoning its fellow and the golden nether-garments to their fate, he desperately leaped from his window into the yard beneath. The other bag, by the way, was subsequently found among the bed-clothes, where it had escaped the robbers' notice. When he recovered himself sufficiently the collector approached the house door, but, perceiving the smuggler sentinel, "he retired to the yard again, and lay covered with straw till about four in the morning" As he was clad only in his shirt, a winter's night on the east coast of Scotland so spent must have been a memorable experience; he himself describes it as "a cold bath"[23]

---

[23] This account of the robbery is taken from the depositions of the witnesses at the trial of Wilson, Hall, and Robertson.—*Criminal Trials illustrative of* " The Heart of Midlothian," 1818.

24

The Hanging of Andrew Wilson.

In the next room to the collector's lay his colleague, Alexander Clerk, supervisor of Excise at Cupar-Fife, who also was awakened by the noise about twelve o'clock. On hearing a cry of "Murder the dogs and burn the house!" the supervisor promptly escaped from his window, but, more prudent than the collector, not until he had resumed his breeches. In these he made the best of his way to Anstruther Easter, where a detachment of the Welsh Fusiliers was fortunately quartered; and orders having been left for the rest of the company to follow, he returned to Pittenweem, under the protection of a sergeant and two men, to avenge, as he believed, the collector's murder.

Meanwhile, Wilson and Hall had effected an entrance through the broken panel, and had secured the purse and pocket-book with their contents, together with such personal mementos of the absent collector as his pistols, seal, pen-knife, Bible, and silver shoe-buckles. Having divided the spoil between them they took their departure unmolested. Robertson was not then at his post, which he had left in the following circumstances:—He had intimidated the landlady and her servants by threatening to kill them if they interrupted the robbery, but the noise of breaking-in the door and the cries of the terrified inmates brought upon the scene such of the neighbours as were within earshot. To these Robertson plausibly represented that the Excisemen were quarrelling with the people of the house, and that he himself by interfering had been "in hazard of being shot." The good folks of Pittenweem were by no means anxious to be mixed up with the revenue officials, and willingly left them to fight their own battles. Two more persistent inquirers, who lingered unconvinced, were invited by Robertson to an adjacent ale-house—liquid refreshment in those benighted times being apparently obtainable at any hour —where their curiosity was easily allayed, one of them philosophically observing "that for his part he would sit still, for what he did not see he would not have in his power to tell," whereupon Mr Robertson gave him a clap upon the shoulder, and said he was wiser than any of them." Robertson thereafter repaired to Anstruther Easter, where, by previous concert, he joined Wilson at the inn.

As Supervisor Clerk and his military escort were leaving Anstruther Easter whom should they encounter but Mr William Hall, quietly making his way to the rendezvous. He was

Captain Porteous.

promptly challenged, but, being of a retiring disposition and averse to notoriety, he attempted flight. The sergeant, however, "hooked him with his halbert," and he was carried in triumph to the public-house Excise-office at Pittenweem, where he was readily identified. On the road he dropped the collector's Bible, which, in the circumstances, may have burned a hole in his pocket. He also had with him that gentleman's valise. The supervisor remarked to Hall "that he was now in for it, and that the best way was for him to discover the rest, which if he would do the deponent would do his endeavours to get him made an evidence." Construing this into a promise of receiving a pardon, Hall disclosed the names of his accomplices, " and that they would be found in the house of James Wilson in Anstruther Easter." The rest of the soldiers having by this time arrived, Hall was left in their custody, and, after a fruitless search for Collector Stark, who was still under the straw in the yard, the supervisor, with a strong guard, once more set out for Anstruther Easter. There, having surrounded the inn, they found Wilson and Robertson in bed, who, being identified by the witnesses from Pittenweem, were duly apprehended. The collector's pocket-book, with the bank notes, was found "upon the bed-head where Wilson and Robertson had lain," but there was no word of the purse of gold. On the way to Edinburgh, however, Robertson disclosed that it had been in the custody of Hall, and the latter, fearing for his pardon, admitted "that he had dropped it, upon his being seized, in a wet fuir near a dunghill," from which unsavoury neighbourhood it was safely recovered. Thus His Majesty's revenue suffered no diminution by reason of the night's adventure.

The three prisoners were removed to Edinburgh to stand their trial for the robbery, and were there lodged in the Tolbooth, the grim and hoary prison of the Scottish capital, celebrated in history and romance under its familiar soubriquet of *The Heart of Midlothian*. This ancient pile towered in the very centre of the High Street at its busiest and most congested part—the north-west corner of St Giles' Church—completely blocking that thoroughfare and confining the traffic to narrow lanes and passages on either hand. "Antique in form, gloomy and haggard in aspect, its black, stanchioned windows opening through its dingy walls like the apertures of a hearse, it was calculated to impress all beholders with a

The Hanging of Andrew Wilson.

due and deep sense of what was meant in Scots law by the
squalor carceris "[24] Much sympathy was felt for the prisoners
by the populace, who regarded any attempt to defraud the
revenue as laudable, this was specially so in Wilson's case, his
contention that, in taking the collector's money, he was but
reimbursing himself for his previous losses at the hands of the
gaugers, and in a manner getting back his own,[25] meeting
with the full approval of the mob Accordingly, when, on
2nd March, 1736, Wilson, Hall, and Robertson were placed
at the bar of the High Court of Justiciary, "indicted and
accused at the instance of Duncan Forbes of Culloden, Esq,
His Majesty's Advocate, for His Highness' interest, for the
crimes of Stouthrieff, Housebreaking and Robbery," the proceedings were watched by the public with angry and jealous
eyes The presiding judges were the Lord Justice-Clerk
(Milton) and Lords Royston, Dun, Newhall, Minto, and
Strichen, all of whom, excepting the last named, occupied
the bench at the subsequent trial of Captain Porteous The
prosecution was conducted by Hugh Forbes, Advocate-depute,
assisted by James Grahame, Peter Wedderburn, and Alexander
Home, while Hugh Dalrymple, William Grant, and Alexander
Lockhart represented the pannels Some of these counsel,
as we shall see, appeared in the later trial William Grant,
afterwards Lord Prestongrange, became the celebrated Lord
Advocate, so familiar to lovers of Stevenson's *Catriona*

The trial presents no features of special interest There
were the usual recondite pleadings common to counsel in those
days, fortified by quotations from ancient jurists and other
venerable authorities, including even King David's reply to
Nathan's parable It was argued for the pannels that the
fact, as charged, did not amount to the crimes libelled, viz,
housebreaking, stouthrief, and robbery, the two last of which
were undoubtedly one and the same, but at most to simple
theft, which was not the crime charged, and, in any case,
that stouthrief—defined by Sir George Mackenzie as " a stealth
committed with violence "—could not be committed except in
presence of the owner of the property, the collector having
raised this point by jumping out of the window at the psycho-

---

24 Chambers's *Traditions of Edinburgh*, 1869 p 95

25 Wilson maintained this in a debate with an Edinburgh minister,
as stated by Patrick Lindsay in his speech in the House of Commons
on the Provost's Bill —*Parliamentary History*, x 254

Captain Porteous.

logical moment   An effort was made to separate Robertson's case from those of the others, as he took no part in actually breaking into the room   All the pannels pleaded inebriety, and sought to represent the affair as an unpremeditated and drunken freak   The facts, upon the evidence for the prosecution, came out as already narrated , no witnesses were called for the defence; and the jury found Wilson and Hall guilty, and Robertson art and part in the crimes libelled.   A poem by the local wit, James Wilson, the eccentric "Claudero," entitled *Elegy on James Robb, Captain of the Tolbooth of Edinburgh*, has the following note —"He [Robb] was chancellor of Andrew Wilson's jury, and gave the casting vote to send him to Elysium, which was the occasion of the unhappy affair of Captain Porteous, that gave Edinburgh and all Scotland much trouble, and was a stumbling-block to many of our clergy "[26]   All three pannels were sentenced to be hanged in the Grassmarket on Wednesday, 14th April

On the 1st of that month, however, the sentence pronounced against William Hall was commuted to transportation for life, "solely on account of the ingenuous and candid part he acted when upon his trial."   From the official record of the proceedings it would appear that Hall, like the Gilbertian House of Lords in *Iolanthe*, "did nothing in particular, but did it very well," as regards the result to himself   No doubt the real reason was the conditional promise of a pardon made to him by Supervisor Clerk, as already mentioned

The two other prisoners, Wilson and Robertson, remained in the Tolbooth to await, with what fortitude they might, the execution of the sentence   For them there was no possibility of a reprieve being granted, as in so aggravated a case the authorities felt that an example must be made   To men of the daring and determined nature of the smugglers the alternative of effecting their escape at once presented itself as possible   One of the peculiar characteristics of their ancient prison was its remarkable incapacity to retain such of its inmates as were blessed with influential friends—a notable example being the escape of Katharine Nairn in 1766 , but Wilson and Robertson had to trust to their own ingenuity alone for obtaining their freedom   Accordingly, at two o'clock in the morning of Friday, 9th April, they made what the

---

26 Claudero's *Miscellanies* Second Number, 1767, p 17, *n*

The Hanging of Andrew Wilson.

Caledonian Mercury terms ' a grand attempt to escape "[27] Having become possessed of certain "spring saws and other accoutrements"—by what means does not appear, but doubt-less through the thoughtful attention of confederates without—they communicated the fact to other two prisoners, Ratcliffe and Stewart, horse-stealers from Arbroath, confined in the chamber above. The latter were lodged in what was known as the Iron Room, and, according to the hospitable use of that apartment, were tettered to an iron bar, the supports of which passed through the floor to the ceiling of the room beneath, being "fixed there with wedges through the eyes" These wedges having been knocked out by Wilson and Robertson, the captives were able to slip their chains off the end of the bar The iron gaud and staple are still preserved, with other curious relics of the old prison, in the Museum of the Society of Antiquaries of Scotland [28] Ratcliffe and Stewart then drew up the files and saws by means of a pack-thread let down from their window, and succeeded in making a hole in the floor of their room large enough to admit of their hauling up Wilson and Robertson The united party next "cut through the great iron bars that secured a very thick window on the inside, and afterwards the cross grate in the window" The noise occasioned by these operations was kept from the ears of the warders by an expedient at once quaint and ingenious Certain of their friends, attired ' in woman-dress." assembled outside the prison, and, having knocked the sentinel on the head as a preliminary to their pious exercises, vigorously sang psalms to drown the sound of the saws, while some sympathetic prisoners, scenting what was afoot, "tuned up another in their apartment" When all was ready Stewart first essayed the window, successfully descended the three storeys by a rope, and got off "scot-free "[29] Wilson insisted in making the next attempt, but, "being a squat, round man, stuck in the grate, and before he could be disentangled the guard was alarmed," so all chance of escape for the rest was at an end Wilson took the sole

---

27 *Caledonian Mercury*, 12th April, 1736

28 For an interesting account of the internal arrangements of the Tolbooth, see Chambers's *Minor Antiquities of Edinburgh*, 1833, pp 122-132

29 Scott assigns this part to Wilson, whose obstinacy in making the first attempt prevents the escape of the others

Captain Porteous.

blame on his unlucky and over-broad shoulders, but made what amends he could for the mishap, as will shortly appear Of Ratcliffe as to whose doings, apart from the above incident, history is silent, excellent use is made by Scott in developing the plot of his romance

But the resources of the doughty free-traders were not yet exhausted On Sunday, 11th April, three days before that fixed for their execution, the prisoners were taken, pursuant to an amiable and ancient custom, to the adjacent Tolbooth Church, one of the three churches into which the modern St Giles' Church was then divided, to hear their own funeral sermon in particular, and generally for the improvement of the public mind [30] Fortunately for posterity, that genial autobiographer, Dr Alexander Carlyle, of Inveresk, was also present on this edifying occasion, as well as at the subsequent execution of Wilson. He describes the scene as follows —" I was carried by an acquaintance to church to see the prisoners on the Sunday before the day of execution We went early into the church on purpose to see them come in, and were seated in a pew before the gallery in front of the pulpit. Soon after we went into the church by the door from the Parliament Close, the criminals were brought in by the door next the Tolbooth, and placed in a long pew not far from the pulpit Four soldiers [of the City Guard] came in with them, and placed Robertson at the head of the pew and Wilson below him, two of themselves sitting below Wilson and two in a pew behind him   The bells were ringing and the doors were open while the people were coming into the church Robertson watched his opportunity, and, suddenly springing up, got over the pew into the passage that led in to the door in the Parliament Close, and, no person offering to lay hands on him, made his escape in a moment—so much the more easily, perhaps, as everybody's attention was drawn to Wilson, who was a stronger man, and who, attempting to follow Robertson, was seized by the soldiers, and struggled so long with them that the two who at last followed Robertson were too late It was reported that he had maintained his struggle that he might let his companion

30 In view of what occurred upon this occasion, the magistrates, on 3rd August, 1737, " ordered that the said usage and custom hereafter be ever discontinued "—*Council Records*

Interior of the Tolbooth Church.

From an Etching by Kay.

have time. That might be his second thought, but his first certainly was to escape himself, for I saw him set his foot on the seat to leap over, when the soldier pulled him back."[31] According to another report of the incident in the *Caledonian Mercury* of that date, "Wilson boldly attempted to break out by wrenching himself out of the hands of four armed soldiers Finding himself disappointed here, his next care was to employ the soldiers till Robertson should escape, this he effected by securing two of them in his arms and after calling out, *Geordie, do for thy life!* snatched hold of a third with his teeth Hereupon Robertson, after tripping up the fourth, jumped out of the seat and run over the tops of the pews with incredible agility, the audience opening a way for him sufficient to receive them both, and in hurrying out at the south gate of the church he tumbled over the collection money"[32] The attitude of the congregation to the fugitive is significant—all did their best to facilitate his escape

After a fierce resistance Wilson was overpowered, and was immediately taken back to the Tolbooth, "without getting sermon, and put in close custody to prevent his escape, which the audience seemed much inclined to favour So that," continues the *Mercury*, "he must pay for all Wednesday next" His credit with the populace was enormously increased by what they deemed his magnanimous conduct, and, indeed, according to Dr Carlyle, Wilson was the better character of the two In Scott's novel this incident is made to occur at the close, instead of the commencement of the service, the author even quoting from the exhortation addressed by the minister to the penitent criminals, while Wilson's act is ascribed solely to his generosity and self-sacrifice

Robertson, meantime, on reaching the Parliament Close, made his escape by the President's Stairs to the Cowgate. Tripping on the steps, he was set on his feet by Mr M'Queen, the kind-hearted minister of the New Kirk, who was coming up at the moment on his way to church [33] In the Horse Wynd he appropriately enough ' made up to a saddled horse, and would have mounted him, but the gentleman to whom the horse

31 *Autobiography*, pp 34-35
32 *Caledonian Mercury*, 12th April, 1736
33 Chambers's *Illustrations of the Author of Waverley*, p 167

Captain Porteous.

belonged prevented him " He then fled by the Potter Row Port and the Cross Causeway to the King's Park, "the crowd all the way covering his retreat," and, having obtained refreshment and a mount at Duddingston, rode off in safety · "nor have we,' says the *Caledonian Mercury*, "since heard any further of him, notwithstanding all the search made." According to the *Newgate Calendar*, "the whole city was instantly alarmed, and Porteous, as usual, sent to search for him, but in vain, for, although he swore the most dreadful oaths that he would have him if he was out of hell, yet Robertson met with a friend who procured him a horse, knocked off his handcuffs, and the same evening he got on board a ship at Dunbar, in which he escaped to Holland In the meantime search was made for Robertson to no purpose by Porteous who knocked down several of the inhabitants for no other reason but that of their telling him they were glad the poor man had got off " A rumour to the effect that Robertson remained in the neighbourhood, for the purpose of attending the obsequies of "his dearly beloved Andrew Wilson," lacks corroboration, and it is much more probable that he at once made the best of his way abroad than that he so hazarded his neck for reasons of mere sentiment With reference to this report, the magistrates, on 29th April inserted in the Edinburgh newspapers an advertisement offering a reward of fifty pounds sterling for his apprehension The advertisement concludes—" *N B*—The said George Robertson is a thin-faced man, about thirty years of age, of a pale complection, and about five foot and a half in stature, well-limbed, lame in two fingers of his right hand."[34] The disreputable young stabler of the Bristo Port has little in common with the aristocratic hero of Scott's story, on whom the author, as was his wont, bestowed "a cocked hat and a sword "; and there is even a painful tradition that the romantic lover of Effie Deans was a married man at the time of his imprisonment Be that as it may, there is no foundation for the picturesque fancy which makes him, disguised in female attire, the ringleader of the Porteous Riot

The following account of Robertson's subsequent career is given in a pamphlet published some fifty years later[35] —"He

---

34 *Edinburgh Evening Courant*, 29th April 1736
35 *Account of the Cruel Massacre Committed by John Porteous*, &c , 1789.

32

The Hanging of Andrew Wilson.

afterwards went to Holland, and settled at Campvere and at Middleburgh, where he tricked many of his countrymen. At last he set up for a private informer, and wrote to the Custom-house officers in several towns on the coast of Scotland, and settled his correspondence with them; and then he sent them over an invoice of the cargoes on board the Scots vessels, the names of the ships and masters, so that the Custom-house officers knew what they brought in and when they sailed; and the Excise yachts went out and caught many cargoes, which ruined many merchants He at last got into some way with the English smugglers, and ruined many of them The Dutch got information of him, and he took the hint and escaped over to London Had he been taken in Holland they would have executed the Scots sentence against him He skulked about in London for some time, and got letters from those he did for in Scotland, and he applied to that hero, William Duke of Cumberland, who procured him a pardon from the King, and at last he died in misery in London" It is fitting that so notable a knave should have found such a congenial patron

In view of the facilities afforded by the populace to the escape of Robertson, and the pronounced feeling of sympathy displayed on all hands for his companion Wilson, the authorities were naturally apprehensive that some attempt would be made to deliver him out of the hangman's hands When the day fixed for the execution, Wednesday, 14th April, drew near, the magistrates therefore considered what steps should be taken to ensure the law not being cheated of its prey The duty of preserving order at public executions devolved upon the City Guard On Monday, the 12th, Alexander Wilson, Lord Provost of Edinburgh, who was *ex officio* commander of the corps, sent for Captain Porteous and told him that there would probably be trouble with the mob at Wilson's execution, and that every precaution must be taken to prevent a rescue He instructed him to call out the whole of the Guard on that occasion, adding that he had given orders to the City Treasurer to furnish them with powder and shot "and such other military ammunition as might be necessary for the use of the men in maintaining the peace of the town and supporting the execution of the laws."[36] We shall later have occasion to consider the precise terms of the instructions

---

[36] Information for Captain Porteous

D

33

Captain Porteous.

given by the Provost to Captain Porteous. Next day (Tuesday), being still apprehensive in spite of these measures, the magistrates placed the hangman in the Tolbooth, lest he should be kidnapped, and doubled the sentinels both within and without the prison The Provost again sent for Porteous and despatched him with a letter to General Moyle, Commander of the Forces in Scotland, " desiring from the general an order for a party of the regiment [the Welsh Fusiliers] lying in the Canongate to enter the city in order to overawe the mob " There was some difficulty in arranging the matter owing to the timidity and vacillation of the Provost, as we shall afterwards see from the evidence given at the Parliamentary inquiry by Major Pool, one of General Moyle's officers, but eventually it was agreed that 150 men, 2 captains, and 4 subalterns should be placed at the Provost's disposal for that purpose This unprecedented step appears to have been bitterly resented by Porteous, who regarded the calling in of the King's troops as a reflection upon the ability of the City Guard to do all that was required in the circumstances, and as an infringement of his own privilege and dignity as their officer It is probable from what afterwards occurred that his men to some extent shared their Captain's feelings

On the 13th, the day before the execution, Porteous attended the Provost in the forenoon and told him that, in obedience to his commands, " the men were all ordered to be in readiness, their arms put in order and loaded, whereof the Provost approved," and stated what arrangements he had made with regard to the Royal forces Accordingly, when, between two and three o'clock on the afternoon of that fatal Wednesday, Captain Porteous, by the Provost's order, drew up his men at the Guard-house, while the two companies of the Welsh Fusiliers marched past him up the High Street, where no drums but his own might lawfully be sounded, and took up their stations in the Lawnmarket, his fury burst all bounds He was, as we have seen, a man of a proud and ungovernable temper ; now smarting under what he deemed a personal affront put upon him before his own men, and, worse than all, in presence of that Edinburgh rabble whom it had ever been his boast to hold in awe ; " and, being heated likewise with wine—for he had dined, as the custom then was, between one and two "[37]—his

---

[37] *Autobiography of Dr Carlyle*, p 36

The Hanging of Andrew Wilson.

passion wrought upon him like a madness. Our old authority, the anonymous biographer, remarks—"His countenance was pale, his eyes rolling and staring, his mouth foaming, his voice broken and confused, his whole gate full of disconcerted and disorderly steps"[38] Unfortunately, there was no legitimate outlet for this intemperate condition, and when Porteous proceeded with his men to the Tolbooth to conduct Wilson to the place of execution, he is said to have behaved with much barbarity to his helpless prisoner. He was especially enraged against Wilson for the part he had played in the escape of Robertson and the ignominy which the Guard had thereby sustained at his hands "When the manacles were too little for Wilson's wrists, and the hangman could not make them meet, he flew furiously to them, and squeezed, the poor man crying, and he squeezing, till he made them meet, to the exquisite torture of the miserable prisoner, who told him he could not have one serious thought, so necessary to one in his condition, under such pain *No matter*, says Porteous, *your torment will soon be at an end Well*, says the other, *you know not but you may come to be in my condition; God forgive you* This behaviour of his embittered the minds of the mob, who were sufficiently exasperated against him before, and it was soon spread in town and country."[39]

At that period criminals were hanged in the Grassmarket at the foot of the West Bow, the gallows being erected when required in a massive block of sandstone with a triangular hole in the middle, which served as a permanent socket for the gibbet The spot is still indicated by a cross formed by the paving-stones in the centre of the street, at the eastern extremity of that "draughty parallelogram" This was the scene of all Edinburgh executions from the Restoration till 1784, when the *locus* was changed to a platform at the west-end of the Tolbooth "There, in the Grass-market, stiff-necked Covenanting heroes offered up the often unnecessary, but not less honourable, sacrifice of their lives, and bade eloquent farewell to sun, moon, and stars and earthly friendships, or died silent to the roll of drums"[40]

When Captain Porteous marched with the prisoner and his Guard up the Lawnmarket, lined by the unwelcome troops,

---

38 *Life and Death*, &c , p 20
39 *Ibid.* p 21
40 Stevenson's *Picturesque Notes on Edinburgh*, p 10

Captain Porteous.

and descended the West Bow to the place of execution, a strangely impressive scene awaited him   The vast area of the Glassmarket was thronged by a densely packed multitude, who watched the proceedings in ominous and lowering silence   Each window of the lofty tenements that reared their cliff-like fronts upon the fatal tree was crowded by well-to-do sightseers, who could afford to pay for their pleasure, and liked to take it at their ease, some of whom were to pay dear enough for it before " the show " was over   Wilson was then delivered over to John Dalgleish, the common hangman, while Porteous and his men surrounded the scaffold erected at the foot of the gibbet   Contrary to expectation, there was no attempt to interfere with the execution of the sentence, and the horrid ritual was duly completed without interruption from the mob. The affair having thus happily terminated in orthodox fashion, Bailies Crockat and Hamilton, who were in attendance officially, adjourned, according to custom, to an adjacent tavern overlooking the gallows, for the purpose of discussing the *deid-chack*, that somewhat ghastly meal to which the city fathers sat down on such occasions [41]   One would think their appetites must have suffered from their attendance at the preliminary function   Half an hour was the usual time allowed before a criminal was cut down, the signal being given by the magistrates pointing a white rod out of the tavern window.   On this occasion, however, after Wilson had hung for only twenty-four minutes, the opening of the window was mistaken by the hangman for the expected signal, and he at once mounted the ladder to perform his office [42]   This action apparently broke the spell which hitherto had held the crowd in sullen acquiescence, and immediately several stones were thrown at the hated official, some of which struck him in the face, drawing blood, and he hurriedly descended and took refuge behind the Guard at the foot of the scaffold.   The rope was unusually long, and Wilson hung within a foot of the ground   At this moment, according to the evidence of Bailie Hamilton, the body of Wilson was cut down by a man standing close to the gibbet, who, describing himself as his brother-in-law, had applied to the magistrates the previous day for leave to bury his

---

41 Chambers states that Provost Creech was the first who had the good taste to abandon this practice —*Traditions of Edinburgh*, 1869, p 127, *n*

42 Examinations of Bailies Crockat and Hamilton

Execution in the Grassmarket.

From an Etching by Skene.

The Hanging of Andrew Wilson.

relative. It was at once removed by his friends in a cart to Leith, various attempts at resuscitation having been made without success No sooner was the body cut down than the mob, probably with a view to divert the attention of the Guard from those who were removing it, began to press upon and attack the party about the gallows. A shower of stones and dirt descended upon the Guard, several of whom were severely injured Two—Alexander Mushet and David Martine —had their shoulder-blades fractured by large stones, the drummer was cut on the head and his drum broken, while others received minor hurts The effect of this assault upon a body of armed men, whose guns were loaded and ready for use, was disastrous Whether it be proved that Captain Porteous either himself fired upon the mob or ordered his men to do so, and, if he did, to what extent he was justified by the circumstances and his instructions, we shall consider when we come to deal with his subsequent trial In the meantime, it is sufficiently clear that certain of the exasperated soldiers retaliated by firing "sharp, dropping shots" among their assailants The consequences of this volley upon the surging crowd around the scaffold was terrible, three persons were killed on the spot, and about twelve others were more or less seriously wounded, some of whom afterwards succumbed to their injuries "The whole tragical scene," as Porteous describes it, lasted only a few minutes

Dr Carlyle, who has recorded his impressions as an eye-witness, was present when a lad of fifteen, along with his tutor, Mr Baillie, and his fellow-pupils—John Maxwell, later a distinguished soldier; John Wotherspoon, afterwards the well-known physician, Sir Henry Nisbet of Dean, and Sir John Dalrymple of Cranstoun "Mr Baillie," writes Dr Carlyle, "had taken windows in a house on the north side of the Grassmarket for his pupils and me, in the second floor, about seventy or eighty yards westward of the place of execution, where we went in due time to see the show, to which I had no small aversion, having seen one at Dumfries—the execution of Jock Johnstone—which shocked me very much When we arrived at the house, some people who were looking from the windows were displaced, and went to a window in the common stair, about two feet below the level of ours The street is long and wide, and there was a very great crowd

Captain Porteous.

assembled.   The execution went on with the usual forms, and Wilson behaved in a manner very becoming his situation There was not the least appearance of an attempt to rescue; but soon after the executioner had done his duty there was an attack made upon him, as usual on such occasions by the boys and blackguards throwing stones and dirt in testimony of their abhorrence of the hangman   But there was no attempt to break through the Guard and cut down the prisoner   It was generally said that there was very little, if any, more violence than had usually happened on such occasions   Porteous, however, inflamed with wine and jealousy, thought proper to order his Guard to fire, their muskets being loaded with slugs; and when the soldiers showed reluctance, I saw him turn to them with threatening gesture and an inflamed countenance   They obeyed, and fired ; but, wishing to do as little harm as possible, many of them elevated their pieces, the effect of which was that some people were wounded in the windows, and one unfortunate lad, whom we had displaced, was killed in the stair window by a slug entering his head   His name was Henry Black, a journeyman tailor, whose bride was the daughter of the house we were in   She fainted away when he was brought into the house speechless, where he only lived till nine or ten o'clock   We had seen many people, women and men, fall on the street, and at first thought it was only through fear, and by their crowding on one another to escape   But when the crowd dispersed we saw them lying dead or wounded, and had no longer any doubt of what had happened   The numbers were said to be eight or nine killed, and double the number wounded, but this was never exactly known "[43]   The very simplicity of this account of the tragedy makes it the more effective in bringing home to the reader's mind the horror of the scene, although the author, writing from memory some sixty years after the event, is, as we shall find, incorrect in several particulars

Meanwhile, the sound of the firing had disturbed the magistrates and officiating ministers in their peaceable enjoyment of the *deid-chack*, and a ball even grazed the side of the window of the room in which they were assembled. They hurried to the scene of the disaster, but Captain Porteous was then

---

[43] *Autobiography*, pp. 36-37

The Hanging of Andrew Wilson.

drawing off his men to the Guard-house by the West Bow, the hostile multitude pursuing them with stones and execrations The harassed soldiers halted mid-way up the steep ascent, and, whether with or without the order of Porteous, those in the rear faced about and again fired upon the people, killing three of them and wounding others Porteous was also said to have himself fired on this second occasion with a musket taken from one of the Guard, but this, as will afterwards appear, was certainly not proved against him During all this time the detachment of the regular troops remained drawn up in the Lawnmarket and took no part whatever in the affray Past this imposing but ineffective body Captain Porteous led his straggling and disordered force—" a thing," he observes, " generally esteemed somewhat inconsistent with guilt, especially such horrible guilt as he is charged with," and arrived without further accident at the Guard-house.

" This unprovoked slaughter," writes Dr Carlyle, " irritated the common people to the last; and the state of grief and rage into which their minds were thrown was visible in the high commotion that appeared in the multitude Our tutor was very anxious to have us all safe in our lodgings, but durst not venture out to see if it was practicable to go home I offered to go, and went, and soon returned, offering to conduct them safe to our lodgings, which were only half-way down the Lawnmarket, by what was called the Castle Wynd, which was just at hand to the westward There we remained safely, and were not allowed to stir out any more that night till about nine o'clock, when, the streets having long been quiet, we all grew anxious to learn the fate of Henry Black, and I was allowed to go back to the house I took the younger Maxwell with me, and found that he had expired an hour before we arrived A single slug had penetrated the side of his head an inch above the ear."[44]

The name of Henry Black is not contained in the contemporary lists of the slain, the lad referred to by Dr. Carlyle being evidently " Henry Graham, tailor in Cannongate, shot through the head while looking out at a window two stairs up," mentioned first in the list of casualties given by the *Caledonian Mercury* It would appear that the published lists were not

---

[44] *Autobiography,* pp 37-38

Captain Porteous.

exhaustive, for that journal states, " It being market day, many people who were in the town about business had the curiosity to go to see the execution, several of whom, having shared in the unlucky fate, retired or were carried off by friends; and we are informed two or three of them have died in the country There are also others in town wounded, who rather incline to put up with their misfortunes than, by publishing the same, alarm their friends "[45]

The magistrates had, somewhat ambiguously, ordered " the killed and wounded to be buried and looked after at the city's expense ", and the following extract from the records of Grey-friars Churchyard gives the names and places of interment of five of the victims —

> " Andrew Wilson, baxter, was execute 14th April, 1736
> His body delivered to his friends.
> " Andrew M'Neill, in Mountainhall [Mortonhall]   Was
> shot 14th April, 1736
> " John Anderson, son to John Anderson, was shot 14th
> April, 1736   Buryed in the West Churchyard.
> " Charles Husband, servant to Paul Husband, was shot
> 14th April, 1736   Buryed in Cannongate Churchyard.
> " Margrat Gordon dyed of ye wounds received at the
> execution of Wilson, 21st April, 1736   She lyes at
> Westhall's stone
> " Hary Graham, taylor   Shot at the execution of Wilson,
> 14th April, 1736.   Lyes in Cannongate Churchyard "

Charles Husband was the person mentioned later in the indictment against Porteous as having been shot dead by the Captain's own hand; and in the information for Porteous it is stated that he was the man " who tumultuously stept in and cut down the criminal "

The body of Wilson was conveyed by his friends across to Fife, and was buried at his native village of Pathhead.   The burial register of that place records that " The corpse of Andrew Wilson, baker, son to Andrew Wilson, baker and in-dweller in Dunnikier (*Qui mortuit Gallifocio Edinburgam*), was interred on the 15th April, 1736 "

The following excerpt from an unpublished account due to

---

the keeper of the Tolbooth, preserved in the City Chambers,[46] relates to Wilson's imprisonment ·—

> "To bread, ale, and brandy to John Dalgleish [the hangman] when in the Tolbooth before Andrew Willson's execution, - - £0 1 6½
>
> "To bread, ale, and candle to four shouldiers when guarding Andrew Willson in the Tolbooth, - - - - - - 0 4 6
>
> "To the masons and smiths when mending the window in the gentleman's chamber and building up the window in the Iron House, 0 5 6
>
> £0 11 6½

The last item has reference to the repairs necessitated by the damage caused in the prisoner's abortive attempt to escape from the Tolbooth on 9th April, as previously described

(3) THE CAPTAIN'S TRIAL

> But Law's a draw-well unco deep,
> Withouten rim fock out to keep,
> A donnart chiel, whan drunk, may dreep
>   Fu' sleely in,
> But finds the gate baith stey and steep
>   Ere out he win
>   *The Sitting of the Session* —Robert Fergusson.

On reaching the Guard-house Captain Porteous drew up his men and sent one of his sergeants to the Provost for orders These were that the Guard should wait on their arms till the King's troops passed, and the latter having marched back to their quarters in the Canongate, Porteous filed off his men into the Guard-house, ordering the sergeants "to keep them close, and by all means not to suffer them to clean their pieces, and at the same time delivered his carabine, loaded as aforesaid, at the Guard door" He then went to the Provost to make his official report upon what he himself calls the " miserable slaughter "[47] The magistrates were assembled in the Spread-Eagle tavern—most of the civic deliberations of those days being held in public-houses, probably as affording ready relief to the dryness of business When the Captain

---

46 Appendix I
47 Information for Captain Porteous

Captain Porteous.

appeared before them he was at once taxed with having ordered his men to fire and firing himself upon the people. He strongly denied both charges, and asked that his firelock be sent for, stating "that it would appear from inspecting of her that she had not been fired" He also produced his cartridge-box, into which he had been seen to put three cartridges that day, then containing only two, the other having been used by him in loading his gun   When his weapon was forthcoming it was found to be still loaded, and apparently had not been fired [48] The magistrates then adjourned to the Burgh Room, accompanied by Porteous and followed by an immense crowd calling for justice upon the murderer   There a more formal inquiry was held into the circumstances of the tragedy; and after various precognitions had been taken, the Lord Provost, as High Sheriff, ordered Captain Porteous to close prison for eight days, and to be afterwards detained in custody till liberated in course of law. He was accordingly removed to the Tolbooth by his own Guard, "without which," remarks the *Caledonian Mercury*, "the mob had unquestionably finished him, so exasperated were they on seeing their innocent fellow-citizens wallowing in their blood, and that the same should have been shed by those nursed up in our own bosom, while, on the other hand, both officers and soldiers of the military detachment behaved with all honour" [49] The *Mercury's* "own bosom," however, was steeled against the Captain from the first, and its attitude towards him was throughout consistently hostile The virtues of the King's troops on this occasion were, as we have seen, purely negative.

The next day fifteen soldiers of the City Guard were sent to keep their Captain company in gaol, seven to the prison of Edinburgh and eight to the Canongate Tolbooth, "it appearing clearly, after a careful examination of all the firelocks of the party, that they were the persons who discharged their pieces." All these men denied having received their Captain's orders to fire.

To satisfy the popular clamour for immediate vengeance, it was at first proposed that Porteous should be tried summarily by the Lord Provost himself, as High Sheriff within the burgh, and a memorial on the subject was submitted to Crown counsel. This interesting document, which, together with the opinion

---

48 Examination of Bailie Hamilton.   49 Appendix III

The Captain's Trial.

thereon, is preserved in the Edinburgh City Chambers, is entitled "Memoriall and Queries touching the Jurisdiction of the Provost and Magistrats of Edinburgh To take Tryall of the Murthers committed by Captain Porteous and part of the City Guard under his Command on 14th Aprile 1736 at the Execution of Andw Wilson "[50] After narrating what happened upon that occasion, and stating that seven or eight persons were killed and ten or eleven wounded, pointing out the desirability of Porteous being forthwith brought to trial, and that the absence from town of the Lords of Justiciary on circuit would cause delay if he were to be tried by the High Court, the magistrates claim for the Provost and themselves the right to try Porteous under a charter of James III and subsequent statutes, confirming them in "the office of Sheriffship and Justiciary of Peace within the said burgh" The memorial then proceeds—"It is also suggested that Captain Porteous may, in order to gain time and perplex his trial, be advised by his lawyers to pretend, and offer to prove as a defence or exculpation, or mitigation, though it be most false and groundless, that he had orders from my Lord Provost and the other magistrates, or some of them, to fire upon the spectators, or possibly he may offer a declinator of the magistrates to be his judges under that pretence" The Provost, at least, as we shall find, had good grounds for feeling nervous as to this line being taken by the prisoner The opinion, which is dated "London, 6th May, 1736," and signed by Duncan Forbes, Lord Advocate, and Charles Erskine, Solicitor-General, states, on the question of jurisdiction, that after the Act 4 James IV par 28, magistrates as Sheriffs "had no jurisdiction in the crime of slaughter but where the offender was taken red-hand, and judged within three suns." With regard to the possibility of Porteous—with or without justification—pleading the Provost's orders in bar of trial, counsel observe, "But this very consideration appears to us a very urgent motive for trying this crime before the Court of Justiciary rather than the magistrates, though these last had, as we think they have not, jurisdiction after three suns "[51]

The evidence of Major Pool, of the Welsh Fusiliers, given at a later stage before the House of Lords, throws some light on

[50] Appendix I
[51] Ibid

43

Captain Porteous.

the Provost's apprehensions on this point   This witness states that the day before the execution of Wilson, General Moyle told him of the Provost's request that a detachment from the regiment be sent to assist thereat, which he (the General) had refused unless the Provost would indemnify his men should any accident happen.   The major met Captain Porteous later in the day, "a little above the Guard," when the Captain told him the Provost would give no such indemnity   Major Pool then said in that case the troops would not be sent; "they [the Guard] would have it all to themselves"   Next morning, however, General Moyle changed his mind, like Pharaoh, and decided to "let the people go," and the major was despatched to inform the Provost, whom he had some difficulty in finding   Eventually he ran his lordship to earth in "Ross s Coffee House," where the details were discussed, but on the city treasurer, who was of the party, remarking "that if the military came into the city, it would give great offence," the Provost at once said he would not have the troops at all   In the end, it was settled that the detachment should be supplied   "As I was going to take leave of him," says the major, "I begged the favour of his lordship that he would not see the King's troops insulted and abused, as they commonly are by the mob in that country, he told me he would take care of that, for he would order their own people (meaning Captain Porteous and his Guard) to be all loaded with slugs—the treasurer was by at the same time—and in case there was any disturbance they should also have his orders to turn out a few of the men out of their ranks and fire at their legs, and if they did not disperse, then he would give his orders to our detachment.   This very same order I delivered to Captain Hickman, who commanded the party"   Whether the Provost, in fact, gave these orders to Porteous is not known, but that he gave them to some one he himself admitted, as will presently appear.   It is difficult to see who but Porteous could have been the recipient   "A few days after the execution of Wilson," continues Major Pool, "I met the Provost at the Cross of Edinburgh, and, after the usual compliments, I told him I was very sorry for the accident that had happened the day I had the pleasure of seeing him last; upon which he told me that he supposed Captain Porteous had been disappointed of some of his whores, which had put him out of humour, to make him act as he did   I told his lordship I thought it was very severe to say so shocking a

44

The Captain's Trial.

thing of a person whom I thought he once had a great regard for, especially in his circumstances I told him that some of the magistrates had owned to some of our gentlemen who supped with them that night [Bailies must sup though burgesses bleed] that his piece was found loaded, and had not been fired; but he told me then that they had since found out the person who had cleand his piece, I then told him that, provided he did fire, it was not without his [the Provost's] orders; he immediately made answer to me that he gave those orders, but he never gave them to Porteous 'Besides, my lord,' said I, 'you use this man exceedingly ill, in my humble opinion, in confining him in a dungeon and stopping his pay,' for I thought it was a very singular instance for a gentleman to have his pay stopped before he was found guilty of the fact "[52] The major proceeds to say that Porteous was then in a starving condition, and that they made a collection for him in the regiment   Why Major Pool was not a witness upon the Captain's trial does not appear, further than that he was not in Edinburgh when it took place   He states that, having received a letter from Porteous " out of prison," desiring his assistance, he called upon Mr. Grahame, one of the counsel for the defence, who afterwards told him that the Lord Advocate would admit his statement as evidence   " Mr Grahame thought his case bad, and that the magistrates were very severe upon him "

On 21st April the Town Council dismissed John Porteous from all his offices—Captain of the Guard, Adjutant to the Train Bands, and Provisor of Coal and Candle—and stopped all payments to him " on account of the premises " On the same date the sum of £5 salary due to him was arrested in the hands of the magistrates at the instance of Thomas Young, brewer at Fountainbridge, who had obtained a decree against the Captain for £3 10s , presumably due in respect of malt liquors supplied to him [53] Next day the *Caledonian Mercury* announces with satisfaction, " Captain Porteous has been removed from the apartment to which he was first confined, whence he had access to converse with the sentinel at the Purses, at least by signs and tangents, and is now in the Iron-house on the east side." The locality favourable to the Captain's military exercises was a narrow defile on the north side of the Tolbooth, known as " The Puir Folks' Purses," from the

52 Examination of Major Pool
53 Appendix I

Captain Porteous.

fact that there the Bedesmen—Fergusson's "Blue-gown bodies" —received the Royal bounty in a leathern purse on each King's birthday, after attending service in St Giles' Church.

On 12th May, in view of the opinion given by Crown counsel on their memorial as above mentioned, the magistrates "resolved unanimously that a criminal prosecution be carried on before the High Court of Justiciary against John Porteous, late lieutenant of the City Guard, and such of the soldiers as were accessory to the horrid murders," and that the same be done at the expense of the city   None of the fifteen soldiers then in confinement was ever brought to trial, for reasons which will hereafter appear   Meanwhile, the unfortunate Captain was having a bad time of it in the Iron-house, for in those days prisons were run on simple and inexpensive lines, the methods of modern philanthropy being then undreamed of   He presented a petition to his late masters, setting forth that he was in a starving condition , and on 28th May the Council, doubtless moved by memories of municipal feasts, handsomely voted him "an aliment at the rate of eighteen pence sterling per day," and adjourned for dinner with an added zest from their generous action   It is to be hoped that Major Pool's subscription was on a more munificent scale

On 21st June the *Caledonian Mercury* informs us—"Thursday last afternoon John Porteous, late an officer of the City Guard, was served with an indictment at the instance of His Majesty's Advocate, for the murder and slaughter, maiming and wounding (on the 14th April last), of the several persons mentioned in the *Caledonian Mercury* of the 15th and subsequent days of the said month, and his trial takes place on 5th July "

Accordingly, on 5th July, 1736, the High Court of Justiciary, panoplied in its ancient and imposing forms, proceeded to the trial of Captain John Porteous   Presiding over that venerable and august tribunal was Andrew Fletcher of Milton, Lord Justice-Clerk, the other judges being Lords Royston, Dun, Newhall, and Minto   The Crown counsel, or, as the record significantly has it, "pursuers," were the Lord Advocate, Duncan Forbes of Culloden, later the great Lord President , the Solicitor-General, Charles Erskine of Tinwald, afterwards Lord Justice-Clerk , and Hugh Forbes, Advocate-depute, assisted by Patrick Haldane, Hugh Murray Kynnynmont, and Sir James Elphinston   The counsel for Porteous, or "prolocutors in

46

The Captain's Trial.

defence," were James Grahame, the future Lord Easdale, Henry Home (Lord Kames); Alexander Lockhart (Lord Covington); James Lesslie, and James Holburne Biographical notes on these distinguished occupants of bench and bar will be found in the Appendix, to which the reader is referred [54]   " The pannel," in the words of the *Justiciary Opera*, " is brought in, guarded " by members of his own Guard , and here it is difficult to resist the following quotation of Maidment's quaint note upon that expression—"Alas ! I cannot insert this word without feelings of the most painful nature !   The Town Guard of Auld Reekie is now no more !   And a gentleman, tried before the High Court of Justiciary, must submit to the indignity of sitting between two nondescripts called policemen, who sport glazed hats and handle no better weapons than batons   How different was it in the days of yore !   How dignified was the cocked hat of the grey-haired veteran !   How imposing his queue !   How awful his Lochaber-axe !   But this is the age of innovation and reform, and a man will, ere long, not even be hanged with common decency !   I wonder the illustrious Hume has not, ere now, pointed out to the reformed House of Commons the absurdity of the country being at the cost of a new rope for each new culprit, when one good one might suffice for a score "[55] A furious multitude crowded the Parliament Close, through which Porteous was, with great difficulty and danger, escorted into Court , indeed, it was admitted by the Lord Advocate in the Parliamentary inquiry that, had it not been for the Guard, the prisoner would have been torn to pieces between the Tolbooth and the Justiciary Room, though not forty paces distant from one another [56]

The indictment, *inter alia*, charges John Porteous—That the pannel, being one of the captain-lieutenants of the said City Guard, was, by the magistrates of the city, ordered to attend, with a detachment of about seventy men of the said Guard, at the execution of Andrew Wilson, sentenced to be hanged by the High Court of Justiciary; and that the said Andrew Wilson, having hung upon the gallows erected for his execution in the street called the Grassmarket until he was dead, at least for a considerable time, and so long that there

---

[54] Appendix XVI.
[55] *Court of Session Garland*, 1839, p 34, *n*
[56] *Parliamentary History*, x, 272.

Captain Porteous.

was ground to conclude he was dead, the said pannel, conceiving a wicked and malicious purpose of destroying, wounding, and maiming the persons, inhabitants of the said city, and others assembled at the said execution, did, without any just cause or necessary occasion, order the said detachment under his command to fire upon the people so assembled, and that some of the men having fired, as it would seem the pannel apprehended, over the heads of the multitude with intention to avoid doing them harm, the said pannel did with threats repeat his commands to fire, calling out to the men to level their pieces and be damned or words to that purpose; and that, at the same time, he levelled the firelock that was in his own hand, taking aim at one Charles Husband, and, having fired the said firelock, the said Charles Husband immediately dropped to the ground, having received a wound or wounds by bullets or large drops of lead, whereof he died in a short space, and that, by the pannel's said example and command, several of the said Guard, to the number of about twenty, did, at the same time, or soon thereafter, fire upon the innocent multitude, by which fire two other persons were killed, and several others wounded, maimed, or hurt, and that the said pannel having thereafter marched off the said detachment of the Guard into that part of the street aforesaid called the West Bow, he did again, without any just cause or occasion, order the men under his command to face about and fire upon the people, and that, at this time, the said pannel did fire a musket that was in his own hand, having either re-loaded, or caused to be re-loaded, his own piece or firelock, or taken another out of the hands of one of the Guard, and that several of the said Guard did, upon that second example and command of the pannel, fire upon the multitude, by which fire three other persons were killed; at least that, by the said firings of the pannel, or of the firings of the other men in the said detachment of the Guard, proceeding from the pannel's order and example, the several persons mentioned in the indictment to have been killed, maimed, or wounded, were all respectively killed, wounded, or maimed; whereby the pannel is guilty of the killing, wounding, or maiming of the said persons; at least is art and part thereof, or accessory thereto, from whence the indictment concludes that the pannel ought to be punished with the pains of law, *i e*, capitally. "To all which," says

The Captain's Trial.

the *Caledonian Mercury*, "and the other facts therein set forth, he pleaded 'not guilty,' and put himself upon trial Then after pleadings by His Majesty's Advocate and Solicitor, Mr Hugh Murray Kynnymont, and Mr Patrick Haldane on the part of the indictment, and Mr Alexander Lockhart, Mr Henry Home, and Mr James Grahame of Dougalstoun upon the relevancy and exculpation, parties were appointed to give in informations for the indictment on Friday next, and for the pannel this day se'nnight. And adjourned till Friday se'nnight"

The debate upon the relevancy, that famous field which of old resounded to "the drums and tramplings" of forensic battle, lasted, according to the *Courant*, for several hours No report of the speeches is preserved, but the arguments, bristling with dialectic subtleties, are contained in the informations respectively lodged in behalf of Crown and pannel, which will be found in the report of the trial From these it appears that various objections were taken to the libel, as not describing with sufficient accuracy the *locus* and the relative positions of the pannel and Charles Husband While it is denied that Porteous, on either of the occasions libelled, fired himself or ordered his men to do so, it is somewhat inconsistently argued that the delivering out of powder and ball to the Guard, the directions received by the pannel to repel force by force, and the other precautions taken amounted to an order from the magistrates to fire when necessary, which necessity arose on the assault upon the Guard by the mob with stones, and the attempt to carry off Wilson's body in hopes of recovering him to life It was maintained for the pannel "that a small degree of resistance of persons in the execution of their duty will justify the persons resisted in the act of killing the resister", that the pannel's duty was not at an end by the mere hanging up of the convict, it lasted till he was executed to the death, which the cutting down of the body by the mob was intended to prevent, that the pannel and his men were still on the spot, and, till marched off at the usual time, must be held as in the execution of their duty, that in the case of soldiers on duty self-defence cannot be required as a plea to justify, or that they shall, in every case, be in imminent hazard of being prevented by violence from executing their duty; it is sufficient if there be reasonable ground to apprehend that they

E

Captain Porteous.

may be in hazard of being defeated in their object and the law set at defiance; that were it otherwise the execution of duty would in such cases "be a very ticklish matter", and, consequently, that the pannel, being *versans in licito* and engaged in the discharge of a lawful duty, if any excess was committed by him, it ought not to be attended with *pœna ordinaria*, or capital punishment.

To this it was answered that, though it were true, which was not denied, that the magistrates gave such orders, these could not justify Porteous in firing, "except all precautions for dissipating otherwise the mob and for legitimating the act of firing upon them had been previously made use of," i e , having the Riot Act read to intimidate the rioters and separate the innocent from the guilty, that his duty, so far as concerned the carrying out of the sentence, terminated when the execution was over and the criminal hanged; that the Guard was not attacked till the sentence had actually been executed; that it was to see to this only that the soldiers were brought there, that after this the pannel 'was no longer an officer employed to that end, for which the fire-arms were loaded, and his actions came to be estimated by the same rules that would have made them lawful or unlawful upon any ordinary occasion, when no particular danger threatened and when no necessary service was in view", that in such circumstances nothing short of being constituted in immediate danger of death without firing could justify him or his Guard to fire It was further argued that the provocation given by the mob by throwing stones and dirt, though it might justify a choleric man in giving a drubbing to any of the mob, could not justify a soldier in firing on a multitude The contradictory accounts given by the various witnesses of the pannel's behaviour were explained by the general confusion and surprise at the time of the tumult, and the fact that "at some other periods of the day he behaved himself in a different manner", and that, whereas the witnesses for the defence could only prove a negative, viz., that they did not see him fire or hear him order his men to do so, the Crown witnesses would swear to what they actually saw and heard to the contrary.

In the information for Porteous a "short relation" is given of the circumstances leading up to the affray, which is of

50

The Captain's Trial.

interest as being his own version of the facts His account of
the Provost's orders as to firing in case of resistance is borne
out by the statement of Major Pool before referred to Some
new points are the allegations that on the morning of the
execution Porteous proposed to the magistrates that they should
issue a proclamation as a caution to innocent sightseers, warning
them of their danger in case of any disturbance or attack made
upon the Guard, that a draft of such proclamation was, in
fact, prepared, but nothing further done, that the magistrates
sent to a bookseller for a dozen copies of the Riot Act, none of
which was used, and that, after Wilson had hung some time,
Porteous, apprehending trouble from the demeanour of the
mob about the scaffold, and fearing that a rescue was intended,
sent to the officiating bailies for permission to have the body
cut down forthwith, but received orders that it should hang a
quarter of an hour longer This is corroborated by Alexander
Thomson, town officer, a witness for the defence Porteous
further states that, when the attack upon the Guard began,
he tried to intimidate the mob by putting his gun to his shoulder
and pointing it around him, threatening "with an audible
voice," if they did not desist, to fire among them; that at this
instant one of the soldiers stepped from behind him and fired
the first shot, which killed Charles Husband; that, on seeing
others of the Guard about to fire, he forbade them to do so,
and even struck up their pieces, that he then did his best to
lead off his men, ordering the sergeants to gather them together
and follow him (which is confirmed by the witnesses for the
defence), and that while marching up the Bow, hearing shots
behind him, he looked back, but thought it best to get his men
away as soon as possible The pannel specially protested
against the accounts of the affair, published "by authority" in
the *Caledonian Mercury* of 15th and 19th April previous,[57]
as calculated to prejudice him in his defence, which he says
"are adorned with some witty sarcasms, very proper to this
melancholy occasion, and painted out with ingenious reflections
and quaint rhetorical invectives, very suitable to the authors
of these historical relations" Four recent instances of firing
upon the Edinburgh mob by men of the Guard, without
orders, were given, the last occurring only a few months earlier
at an execution when Captains Lind and Fergusson commanded

[57] Appendix III

Captain Porteous.

the detachment; and attention was drawn to the fact that several of the Guard had vowed vengeance against Wilson and his friends after the escape of Robertson   Among the precedents cited in behalf of the pannel were the cases of James Gordon, messenger, and others, 1691 (homicide on resistance of civil process), Captain John Wallace, 1692, and Corporal Macadam and Private Long, 1735 (homicide by soldiers in their duty), in each of which the defence was successful   In the case of Macadam and Long the sentence of the Court of Admiralty was reversed on review in the Court of Justiciary

The information for Porteous concludes as follows — "If the pannel is guilty of the charge in the precise way and manner it is laid against him in the indictment, he is of opinion himself he deserves to suffer, but if, upon the other hand, it shall come out that he is entirely innocent of the blood of those men wherewith he is charged, he thinks his case deserves singular commiseration, because, if bonds and imprisonment, loss of employment and bread, obloquy, and reproach of blood-guilt and massacre, and, of consequence, loss of character, be calamities in human life, then he has had as great a share of them as ever attended innocence "

On 16th July the Court met, and, having considered the indictment and debate thereupon, found the facts libelled relevant to infer the pains of law, " but allowed the pannel to adduce what evidence he could with respect to his behaviour at the time the foresaid crimes are libelled to have been committed, for taking off the circumstances which should be brought for inferring his being guilty, or art and part of the crimes libelled, and remitted the pannel and the indictment as found relevant to the knowledge of an assize " The Court then continued the diet " till Monday next at seven of the clock in the morning," and ordained the pannel to be carried back to prison

With reference to the interlocutor on the relevancy, Burnett observes—" Nothing is here said of the conduct of the mob, the true, indeed, the only ground of justification on the part of Porteous, but his defence is made to rest solely on his behaviour at the time   There was, indeed, both in the information for the prisoner, and in his petition afterwards to Queen Caroline, too much said on his supposed conduct at the time (his not firing or giving orders to fire), and too little on

the general argument in justification, arising from the conduct
of the mob, and the consequent plea of duty on the part of the
soldiers "58   Lord Dreghorn states it was objected for
Porteous that this interlocutor circumscribed his proof too
much, and that he ought to have been allowed a proof of all
circumstances he judged material for his defence   Upon this
point his lordship quotes the following observations, taken
from an unprinted paper preserved in the collection of a
gentleman who was at the time of this trial in the King's
service.—" It was answered, 1st. A proof at large cannot
be allowed, consistent with the rules established, in favour of
the person who stands his trial   To check the witnesses, and
for the more thorough information of the jury, and to prevent
as much as possible the jury from returning verdicts contrary
to evidence, all the depositions or examinations are entered
upon record, signed by the witnesses and one of the judges
Counsel is allowed to plead for the defendant, which necessarily
take up so much time that, if the defendant was left at liberty
to prove what he pleased, human nature could not stand under
the fatigue of a trial, and breaking off in the middle and
taking it by parts is both contrary to law and extremely
dangerous.

"2nd. The defendant is at liberty to offer what he pleases
in his defence to the Court, and if he made it appear by his
counsel that it is material for him, the Court allows a proof
In the trial the counsel for Captain Porteous insisted upon
circumstances previous, circumstances subsequent, and his
behaviour during the execution of Wilson   The circumstances
previous were the orders said to be given by the magistrates
the day before the execution   Now the orders could be no
other than to fire if it was necessary, and that he could have
done without orders   If they had ordered him to fire without
necessity such apparent unlawful order could not defend him

"If the magistrates had upon the spot given orders his
case was more favourable; wherefore the Court could not
sustain these orders as a defence nor regularly admit a proof
of them

"But in the *next* place every circumstance insisted upon by
the defendant in relation to these orders are fairly admitted
by His Majesty's advocate in his information, and this

---

58 Burnett's *Criminal Law*, 1811, p 73, *n.*

Captain Porteous.

admission is accepted of in the information for the pannel, so that, had this circumstance been material, he had all the advantage he could hope from a proof, though, in truth, it was altogether immaterial

"As to all that happened in the Grassmarket he had a proof allowed him

"It has, indeed, been objected that here he was limited to evidence with respect to his behaviour   But as *behaviour* is a relative word, it necessarily led him into a proof of the behaviour of every person there present; and this is apparent from the proof taken . and it is the word the pannel's lawyers chose in setting forth his defence, as is apparent from the 19th page of their information in the first paragraph

"As to circumstances subsequent one only was insisted on, viz , that his gun appeared not to have been fired   It was in itself immaterial   For, 1mo, it did not exculpate from giving orders to fire; 2do, he might have fired the gun of one of the soldiers under his command; 3tio, to make it an ingredient of any force, he behoved to offer a proof that the gun inspected after the affair was over was, during the whole time of the execution and until it was inspected, in his hands , which was not offered to be proven

"But in the *last* place, even this circumstance was allowed to be laid before the jury, for, upon the request of the pannel's counsel, the magistrates present did, in open Court, declare the gun produced to them by Captain Porteous when, after the misfortune they were proceeding to take a precognition, appeared to be clean "59

When the Court sat again on 19th July a jury was em-panelled, which included Sir John Inglis of Cramond and six other local landowners, the remainder being Edinburgh tradesmen   The pannel then judicially confessed that the several persons mentioned in the indictment " were killed or wounded by firing proceeding from the party of the City Guard then under his command," and the evidence for the prosecution was led

It is to be regretted that in the official record of the trial, which is the only report available, the evidence of the witnesses is given in the then customary form of depositions, and not by way of question and answer.   The old

---

59 Maclaurin's *Arguments and Decisions*, 1774, Introduction, sec 3.

54

The Captain's Trial.

method adopted, besides being much less full and interesting, draws no distinction between facts elicited on examination-in-chief and those obtained by cross-examination, further, it entirely obscures the individuality both of witness and counsel "The evidence printed," writes Mr Andrew Lang, "leaves the question of facts obscure", and he also refers to ' the discrepancies in the hostile evidence, which were great."[60] Scott, in his *Tales of a Grandfather*, describes the evidence as "perplexed and contradictory"

Twenty-eight witnesses were examined in behalf of the Crown, including such "representative citizens" as Sir William Forbes, advocate, the Hon William Fraser, a son of Lord Saltoun, and Mr Dewar of Vogrie, together with sundry merchants, artificers, and soldiers of the Guard Of these, nineteen expressly swore that they saw and heard Porteous fire the first shot in the affray, most of them adding such "corroborative detail' as the flash of powder in the pan and the smoke from the muzzle of his gun They viewed the scene either from windows overlooking the gibbet or from various positions in the street, some being thirty yards distant at the moment, while others were within a yard or two of him The facts brought out for the Crown from the tangled testimony adduced appear to be briefly as follows ·—That when the attack was made upon the Guard Porteous was on the causeway at the north-east side of the scaffold, between it and the Bowfoot Well, that he advanced a few paces westward in front of his men and pointed his gun at the people, as if threatening them that he would fire, that, being struck by one of the stones, he did fire, the shot killing Charles Husband, then standing at the foot of Robertson's Close, and tearing the coat of the witness Andrew Daw, who stood beside him that immediately thereafter Porteous called to his men to "fire, and be damn'd !" whereupon some twenty shots were fired by the Guard, with the fatal results which we know The contention of the defence was that the first shot was fired by a soldier, who advanced from behind Porteous on his right hand Five of the Crown witnesses deponed, presumably in cross-examination, as to this point, four of these saw no soldier near him when he fired, but the other, George Drummond, one of the Commissioners of

---

60 *History of Scotland*, iv 430

Captain Porteous.

Customs, directly corroborates the witnesses for the prisoner With regard to the gun used by Porteous the statements are very confusing   Archibald Yates, William Murray, William Jameson, and John Moffat say he fired twice, first with his own gun and next with a gun taken from one of the Guard, Yates adding, "That at the time when the pannel took the gun from the soldier he laid his own upon the scaffold", William Johnstoun says he fired once, with the soldier's gun, and "appeared to be in a passion, and it was some short time before he was master of the gun"; John Stewart says he saw Porteous "jump down from the south side of the scaffold and walk up briskly towards the place where the disturbance was, but nothing in his hand but a cane," and that he then took a gun from a soldier and fired, the other witnesses say he fired once only, and with his own gun.   As to the position of Porteous when he fired there is also a conflict of evidence among the Crown witnesses, but the majority depone to that above mentioned. To increase the complexity of their evidence, John Ritchie says that three shots were fired by the Guard before Porteous himself fired, while William Murray depones that two soldiers fired first, and that Porteous then pursued a man for thirty or forty yards and shot him down   Murray is the only witness who mentions this incident, but it appears he had been deaf for seven years, so perhaps, as a compensation, he saw more than other people.

With regard to the alleged orders by Porteous to fire, ten of the witnesses for the prosecution swore positively that they heard these given   James Nasmith and David Brown, two of the workmen who were beginning to remove the scaffold, heard the words as the Captain passed them at a distance of a yard or so   Most of these witnesses concur as to the expression used—"Fire, and be damn'd!" but the deaf gentleman, in spite of his infirmity, is able to condescend upon even more impolite and forcible terms

All the Crown witnesses minimise the seriousness of the assault upon the Guard   James Drummond speaks of "some small stones thrown by the mob at the executioner, some whereof the deponent believes might have fallen upon the Guard"; George Drummond "did not think that the stones that were thrown did give any just cause for the firing," but admits that they damaged the hangman, and "observed his

The Captain's Trial.

nose blooding", and Mark Sprot depones "he did not observe
that there was any greater disturbance than usual at executions" No evidence seems to have been led by the Crown
with reference to the last firing, when the Guard were being
withdrawn by Porteous up the West Bow, his renewed orders to
fire there, and his firing himself upon that second occasion,
all as libelled in the indictment The witnesses who depone
to his having fired twice cannot refer to this incident, as they
state the shots referred to were both fired at the beginning
of the affray, in the vicinity of the scaffold

Sixteen witnesses only were adduced for the defence, although
the *Courant* records, on 5th July, that "upwards of one
hundred witnesses are summoned to the pannel's exculpation."
Eight of these swear that they distinctly saw one of the Guard
soldiers fire the first shot, all of them, having the same opportunity of judging as the Crown witnesses, say that Porteous
merely threatened the mob with his musket, and never fired
at all Thomas Harton, surgeon in the Welsh Fusiliers,
depones "that he had his eyes strictly upon the pannel all
this time", John Clark, sergeant in the same regiment,
"during that time had his eye fixed upon those who fired, and
did not observe Captain Porteous fire', and Mr Campbell
of Ardonnick (Ardeonaig) states that he watched Porteous—
who, notwithstanding the disturbance, behaved ' very civilly "
—until the first shots were fired, "which firings took the
deponent's eyes from off the pannel " Sergeant Clark's
evidence is interesting He had been sent down by the officer
commanding the detachment of regular troops in the Lawnmarket to receive any orders relative to their movements, and
was, at the time of the attack by the mob, in conversation
with Porteous upon the scaffold. He was struck by a stone
"about the bigness of his two fists," whereupon he and the
Captain came down from the scaffold together, the latter
"endeavouring to keep off the mob with his fusee, waving it
to and again, telling them to keep off or he would fire, but
there was no fire at that time " The crowd was pressing
upon the Guard, "and drove them about four or five yards from
the place where they were posted at first " The witness goes
on to state that he saw the soldier fire while Porteous was
beside him, "and observed a man [Charles Husband] drop
at the entry of Robertson's Close " Another witness, John

57

Captain Porteous.

Robertson, confirms this. George Vint depones to the same effect, describing the soldier as "a black-haired man" [not the usual "powder'd pow'" of the City Guard], "upon which the pannel turned about to him and pushed him into his rank."

With regard to the gun carried by Porteous, Dr Harton depones, "That when the pannel was upon the scaffold he had no gun in his hand; but when he came off again he took a gun from a soldier" William Meanie, sergeant of the Guard, says "that the pannel gave the deponent his fusee, which was the fusee the pannel ordinarily carried, to keep while he attended the execution and the players, which the deponent returned to the pannel again upon the sign being given to cut down Wilson, and before the pannel came down from the scaffold"

As to the orders given by Porteous, three soldiers of the Guard gave evidence Matthew Howert, who was close to him, depones that, just before some of his fellows fired, "he heard the pannel say to the soldiers twice, 'Do not fire,' and heard the soldiers say one to another, 'Fire, or we shall all be knocked down'", David Maitine says "before there was any firing he did hear the pannel call to them not to fire", and William Byres, after the first shots, "heard the pannel call unto the soldiers to fall into their ranks and follow him, which accordingly the deponent and the rest did, falling in gradually as they were able" It is observed, with much force, in the information for Porteous that at the time of the alleged orders to fire, the men were not drawn up in a regular line or band, but were either straggling, mixed with the mob, or in a circular formation surrounding the scaffold, which excluded the possibility of any general order to fire, "unless it be supposed that the pannel was a madman, seeing any compliance with such order must have led the men to fire each in his opposite neighbour's breast and a great many into that of the pannel"

The evidence for the defence shows the attack on the Guard to have been a much more serious affair than either Dr Carlyle or the Crown witnesses represent Dr Harton says the stones thrown by the mob at the soldiers were "of such bigness that was sufficient to have killed them, in case they had hit them in a proper place" Sergeant Meanie speaks to "showers of stones,' and "particularly one big stone, which

58

The Captain's Trial.

lighted betwixt the deponent and Sergeant Finlay, above three pounds weight"; Matthew Howert tells of "a great many stones, both great and small," striking the soldiers, David Martine "had his shoulder-blade disjointed with a stroke he received upon it with a stone", and James Armour, Writer to the Signet, who saw the affair from a window, "observed the crowd of people throwing stones of considerable bigness" about the scaffold, and when the soldiers were retiring 'the crowd pursued after them, renewed the throwing of great stones, and in great numbers" Another Edinburgh writer, George Smeiton, depones that one of the mob grappled with Porteous as the latter descended from the scaffold, which statement is supported by Dr Harton, who adds that Porteous was then "endeavouring to get his men together, which he could not well do, they being so much interspersed with the mob" There can be no question of the dangerous character of the assault upon the Guard, for Sergeant Meanie's account of the injuries sustained by the soldiers from these missiles is corroborated by the evidence of Dr Kennedy, an Edinburgh surgeon, who describes the hurts of such of the men as he attended professionally after the affray.

It also seems to be clearly proved that Porteous had nothing whatever to do with the second firing in the West Bow David Rennie, looking from his own window in that street, as the Captain led his men past below, heard the shots fired further down by those in the rear, who were out of his sight, Matthew Howert and William Byres were marching after Porteous up the Bow, and heard the firing behind them, Mr Armour observed the soldiers in the rear turn upon their pursuers, "and then heard a good number of more shots fired, which, to his grief, he saw did great execution", while Peter Colstoun, from the north-west corner of the Cornmarket, "saw the pannel march the Guard under his command up the West Bow, and saw several of the rear of that Guard fire upon the people assembled at the execution, and at the time observed, the pannel was within the first turn of the West Bow, and so out of the deponent's view"—the significance of the last statement being that if Captain Porteous, at the head of his men, had rounded the first bend of the Bow, which rose in a sharp zig-zag to the Lawnmarket, it was impossible for him either to see or control

59

Captain Porteous.

the movements of those in the rear, who had not yet turned the corner

The *London Magazine* for September, 1736, states—"We are assured that, after the depositions against and for Captain Porteous, the counsel for him urged that two of the magistrates of Edinburgh and a gentleman, one of the counsel against him, which three persons were present in Court, might be examined, to give some satisfaction to the Court and jury of the condition his piece or firelock was in immediately upon his return from the execution of Wilson, and before he had entered any house And the said three persons, being so examined, did all severally declare that upon his return from the execution aforesaid he did directly come up to the magistrates of the city, assembled at their Council House, and desired that his piece or firelock might be inspected , and that the same having been accordingly inspected by the said magistrates it was found loaded, and in such condition of cleanness that it was apparent it could not have been fired, unless it had been thereafter cleaned. But these declarations don't enter the record " This is corroborated by Bailie Hamilton's examination and the paper printed by Lord Dreghorn

In view of the contradictory and inconsistent character of the evidence adduced, it is unfortunate that the addresses of counsel for the prosecution and defence are omitted in the official record of the trial The only reference to these extant is contained in the following paragraph from the *Caledonian Mercury* of 20th July, 1736 —"Yesterday, at seven in the morning, the Right Honourable Lords of Justiciary sat down again on the trial of John Porteous, and appointed the jury.

The examination of witnesses for the indictment was not finished till near six at night, and those for the pannel not till after one this morning In summing up the evidence (by His Majesty's solicitor) for proving the pannel's firing among innocent people and giving orders so to do, the atrociousness of these crimes was most learnedly set forth sub-summing, that no negative evidence could at all enervate positive proof The evidence for the pannel tended in general to prove his innocent behaviour all the time libelled, and the provocation the populace gave him to act another part all which were very judiciously treated by Mr. James Grahame, junior At two in the morning the jury inclosed (with the proof and a plan of the place of execution); about nine o'clock

The Captain's Trial.

they broke up, and at four this afternoon are to return their verdict." In arriving at their decision the jury had not the benefit of any summing up of the evidence by the presiding judge, tho practice of charging juries being then unknown This custom was first introduced by Lord Kames at the remarkable trial of Katharine Nairn in 1765, where exception was taken to it in behalf of the prisoner as being illegal, but later it became the uniform usage

As Sir Walter Scott observes, "A jury of incensed citizens took the worst view of the case", and on 20th July, under the hands of Sir John Inglis of Cramond, their Chancellor, and James Davidson, bookseller in Edinburgh, their Clerk, they returned a verdict of guilty in the following terms·— "They all in one voice fand it proven, that the said John Porteous, pannel, fired a gun among the people assembled at the place of execution and time libelled   As also that he gave orders to the soldiers under his command to fire; and upon his and then so firing the persons mentioned in the indictment were killed and wounded   And fand it proven that the pannel and his Guard were attacked and beat by several stones of a considerable bigness, thrown amongst them by the multitude, whereby several of the soldiers were bruised and wounded "   The *London Magazine* for that month records— "The number of jurymen in the pannel was fifteen, eight of whom were for the verdict as brought in, and seven against it "   So the Captain's fate was decided by a majority of one. The Court then pronounced sentence of death in the usual form, " by the mouth of John Dalgleish, dempster of Court," adjudging John Porteous to be hanged in the Grassmarket upon Wednesday, 8th September, between the hours of two and four, by the hands of the executioner ; and the proceedings terminated

Commenting on this trial, Burnett quotes an *obiter dictum* of Lord Royston in a similar case, that " the Court was not inclined to give too much encouragement to soldiers, even though acting by orders, military execution being an extraordinary remedy, and not to be used but in cases of necessity " Burnett remarks—" This principle seems to have ruled in the noted case of Porteous, which happened a few years thereafter, though, considering the violence of the mob, the actual assault made on the soldiers, and the notoriety of the avowed purpose which brought the greater part of the mob there, this

Captain Porteous.

principle ought not to have had effect in such a case, and
certainly would not now be followed were a similar case to
occur.   It is plain, from the interlocutor of relevancy, and
still more from the sentence following on the verdict (which
last expressly found that the pannel and his Guard were
attacked and beat, and several of the soldiers bruised and
wounded), that the Court were influenced by the circumstance
of Porteous's conduct at the time betraying symptoms rather
of a revengeful and malicious purpose, than showing that he
acted from a sense of duty "[61]

Hume, treating of *Homicide by Soldiers in Discharge
of their Duty*, observes—"But between the case of
Porteous and the precedents which have been cited on
the other side there is one material distinction, that this
assembly of people was not a licentious and criminal, but a
lawful, and (as it must be esteemed) even a laudable, assembly,
in which by far the greater part of the persons present were
innocently and peaceably met, and neither in truth did nor
could in law be held to partake of the evil purposes of those
among them who came there to rescue the convict   Now, to
justify the firing on a multitude of this description would
have required far higher provocation than any that is mentioned in the verdict, and circumstances also of delay, warning,
and forbearance, beyond what are necessary in the case of an
unlawful meeting, and which could not be alleged for this
unfortunate pannel.   The tumult had not been of long con-
tinuance when he gave orders to fire, and he did so without
any authority from the magistrates of the place, who were
at hand to be consulted on the occasion   Neither does it
appear that he ever warned the people to desist, or gave
notice of his intention to fire,[62] or allowed time for the peaceable and well-disposed to separate or withdraw   Moreover, the
fire was not directed to that quarter only from which the
stones were thrown, and, stepping out of his proper duty,
Porteous acted the part of a private soldier, and was himself
the first to discharge his piece   Certainly, in these circumstances, his conduct could not be justified   Whether his
offence might not properly have been referred to some of the
lower species of homicide if the jury had stated in their verdict

---

[61] Burnett's *Criminal Law*, 1811, p. 73, *n.*
[62] On the contrary, it seems to be clearly proved that he did both.

62

The Mob's Revenge.

all those extenuating circumstances which were warranted by
the proof; nay, whether there was not room for this construction on the verdict as actually returned; and whether,
on the whole case, there might not bo sufficient grounds for
the interposition of the Royal mercy to mitigate the sentence—
these are different questions, and perhaps not so clear against
the sufferer as one would wish them to have been " And in
a note on this passage Hume adds—"It was admitted on the
part of the Crown that the magistrates, in fear of a rescue,
had given orders for the Guard to load before proceeding to
take charge of the convict, and that a body of the King's
forces had been called into the city, and assurance given them
of permission to fire, if they were attacked Further, it
seems to be proved that before the order to fire the convict's
body was actually cut down by the mob, that the Guard were
pressed upon and thrown into disorder, that the executioner
was cut in the face with a stone to the effusion of his blood,
that a drummer was cut in the head to the effusion of his
blood, and his drum beaten to pieces by a stone, that a
soldier of the Guard had his shoulder-blade broken, and that
the pannel himself was struck with a stone before he fired
The verdict does not state any of these things, and the Court
could not consider them But even upon what is found by the
verdict it has not to every person seemed clear that the case
fell to be construed as a case of murder "[63]

(1) THE MOB'S REVENGE

Glowr round the cawsey, up an' doun,
What mobbing and what plotting !
The Election.—Robert Fergusson

No doubts as to the soundness of the verdict or the justice
of the sentence clouded the intense satisfaction with which the
Edinburgh populace hailed the result of the trial It is
worthy of note that, although it clearly appeared from the
evidence of all the witnesses that some twenty shots had been
fired by soldiers of the Guard, there was no popular outcry
against them, nor any demand that they should be brought to
trial for the crime, on account of which fifteen of them were
then in gaol It was upon Captain Porteous, and upon him
alone, that the popular fury fell; he only was the object of

---

63 Hume's *Commentaries*, 1819, 1 207, and *n*

Captain Porteous.

the people's vengeance   The Provost, who ordered him to repel force by force and had his men supplied with powder and ball to that end : the soldiers, of whom, in the uproar and confusion of the tumult, scattered as they were by their assailants, and each fighting for his own hand, some at least must have fired voluntarily (as those in the West Bow plainly did), were alike blameless in the eyes of the rabble so soon as their scapegoat's fate was sealed.   It only remained to kill time till the welcome day should dawn when something more tangible was to be destroyed, and that good old custom of blood for blood could be lawfully indulged

Porteous, however, had powerful friends, and there were not wanting men of sober judgment, unblinded by the common hatred of the culprit, who regarded the proof of his guilt as doubtful and inconclusive   Apart from this, many thought it hard that what was at worst an excess committed in the performance of a public duty should be punished with death, and considered the case eminently one for the exercise of the Royal prerogative, with a view to a mitigation of the sentence Though Captain Porteous had frequently attended other executions in his official capacity, the propriety of his conduct on such occasions had never been questioned—indeed, the Lord Advocate admitted in his information, ' the prosecutor never heard, nor, so far as he knows, did ever any man before this time complain, of the wickedness or inhumanity of the pannel ; and he has received no information by which he can be induced to think that for any considerable time before the fact complained of the pannel had premeditated the destructive action of which he is accused "   Porteous was accordingly advised to present a petition to Queen Caroline, then guardian of the realm during one of her august consort's chronic visits to his beloved Hanover, setting forth the peculiar circumstances of his case, while it was arranged that other petitions in his favour should be forwarded at the instance of his friends and well-wishers   He would seem himself to have been dubious as to the result of these applications, and to have been prepared for the worst, for we read in the *Caledonian Mercury* of 9th August—" Yesterday John Porteous, under sentence of death, was, at his own desire, prayed for in all the churches and meeting-houses of this city "

In illustration of the feeling in favour of Porteous above
64

The Mob's Revenge.

referred to, an interesting letter from the papers of General Wade, Commander-in-Chief of the Forces in Scotland, written to enlist his interest in behalf of the condemned man, is printed by Chambers [64] The writer, Catharine Allardice, was a daughter of George Allardice of that ilk, by his wife Lady Anne Ogilvy, daughter of the fourth Earl of Findlater; and the letter is valuable, not only as showing the influential persons who were moving in the matter, but as a curious example of the literary attainments of the Scots gentlewoman of that day The letter, the original orthography and punctuation of which are preserved, is as follows —

"I dute not Dear general waid but by this time you may have heard the fattel sentence of the poor unhappy cap[t] porteous how in six weeks time most dye if he riceve not speedy help from above, by the asistance of men of generosity and mercy such as you realy are it is the opinion of all thos of the better sort he has been hardly deelt by, being cond'mned but by a very slender proof, and tho he was much provokted by the mob and had the provest and magestrets order to fire which th'y now sheamfuly deney nor had he the leeberty to prove it tho even in his own defence, but the generous major powl [Pool] will assure you of the trouth, and yet tho the cap[t] had thos crule orders it is proven my [by] commiscrci wesly mr Drumond doctor horton and severel other gentelmen of undoubted crided he realy did not make use of them, that there eyes were fixed on him all the while and have declar'd upon oth he deed not fire, true it is he presented his firelock in hopes to frighten the mob when ane unlucy felow at the same time and just by the cap[t] fired which lead the two witness into the fatel mistake that has condemn'd him the unfortenat pannal both befor and after the dismal sentence protested befor god and the judges he was entirely inesent putting all thes circomstances to gether the miserable state he now is in most draw your generous pity on his side ther'for dr general waid continwa your uswal mercy and plead for him and as our sex are neturly compassinot and being now in the power of the quin, so generous a pleader as you may easely persuad, considring it is a thing of great concquenc to the whol army which yourself better knou then I can inform the duke of buccleugh, marques of Lowding [Lothian]

---

64 *Domestic Annals of Scotland*, iii 595, n

Captain Porteous.

Lord morton geneal myls [General Moyle] all the commissioners and chiff baron are to join their intrest with yours in this affair, by your own generous soul I beg again Dear sir you will do whats in your power to save him, thos that think right go not through this poor short life just for themselves which your good actions shou you oft consider, and as many just now put a sincer trust in your generous mercy I am sure they will not be disapointed throgh aney neglect of yours let this letter be taken notes of amongst the nomber you will reseve from your frinds in Scotland in behalf of the unfortunat capt which will intierly oblidg

"Dear general waid

"your most affectionat and most

"obident humble servant

"CATHARINE ALLARDICE

you would be sory for the unexresable los I have had of the kindest mother, and two sisters I am now at Mrs Lind's where it would be no smal satesfaction to hear by a Line or two I am not forget by you drect for me at Mr. Lind's [captain of the City Guard] hous in Edenburg your letter will come safe if you are so good as to writ Mr Lind his Lady and I send our best complements to you, he along with Lord aberdour and mr wyevel how has also wrot to his sister Mis pursal go hand and hand togither makeing all the interest they can for the poor capt and meet with great sucess they join in wishing you the same not fearing your intrest the generals Lady now is his great friend were this day to speak to the Justes clarck but I have not since seen her so that every on of compassision and mercy are equely bussey forgive this trouble and send ous hop"

    Two petitions, differently worded, by Porteous to the Queen are among the Scottish State Papers in the Record Office One, setting forth his case at length in a very lucid and able manner, is unsigned, and is apparently a draft or copy; the other is shorter, and signed "John Porteous" Two petitions in his behalf by "Noblemen and others" in identical terms are extant, one in the Record Office and the other in the possession of the Society of Antiquaries of Scotland [65] The

---

[65] Copies of these four documents will be found in Appendix II

66

The Mob's Revenge.

former is signed by fifty persons of position and repute, including the Duke of Buccleuch, the Earls of Moray, Morton, Home, Cassillis, Lauderdale, Balcarres, and Wigton, Viscount Primrose; Barons Elphinstone, Napier, Torphichen and Lindores; Lords Aberdour, Doune, George Ilay, Edward Murray, and Charles Hay; four baronets, two Sheriffs, General Moyle; Colonels Duroure and Peers, and others   The second petition, which does not appear to have been presented, is signed by Baron Saltoun, Lord Drummore (one of the Lords of Session), and seventeen landed proprietors   The petitioners, *inter alia*, state—"That we beg leave to submit it to your Royal wisdom whether there are not some circumstances attending the case of the said John Porteous that may plead our excuse for thus presenting him to Your Majesty as a proper object of the royal clemency? and whether, if the said sentence shall be executed to the rigour, it may not encourage wicked and evil-disposed persons to adventure upon resisting the just execution of the laws? and therefor if, in respect of the attack upon the Guard so found proven by the jury, the said John Porteous may not merit some mitigation or commutation of the sentence pronounced against him"   The two petitions of Porteous, both of which are undated, are pinned together, and each is endorsed "in the Lord Justice-Clerk's of Aug 25th, 1736"   The petition in his favour at the Record Office is similarly endorsed.   On that date Lord Milton writes to the Duke of Newcastle, Secretary of State for Scotland—"At the desire of persons of quality and distinction, I have taken the liberty of troubling your Grace with the enclosed petition to Her Majesty in favour of John Porteous, now under sentence of death, together with a petition from himself to the Queen, and it is their request your Grace may be pleased to present them to Her Majesty as soon as may be convenient, because the 8th of September is the day fixed for the execution '[66]

Mr Omond, in his interesting article on the Porteous Riot, remarks that the Government was, from various causes, then so much weakened in Scotland " that, though anxious to support the authority of the law by saving Porteous, whose offence they regarded as merely an excess of zeal in the performance of his duty, the Ministers were afraid to grant the prayer of his petition   Another petition was therefore prepared at the

---

[66] Copies of this and other letters afterwards quoted will be found in Appendix XIII.

Captain Porteous.

same time, which the Ministry privately agreed to support, on condition that the opposition, as well as the friends of the Government, should sign it   This condition, which was kept a profound secret at the time, was insisted on, lest the opposition should make political capital out of the reprieve of Porteous, which, it was well known, would be highly unpopular in Scotland "[67]   There is no doubt, however, that the reprieve was actually granted by the Queen before these documents reached London.   General Wade, in the House of Lords inquiry, after deponing as to the promotion of the petition in favour of Porteous, remarks, ' But Her Majesty being graciously pleased, out of her great goodness and mercy, to grant a reprieve before this petition was delivered, it arrived at Edinburgh about a week before the time appointed for his execution [68]   On the 26th August, the day after the Lord Justice-Clerk's letter above mentioned was despatched, the Duke of Newcastle, in a letter directed to the Lords of Justiciary at Edinburgh, signified "Her Majesty's pleasure that the execution of the sentence pronounced against the said John Porteous be respited for six weeks from the time appointed for his execution "   The Royal reprieve reached Edinburgh on Thursday, 2nd September, and on that date the *Caledonian Mercury*, in notifying the respite, observes—" The grace extended to John Porteous seems to have anticipated the second application made in his favours "   This, the only notice of a previous application, no mention of which appears elsewhere, probably refers to the private efforts of friends exerted in his behalf, as indicated in the letter of Catharine Allardice to General Wade, above quoted

On Friday, 3rd September, in obedience to the Queen's command, the High Court of Justiciary pronounced an order prohibiting the magistrates and all other officers of the law from putting the sentence of death in execution until the 20th of October following, on which day it was required to be carried out by them as formerly ordered   The effect of this reprieve upon the populace of Edinburgh is eloquently described in the fourth chapter of the *Heart of Midlothian*, of which it forms one of the most impressive scenes, the author comparing it to the feelings of a tiger deprived of the meal he

---

[67] *Scottish Review*, July, 1892; see also the same author's *Lord Advocates of Scotland*, i 351 and authorities there cited
[68] Examination of General Wade

The Mob's Revenge.

was about to devour. But it is to be noted that the novelist,
with a view to secure a striking situation, has taken
unwarrantable liberty with historical truth Scott postpones
the arrival of the respite to the dramatic but imaginary
moment that a fictitious mob are waiting round a non-existent
gibbet for the hanging of Captain Porteous on the day
originally fixed for the execution, Wednesday, 8th September,
when that unfortunate officer was, in fact, lying dead in Grey-
friars Church The gain of thus heightening the effect of
the tale is immeasurably overbalanced by the improbability
of making the subsequent conspiracy for Porteous's murder the
work of a single afternoon, instead of being, as it actually was,
a deep-laid and elaborate scheme which required five full days
to mature and execute "Not even the most romantic reader
of novels,' says Chambers, "supposing him to understand
the case to its full extent, would deceive himself with so
incredible an absurdity "[69] But the picture of the wild beast
robbed of its prey is so admirable and convincing that one
feels the incident ought to have happened as depicted, and
that for once fiction is stranger than truth As a matter
of fact, however, no overt hostility was at first displayed by
the people to the action of the Government in granting the
reprieve, and the Lord Justice-Clerk, in acknowledging its
receipt to the Duke of Newcastle on 4th September, writes,
"This act of Her Majesty's Royal mercy, and as it points to
further, meets with almost a general approbation, especially
among those of the higher rank and greatest distinction. And
the few who grumble are only of the meaner sort, or such as
either have confined ways of thinking, or such as seem determined to complain whatever happens " His lordship was
soon to find that the malcontents could do something more
than grumble

"The mob of Edinburgh," says Scott, "when thoroughly
excited, had been at all times one of the fiercest which could
be found in Europe, and of late years they had risen repeatedly
against the Government, and sometimes not without temporary success " One instance of its temper and power is
furnished by the notable case of Captain Green, executed for
piracy and murder in 1705 Green and some of his crew
were found guilty of a crime, which they were not proved to

---

[69] *Illustrations of the Author of Waverley*, p. 169

Captain Porteous.

have committed, by a jury blinded by national prejudice and local passions   When the Privy Council met to consider the prisoners' petition for mercy, and were disposed to rectify so scandalous a miscarriage of justice, a howling mob thundered at the doors, demanding the lives of the condemned men with such fury that the Council was afraid to interfere with the sentence   "The mob, imagining that the criminals were reprieved by the Privy Council's sitting so long, did attack the Lord Chancellor in his coach with stones and sticks, who with great difficulty escaped, his coach being broke to pieces, and my lord run up the stairs of a house "[70]

It was, therefore, not to be supposed that such a people would tamely acquiesce in the benevolent intentions of the Government towards the object of their peculiar hate   The joy with which the death sentence had been received in July was tempered by some uneasiness lest the Crown should intervene, and Porteous, in the expressive vernacular, "cheat the wuddy" after all   The promotion of the petition for a reprieve added to the rabble's apprehensions, and on the receipt of the respite their worst fears were realised   "The mob," writes the author of the letter belonging to Mr Farley, before referred to, "who had the spirit of revenge kept strongly alive in them by those true trumpeters of sedition and cruelty in all countries, the dam'd priests, dropt some threatening letters, and many reports were spread of what they would do if Porteous was not executed on Wednesday, the 8th inst., according to the tenor of his sentence "[71]   That the ministers were no advocates of the quality of mercy also appears from an unpublished "Brief Account" of the riot among the Newcastle MSS in the British Museum, which states—"Before the murder of Porteous some of the clergy from their pulpits said that the land was defiled with blood, and that the judgments of God would hang over their heads till the bloodshedders were delivered into the hands of the avenger   And afterwards some of them said that God often made use of mean instruments to bring about His blessed will and purpose "[72]

Fortified by these ghostly counsels, the evil passions of the

---

70 For this and other examples of the behaviour of the Edinburgh mob, see Appendix VIII
71 Appendix IV   72 Appendix V

The Mob's Revenge.

people were wrought into a deadly design, and the rumour that lynch law would carry out what official justice had failed to effect was current on every hand. According to the "Brief Account," it was publicly said, in all conversation both in town and country, "that Porteous would be hanged the day he was sentenced to die, without any regard to Her Majesty's reprieve; and this was industriously spread through the country fifty miles round Edinburgh to induce them to come and assist in that execrable murder "[73] "These reports of this intended murder," says General Wade, "were so public that it was the topic of conversation for a week before it was committed, both at taverns, coffee-houses, tea-tables, and even at the Market Cross of Edinburgh; it had spread likewise to Glasgow, Stirling, Perth, and was talked of at Carlisle and at Berwick for some days before, and even at London the day after it was committed "[74] In support of the last statement the general relates how a Scots tradesman, whom he employed in London, told him that he gave a fellow-countryman a bed on the night of the murder, Tuesday, 7th September. Next morning he asked his lodger what news there was from Edinburgh, and received the answer, "that all the news he could tell him was that Porteous was hanged last night." On the landlord reminding him that Porteous had been reprieved ten or twelve days before, "'Tis all one for that," replies the man, "you will find he was hanged last night," which some time after, to his great surprise, he found to be true.[75] Patrick Lindsay, ex-Lord Provost of Edinburgh, and then member of Parliament for the city, admits that he early heard the report of the mob's intention from several persons, but considered it improbable. "I remember," he says, "that a few days before the thing happened, one Mr. George Gordon, brother-in-law of Porteous, and one who was very solicitous and anxious to have a reprieve for him, told me, laughing, 'You have no doubt heard the story that the mob are to hang poor Porteous. I wish we had nothing else to fear.'"[76] It is curious, by the way, if Porteous was the type of husband he is said to have been, that his brother-in-law should take such interest in his preservation.

---

[73] Appendix V.
[74] Examination of General Wade.   [75] Ibid.
[76] Examination of Patrick Lindsay.

Captain Porteous.

Captain Lind, of the City Guard, states that the rumour of the intended riot was the common talk of the whole town—"in all coffee-houses upon the street"—for eight days before it happened, and that he received definite intelligence regarding same from an unnamed informant on Friday, 3rd September On Saturday, between eight and nine at night, he called at the Provost's house and communicated this information to him, in presence of Mr. Lindsay, the town treasurer, and the dean of guild If Provost Wilson was, as he asserts, till then entirely ignorant of the gathering storm, he must have been a singularly ill-informed and unobservant official But the "Brief Account" states that "the Provost received several letters from different hands acquainting him with the intentions of the mob, and some threatening him that if he did any act or thing that should defeat their design of hanging Porteous he might expect to be hanged in his place " As to what passed at this interview on Saturday, the 4th, there is a conflict of evidence between the parties The Provost says he told Lind to inquire into the truth of the matter, and to report further thereon to him; Lind denies that any such orders were given, and adds that his suggestions that Porteous should be removed for safety to the Castle, and the city train-bands called out, met with no response Lindsay was of opinion that the affair ought to be carefully inquired into, "for those things are easier prevented by being crushed in the bud than suppressed when they come to any height " Later events must have confirmed him in this judgment

Captain Lind, having prosecuted his inquiries, was satisfied that there was grave cause for alarm, and on Tuesday, the 7th, he again sought an interview with his superior officer, the Provost "The report was a great deal stronger," says Lind "There was more talk of it than there had been for three days before " and, Wednesday being his day for commanding the Guard, he wanted to have his lordship's orders, as it was the invariable custom, when there was to be "an augmentation of the Guard," to give out these the previous night Twice in the course of the forenoon, and again in the afternoon, he called for the Provost at the Council Chambers, without result; but hearing about five o'clock that this elusive functionary was then in Muirhead's Coffee-house, he sent up word by the servant that he desired to see him. The reply was that the Provost was busy, but would be at the Council Chambers in an hour.

72

The Mob's Revenge.

The parties met there at six o'clock   According to the Provost,
Lind reported that the rumour turned out to be merely "common clatter among common servants and children"; this Lind
positively denies   Both agree that no orders were given except
the parole for the night, and that Lind should come again on
the following day for instructions   Lindsay entered the
Chambers just after Lind left, and to him the Provost stated
that the latter had reported the rumour to be groundless, but
that the Council would meet next morning to arrange for the
Guard being under arms in case of any disturbance   It is
to be kept in view that all these surmises and reports pointed
to some attempt against Porteous on Wednesday, the 8th, the
day originally fixed for his execution, and not the night before,
as actually happened [77]   This was doubtless a device of the
conspirators to put the authorities off the scent, but the fact
that the City Guard were, on the Tuesday, entirely destitute of
ammunition, which could only be supplied by the Provost's
order, indicates something worse than negligence   The other
magistrates examined by the House of Lords denied all knowledge of the rumour, with the exception of Bailie Colquhoun,
who, while admitting he had heard it, said, "It was only among
the lower sort of people, the better sort gave no credit to it
All the foundation I could learn of it was, one said, 'My boy
brought it from school,' and another, 'My servant brought it
from market'   Even the surmise was always mentioned to be
on the 8th, but never upon the 7th "[78]

Meanwhile, the bruit of the threatened outrage had penetrated the massive walls of "the very reverend Tolbooth itself,"
and had reached the ears of the person chiefly concerned.
Bailie Colquhoun states that "both Captain Porteous and a
good many of his friends and well-wishers did hear the surmise,
as well as everybody else, but they gave as little credit to it
as anybody "   How little the prisoner suspected the imminence

---

[77] At the Parliamentary inquiry two witnesses, Bailly and Din, said
they had heard long before the riot that it was to take place on the
Tuesday, and the "Brief Account" states—"Captain Lort of General
Sabine's (who is now in town) was told by the turnkey of the prison
that he had notice given him, the 7th September, in the morning, that
the prison would be attacked that night, which he told to the head
keeper, desiring him to acquaint the Provost of it "   General Moyle,
writing to the Duke of Newcastle on 9th September, also refers to this
incident

[78] Examination of Bailie Colquhoun.

73

Captain Porteous.

of his doom appears from certain unpublished depositions, preserved in the City Chambers, by friends who visited him on the fatal Tuesday, his last day on earth [79] John Ure, writer in Edinburgh, declares that he dined with the Captain on the day of his death, a son of George Gordon, writer—probably his brother-in-law—and one Haswell, an Edinburgh merchant, being of the company During dinner Ure referred to the report, which he had been discussing with Captain Fergusson of the Guard, " to which Captain Porteous answered that he was in no manner of way afraid of any mob, and that if the door was opened to him, he would venture to go to the Cross with his cane alone in his hand, and at the same time he told the declarant that on the morrow thereafter, which was the day appointed for his public execution, the Lord Drummore's [80] son was to dine with him, and he invited the declarant to come and take part of his next day's dinner to bear company with Mr Dalrymple " One Dishingtoun, calling the same afternoon, told Porteous he wished he were safe in the Castle, the Captain, however, replied that he could have been there if he pleased, " but that he did not desire it, for that he had undergone a great change in his constitution upon being committed to the Tolbooth and during his stay in it, and that he was afraid he might have run the risk of another change if he had been sent to the Castle " The insalubrious hospitality of the " Heart of Midlothian " was evidently having a bad effect upon its unwilling inmate, and he seems to have preferred rather to endure his unhealthy surroundings than go further to fare no better in the Castle dungeon Dishingtoun adds—" Mr Gordon, a gentleman in company, told Porteous that he was going in a few days to the West country, but Mr Porteous desired him to stay a week or so, and he would go along with him " Other visitors were William Ure, goldsmith, and " Mr Robt. Yetts, preacher of the Gospel in Edi.," who remained from four o'clock till seven that evening The pastor prophetically warned Porteous " that he should take care of whom he gave access to come in to him, for that he was afraid some evil might come over him , upon which the Captain said that he understood what he meant was until the next day should be over, but that he was in no apprehension of danger that way " The persons

---

79 Copies of these documents will be found in Appendix I
80 Hew Dalrymple of Drummore (1690-1755), one of the Senators of the College of Justice

74

The Mob's Revenge.

named appear to have been the Captain's only visitors on that fateful afternoon, and the jovial entertainment described by Scott as given by Porteous to celebrate his reprieve, which left him "full of bread, hot with wine, and high in mis-timed and ill-grounded confidence," when the shouts of his murderers broke in upon the feast, is a creation of the novelist's fancy

Before proceeding to the affair of the riot, the reader unfamiliar with the topography of old Edinburgh would do well to refer to that part of Edgar's plan of the city in 1742 reproduced in the present volume   In Porteous's day the famous Flodden Wall encircled the city proper and its principal thoroughfares, the High Street and the Cowgate, with the maze of wynds and closes leading from the one to the other The upper portion of the High Street, between the Tolbooth and the Castle Hill, known as the Lawnmarket, communicated by the "sanctified bends" of the West Bow with the oblong area of the Grassmarket   There was situated the West Port, one of the five ports or gateways with which the town wall was pierced, forming the main entrance to the city from the west, beyond which lay the suburb of Portsburgh   Bristo Port. at the head of Candlemaker Row, and Potter Row Port (anciently Kirk-of-Field Port, the scene of Darnley's murder), at the head of the Horse Wynd, gave access from the south Eastward was the Cowgate Port, at the foot of St. Mary's Wynd, at the head of which the stately structure of the Nether Bow Port—the Temple Bar of Edinburgh—divided the High Street from the old Court suburb of the Canongate, and formed the principal entrance to the city on the east   Each of these ports, which were closed every night, was in charge of a keeper and his subordinates, who were known as "waiters", and after the great gates were shut wayfarers could only obtain "ish and entry" on paying toll to the waiter, who attended at a wicket for that purpose   Entering the city at the Nether Bow, and, proceeding westward up the High Street, the visitor in those times would find, stranded in the middle of the fairway, the low, black hulk of the City Guard-house, beyond which the slender shaft of the Market Cross rose from its castellated base He would next encounter the tall pile of the Luckenbooths, blocking his passage for the length of St Giles' Church, and, having traversed the lane on either side, he would see before him the gaunt mass of the Tolbooth further embarrassing his progress   Above this point the wider Lawnmarket opened a

Captain Porteous.

clear space to the head of the West Bow, where the traffic was again impeded by the clumsy fabric of the Weigh House Descending the sharp and angular slope of the Bow to the Grassmarket, and reaching the Bowfoot Well, he would observe in the centre of the street the Cornmarket, with its range of pillars, and fronting it, to the west, the ominous bulk of the gallows stone, the scene of Wilson's death and his avengers' triumph

The most reliable contemporary account of the proceedings of the rioters is furnished by the depositions of the witnesses at the abortive trial of William Maclauchlane for complicity in the riot in 1737, to which we shall later refer, and the reports in the *Caledonian Mercury* of 9th and 13th September, 1736, state the facts so far as that enterprising journal could collect them at that time   To these we are able to add many new details of interest from the various original documents before mentioned, viz , the Examinations of the witnesses before the House of Lords, the Lord Justice-Clerk's Narrative, the Brief Account of the Riot, the official correspondence, and private letters

Between nine and ten o'clock on the night of Tuesday, 7th September, shortly before the closing of the ports a body of persons, armed with staves and cudgels, assembled in the suburb of Portsburgh   Their first act was to beset the house of the burgh drummer, demanding his drum , and, when he asked what they wanted with it, he was told that " they were going to sacrifice Captain Porteous "   Seizing the drum, the rioters tied it about the neck of the drummer's son, and compelled him to beat a call to arms, at the same time crying out, " Here ! all who dare to avenge innocent blood ! "   They then forced the keys of the West Port from the waiter, and dragged up to the Port the man whose duty it was to shut the gates, ordering him to make them fast, which he was too frightened to do , whereupon some of them locked and nailed up the gates themselves, " that the enemy might not get in upon them and hinder them to execute the design they had at that time to hang Captain Porteous "   Having thus secured the port, the rioters proceeded along the Cowgate—the reluctant drummer beating for his life—till they reached the Cowgate Port, the keeper of which, aware of their approach, had hidden himself, along with his keys   But the mob " secured it with great stones,

The Mob's Revenge.

and kept a guard at it till the murder was over, and then they opened it themselves" Here the mob openly stated that "they were going to put Captain Porteous to death" Despatching some of their number to take possession of the Bristo and Potter Row Ports, the main body of the rioters rushed up Gray's Close and poured into the High Street, a little above the Nether Bow At a quarter to ten o'clock the keys of the Nether Bow Port were forced from its aged keeper, and the gates locked, the rioters taking the keys with them as they turned westward up the High Street towards the Guard-house While they were fastening the gates the waiter "heard the mob speaking that their design was upon Captain Porteous." They left no sentinels at this gate, "but every now and then some of the said mob came down and visited the said port" It will be observed that the rioters made no secret of their intentions, though Scott says that, until they had captured the Guard, they "preserved silence on the ultimate object of their rising" The strategic importance of securing the Nether Bow Port cannot be over-estimated, for by so doing the mob, as we shall see, prevented the magistrates from obtaining the assistance of the regular troops quartered in the Canongate The triumphant shouts of the rioters and the continuous beating of the drum as they moved up the High Street to attack the Guard attracted to the spot a crowd, partly composed of curious spectators, but mainly of those in sympathy with their design, whose numbers swelled the original band of conspirators into a formidable mob

We must now see how the responsible guardians of the peace of the town were discharging their duty Provost Wilson, Bailie Colquhoun, and Mr Lindsay, late Provost, and then member of Parliament for the city, were passing the evening at a tavern kept by Robert Clerk, vintner, in the Parliament Close, where they had been since eight o'clock, in company with Mr Bur, midshipman, and other officers of H M S *Dreadnought*, then stationed in Leith Roads At a quarter to ten,[81] the Provost received a verbal message from his niece, which he states was to the effect "that there were a few boys beating a drum in the Grassmarket" Bailie Colquhoun says the message referred to "a mob" there The messenger was sent to fetch Captain Lind, who was readily accessible, being in the next room Lind, having heard nothing of the mob, was ordered

---

81 According to the Provost; the Bailie says 9 40, and Lindsay, 9 30

Captain Porteous.

to go to the Guard-house, which was not above a hundred yards from the tavern, and make inquiries There he found everything quiet, and despatched one of his men to the Grassmarket for intelligence. In the street he met "one Mr Hunter," who informed him there was a mob of four or five thousand people at the Nether Bow, at that moment he himself heard the drum beating as the rioters left the Port, and "run as hard as he could to the Provost," whom he found 'still in the same room with Mr Lindsay where he had left him " The latter told him to go at once and turn out the Guard and that the magistrates would follow him to give orders Hunter says that he warned the sergeant at the Guard-house that the mob was up "and seemed resolved to have their will," and that when Captain Lind "saw the mob gathered together towards the head of Blackfriars Wynd, he clapt his hand to his sword and cried, 'God's mercy! what's this?' and away he ran as fast as his feet could carry him " Curiously enough, on this eventful night, instead of the usual squad of thirty men, the Guard mustered only a corporal, sergeant, drummer, and ten privates, of whom three were on sentry duty at the Guard-room and Tolbooth doors and the Parliament Close respectively, while a fourth had been sent by Lind to the Grassmarket None of the men as we have seen, was provided with ammunition—"there was not a flask of powder nor a pound of shot amongst all the Town Guard "— so that, in the event of any emergency, the King's peace was in precarious keeping

Meanwhile the rioters had surrounded the Guard-house, surprised and disarmed the sentinel, and, rushing in, seized all the arms they could find, 'being ninety firelocks in number, besides several Lochaber-axes," possessed themselves of the town drums,[82] set at liberty such minor offenders as were then confined in the cells, and turned out their astonished guardians When Captain Lind for the second time approached the Guard-room he found it invested by the mob, who were arming themselves with the firelocks and Lochaber-axes of the Guard, handed out through the windows for distribution by those

---

82 According to Scott their first act was to destroy the drums, " by which they supposed an alarm might be conveyed to the garrison in the Castle, and for the same reason they now silenced their own ", but there is ample evidence that these drums were beaten up the High Street, at the Tolbooth, and during the murder of Porteous The Portsburgh drummer escaped while the mob was attacking the Guard-house

The City Guard House.

The Mob's Revenge.

within Some of the crowd were about to attack him but others cried, ' Spare him, we have nothing to do with him ", and he once more fled back to tell the magistrates what had happened These worthies had at length quitted their tavern, and encountered Lind at the Market Cross as the town clock struck ten 'After this," says Lindsay, "some called out, 'Get away ! for the mob are moving this way,' and we stepped to the side of the street, a little above the Coffee-house stairs, where it was proposed what was to be done They all agreed there was no hopes of relief but by assistance from the King's troops [in the Canongate], and one of the company said, 'Then let us go back to the house and contrive a letter to the general [Moyle]'; upon this Mr Colquhoun said, with great concern, 'God's mercy ! if we stay till you write three lines we shall be all of us in the hands of the mob and then we shall have no hope of relief,' and said, Why may not Mr Lindsay go —he is well known to the general—and acquaint him of our situation?' Upon this I turned and said, 'Lord Provost, if you desire me, I will go', he answered, 'By all means, make what haste you can, for there is no time to be lost !'" Bailie Colquhoun states, "There was a dispute at first whether to send Mr Lindsay, because we were of opinion that Mr Lindsay would be very useful to be with us in directing, but as the mob were pouring out in swarms, we were apprehensive it would be dangerous to lose time, and therefore agreed to send a verbal message by Mr Lindsay, who was very well known to the general, which at that time we thought would have equal credit with a letter from the Provost sent by an indifferent hand " Had the precious moments wasted in this discussion been employed by the Provost in writing half a dozen words to General Moyle he would have saved not only the life of Porteous, but also what, had he foreseen it, might have weighed with him more, much tribulation to himself It was a further misfortune for all concerned that of the three persons then present the only one who was *not* a magistrate was selected for the purpose. The magistrates then returned to Clerk's Tavern, and Lindsay departed to seek the general's aid How he fared upon his errand we shall see later

The rioters in the meantime, "having furnished themselves with shot by breaking open the shop of one Alexander Dunning, wherewith they had loaded the pieces they had seized in the

79

Captain Porteous.

Guard," concentrated their whole force upon the most difficult part of their design, the taking of the Tolbooth. Having secured the various approaches to the prison by placing strong bands, armed with muskets, across the street at the Purses and upper end of the Luckenbooths, on the north side of the Tolbooth, the main body assembled at the foot of the turret nearest the High Kirk, with "huzzaing and drums beating," before the massive portal of that grim and formidable pile. But its obdurate walls, less subject to the influence of martial strains than those of Jericho, defied, for upwards of an hour, the utmost efforts of the besiegers. The assault was commenced with sledge-hammers, the crash of which, as we shall find, reached even to the garrison in the Castle, but, though hundreds of hands willingly helped in what was to them a labour of love, the stout door still stood fast

The magistrates were in vain seeking inspiration in the tavern. They thought of raising the train-bands, and sent "one Hallyburton, their commander, to the house of Mr Rollo, at whose house were the books which contained the names and places of abode of every captain of a company, but when he came there he was denied access by Mr Rollo's wife, who desired him to begone. They then proposed to ring the alarm bell, but found the mob had taken the precaution to secure the tower in which it hangs [the steeple of St Giles' Church]. They then sent to the magazine for arms, but it appeared by the evidence of Hislop, the storekeeper, and others that the mob had likewise secured that." It is surprising that not until Lindsay had left and these other means had failed did any one suggest the obvious and simple course of sending a letter from the Provost to Major Robertson, who commanded the garrison of the Castle. Bailie Colquhoun alone has the credit of proposing that this should be done, but the Provost and others thought the major would not act without orders from General Moyle. The general occupied the mansion-house of Abbey Hill, over a mile distant, beyond the walls, and Mr Lindsay, leaving the Cross very shortly after ten, did not arrive at his destination till fourteen minutes to eleven. A few minutes would have sufficed for a messenger to reach the Castle, and though Scott says that more than one was despatched by different ways, all of whom were intercepted and turned back by the mob, it is clear from the evidence of the magistrates themselves that they made no attempt what-

The Mob's Revenge.

ever to communicate with the garrison The omission is the more remarkable since it appears from the evidence of General Wade that Major Robertson, warned of the riot by a servant whom he had sent to the town between nine and ten to post a letter addressed to the Earl of Orkney, Governor of Edinburgh Castle,[83] had the whole of his hundred men under arms, marched fifty of them, furnished with hand-grenades, to the lower gate, where he waited till two in the morning "in expectation of having his assistance required by the civil magistrate, and had the mortification to hear from the works of the Castle the hammers striking against the prison gates, and to see the fire that was set to it to burn it down " The general adds that Moyle had "no power in the Castle," and that Robertson would have obeyed the Provost's order to disperse the mob Of course, with the object-lesson of Porteous before his eyes, the major was not so foolish as to interfere without personal or written authority from the magistrates

Half an hour after the departure of Lindsay these intrepid guardians of the city decided to oppose the rioters in person. Treasurer Young was sent for a copy of the Riot Act, but, without waiting for his return, the Provost and Bailies Colquhoun, Blackwood, and Hamilton, accompanied by Captain Lind and others, to the number of twenty-six, issued from the peaceful precincts of Clerk's Tavern and approached the Tolbooth from the head of Mary King's Close, on the north side of the High Street Some of the party carried lighted torches, but none of them were armed—even the captain, who led the attack, having only "a flambeaux in one hand and his cane in the other hand " So soon as they got the length of the Advocate's Close, "over against the Stinking Style," they encountered the outposts of the mob at the north-east end of the prison, who received them with a shower of stones and, to the dismay of the Provost, "snapped their firelocks" at them, some of which flashed in the pan [84] "Though our

---

83 The man was questioned as to his business by some of the mob, who examined the letter by the light of a link, and actually escorted him to the post-house

84 Except for thus frightening the magistrates, the rioters made no use of their firearms, the only casualty being a person who was shot in the eye at the Guard-house, evidently as the result of an accident, when the arms were being distributed among the mob

Captain Porteous.

number was twenty-six when we came out of the tavern,"
says Bailie Colquhoun, naively, "yet when we got to the north-
west end of the prison it was much smaller, and we were
under a necessity of retiring—we were not able to quell the
mob" Lind, with some of the bolder spirits pushed on
till they came near the prison door, when his flambeau was
captured and himself beaten back   Only one of the party,
John Hislop, "with a link in his one hand and a firelock in
the other hand, which he found upon the street," turned the
corner of the prison, and saw the mob endeavouring to break
in the door, but he was at once attacked, 'upon which he
thought it full time to retire, which he accordingly did down
Best's Wynd," on the south side of the gaol. So ignominiously
ended this impotent attempt to vindicate law and order, which
left the rioters absolute masters of the field

Meanwhile the patience of the mob was becoming exhausted
More than an hour had been wasted in the assault upon the
Tolbooth door, and yet their design was no nearer completion,
Force having been tried in vain, they decided to employ the
subtler medium of fire   'A parcel of broom, furze (or
whins), with other combustibles, and heaps of timber placed
over a barrel of pitch" were quickly massed against the door,
the torches taken from the magistrates were applied to the
pile and in a few seconds the sombre gateway was wrapt in
a sheet of roaring fire [85] The strong fabric, which had so
bravely withstood the blows of the sledge-hammers, crumbled
and cracked as the flames did their stealthy work, and, " before
the prison door was near burnt down," several of the rioters
burst through the blazing wreck   "But as there was," writes
the author of Mr Fanley's letter, "a few paces within that
a much stronger door than the outward door, viz , a huge,
massy, iron one, they must necessarily have been detained
above an hour more there, as Bailie Colquhoun owned to me
himself next day if, unhappily, through stupidity or rather
worse, the keeper had not staid in the way, and him they
obliged to unlock the door "   Thus, at half-past eleven
o'clock, the Tolbooth was in the hands of the mob   Having
taken the key from the keeper, some of the rioters rushed

85 As showing the determination and singleness of purpose which
characterised the actions of the mob throughout, it is recorded that they
" provided water to keep the flame within its due bounds," so as to avoid
causing more damage than was necessary to effect their object

The Tolbooth of Edinburgh.

From an Etching by Skene.

The Mob's Revenge.

up the turnpike stair to the Iron Room on the floor above in which Captain Porteous was confined, "though they could scarce see one another for the smoke," while the rest "seized the turnkeys, forced them to open every ward in the prison, and dismissed all the prisoners" According to the *Caledonian Mercury*, "No less than seventeen criminals escaped from the city jail on this occasion, among whom are the dragoon who was indicted for the murder of the butcher's wife in Dunse, the two Nowhaven men lately brought in from Blackness Castle for smuggling, seven sentinels of the City Guard, &c "[86]

The account of the murder of Porteous given by Scott differs in some particulars from that afforded by the contemporary evidence In the novel the terrified Captain conceals himself in the chimney, whence he is ignominiously dragged—a sorry sight—by his self-appointed executioners The fact appears to be that when they burst into the chamber, calling, "Where is the ——?" he quietly faced them with the answer, "Gentlemen, I am here, but what are you to do with me?" To which they replied, "We are to carry [conduct] you to the place where you shed so much innocent blood, and hang you." Another point is the behaviour of the murderers to their helpless victim, which the novelist represents as the stern but impartial demeanour of men who were carrying out what they believed to be an act of justice "Let no man hurt him," says their leader; "let him make his peace with God, if he can, we will not kill both his soul and body " We shall see how these humane professions were fulfilled in fact.

The prisoner, attired in his nightgown, cap, and breeches, was dragged by the legs down the stairs to the street, where he was set upon his feet, "some seizing him by the breast and arms, while others pushed behind, thus conducting him to the Bowhead, where they stopped a little, at the pressing solicitation of some citizens, that so he might die peaceably, but whose real view was to gain time, expecting every moment the Welsh Fusiliers from the Cannongate " George Wilson, a witness at the subsequent trial of Maclauchlane, depones that when the

---

[86] Contemporary MSS in the possession of John A Fairley, Esq, give the names of thirteen of the prisoners who thus escaped from the Tolbooth as follows —*Soldiers of the Guard*—John Paterson, John Kello, Andrew Tod, David Gilchrist, Matthew Buckles, John Lesly, and Robert Brown *Other persons*—Christian Goudie, William Stodhart, James Balfour, Alexander Sydie, Robert Ferguson, and Isobell Prats

Captain Porteous.

crowd came " to Stewart's sign-post, near the Bowhead," some
of the mob proposed to hang Captain Porteous there, but
others were against it, and that when they reached the
Weigh House, it was proposed to hang him over the Weigh
House stair, but this was also rejected   William Turner,
another witness, corroborates this, adding that the rioters
said "they would carry him to the place where the deed was
done "   "By this time the deponent [Wilson] happened to
get pretty near to Captain Porteous, and as the mob was
carrying the said Captain Porteous down the Bow one of the
mob, in a woman's dress, knocked the deponent down, and
that as they were going alongst before this the deponent
interceded with the mob to give Captain Porteous some time to
pray   The answer made by the mob was that the said
Captain Porteous never prayed for himself, and did not give
them time to pray that he had killed, and that he should be
damned before he got time to pray ''   The devout Mr Butler,
thoughtfully retained by the murderers to prepare their victim
for his sudden death, is an amiable and pious fiction   He
begged for mercy,' says the writer of Mr Fauley's letter,
"but alas ! the mercies of a mob, like those of Churchmen,
are barbarities and cruelties, for as they carried him to the Grassmarket they run torches in his face, which they had with them,
though the moon made it as light as day, and beat and punched
him most unmercifully "

Most of the accounts concur in stating that the rioters broke
open a shop in the West Bow, from which they took a coil of
rope wherewith to hang their victim, leaving a guinea upon the
counter to pay for the damage   Chambers,[87] however, writing
of the West Bow, gives a different version of the incident—
"About twenty yards farther down the street, on the north
side, bearing the number 69, is the shop in which the rioters
of 7th September, 1736, obtained the rope with which they
hanged Captain Porteous   It was then the shop of a dealer
in smallwares, by name Mrs Jeffrey, who added a traffic in
ropes to her other motley business   When the rioters asked
for a coil of rope, the woman asked 'if it was to hang Porteous
with?' and, on being answered with a hearty affirmative, she
cried that she would willingly give all the ropes in her shop for
so good a purpose, and they laid a guinea upon the counter,

---

[87] *Traditions of Edinburgh*, 1825, i. 142

The Mob's Revenge.

as the price of the rope, which she handed to them." The other authorities make no reference to this bloodthirsty dame

When the mob at length reached the Grassmarket, it was at first proposed that Porteous, with poetic justice, should be hanged at the gallows stone, in atonement for the blood shed by him on that spot. Some began to pull up the stones that filled the socket into which the gibbet was ordinarily fixed, while others tried to uproot a dyer's pole which stood at the head of Hunter's Close, on the south side of the street, over against the place of execution. John Nisbet, another of the Maclauchlane witnesses, saw this from his window in Orr's Land, "under which window the dyster's tree was fixed." He then heard one of the mob cry out, "You had much better hang him over the dyster's tree than give yourselves so much trouble," whereupon those who guarded Captain Porteous brought him towards the spot, while others made ready the rope. "Then he begged for mercy again," says the writer of Mr. Fairley's letter—under date 11th September—'which being with imprecations denied, he entreated they would allow him half an hour to pray. While they were debating this among themselves for about two minutes, he spied John Carmichael, the merchant (from whom I had it), who had followed the mob to see if he could do him any service in mollifying them, and, beckoning him up to him, he slipped a purse with twenty-three guineas into his hand, and twice whispered him to give it his brother, which, as he knew it, would be of service to him, as being a poor man, was surely an astonishing instance of presence of mind [88]. The mob then called out to Mr. Carmichael and asked him what Porteous said, to which he readily replied he had only been taking leave of him. Upon this the monsters threw the rope over a dyer's tree, which happened to be close by, and is, you know, in the form of a gallows, about fifteen foot high, on which they dry their worsteds and cloths, and immediately hauled him up. After he had hung about three minutes, the barbarians let him down again, quite alive, and stripped off his nightgown and shirt, which last they tied about his head, but not his face, and then, with huzzas, pulled him up again; but as his hands were

---

[88] This incident is spoken to by Mr Carmichael himself at the trial of Maclauchlane, and does not accord with Scott's story of Porteous, before leaving the Tolbooth, being allowed by his captors to give his money to " a person confined in the jail for debt "

Captain Porteous.

not bound, he struggled, poor creature, very much, upon which one of the villains up with a Lochaber-axe and broke his right arm and shoulder, and then they kept jerking him up and down about an hour When they were sure he was dead, they wound the rope, as it was very long, about one of the supporters of the gallows, and, nailing the end of it with several great nails, left him hanging till five in the morning "

The above account of the murder is quoted at length as being not only a new but very vivid description of the scene Some further details may be added from other authorities, which, in the main, corroborate it " To show the insolence of these devils to the Government," the writer of this letter mentions an exceedingly coarse allusion made by the mob to Queen Caroline and 'her bonnie reprieve" of which the author of an unpublished "Letter from Edinburgh" in the Record Office[89] gives, on the same date, a more genteel version—" I had forgot to tell you that the villains had the impudence to have a watchword, which was *Hanover*, speaking on all occasions very disrespectfully of the Queen who granted the reprieve, and at every interval of letting him down from the tree, cried, insulting Porteous, 'Where is your reprieve? Show it us, and we'll save you!' and then, with insulting curses, hung him up again " This letter also states that Porteous ' humbly implored time to make a short prayer, which they refused, and on lifting up his hands, one of them struck him over the arm with a Lochaber-axe and broke his arm, and hung him up; and after he had hung about four minutes, they let him down, in order to augment his terrors and increase his tortures, at the same time cutting him over the head and burning his foot that had the shoe off with a torch [90] Thus they used him in this barbarous manner three times, so that he was near expiring when they hung him up the last time The tragedy being ended

---

89 Mr Omond, quoting from this letter in his article before cited, describes it as written by the Lord Justice-Clerk to the Duke of Newcastle The original copy in the Record Office, however, has no address or signature, and, from internal evidence, is apparently written by an officer of one of the regiments then stationed in the Canongate; certainly not by the Justice-Clerk

90 The writer had previously stated that Porteous, while being dragged by the mob to the Grassmarket, " lost one of his shoes, which they would not suffer him to put on " In the novel, " they stopped, sought for it, and replaced it upon his foot with great deliberation " The actual murderers were less considerate than Scott's courteous assassins

The Mob's Revenge.

they all dispersed, it being then within a quarter of twelve at
night, and left him hanging, where he continued till five next
morning "

Many of the witnesses at the trial of Maclauchlane give additional particulars of the tragedy from their own observation.
Andrew Finlayson, the waiter at the West Port, who witnessed
the scene from Heriot's Work Bridge, after describing the
murder, says—"During all this while the mob had a drum,
which they incessantly beat, which hindered him to hear
anything that passed, but he distinctly saw as above, the moon
shining at the time, as also they had lighted flambeaux at the
place of execution " George Wilson, who was knocked down
as above mentioned, having been "run over by a good many of
the mob," picked himself up and followed them to the Grassmarket, where the mob threw down their arms. He saw
Porteous give his purse to Carmichael, and the rope put about
his neck ; "but he was not drawn up until they heard that the
military were coming from the Canongate, in by the [Trinity]
Hospital, at the foot of Leith Wynd"—a false alarm He
depones that Porteous was "three times hung up, and twice
let down again ; that the first time Captain Porteous was hung
up he heard some of the mob make a proposal of cutting his
ears out, and others proposed to geld him, and at the last time
he was hung up he saw some of the mob strike him upon the
face with a Lochaber-axe " Such bloody propositions would
have shocked Scott's conscientious murderers, "whom Heaven
and their righteous anger had stirred up to execute judgment "
John Nisbet, from his window overlooking the spot, "observed
one of the mob to bring a coil of ropes, one end whereof the
rioters threw over the dyster's tree, which a party of them, on
the east of the said tree, laid hold of in order to be ready to
pull him up, while another party, to the west of the tree, about
ten yards, endeavoured to tie the other end of the rope about
his neck, and in the struggle he was brought down to the
street and laid upon his back, and they, having there fixed
the rope about his neck, dragged him thereafter towards the
foot of the tree, and then the other party drew him up, and
then the deponent observed one of them that pulled him up,
being a thin man, well set on his joints, and tall, with a blue
coat, a lighter-coloured waistcoat, a black roller about his neck,
a hat, and a dark-coloured periwig, take hold of a Lochaber-
axe and gave the deceased Captain Porteous two strokes with

87

Captain Porteous.

it " This is the only witness who ventures to describe the appearance of any of the rioters George Gordon, writer in Edinburgh, his brother-in-law, " saw the mob hang the deceased Captain Porteous over a dyster's tree, and when he had hung for some time he saw some of them pulling at his feet, and saw him laid down again to the ground, but whether he was then dead the deponent did not know, but they drew him up again; and thereafter saw some of them put up their hands to see if he was dead, and heard them call out, 'He is dead enough, I warrant you!'"

Its end accomplished, the mob melted away as swiftly and mysteriously as it arose Up in the Lawnmarket the scorched and blackened gateway gaped from the empty prison, scattered arms and smouldering torches lay thick about the Bowfoot Well, beneath the grim shadow of the dyster's tree the silent figure swayed lonely in the moonlight Save for these traces of its passing, the riot of the night seemed but an ugly and fantastic dream

(5) THE MYSTERY OF THE MOB

A tale that never fail'd to be the pride
Of grannies spinnin' at the ingle-side
An Eclogue—Robert Fergusson

When Patrick Lindsay (of whom some account will be found in the Biographical Notes appended to the present volume) left the magistrates in the High Street shortly after ten, with their message to General Moyle, he walked as fast as he could down to the Nether Bow Port, which he found was shut, " and a very great number of [the] mob at it and some few of them with firearms " The direct road to Abbey Hill, by way of the Canongate, being thus closed to him, and the crowd about the Port appearing suspicious of his business, he concealed himself for a little in a neighbouring close, and then retraced his steps as far as the Guard-house, where he " stepped into another close-head to listen what the mob were saying " and devise some means of escaping from the town. " Then it struck me in the head," as he says in his examination, from which this account is taken, " that they might have neglected the Potter Row Port, and I immediately crossed the street, went down Marlin's Wynd [on the east side of the Tron Church], crossed the Cowgate, went up the College

The Mystery of the Mob.

Wynd, and came to the Potter Row Port, which I found locked and nobody near it but the keeper, who opened the wicket and let me out.[91] From thence I was obliged to go in my way to Abbey Hill, where the general's house was, round by the King's Park wall." So much time was lost in following this devious route that it was not until fourteen minutes to eleven that he reached the mansion-house of Abbey Hill

General Moyle states in his examination that he had been "ill a long time, and seldom went up to the town", but, in common with everybody except the Provost, he had heard, in his seclusion, the rumour of the threatened rising On Saturday, the 4th, one of his officers, Captain Gumley, spoke to him of the report, "as he was going to dine with the Lord Justice-Clerk," and next day informed the general that his lordship considered "that it was without ground"

Moyle was not unprepared to receive the tidings brought by Lindsay On 9th September he writes to the Duke of Newcastle—"Last Tuesday night, about a quarter of an hour after ten, being then in my bed, Colonel Pears, who commands Lieutenant-General Sabin's regiment in the Canongate, came and told me there was a great disturbance in the city, on which I immediately ordered him to assemble the six companies quartered here, and to parade them near the Guard in the Canongate, and to send for the three companies from Leith, which was done with as much expedition as possible, for some of the companies are quartered a great distance from the Canongate. I dressed myself as soon as possible in order to join the regiment." He was 'scarce dressed" when Mr Lindsay arrived

There was later much ill-feeling between the parties to this interview, of which very different versions were given by each, with a view to casting the blame of the result upon the other, and their mutual recriminations caused the legal authorities some trouble The Earl of Ilay, Lord Justice-General of Scotland, who came from London, as we shall see, to inquire into the affair of the mob, writes to the Duke of Newcastle on 15th October, "I have great difficulty to prevent disputes arising between General Moyle and Mr Lindsay I have begged of them both to consider that the duty of the King's servants

---

91 The keeper afterwards said that Lindsay had not been gone two minutes when some of the mob seized this gate and took away the keys

Captain Porteous.

and the friends of the Government is to assist one another in detecting and bringing to justice the criminals, instead of wrangling about facts which are altogether immaterial in that respect" Writing to Sir Robert Walpole the next day, Lord Ilay puts the matter more plainly, "Moyle says that Lindsay was drunk, and never asked his assistance, Lindsay says that he told him he came from the magistrates to ask his assistance I have, as far as it was in my power, enjoined silence upon this subject or any other of the like nature"

We are now able to see from the examinations what were the official accounts given by the disputants Lindsay says, "As soon as I had access to the general, I made an apology for disturbing him at so unseasonable an hour I told him the present unhappy situation of affairs in Edinburgh made it necessary, that a mob had surprised the City Guard, drove away the soldiers, and seized the arms, and I was come from the magistrates to acquaint him of it and to desire his assistance The general upon this told me that he had notice of the thing before I came, but no such particular account of it; that on the first notice he had ordered all his men in Canongate to be under arms, and likewise all his men quartered in Potter Row and West Port to be got under arms, lest the mob should also surprise them and seize their arms, and then he said, 'Sir, I will do more,' and immediately called for a servant and ordered him to take horse and go to Leith, and to acquaint the Commanding Officer there that it was his orders that he should get his men together with the greatest secrecy, get them under arms, and march them up to join the Canongate Guard Upon this I said, 'If we wait till these three companies come from Leith I am afraid it will be too late; the mob are now absolute masters, they are acting without control, and no mortal can answer for the mischief they may do, unless they are speedily checked and dispersed' Upon this the general made answer that he could not allow one man to march from the Canongate Guard without a warrant from the Lord Justice-Clerk or a Lord of Justiciary—I do not remember which Upon this I was very much at a loss The nearest judge of that Court, to the place where I was, was the Justice-Clerk I told the general that if I knew any way of sending to him I would write a letter and acquaint him what had happened and what he had done Upon this Mrs Moyle, who was in the room, desired me to walk into the next room, and gave me

The Mystery of the Mob.

paper, pen, and ink, and told me there would be a servant and a horse ready to carry the letter to him by that time it was wrote I wrote a short note to the Justice-Clerk to acquaint him what had happened, what the general had already done, but that he would proceed no further without a warrant from his lordship This is the substance of all that passed " Later in his evidence he says, "The general, while I was with him, asked me whether there was any access to the Castle without going through the town, and proposed to send an orderly sergeant thither, but I told him there was no access to the Castle but through the town "[92]

General Moyle's evidence on the subject is as follows .—" On Tuesday, fourteen minutes before eleven o'clock at night, Mr Lindsay came to my house and told me there was a great mob in the city to the number of three or four thousand, that they had seized the city gates, as also the arms of the City Guard, and told me he had got out at a wicket and gave sixpence to the person to let him out, and believed by this time his house was pulled down I told him I had heard the report of a mob before, and, upon his not producing a letter from the Provost, I told him my hands were tyed up, I could not take upon me to order the King's forces to break open the gates of the city without an order from the civil magistrate He did not acquaint me that he was a Justice of the Peace or a magistrate, if he had, I would have asked him to have headed the King's troops, and I would have given them orders to march If he would have gone with them and given them authority, I would have ordered them to have broke open the gates Q. Would you have given orders to the troops if Mr. Lindsay had brought you a written order from the Lord Provost or any of the magistrates?—A I never refused them when so applied for, or I would have given orders to the troops if a civil magistrate would have gone with them, or if a written order had been brought from the Provost, empowering me to break open the gates Finding there was no letter come nor any magistrate, I asked Mr Lindsay if the Lord Justice-Clerk was in town, Lord Royston, or Lord Newhall. He told me Lord Justice-Clerk was not in town, Lord Royston was not in town, Lord Newhall was, but not to be come at Upon which I desired Mr Lindsay to write to the Lord Justice-Clerk, in my name, to desire that

---

92 Examination of Patrick Lindsay

Captain Porteous.

he would send me an order for forcing open the gates of the town Mr Lindsay accordingly did write a letter, which my servant carried to the Lord Justice-Clerk He galloped all the way thither, but was detained above an hour before he got an answer, so that the latter did not come till long after Porteous was murdered It was above two hours from the writing of the letter till the time the servant returned "[93] General Moyle further says, in reply to a question, " I had a good deal of reason to believe he [Lindsay] did not come from the magistrates, because he produced no order from them," and adds that Lindsay did not offer to return to the Provost for a letter, as " he was afraid of being murdered if he went back to the town "[94]

Writing to the Duke of Newcastle on 8th September, Moyle gives practically the same account of the interview. " He [Lindsay] made no demand of a guard to assist them," he writes " This unheard-of barbarity had been concerting several days, and I am surprised the magistrates were not more upon their guard. The town soldiers, instead of resisting, delivered their arms to the mob On their suspecting the mob would rise that night, the care of the port next to the Canongate ought to have been put under the guard of the King's forces, and then the communication between the city and the suburbs would have been kept open I have to add that had the troops forced their way into the town without a legal authority, Your Grace would soon have had a terrible complaint from the magistrates
     . They charge me with procuring Porteous's reprieve, and threaten to murder me in my bed ; but I despise them all."

After Lindsay left, the general mounted his horse and rode up to his regiment at the Canongate-head where he remained waiting for the Justice-Clerk's answer or any further orders from the magistrates, until he heard that Porteous was dead [95] It is a remarkable circumstance that at each end of the town an officer was waiting at the head of a regiment for proper

---

[93] The house of Brunstane, where the Justice-Clerk resided, was situated over three miles off, Lord Newhall lived near the Potter Row Port, " just without the gate " Why the latter was not applied to instead, Lindsay fails to explain

[94] Examination of General Moyle

[95] Walter Ruddiman told the general that he had prepared a paragraph to this effect for insertion in his newspaper, the *Mercury*, but he was threatened to be sent to prison if he did so, and was obliged to strike out —*Ibid*

The Mystery of the Mob.

authority to support the law, while between them the rioters were leisurely working their will   General Moyle, on his examination, produced a letter from General Wade, dated 13th March, 1735, containing the orders given by the latter upon which he acted ,[96] and General Wade, in his evidence, gives his reasons therefor [97]   Had Moyle seen his way to act without a written warrant he would doubtless have been able to save Porteous's life , but if his unauthorised interference had resulted in bloodshed, as would in all probability have happened, his own case might have been little better than that of the unfortunate Captain

Lindsay, on his way back to the town, reached the Canongate at eleven o'clock, where he met one Mr Baird, who, at his own request, had been allowed by the Provost to follow Lindsay to hasten the coming of the military   He also asked the Provost to give him a letter to the general in case Lindsay's mission failed, but his lordship said, " There is no occasion." This gentleman had scaled the town wall by means of a rope tied to a tree in an adjacent garden, and let himself down into Leith Wynd   ' For God's sake!" said he on seeing Lindsay alone, "how come you not to have the troops with you?"   To which the latter replied, "I come from the general , I have done all that could be done , and an express is gone to Lord Justice-Clerk to obtain a warrant "   Mr Baird then returned the way he came to inform the Provost, ascending the wall "by the help of a cart which stood near the place he came down "   Lindsay, being apparently unequal to this feat, walked round the wall from gate to gate, until the West Port was opened by the mob, by which he entered the city [98]

The magistrates in the meantime had continued their sederunt at Clerk's Tavern, apparently satisfied that they had done all that was possible in the circumstances.   After Lindsay rejoined them, the long-delayed letter from the Justice-Clerk reached him at two o'clock in the morning   His lordship writes—" I am just now awakened at your unlucky news   I am sorry the magistrates have had so bad intelligence, else all this might easily been prevented [sic]   What is now to be done it is impossible for me, at this distance, to judge, when

96 Appendix XIII   97 Examination of General Wade
98 Examinations of Lindsay and Colonel Duroure

93

Captain Porteous.

every minute may change the face of affairs, and possibly, by this time, all may be over   At the same time I suppose, upon your application, the general will think it reasonable to endeavour to save the magistrates and town from the power of the mob   It will be proper you go along with them, and get constables to read the proclamation   In case they shut all the gates, while the regiment is beating to arms in the Canongate, some companies might try to get in by the foot of the Castle, but as you know the pass, you can better judge how far it is advisable   To me, it seems the way to get into the town with the least harm "

Hearing nothing further of the rioters, and believing that the worst was over, Lindsay and some of the others plucked up sufficient courage to venture into the streets, where everything was quiet   They went down to the Nether Bow Port, which they found still locked, the mob having taken away the keys, but the Cowgate Port was open, the barricade having been removed by the rioters themselves   It was by this gate that many of these left the town after the murder, while others departed by the West Port, which was also opened by them Lindsay deponed before the House of Commons Committee that, when he returned from General Moyle, " the mob was pouring in vast shoals out of the town into the country, and that he did not remember any one face of the many hundreds he met with, though he had lived and borne the highest offices in the city for several years."   There is no evidence as to the condition of the other two ports after the tragedy   The party " seized three fellows who could not give a sufficient account of themselves," and lodged them in the Canongate Guard, from which they were later released, as there was no evidence against them   After this, says Lindsay, they proceeded to the Grassmarket, where, " several of the inhabitants having joined us, we took down the body and sent it into a church [Greyfriars] just by   It was then just break of day "   Between five and six o'clock the magistrates met in the Council Chamber, and took what measures they considered adequate ' to take care of the peace and safety of the city," which were of the nature of the proverbial locking of the stable door after the steed is stolen.   They ordered the Train-bands to mount guard nightly, armed with one hundred firelocks and bayonets from the city armoury, dismissed as incompetent all the soldiers of the City

The Mystery of the Mob.

Guard ; caused the gates of the Nether Bow Port to be chained back , and ordered a new door for the Tolbooth [99]

The body of Porteous, " his neck broke, his arm wounded, and his back and head bruised," was laid the next forenoon in its " resting grave," conform to the following extract from the burial records —"John Porteous, captain of the City Guard   Buried 9th September 1736   Lyes 3 dble pace from the S corner Chalmers' tomb, Greyfriars' Churchyard " The grave, which is situated about the centre of the western boundary of the churchyard, may still be visited by the curious There is

> No sculptur'd marble here, nor pompous lay,
> No storied urn, nor animated bust ;

but the place is marked by a wooden post, bearing the number 32

When the Justice-Clerk came to town in the forenoon of Wednesday, 8th September, he received from the magistrates a report of what had happened in the night, which was embodied in the " Narrative " before referred to   This document was evidently prepared from information furnished by the magistrates, as its terms are similar to the account of the occurrence given in the Council minute of that date   The same day his lordship writes to the Duke of Newcastle—" The mob in Edinburgh having last night, in contempt of the authority of the Crown, as well as in defiance of the laws of the land, barbarously murdered Captain John Porteous, I thought it my duty without loss of time to transmit to Your Grace a short narrative of that unheard-of cruel action, as far as I have yet been able to discover   The mob are now so insolent, and the Town Guard so dispirited and in such contempt, that I find it would be in vain for the magistrates, upon their own authority, to attempt to inquire after and seize the authors or actors of this barbarity, and at the same time, considering what ill blood it might occasion to bring in the military into the city, contrary to their privilege, till I receive further directions, I have prevailed with General Moyle to double his guard in the Canongate, and to send fifty men to the Castle

---

[99] This was the door which, together with the stones of the historic gateway, was obtained by Scott on the demolition of the Tolbooth in 1817, and employed by him " in decorating the entrance of his kitchen-court at Abbotsford "—*Heart of Midlothian*, Note 11 , " Tolbooth of Edinburgh "

Captain Porteous.

of Edinburgh, to be daily relieved by the same number marching through the city, to be in readiness in case of necessity."

It was the summer vacation, the chief law-officers of the Crown, the Lord Advocate and Solicitor-General, were both absent from the city and while awaiting instructions from the Government, the Justice-Clerk made what inquiry he could into the mysterious business Lindsay says that he and Bailie Colquhoun were sent to interview Mr Nisbet, who had witnessed the scene from his window, as already narrated "He told us he looked on all the while, and took such marks of several of them that he should know them again if he saw them, but was a stranger to all their faces" Another gentleman, Mr Buchanan, told them "that he was within sight of the prison door all the while the mob were breaking and burning it, that he looked on many of their faces, but knew none of them, that they were all dressed like tradesmen's servants, but, in his opinion, by their linen and the colour of their hands, some of them seemed to be persons of better condition "[100]

That the moving spirits of the mob were strangers to the town, and were not members of the lowest class, was the common opinion at the time The *Caledonian Mercury* of 13th September observes—"Neither the gentlemen who conversed with them at the Tolbooth, nor those who were sent out by the magistrates to see if they knew any of the rioters, could say they had ever seen any of them before, though the flames rendered it as light as at noon. So that it is generally believed no citizen acted any principal part in this tragedy; though, indeed, it is certain that many of the inhabitants, led by curiosity, stept out to behold the surprising boldness and incredible extravagance of the scene Upon the whole, it would seem their plot was concerted with judgment, conducted with secrecy, enterprised with resolution, and execute in the space of two hours, with unexpected success" The *Edinburgh Evening Courant* of the following day remarks—"Nothing of this kind, perhaps, was ever so boldly attempted, so secretly kept, nor so successfully executed, which makes people apt to believe that persons above the vulgar rank had a hand in it, the rather that the keeper of the prison declares that they were

[100] Examination of Patrick Lindsay

persons in good dress who took out the prisoners, though disguised with leather aprons, &c "

With reference to the innocent spectators of the riot, it is recorded that James Burnett, later the eccentric Lord Monboddo, who had been studying civil law in Groningen, returned to Edinburgh on the day of the murder   As he was going to bed, he heard the noise of the tumult, and went into the street, half-dressed, to ascertain the cause   He was carried along by the crowd to the Grassmarket, and witnessed the last act of the tragedy   ' The scene made so deep an impression on his lordship that it not only deprived him of sleep during the remainder of the night, but induced him to think of leaving the city altogether as a place unfit for a civilised being to live in "[101]

In giving the result of his investigations into the circumstances of the riot on his examination before the House of Lords, General Wade stated—"I was informed it was a very clear, moonlight night, that any person's face might be known from one side of the street to the other, and I never heard that they [the magistrates] ever sent any of them under officers or emissaries to mix among this great crowd of people to inform them who were the most active in the murder   I never heard there was any care taken by the magistrates the morning after the murder was committed, when they might have had the assistance of the regular troops, to secure the gates of the city till a strict examination was made; for I was informed by gentlemen of unquestioned credit and reputation that those that came in from the country to assist in this inhuman murder, returned by the several roads that lead to and from the town, in clusters, triumphing, valuing themselves upon what they had done ' [102]

Dr Carlyle, referring to the tragedy, remarks that, so strongly was the popular mind impressed with the expectation of something extraordinary taking place, he, on the night of the murder, at Prestonpans, nine miles from Edinburgh, dreamt he saw Captain Porteous hanged in the Grassmarket   Early next morning he was told by one of his father's servants, who was thrashing in a barn by the roadside, that several men on horseback had passed about five in the morning   Being asked for news, they replied there was none, except that

---

101 *Kay's Portraits,* i 19
102 Examination of General Wade

Captain Porteous.

Captain Porteous had been dragged out of prison and hanged on a dyer's tree [103]

On 16th September the Justice-Clerk writes to the Duke of Newcastle that, in obedience to Her Majesty's commands, he has consulted with the magistrates as to "the proper measures for restoring and preserving the peace of the city, and for discovering the authors and actors of the late wicked and audacious proceedings." The means adopted as to the former were the arming of the Train-bands and the enlistment of new men in the City Guard With regard to the latter, his lordship writes—"As this outrage was committed, not by an ordinary sort of mob guided by sudden rage, but by a well-contrived scheme, executed by a cool, resolute gang, taking evidently to themselves authority over the mob, and restraining them from every folly but the wickedness they had determined to perpetrate, to which they kept them close at work, there is great reason to believe that some of that abandoned gang of smugglers had a chief hand in all this One of the first things they were observed to do was to liberate two smugglers then in prison ; and all this being done in the night time, though some moonlight, it was not easy for bystanders to know persons in the least disguised Some of the magistrates and I have spoke with several persons who were eye-witnesses to most of the tragical scenes, and yet did not know one of the actors, though they spoke to some of them I have got some hints of some of the principal actors, but doubt much of getting evidence against them, except from such as, if they were not actors, were at least abettors ; and they will never speak out, I am afraid, unless they be assured of their pardon and also some encouragement of living elsewhere, in case, as they all dread, they could not live here if they make any discovery " Having referred to the great importance of detecting and punishing the perpetrators, to which end " all methods are set agoing," his lordship states that, as commanded by the Queen, he has summoned the Lord Advocate and Solicitor-General to assist in the investigation

The Solicitor-General arrived from Annandale on the 18th ; but the Lord Advocate, who was then at his house of Culloden, near Inverness, at first delayed his return, as he writes to the Duke of Newcastle on 1st October, owing to the state of his health, " and recollecting that nothing

103 *Autobiography*, p. 39

Archibald, Earl of Ilay Lord Justice-General.
From the Portrait by Aikman in the Parliament House.

The Mystery of the Mob.

was to be done but to make the strictest inquiry after the authors and principal actors in that daring insult, which Mr Solicitor-General was actually examining into" But on hearing from the Duke that the Queen desired him to dispose of the matter at once, he proceeded forthwith to Edinburgh, where his lordship was to find the duty more difficult than he anticipated On the 4th the Earl of Ilay, Lord Justice-General, came from London to take charge of the affair, the Government being determined to probe it to the bottom, and adequately avenge so notable an affront to the Royal authority, while General Wade was brought from his great work of road-construction in the Highlands to make straight the crooked path of the inquiry—a task beyond even his engineering skill

Meanwhile Provost Wilson had received from the Duke of Newcastle a letter expressing the dissatisfaction of the Government with the magistrates' behaviour, to which he obsequiously replied on 22nd September ' This abomination," he writes, " both astonished and greatly afflicted me and the other magistrates, and I take the liberty to assure Your Grace that, as far as the surprise and the uncommon circumstances that attended it did allow of, the magistrates did exert themselves to have quelled the mob and to prevent the mischievous consequence that ensued , but it was got to so great a height before we had any notice of it, that our endeavours were in vain." He acknowledges, " with great thankfulness, Her Majesty's great goodness and care of the peace of the city ', and refers to " His Majesty's most just and wise administration, upon which our own and the nation's happiness entirely depends " These loyal protestations, however, were insufficient to save him from the consequences of his conduct Writing on the following day to the Duke of Newcastle, General Moyle observes—" When I have the honour of seeing you, I shall be able to convince Your Grace it was not by any neglect of mine the poor man lost his life Had the Lord Provost given me as early notice as he got himself from a relation of his own, I could with ease have prevented what happened without the effusion of blood But it was a conceited affair that the poor man should die, to prevent the resentment of the mob falling on a certain person "[104]

---

[104] On his examination before the Lords, the general adhered to this opinion, and stated that the person referred to was the Lord Provost

Captain Porteous.

The Queen, mistrusting the retentive capacity of the Tolbooth, had commanded that such prisoners as might be apprehended should be lodged in the Castle—a course strongly recommended by General Moyle The Justice-Clerk, writing the Duke of Newcastle on 23rd September, submits whether this "may not have the appearance of too great weakness in the Government, and may not tend to lead the mob to fancy themselves more considerable than they are " He mentions that he has caused one of the gates of the Nether Bow Port to be removed, on pretence that it stood in need of repairs "I choosed this should be done by degrees," he writes, "and in the easiest way, because the populace fancy some of their privileges are wrapt up in their gates " Later the Government found in these fancied privileges a means of punishing the citizens The Justice-Clerk adds—"The Solicitor-General came to Edinburgh on Saturday, and all hands have been at work to make discoveries, in which some progress has been made. Being informed that some of the principal actors came from the country, I have sent proper persons, in disguise, to try to get into the secret This day I prevailed with one of the mob, after promising him pardon, &c , to discover some of the aiders and abettors, which I hope will lead us into a full discovery of that mystery of iniquity " The problem, however, was not to be so easily solved

On 25th September a Proclamation by the Queen was published, offering a pardon to any of the rioters who, before 20th November following, should discover or apprehend any of the others, and also a reward of £200 for every person so discovered or apprehended on their being convicted

The whole machinery of the law was now set in motion ; the ablest men in Scotland were concentrating all their powers upon the inquiry , neither time, pains, nor money was spared. and no means which their skilled ingenuity could suggest were left untried for bringing the matter to a successful issue , but, despite their utmost efforts, the conspiracy of silence by which they were opposed proved too strong for them in the end The difficulties that beset the investigators from the first, increasing rather than diminishing as the inquiry dragged its lengthy course, and the disappointing results by which their labours were attended, can best be appreciated from the

The Mystery of the Mob.

unpublished letters, preserved in the Record Office, reporting from time to time their progress—or, rather, want of it—to the Government. The letters tell their own tale.

On 25th September the Solicitor-General communicates to the Duke of Newcastle his opinion of the situation. "Since I came to this place," he writes, "with great attention I pursued every light offered to discover the authors and actors of these most dangerous and detestable crimes; and one would naturally think it should not be hard to come at the knowledge of these impudent monsters, who, in open defiance of laws and humanity, committed, and from wantonness lengthened out their wickedness, in the face of so many spectators. Yet the disguise in which they had put themselves, the panic that seized the innocent, and the unwillingness in some, arising partly from fear of the mob, to discover what they know, has hitherto obstructed in a great measure the success of our endeavours. However, some discoveries are made, and greater seem to be in view. We were unwilling to begin the apprehending such against whom we have information until we saw the event of a further inquiry now carrying on, because I am persuaded that, so soon as any warrant is out, it must start the whole gang."

On 1st October Sir Robert Walpole, writing to his brother Horace, says that nothing remains to be done but to discover and punish the criminals. "But here," he continues, ' lie my greatest apprehensions that we have as yet no prospect of coming at either, although it is impossible but the chief agents must be known to great numbers of people. But so great a panic seized them at the time, and such a terror seems to me to continue upon them, that I very much fear it will be difficult to persuade them to do anything that may expose them again to the same ill consequences. I speak this as my own private observations, notwithstanding which I think nothing must be omitted that can possibly be done to make examples of such an unheard-of attempt. Lord Ilay goes for Scotland this week, and I think is determined to exert himself to the utmost upon this occasion. The Queen's orders are likewise sent to General Wade to repair immediately to Scotland, to countenance and assist the Government in their further proceedings."

Lord Ilay writes on 5th October to the Duke of Newcastle— "I came hither last night, and have spent all this in looking into the state of the intelligence already procured of the

Captain Porteous.

criminals; and, finding that some have absconded, that the news of the proclamation alarmed them greatly, I thought no time was to be lost in endeavouring to seize such as we have information against, and therefore immediately signed warrants against seven of them, and the Justice-Clerk has signed warrants against three more We shall attempt to execute them to-morrow morning all at once by several civil officers, each of which is to have some soldiers to assist I cannot pretend to foresee what success we shall have, but I have endeavoured to take all precaution that the nature of the thing and the various circumstances attending this case do admit of ' On the 7th Ilay reports that, as the result of these measures, five persons were then in custody   "There was some little grumbling," he writes, "among the mob who gathered together upon the seizing of the criminals, such as saying to one another, 'We will not suffer our fellow-citizens to be thus dragged away', but upon the first beat of the drum that attended the party which marched up the street, in order to conduct them to the Castle, all was entirely quiet.   The Solicitor, Mr Erskine, will go to the Castle to-morrow to try if he can bring any of them to confess It is incredible how much everybody here is afraid of appearing as evidences, the mob having industriously spread rumours that all were to be murdered that acted against them   Those who are taken are shopkeepers or servants, but I am fully satisfied that there was a few in woman's clothes or other disguises who had the conduct of the whole "

On the 9th Ilay writes to Newcastle—"To-day I believe we shall catch one, who is a footman to a fair lady, and assisted the mob in his livery " On the 15th he mentions that the Countess of Wemyss' footman, whom he had ordered to be apprehended, had gone with his mistress to Haddington, and that he had sent a proper person to catch him there   "The Advocate and the Solicitor," he continues, "sit together three hours every morning to examine persons concerning the murder They daily seem to get some farther light into it by comparing the several examinations they take, but all the evidence they are yet masters of relate only to the inferior actors, and I think it is morally impossible but that the authors of the conspiracy are persons of more distinction than those I have taken up or have signed warrants against There is a master carpenter

The Mystery of the Mob.

here who pretends great innocence, and as yet we have no manner of evidence against him, but [he] had no less than four of his workmen in the insurrection, and active He was examined by the Advocate and Solicitor to-day, to very little effect He is a great favourite of one of the magistrates who I suspect of somewhat more than neglect This inquiry will of necessity take up a long time" He adds, "I shall desire the Advocate and Solicitor to draw up, before I leave this place, a state of all the information they have, and the evidence they have to support it, that the King's servants may be better able to give them their directions."

Next day Lord Ilay writes to Walpole—"It is a great concern to me to find it so difficult hitherto to make discoveries of the murderers I am sure there is all the pains taken in it that is possible, and I never before had the pleasure to see all the King's servants here act so uniformly together in the discharge of their duty. On the other side, the secret patrons of the mob seem to be as busy in preparing false evidence to acquit the criminals, as we all can be to bring them to justice They that are in prison have already in their mouths the names of persons who, they say, will swear to their innocence, that is, their accomplices in the murder will easily perjure themselves to save their friends The most shocking circumstance is, that it plainly appears the High Flyers of our Scottish Church have made this infamous murder a point of conscience One of the actors went straight away to a country church, where the Sacrament was given a vast crowd of people, as the fashion is here, and there boasted of what he had done All the lower rank of the people, who have distinguished themselves by pretence to a superior sanctity, speak of this murder as the hand of God doing justice, and my endeavours to punish murderers are called grievous prosecutions I have conversed with several of the parsons, and I have observed that none of those who are of the High party will call any crime the mob can commit by its proper name Their manner of talking, were it universal, would extirpate religion out of the world for the good of human society, and, indeed, I could hardly have given credit to the public reports of the temper of these saints if I had not myself been witness of it, and been admonished by one of them to have regard to the Divine attribute of mercy—(in English) to protect the rebels and murderers Under these and other

Captain Porteous.

difficulties, particularly the dread all the common people are in of being murdered if they make discoveries, the inquiry goes slowly on; but I cannot but hope that by degrees this matter will come to light " " The behaviour of the magistrates," he adds, " was certainly worse than can well be imagined, and some of them, I have reason to suspect, were wilfully neglectful " He states that he has ordered them to obtain returns from the merchants and tradesmen of the city as to such of their apprentices and servants as had absconded since the riot   This measure was duly adopted by the Town Council on 20th October, with the results after mentioned

On the 30th Ilay reports—" The footman of the Countess of Wemyss is taken, and seems, by the account given of him, to have been very active in the murder.   I have sent proper persons to-day 18 miles out of the town to Falkirk, in Stirling-shire in hopes of seizing a person who walked behind Captain Porteous all the way, with a hatchet in his hand, in order, as it is thought, to kill him in case they had been attacked. One of the King's chaplains being, the other day, to preach at the giving the Sacrament (which they do here while the communicants are sitting round a very long table, which holds great numbers), I sent to him to desire that he would use some proper expressions upon the late murder of Captain Porteous He accordingly did it by warning all sorts of impenitent sinners, and, amongst the rest, the murderers of Captain Porteous The effect of it was that above a hundred, as I am told, withdrew and did not receive, but the minister, who immediately preached next, gave many hints of his being of another opinion *Tantum religio potuit* "

The last important letter of this series is that written on 4th November by General Wade to the Duke of Newcastle " I send Your Grace enclosed," he writes, " a list of the persons who have been sent prisoners to the Castle of Edinburgh for the murder of Captain Porteous   These have been committed since the arrival of Lord Ilay, for before I do not find there was any inquiry made after them by the magistrates, who, by the best information I have been able to procure, not only permitted the murder to be committed (which they might easily have prevented), but suffered all who were conscious of their guilt to make their escape   And I fear it will be difficult to find a jury who will not acquit those who are now prisoners "

The Mystery of the Mob.

The list referred to contains the names of William Stirling, James Braidwood, William Stoddart, Peter Trail, John Binney, and William Maclauchlane, the first five being Edinburgh tradesmen or their assistants, and the sixth, the footman of the Countess of Wemyss

The proceedings in respect of these persons and others is described at length in a memorial,[105] drawn by the Solicitor-General on the instructions of Lord Ilay as above mentioned, of which Scott possessed a manuscript copy, and printed it for the first time in his notes to the *Heart of Midlothian* Another copy, endorsed " Copy of Mr Solicitor Erskine's Memorial concerning the Murder of Captain Porteous, delivered by him to General Wade, on the 16th December, 1736," is in the Hardwicke MSS in the British Museum;[106] the original of this interesting document is among the Scottish State Papers in the Record Office The memorial covers the same ground as the letters already quoted, and summarises the difficulties by which the investigation was hampered The magistrates, on the Solicitor's arrival, "seemed to be all struck of a heap", they gave him no assistance ' worth mentioning ". and he entered upon the inquiry "groping in the dark " Before he arrived the guilty parties "had either run off, or at least kept themselves upon the wing," awaiting the turn of events So sensitive was the public conscience that the Solicitor pathetically records, " Very few people had so much as the courage to speak to him on the streets " To meet the susceptibilities of bashful informers, he examined the witnesses " in the privatest manner, before himself in his own house, and for six weeks' time, from morning to evening, went on in the inquiry without taking the least diversion, or turning his thoughts to any other business ' He even employed no clerk, taking down all the declarations with his own hand But, in spite of these precautions, no reliable evidence was obtained " He could get nothing but ends of stories, which, when pursued, broke off; and those who appeared, and knew anything of the matter, were under the utmost terror lest it should take air that they had mentioned any one man as guilty " The memorial concludes as follows —" This is a summary of the inquiry, from which it

---

105 Appendix VII
106 Scott remarks that the document " seems to have been drawn up by the Solicitor-General " This endorsation settles the point

Captain Porteous.

appears there is no proof on which one can rely but against Maclauchlane   His Majesty's Advocate, since he came to town, has joined with the Solicitor, and has done his utmost to get at the bottom of this matter, but hitherto it stands as is above represented   They are resolved to have their eyes and their ears open, and to do what they can   But they laboured exceedingly against the stream, and it may be truly said that nothing was wanting on their part   Nor have they declined any labour to answer the commands laid upon them to search the matter to the bottom "

In addition to the six prisoners in the Castle, it appears from the memorial that three others—Matthew King, John Crawford, and James Wilson—were then confined in the Canongate Tolbooth, while warrants had been issued for the apprehension of seven more who had absconded as aftermentioned   The names of the latter were William Whyte, Robert Taylor, Thomas Burns, Robert Anderson, Thomas Linnen, James Maxwell, and James Waldie   They were all young Edinburgh journeymen

In accordance with the instructions of Lord Ilay, the magistrates, on 20th October, had ordered returns to be made by merchants and masters of the various crafts, showing how many of their servants and apprentices had left their service at and since 7th September   These were duly lodged, and on 19th January, 1737, the magistrates passed an Act of Council containing a list of the names and designations of one hundred persons who had so deserted their masters   The Act, which was ordered to be printed and published, required those named in the list to return to their service on or before 20th March, and also to notify the magistrates of their willingness to justify themselves from the imputation of complicity in the riot   On 12th April a list was laid before the Council containing the names of thirty of the deserters who had returned, and stated, in presence of the magistrates, their willingness to justify themselves, in terms of the Act [107]   The remaining seventy who failed to do so were declared to have thereby forfeited their rights of citizenship

Of all these potential pannels, two only were destined to occupy the dock of the High Court of Justiciary, whence each, so far as the charge was concerned, was to

---

[107] No further proceedings were taken against any of those who thus returned   but sentence of fugitation was pronounced against the others by the High Court of Justiciary on 13th June, 1737

The Mystery of the Mob.

retire in turn with flying colours   On 11th March, 1737,
William Maclauchlane was placed at the bar, charged with
being accessory to the murder of Captain Porteous [108]   " During
this trial, it having been surmised that a body of footmen had
conspired to carry off the pannel, the magistrates ordered the
City Guard to be all under arms, and all the officers of the
Train-bands and the constables, with long battons, to attend in
the burgh room, and the magistrates sat in the Council Chamber
all night, which prevented all manner of disturbance' [109]
Informations for the Crown and pannel, of the usual abstruse
and lengthy sort, were respectively lodged on 14th and 17th
March, on the 18th the libel was found relevant; and the
hearing of evidence on the 21st lasted from seven in the
morning till eight at night, when the jury inclosed.   ' The
pannel was afterwards conducted to the Castle by the City
Guard, two of the magistrates, with white rods, preceded by
their officers, with lighted flambeaux, and attended by the
constables, walked before them to the Castle gate, and two
companies of the Train-bands mounted guard, by way of precaution "[110]   On the 22nd the jury unanimously found the
pannel not guilty of the crime charged, and he was accordingly
dismissed from the bar

The only good purpose served by this trial was the production
of the testimony of eye-witnesses, throwing valuable light upon
the behaviour of the mob, which we have already considered
As regards the prisoner's guilt, the evidence adduced by the
prosecution was ludicrously inadequate, although the memorial
says, " the proof seems very heavy against him "   No doubt
the depositions sworn to in the witness-box fell far short of
the statements made on precognition   It appeared that the
pannel was seen among the crowd in the Lawnmarket with a
Lochaber-axe, given to him by some of the mob, in his hand,
which he used not for purposes of offence, but as a physical
support, he being " vastly drunk " during the whole time of the
riot, and unable either to stand alone or speak   He was wearing
" my Lady Wemyss' livery," and so was readily identified   This
grotesque figure, staggering across the stage in the glare of

108 For a report of Maclauchlane's trial, see *Criminal Trials,
illustrative of* " The Heart of Midlothian," Edinburgh, 1818
109 *Gentleman's Magazine*, March, 1737
110 *Edinburgh Evening Courant*, 22nd March, 1737

Captain Porteous.

the murderers' torches, supplies some comic relief to the grim horror of the tragedy It is hard to believe that the Crown counsel expected to secure a conviction ; the probability is that some one had to be tried in order to appease, if possible, the Royal wrath, and the unlucky footman was selected as scapegoat. Writing to the Duke of Newcastle on 15th October, 1736, Lord Ilay remarked, It seems to be of the last importance to begin the first trial with one against whom there is the strongest evidence ", and if the case against Maclauchlane was of this description, it is not surprising that none of the other prisoners was required to ' thole his assize " A quaint sequel to Maclauchlane's trial is recorded by Chambers The children of the Countess of Wemyss, proud of the family's connection with the affair, arranged among themselves a dramatic representation of the tragedy, the future earl being cast for the leading part But so realistic was his sisters' conception of the scene that the helpless impersonator of Porteous was black in the face before they saw the necessity for cutting him down.[111]

Not till a year later was Justice again called upon to unsheath her sword, when, probably much to the annoyance of the Crown officials, Thomas Linnen, formerly apprentice to Colin Alison, wright in Edinburgh, returned to his native city, and, "conscious of his own innocence, did, on Saturday last, present himself to the Lord Justice-Clerk, craving that he might speedily be brought to trial" This youth was one of those who absconded, as already mentioned, and against whom sentence of fugitation had been pronounced on 13th June, 1737 After various delays the trial took place on 16th June, 1738 " The evidence brought against him proved his withdrawing and absconding; and two of the witnesses proved his being seen on the streets the night of the riot and murder, one of them having talked with him not far from the Tolbooth door, when it was broke open, and the other saw him standing within a very few persons of Captain Porteous himself, at the place where he was murdered But both these witnesses deposed that they saw him have no weapon in his hand, nor anyways active in the proceedings of the rioters Many other witnesses were also examined, who had been upon the streets and spectators of the actings of the mob, and being interrogated if they saw

---

111 *Traditions of Edinburgh*, 1825, ii 204

The Mystery of the Mob.

the prisoner there, and if he acted any, or what part in the riot or murder, deposed in the negative, most of them adding that they had never seen him before he appeared upon his trial   This being the whole of the pursuer's evidence, the counsel for the pannel did not think it necessary to call any, upon which the jury, after withdrawing a little while, returned, and brought in their verdict, unanimously finding him not guilty   Whereupon he was acquitted by the Court and dismissed from the bar "[112].   Thus ended the last judicial attempt to vindicate the outraged majesties of Queen Caroline and the law

The reader will remember that, on the day after Wilson's execution, seven soldiers of the City Guard were imprisoned in the Tolbooth of Edinburgh and eight in the Canongate Tolbooth for having fired their pieces upon the crowd   The former, as we have seen, were liberated by the mob at the taking of the prison—an instance of magnanimity in striking contrast to the treatment reserved for their Captain, with whom they were equally guilty of the people's blood   The others, less fortunate, continued in close confinement, until, on 26th July, 1736, according to the *Courant*, one of them, William Allan, "found means to make his escape from the Canongate Tolbooth in women's habit, by the assistance of a linen washer, who had conveyed the same to him, along with linen for the other prisoners "—" and then there were seven "   We hear nothing further of the rest until 27th November following, when the *Caledonian Mercury* announces—' Last week Archibald Campbell, William Hunter, George Robertson, Francis Williams, William Gun, and Andrew Macilfreish, being the last six of the sentinels of the City Guard who were in prison on account of the havoc committed at the execution of Andrew Wilson, petitioned the Right Honourable the Lords of Justiciary that they having now run their letters, might be liberate   Accordingly, a warrant for their enlargement from the Canongate Tolbooth was expede   But the magistrates caused take the city clothes from them, having no further employment for them "   What became of the seventh man does not appear, though Bailie Crockat stated, in the House of Lords inquiry, that " the other seven applied, according to an old statute,[113]

---

112 *Edinburgh Evening Courant*, 19th June, 1738
113 Act 1701, c. 6

Captain Porteous.

either to be tried or set at liberty", and, after the sixty days had run, obtained a warrant for their release Bailie Colquhoun, on the same occasion, explains why none of the soldiers were brought to trial It was, he says, the opinion of "the city lawyers, Mr Haldane, Sir James Elphinstoun, Mr Hugh Murray, and Mr Hugh Forbes," that, as Captain Porteous was proved to have given orders to fire, his men could not be prosecuted for obeying same [114]

What, then, is the key to the Justice-Clerk's "mystery of iniquity"? Who were the moving spirits of the mob? And why was the conspiracy of silence so completely successful? It must have been evident to every reader of the foregoing narrative that the conduct of the rioters presents many singular features in contradistinction to the actings of an ordinary mob That this was no fortuitous ebullition of popular fury, but rather a deliberate plot cunningly contrived and carried out, was the opinion of so experienced a strategist as General Wade, who, in his speech in the House of Commons upon the Provost's Bill, complimented the rioters on their methods "If we take a view of the whole proceedings in that barbarous murder," said he, "we find nothing in it that looks like the precipitate measures of a giddy mob, no, they went coolly and regularly to work, and, for my share [part], I never was witness to, or ever heard of any military disposition better laid down, or more resolutely executed, than their murderous plan was "[115] But apart from their tactical ability, the rioters are also remarkable for the singleness of purpose by which their acts were governed Here was no riot, in the common sense, no deed of robbery or violence, no injury to person or property, excepting such as was inseparable from the mob's design, can be laid to their charge, water is provided to limit the power of the flames to its appointed task, the weapons taken from the Guard are left upon the street : even the rope is paid for The attitude of the rioters to the soldiers of the City Guard, doubly detested since the massacre in the Grassmarket, is also highly significant At the storming of the Guard-house no reprisals are attempted, nay, more, the seven soldiers confined in the Tolbooth, who had actually killed and wounded their fellow-citizens, are set at liberty along with the other felons The "Brief Account,"

114 Examinations of Bailies Crockat and Colquhoun
115 *Parliamentary History*, x, 291

The Mystery of the Mob.

befoie iefeiied to, emphasises the following facts.—" It was so clear a moonlight when Poiteous was murthered that the face of any peison could be known from one side of the stieet to the other   The Giassmaiket, where the murther was committed, was filled with people, and is large enough to contain four or five thousand in numbei "[116]   In addition to this natural illumination, the scene was biilliantly lighted by the torches of the conspiiators, yet no single membei of so great a multitude, save the iidiculous and drunken footman, could ever be discovered

Theie is ieason to believe that the Goveinment at first attii-buted the affaii to the influence of the Jacobites, and, with the compaiatively iecent events of 'the '15" fiesh in the public memory, feaied it was but the beginning of a geneial dis-affection   To others, the Westein Covenantcrs weie objects of suspicion   Di Carlyle, iefeiiing to this point, obseives— " It was represented as a dangerous plot, and was ignorantly connected with a gieat meeting of zealous Covenanteis, of whom many still iemained in Galloway and the West, which had been held in summei in the Pentland Hills to ienew the Covenant. But this was a mistake, foi the muidei of Porteous had been planned and executed by a few of the ielations and fiiends of those whom he had slain, who, being of a iank supeiioi to mere mob, had caiiied on their design with so much secrecy, ability, and steadiness as made it be asciibed to a still higher order, who weie political enemies to Goveinment "[117]   It is, howevei, unlikely that the victims of the affray at Wilson's execution, who, as appears fiom the published lists of casualties, were either small tradesmen or seivants, would have ielations and friends of superior rank   The only one with any claim to "gentrice" was "Patrick Spalden, son of —— Spalden of Ashintully, Esq, and appientice to Mr David Mitchell, jewellei," who, like many younger sons of good family in those days, was destined for a commeicial caieei   But neither Jacobites nor Covenanters, nor, pace Dr Carlyle, the relatives of the slain, were the mainspiing of the movement, though, doubtless "the grief and concern of the friends and relations of those whom he [Porteous] had muidei ed and wounded came in to increase the flame against him "[118]

116 Appendix V
117 *Autobiography*, p 39
118 *Life and Death*, &c, p 18

Captain Porteous.

"It was very clearly the work of no ordinary rabble," says Mr Hill Burton, "subject to the momentary impulses of ferocity and of regret, which actuate such a body, ready to perpetrate an atrocity at one moment, disposed to conciliate and secure their personal safety from the consequences at another It is difficult to believe that Forbes could have failed to see how much his own favourite exclusive trade system and formidable revenue laws had their influence on the national feelings, of which this act, and the mystery in which it was shrouded, were the types "[119] There was a bold and powerful class in Scotland whose comprehensive hate embraced at once the Government and all its works in general, and the Custom-house and its officials in particular—the smugglers A leading member of this fraternity, dear to the heart of the *profanum vulgus*, had, as we have seen, come within the clutch of the law and miserably perished, his last moments embittered by the barbarity of Porteous. His brother-in-law and his friends, in their attempt to pluck him from the jaws of death, caused the lamentable loss of life which followed, these same persons were almost certainly ' the only begetters" of the conspiracy by which he was avenged There is little doubt that Scott had his hand upon the key of the mystery when he lighted on the tale of the twelve young men belonging to Wilson's native village of Pathhead, who, determined that Porteous, despite the reprieve, should not escape his lawful doom, crossed the Forth at different ferries, assembled in the Portsburgh (probably on Monday, 6th September), and supplied the spark which, in the then state of public feeling, was all that was required to fire the train of popular fury [120] It is unfortunate that Scott in his inquiries was baffled by the not unnatural reticence of a deceased conspirator's son He himself considered the story so simple and satisfactory an explanation of the facts "that although," he remarks, " the degree of proof, upon investigation, fell far short of what was necessary as full evidence, I cannot help considering it as the most probable account of the mysterious affair " Owing to the failure of the authorities to

---

119 *Lives of Forbes and Lovat*, 1847, p 350

120 " The rioters, as far as Perth, Stirling, Fife, and Dumfries-shires, having gathered together, as they say, and skulked in and about the town upon Monday, assembled in greater bodies in close-heads, turnpikes, and stairs upon the Tuesday night, within the town "—*Life and Death*, &c , Introduction

The Mystery of the Mob.

take immediate action, the original devisors of the scheme fled to foreign parts before the hue and cry began, which, in Scott's opinion, accounts for nothing being found out as to the origin of the riot, "since, though in itself a great conflagration, its source was from an obscure and apparently inadequate cause."[121]

It is evident that the design was known and approved in Edinburgh beforehand, for the Solicitor-General states in his memorial that James Maxwell (who, like his fellow-servant, Thomas Linnen, had absconded after the murder), "is proven to have come to a shop upon the Friday before [3rd September, the day the reprieve was published], and charged the journeymen and 'prentices there to attend in the Parliament Close on Tuesday night, to assist hang Porteous, which," as the Solicitor-General justly observes, "is pretty remarkable" This Maxwell was one of the Crown witnesses at the trial, and gave strong evidence against Captain Porteous The fact that some seventy Edinburgh journeymen and apprentices fled the country after the riot shows how hearty was the co-operation given to the original conspirators at the time; while the incident mentioned by Lord Ilay, when over a hundred members of an Edinburgh congregation withdrew from the Communion table rather than hear the murderers denounced as sinners, speaks volumes for the state of the public feeling, and explains why no evidence against them could afterwards be obtained

The hero of the historic guinea has, for many years, been the ancient mariner, Alexander Richmond, who disclosed his identity to a friend of his youth upon the pier of Leith [122] The story of the bold baxter lad, sent early to bed by his father on the night of the mob, and prudently deprived of his clothes lest he should be tempted to join it, escaping by the window in his sister's garments (which presumably contained the lady's purse), becoming the ringleader of the rioters, and paying for the appropriated rope, is more picturesque than probable His going to sea to escape detection, and, finally, returning in his old age to tell the tale, does not square with the fact that his name is not found in the list of those who absconded after the murder, and makes one doubtful of the

---

121 *Heart of Midlothian*, Note iii , " The Porteous Mob ", *Tales of a Grandfather*, Standard Edition, 1898, p 973
122 *Illustrations of Geikie's Etchings*, p 8

Captain Porteous.

hero's veracity   Be that as it may, there is now another "Richmond" in the field   The late Dr Robert Goodsir, of Edinburgh, writing (in 1884) the reminiscences of his boyhood in Anstruther, under the title *Linked Memories*,[123] refers to the recollections of a venerable resident, named Mrs Black, who, he says, "could tell about the Porteous Riot, for that was only a story of yesterday in her young days   . She could tell about one Bruce, a wild Anster youth, who procured, by rather unjustifiable means, the rope for which a guinea was left in exchange, and with which rope they proceeded forthwith to hang the wretched, bullying, wife-beating Jock Porteous Mrs Black's story went on to tell that Bruce, the West Port rioter, afterwards, when things had blown over, returned to Anstruther, and resumed his peaceful avocation of a shaver and wig-dresser." It is quite possible that this Bruce may have been one of Scott's young men from Fife

Mr Charles Kirkpatrick Sharpe was a firm believer in the traditional guinea, but ridiculed the idea of its being left by any member of an ordinary Edinburgh mob "Even if beset with the whim of maintaining a character for honesty, who among such a rabble had a guinea to spare?   More likely a pund Scots, or twal' pennies sterling!"[124]   He rather regarded the incident as a proof that people of good position were implicated in the riot   "From many old persons I have heard," he writes, "that people of high rank were concerned in the affair   My great-grandfather, Lord Alva, told my grandfather that many of the mob were persons of rank, some of them disguised as women—Lord Haddington, for one, in his cook-maid's dress   I have been told that my great-grandfather, Sir Thomas Kirkpatrick, had a hand in it, as other people of quality unquestionably had.   I have often since suspected, from words let fall by my grandfather, and still more from hints of my aunt, Lady Murray of Clermont, that my grandfather knew more about the whole affair than he cared to tell The upper ranks of society then had a strong power over the lower, wholly unknown now   On this head I could mention many things scarcely to be believed "[125]   It is, however,

---

123 The original MS is in the possession of John A Fairley, Esq , to whose courtesy the Editor is indebted for the use of same

124 Wilson's *Reminiscences of Old Edinburgh*, ii 84

125 *Ibid* ii 83

The Mystery of the Mob.

difficult to understand what object these distinguished persons could have in assisting at the slaying of Porteous, who was, as we have seen, on terms of intimacy with people of position

Sir Daniel Wilson mentions a curious allusion to the Porteous mob which occurred in the defence of the celebrated John Horne Tooke, on his trial for libel before Lord Mansfield in 1777 His lordship, who had been one of the counsel for the City of Edinburgh in the proceedings on the Bill of Pains and Penalties aftermentioned, and was himself suspected of having been among the rioters, was thus addressed by the prisoner— "I shall not trouble you to repeat the particulars of the affair of Captain Porteous at Edinburgh These gentlemen are so little pleased with military execution upon themselves that Porteous was charged by them with murder ; he was prosecuted, convicted, and, when he was reprieved after sentence, the people of the town executed that man themselves, so little did they approve of military execution Now, gentlemen, there are at this moment people of reputation, living in credit, making fortunes under the Crown, who were concerned in that very fact, who were concerned in the execution of Porteous I do not speak it to censure them, for, however irregular the act, my mind approves it."[126] This statement affords, in Wilson's view, a singular corroboration of the traditions that represent the higher classes to have furnished the chief leaders in the Porteous mob Mr Andrew Lang, however, is of a different opinion "Men of intelligence," he writes, "certainly directed the mob, but only anecdotes of their courtesy to ladies, given by Scott, suggest that any of the leaders belonged to the class of gentry" [127]

Chambers, writing in 1825, states that he was informed by a very old man, who had been an apprentice in the Fleshmarket of Edinburgh some fifty years before, "that in his younger days it was well known among the butchers, though only whispered secretly among themselves, that the leaders of this singular riot were two brothers of the name of Cumming, who were, for many years after, fleshers in the Low Market, and died unmolested at advanced ages They were tall, strong, and exceedingly handsome men, had been dressed in women's clothes on the occasion, and were said to have been the first to jump

---

126 *Memorials of Edinburgh*, 1848, ii 209
127 *History of Scotland*, iv 434

through the flames that burnt down the prison door in eager-
ness to seize their unfortunate victim." [128]   Another account
of the riot is given by Forsyth in 1805, on the authority of
an unnamed informant, 'who resided in the upper part of
Lanarkshire, and had a relation killed by the fire of the Town
Guard   Hearing the rumour of the intended rising, this
person proceeded to Edinburgh on Tuesday. the 7th, where he
found the inferior sort of inns in the Grassmarket full of people,
and saw many persons, apparently strangers lurking in the
different houses "   He joined the rioters at the beating of the
drum in the Portsburgh, and assisted in putting Porteous to
death [129]

The reader has now before him all the available evidence
upon which to form a judgment, and must answer the riddle
for himself

(6) THE PROVOST'S BILL.

Lang s their debating thereanent
The Election —Robert Fergusson

Plagu'd wi' pamphlets, dunn'd wi' cries
Auld Reikie —Robert Fergusson

"The annual friendly meeting of the gentlemen of the name
of Wilson was held at the house of Jean Wilson spouse to
Arthur Cumming, periwig-maker, opposite to the City Guard ,
the Right Hon Alexander Wilson, Lord Provost of the city,
preses   There were present about forty gentlemen and others
of that clan, who were served at supper by persons of the
name   The entertainment was sumptuous, and choice wines
went merrily round "[130]   This paragraph gives us a pleasant
glimpse of the Provost in his careless hours, before the shadow
of the Porteous affair had darkened his lordship's days

The anonymous author before quoted pays, in his *Life and
Death of Captain John Porteous*, &c , the following tribute
to the merits of Provost Wilson —" The Provost is the son of
a substantial farmer in Mid-Lothian ; he ply'd the trade of a
brewer, and succeeded very well that way   He had been
long in the magistracy, and behaved so well that he was
chosen Lord Provost of the city   He was much

---

128 *Illustrations of the Author of Waverley* p 171
129 *The Beauties of Scotland*, i 235
130 *Caledonian Mercury*, 19th January, 1736

Alexander Wilson, Lord Provost of Edinburgh, 1735-1736.

From a contemporary Portrait.

The Provost's Bill.

regarded for industry in his trade, great honesty in his way of dealing, and an unalterable veracity, from which he would not deviate even in trifles. He has that cheerfulness of temper in a most inoffensive way, that justice, humanity, and compassion in his decisions when in public authority, that there is none who knew Bailie Wilson who did not love him In one word, he was a good friend, a good neighbour, and a good subject He hated politicks as much as he loved truth, openness, and plainness " In the matter of Porteous, however, these shining qualities would seem to have suffered a temporary eclipse

On 1st February, 1737, the first mutterings of the Parliamentary storm, which was to strip this estimable gentleman of his office and imperil the privileges of the city, were heard at Westminster in the speech from the Throne on the opening of the session. When His Majesty returned from Hanover in the beginning of January, he found that a spirit of discontent and insurrection was abroad Riots had occurred in London and other parts of the country, principally owing to the execution of the Gin Act, there had been tumults among the Spitalfields weavers, and disturbances in connection with turnpikes in the West, while the signal affront offered to the authority of the Queen Regent by the Edinburgh mob, specially repugnant to the Royal pride. called for immediate chastisement [131] The general allusion in the King s speech to these disorders was answered by loyal addresses from both Houses, reprobating such outrages, and expressing their resolution to support the Royal authority On 10th February, in the debate which followed in the House of Lords, Lord Carteret, although in opposition to the Ministry, spoke strongly in favour of a searching inquiry being made into the circumstances of the tumult at Edinburgh The murderers of Porteous must, he argued, be well known to the magistrates and citizens, the former having encouraged the riot and some of the latter being concerned therein ; and if they concealed their names the city should be punished by the removal of the Courts of Justice and the forfeiture of its charter

---

131 " The legend that Queen Caroline threatened ' to make Scotland a hunting-ground,' and that Argyll replied, ' In that case I will take leave of Your Majesty, and go down to my own country to get my hounds ready,' is better known than attested "—Lang's *History of Scotland*, iv 431.

Captain Porteous.

A valuable account of this and the subsequent proceedings in the House of Lords is given by George, Earl of Morton, in his letters to his son, Lord Aberdour [132] "He" [Lord Carteret], writes Lord Morton on 10th February, 1737, "was answered by the Duke of Newcastle, who spoke as modestly as that horrid subject could bear, and the Lord Batters [Bathurst] spoke, and seconded Lord Carteret, then the Earl of Ilay (who has not yet recovered his late illness) spoke in a very handsome manner, and though he condemned the horridness of that mob and the cruelty which they had committed, yet spoke very strongly against taking away the privileges of the city or removing the Courts of Justice to another place, which was proposed by the Lord that opened the debate " Lord Carteret then made the following motions, which were all agreed to, viz :—(1) That the Provost and four bailies[133] of the city of Edinburgh in the year 1736 be ordered to attend this House   (2) That the person commanding the City Guard at the time of the riot in which Captain Porteous was murdered be ordered to attend this House   (3) That the Officer Commanding-in-Chief His Majesty's forces in that part of Great Britain called Scotland, and residing there at the time of the said riot, be ordered to attend this House   (4) That an authentic copy of the trial of Captain Porteous, and all the proceedings relating thereunto, he laid before this House   (5) That an humble address be presented to His Majesty that he will be graciously pleased to give order that the accounts transmitted hither of the murder of Captain Porteous, and what passed thereupon, together with the orders and directions sent from hence relating thereunto, as likewise a copy of the reprieve of the said Captain, granted by Her Majesty, as guardian of the kingdom, be laid before this House   (6) That the attendance of the several persons aforementioned be on this day month [134]

On 10th November, 1736, the Town Council, in respect that Isobel Gordon, the widow of Porteous, "is left utterly destitute, without any means of subsisting unless some aid be given her by this city," had granted her an annual pension of £10 sterling ' On 26th January, 1737, the lady wrote a letter to

---

132 Appendix X

133 The bailies of Edinburgh figure, throughout these proceedings, under what Mr Hill Burton calls " the equivocal title of ' Bailiffs ' "

134 *Parliamentary History*, ix 1310.

The Provost's Bill.

the Provost, exonerating the magistrates from all responsibility in connection with the Captain's murder, gratefully acknowledging their bounty, and regretting that she, "the widow of so unfortunate a husband," is unable to make any other return "than putting up her fervent prayers to heaven for the welfare and peace of this city." So pleased were the Council by the propriety of these opportune sentiments, that they increased her pension to £12 The prayers of the grateful widow were destined to remain unanswered, but her letter was taken to London by the magistrates as a certificate of their impeccability, along with the lists showing the number of persons who had absconded after the murder [135]

On 21st February the Provost and bailies, accompanied by Mr Irvine, the town-clerk, set out for London, in obedience to the order of the House of Lords, Captain Lind, who since the riot, had ceased to enjoy the Provost's favour, following the next day Lord Morton writes, "I suppose the ministers will forgive them [the magistrates] for travelling on Sunday, being a case of necessity" On 3rd March the Duke of Newcastle presented to the House the authentic copy of the trial of Captain Porteous and other documents called for, and on the 10th the House resolved itself into a committee to consider the affair, and agreed to fifteen interrogatories, upon which the Provost and the four bailies were examined; after which General Wade, Patrick Lindsay, Major Pool, and Colonel Duroure, whose names had been mentioned in the examinations, were likewise ordered to attend On 17th Captain Lind was examined upon eleven interrogatories, as also were Mr Lindsay and General Moyle With the substance of these examinations we have already dealt, and copies of same will be found in the Appendix [136]

Writing on the 10th, Lord Morton says that the Provost's examination that day lasted till seven o'clock, "and really he behaved very well, and much better than was expected" A contemporary account mentions a humorous incident in connection with his examination.[137] The Duke of Newcastle, having asked the Provost what sort of shot was used by the City Guard on the occasion of Wilson's execution, received the

135 *Council Records*
136 Appendix XII
137 *Life and Death of Captain John Porteous, &c*, 1737, p 34

Captain Porteous.

surprising reply, " Ou, juist sic as ane shutes dukes and sic-like fules wi' ! " This answer was considered as contempt of the House, and the unfortunate Provost was about to pay dearly for his vernacularism, when the Duke of Argyll hastened to translate the offensive words into their English equivalents of "ducks and water-fowl" Scott refers to the anecdote in the *Heart of Midlothian*

Lord Morton, who was prevented by an attack of gout from attending the examinations of the bailies, heard Captain Lind examined, "who," he writes, "answered very distinctly and very pointedly, but differed in several questions from the Provost, and I am afraid that the poor Provost does not stand in so good a light as he did." With regard to Lindsay s examination, his answers "were as favourable for the conduct of the magistrates and himself as the nature of the thing would bear, but it still appeared they were very negligent and deficient in their duty" General Moyle "said very much for his own vindication, and blamed the magistrates and Mr Lindsay." Morton adds, "I think it seems to be agreed on all hands that the magistrates have been very deficient, and I am afraid the Provost will not come off so well as I could wish him." On 22nd March he writes, "I was obliged to go to the House of Peers this day, where I heard Colonel Duroure, Major Pool, and General Wade examined, which continued near five hours, they do not make for the magistrates I suppose you'll soon hear that Lord Milton, Lord Royston, and Lord Dun are ordered to attend the House, which motion was made yesterday by the Duke of Newcastle, which, if it had not, I believe the other party would have moved this day to have brought Lord Milton by himself "[138]

On the 26th Lord Morton reports that the evidence of the witnesses was read before the House, " which really comes out pretty strong, and it was moved by a Lord [Strafford] that the Provost should be sent to Newgate for prevaricating in his examination, but, the consideration of the whole having been put off till Thursday, it was let drop till the whole was before them, and then, I am afraid, it will be very heavy on his lordship " He concludes by hoping that before that date Maclauchlane,

---

138 Such a motion, intended as an impeachment of the Justice-Clerk, was made by Lord Lovel on 18th March ; it was superseded, however, by Newcastle's motion to summon also the two senior judges who had tried Porteous —*Parliamentary History*, x, 197-198

The Provost's Bill.

who was then upon his trial before the High Court of Justiciary, would be convicted, "otherwise we shall be all affronted" The news of the prisoner's acquittal was received at St. Stephen's as a fresh proof of the contumacy of the Edinburgh citizens and Lord Morton considered it would be "of ill-consequence to the magistrates." On the 29th he writes—' I admire they should have tried this fellow without having clear evidence against him, for it has brought a scandal upon the whole nation, and God knows what the consequences may be It has made good what Generals Wade and Moyle wrote to the Duke of Newcastle, that no jury in Scotland would condemn any that were concerned in the murder of Porteous, and I now make no doubt but all England believes it " The abortive result of the trial unquestionably intensified the irritation of the Government, and as Lord Morton says in another letter, "occasioned a great spight against the Provost" On 3rd April, in pursuance of the several resolutions which were reported and agreed to,[139] the Provost was ordered to be taken into custody of the Gentleman Usher of the Black Rod, and the following bill was ordered to be brought in —*To disable Alexander Wilson, Esq , from taking, holding, or enjoying any Office or Place of Magistracy in the City of Edinburgh, or elsewhere in Great Britain, and for imprisoning the said Alexander Wilson: and for abolishing the Guard kept up in the said city, commonly called the Town Guard, and for taking away the gates of the Nether Bow Port of the said city, and keeping open the same* [140] The motion for bringing in the bill was carried on a division by 82 to 17 Next day the bill was read a first time, and ordered to be read a second time On the 19th the Provost was admitted to bail, himself being bound in £2000, and his two securities in £1000 each

A detailed account of the preparations made by the magistrates for opposing the bill is contained in the Council minute of 12th April,[141] the Provost's letter from London on the situation, and the Council's answer thereto, being quoted in full The latter gives an outline of the proposed defence of the city, as advised by James Grahame and William Grant,

---

139 Copies of these eight Resolutions will be found in the *Courant* of 7th April, 1737

140 Appendix IX

141 *Council Records.*

Captain Porteous.

advocates, who were consulted in the matter "It was by them judged needful," Bailie Crockat writes to the Provost, "to discriminate and separate the case of the community or burgesses and inhabitants of the town from your particular case They thought that it would be highly inconvenient, considering the temper of these times, to mix or blend them together, and that it was a point of prudence to endeavour to make the town's defence with as great caution as possible" Evidently, in the opinion of counsel, the Provost had a bad case The bailie mentions a suggestion by Mr Grahame as to whether it would not be better 'to let this storm blow over till persons' blood cool somewhat, and even suffer the Guard to be laid aside, and then, upon the contusion and anarchy into which this city must necessarily be drawn, to apply to have things again put upon their ancient footing " This course, however, was not adopted, and a petition was presented by the magistrates and Town Council to the House of Lords, praying that they might be heard by their counsel against the bill on the second reading. Along with this petition, the various Charters, Acts of Parliament, and Acts of Council mentioned in the minute were transmitted to London

On 26th April an important debate took place, upon a motion made by Lord Carteret to have the verdict and sentence pronounced against Captain Porteous declared erroneous.[142] " In examining the proceedings of the trial," says Coxe, " it plainly appeared that Porteous was fully justified, from the principles of self-defence. in firing upon the mob, and that the reprieve granted by the Queen was founded on law and justice, and, as the constitution of the criminal law in Scotland was different from that in England, it appeared incomprehensible to most of the peers that a person could be condemned to death upon a verdict so inconsistent with common justice "[143] The motion, however, was not insisted in, nor was there any division upon it The chief speakers for the motion were Lord Carteret, Lord Bathurst, the Earl of Winchelsea, and Lord Lovel The Lord Chancellor and the Bishop of Salisbury spoke against the trial, ' but thought they had not sufficient lights to pass any censure upon it ", and the chief speakers against the motion and in favour of the trial were Lord Hervey, the

---

142 *Parliamentary History*, x 201-213

143 *Memoirs of Sir Robert Walpole*, i 494

The Provost's Bill.

Earl of Findlater, the Earl of Ilay, the Duke of Argyll, and the Earl of Scarborough.

The temper in which the proceedings were conducted had already roused the national spirit of the Scots peers, and their feelings were further embittered when, on 29th April, the question was raised as to whether the three Lords of Justiciary, who had been summoned to attend the House, should be examined at the bar, at the table, or upon the Woolsack. Lord Morton, writing on 3rd May, gives an account of the debate "Yesterday we had a long debate about the manner our judges should appear, and it being found by the records of Parliament that never any judges that were called by the peers had been allowed to sit among the English judges, but one single instance of two that had been called by the Convention at the Revolution, and afterwards were dismissed and never allowed to come to the House again But it appeared upon many occasions that the Keepers of the Great Seal, the Chancellor of the Exchequer, always appeared at the bar, and even the great Lord Chief Justice Holt, being once called, appeared likewise at the bar, so it was put to the vote, and it carried that they should come to the bar, 48 against 37. So they were ushered in by the Keeper of the Black Rod and chairs set for them, though they had no occasion to sit down, and every question that was asked at them was put in writing, and joining their heads together Lord Dun, who was appointed to answer first as being youngest, gave his answer, and next Lord Royston, and then the Justice-Clerk, and they all answered very exactly to every question as they were put to them, so they were ordered to withdraw, and I don't hear that they will be called again " In the debate, the principal speakers for calling the Scots judges to the bar were the Earls of Abingdon, Aylesford, Chesterfield, Strafford, and Winchelsea, the Lord Chancellor, and Lords Delawar and Bathurst, against it were the Duke of Argyll, Earl of Ilay, Duke of Newcastle Lord Hervey, Duke of Athole, and the Earls of Crawford and Findlater [144] The result of this debate was regarded by the Scots people as a deliberate slight upon the dignity of their judges

Ramsay records an amusing anecdote of the appearance of the Lords of Justiciary at the bar of the House, told him by

---

[144] *Parliamentary History*, x 213-238

Captain Porteous.

Lord Kames, who was in London at the time "The night before, he [Kames] was invited to sup with them, when Lord Dun, who was a very worthy, but withal a very pompous man, said to his colleagues, 'Brethren, I am sorry to say neither of you will be understood by the House to-morrow I am, you well know, in a different situation, having made the English language my particular study' To-morrow came, when, Lord Kames said, Lord Royston was hardly intelligible, Lord Milton, though no elegant speaker, was well heard, and his meaning comprehended, as for Lord Dun, 'Deil ae word, from beginning to end, did the English understand of his speech ' "[145]

The Lord Provost and the City of Edinburgh having been admitted to be heard by their counsel against the bill, that hearing began on 4th May, and was continued every day till the 7th Then the bill was committed for the 9th, when it passed in committee, and on the 11th was read a third time, and passed on a division, 54 Contents to 22 Not Contents [146]

Upon the third reading the Duke of Argyll concluded an eloquent and powerful speech against the bill as follows —
' This riotous and rebellious spirit of theirs does not proceed from any oppression in the governors or civil magistrates of that country, as has been strongly insinuated, but from a few fanatical preachers lately started up in that country, who, by their sermons and otherwise, instil into the minds of the vulgar and ignorant such enthusiastical notions as are inconsistent with all government, by making sedition and rebellion a principle of their religion From this cause, I am inclined to think, the tumult at Edinburgh proceeded, and to this is owing that ill-judged fidelity of the guilty towards one another by which the secret was, before the execution, made impenetrable, and by which the discovery of the persons concerned has since been rendered impossible But of the inhabitants of Edinburgh, I am convinced, there are very few tainted with such principles, because they seldom or never hear any such doctrines I have now, my Lords, given my opinion with respect to the present bill, so far as I have had opportunity to know anything of its tendency, or the evidence upon which it is founded, and I think that, if we consent to

---

[145] *Scotland and Scotsmen*, ii 543, *n*
[146] *Parliamentary History*, x 238

124

John, Duke of Argyll and Greenwich.

From an Engraving after Kneller.

The Provost's Bill.

the passing it into a law, at least in the shape it is now in, we shall do what is both imprudent and unjust."[147]

The Lord Chancellor (Lord Hardwicke), who spoke next, warmly supported the bill, and said—"I believe, my Lords, there have been very few bills brought into this House with which your Lordships, however differing in opinion in other respects, will more heartily concur than with the present. We have seen bills of this kind before, and we have heard many plausible arguments advanced against them, but I cannot imagine how any one who wishes well to his King and his country, can look upon this present bill, which is calculated only to punish a visible neglect of the interest of both, as a job, and refuse his concurrence to it on that account. The time was, indeed, when races of popularity were run, and when gaining a borough or a county might have been the motives of dissent from a bill of this nature: but I hope there are no such persons nowadays—at least, I hope there are none among us—who will sacrifice the honour of the Government in general to any job or to any selfish views whatever. Some think to govern nations by a party, without any view to the good of government in general, but it is a pitiful way of governing. A man who acts zealously for the good of his country will make the rule of his conduct the interest of the whole, which is as much supported by the maxims of punishing open violations of, as rewarding particular services done to Governments in general. Whoever, I say, acts in this manner acts for the good of the whole."

The Duke of Argyll, regarding this peroration as aimed at himself, made a spirited reply, in the course of which he said—"My Lords, I am no minister, and I never will be one. Time was when I might have been a piece of a minister, but I was too sensible of my own want of capacity to engage in any State affairs, and I thank God I had always too great a value for those few abilities which Nature has given me to employ them in doing any drudgery or any job of what kind soever. I have, ever since I set out in the world (and I believe few set out more early), served my Prince with my tongue, I have served him with any little interest I had, and I have served him in my trade, and were I to-morrow to be stripped of all the

---

147 Reports of this and the other speeches aftermentioned will be found in *Parliamentary History*, x 238-247

Captain Porteous.

employments which I have endeavoured honestly and faithfully to deserve, I would serve him again to the utmost of my power and to the last drop of my blood." Whereupon the Lord Chancellor rose and explained that, personally, he entertained the highest opinion of the noble Lord's integrity, that the words which had given offence to the noble peer were only to be understood in a Hardwickian sense, as referring to no one in particular, and "that the noble Lord was the last man in the world to whom he would have them applied."[148]

On 16th May the famous bill was received in the Commons from the Lords.[149] It is certain that the Ministry had not sufficiently considered the nature of the Scots Constitution as settled by the Act of Union, and that the evidence was wholly inadequate to justify the penalties sought to be imposed. The measure was purely vindictive. "It was," says Mr. Hill Burton, "the threat of angry enemies, not the wise legislation of a national Parliament." The abolition of the City Guard and the removal of the Nether Bow Port resembled the treatment meted out to a conquered city by a victorious foe. and the proposed humiliation was resented accordingly by the Scots members. The reception given to the bill was singular. Befriended by some of the most violent opponents of the Ministry, the measure was attacked by supporters of the Government, notably the Lord Advocate and Solicitor-General, the principal law-officers of the Crown for Scotland. Such prominent English members as Sir John Barnard, the representative of the City of London, Sir William Wyndham, and "Honest Shippen," denounced, in strong terms, the dangerous tendencies of the bill.

On the motion for the second reading, Patrick Lindsay, the member for Edinburgh, defended his constituency in a long and vigorous speech, in the course of which he attributed the particular instance of the *perfervidum ingenium Scotorum* then under consideration to the malign influence of certain of the Scots clergy, who, if any law, *e g*, that of patronage, stood in their way, "abuse the unwary people, and spirit them up to despise and disobey the law by this seditious doctrine, too often inculcated upon such occasions, that such a law is iniquity

---

148 This scene quaintly anticipates, by just one hundred years, the familiar passage between Mr. Pickwick and Mr Blotton (of Aldgate)

149 *Commons' Journals*, 16th May, 1737

The Provost's Bill.

established by law" As the result of these amiable precepts,
their parishioners "look upon every law that interferes with
their passions to be iniquity" This doctrine, he adds, "is
preached up by those wild, hot-headed, violent High Church
clergy, who are not to be satisfied with any power unless they
possess all power, and by them only Yes, sir, I am sorry to
say it, we have High Church Presbyterians who have higher
notions of clerical power than any Protestant clergy whatever" These observations were so badly received by his
clerical constituents that Lindsay had, later, to address an
open letter to the Edinburgh journals expressly excluding
"the reverend ministers of the city" from the scope of his
remarks, "which makes us wonder," says Mr. Andrew Lang,
"who the High Flyers mentioned by Ilay can have been—the
ministers who thought killing no murder "[150] The motion
for the second reading was carried, upon a division, by 146
to 99

The opposition to the bill continued violent and strenuous,
and its progress was resisted in every possible way. The
witnesses who had been called before the House of Lords were
examined *de novo*, and some fresh evidence was taken, new
petitions by the Lord Provost for his own interest, and by the
magistrates and Town Council in behalf of the city were
presented to the House, and counsel were heard against the
bill An interesting account of the hearing of counsel and
examination of witnesses is given in a contemporary 'Letter
to a Gentleman, containing a summary account of the proceedings in the Lords' bill for punishing Provost Wilson, &c "[151]

On 9th June the Attorney-General moved that the bill be
committed, the motion being seconded by the Solicitor-General
for England,[152] who delivered a forcible indictment of the
Provost Then the Lord Advocate, Duncan Forbes of
Culloden, in a dignified and weighty speech, raised his voice
for the independence of his country He warned the House
against the danger of acting under the influence of national
prejudice, and supplied, from his own experience, a singular
instance of the fatal result of so doing in the case of Captain
Green, at whose trial for piracy and murder he had been

---

150 *History of Scotland*, iv 433

151 Appendix XI

152 Reports of these speeches, as also those aftermentioned, will be
found in *Parliamentary History*, x 274-292

Captain Porteous.

present, and of which he gave a striking account Green, who "seemed to have no other crime but that of being an Englishman," and was undoubtedly innocent of the charge against him, fell a victim to the popular hatred of England So impressed was Forbes with this scandalous injustice that he attended the execution in deep mourning, and "carried the head of Captain Green to the grave " The Lord Advocate concluded his speech as follows —"Thus, Sir, 1 have given my opinion with respect to the insufficiency of the evidence for passing the present Bill into a law, and I have done it in the sincerity of my heart, for what motive can I have in what I have spoken, but the discharge of my duty as a member of this House? It is more than probable, Sir, that I shall never trouble you again with my sentiments upon this or any other subject, but my conscience would ever afterwards have accused me if I had quitted my seat before I had given my reasons why I think the present Bill should not be committed "[153]

General Wade, who spoke next in support of the motion, dwelt upon the currency of the rumour as to the intended murder of Porteous, and defended General Moyle for his caution in refusing to act without legal warrant. The aversion of the people of that country,' said he, ' to the gentlemen of the army is very great, and Mr. Moyle undoubtedly acted the wisest part, for there is no room to suppose he would have met with much favour from the witnesses had his conduct been brought to trial in a civil Court " Other speakers in this debate, whose speeches are reported in the *Parliamentary History*,[154] were, in favour of the committal, Mr Serjeant Skinner, Henry Fox, Sir William Yonge, and Sir Robert Walpole: against the motion, William Shippen, Solicitor-General Erskine, Lord Cornbury, Lord Glenorchy, Mr Oglethorpe, James Erskine of Grange,[155] Lord Polwarth and Sir John Barnard Walpole spoke last, and concluded a very moderate speech as follows —' If, after it is committed, gentlemen should think fit to make such amendments upon it as may leave the privileges of the Incorporation of Edinburgh

153 The office of Lord President of the Court of Session was then vacant by the death of Sir Hugh Dalrymple Forbes was appointed his successor, and took his seat on 21st June, 1737

154 Vol x 292-317

155 For some account of this remarkable man, the notorious Lord Grange, see Appendix XVI

The Nether Bow Port.

From an Etching by Skene.

The Provost's Bill.

untouched, and remit the most penal part of the punishment of the Lord Provost, and if these amendments should be founded upon reason and equity I shall be by no means against them " The motion was carried, upon a division, by 124 to 118

On 12th June the House went into Committee, where the preamble and every clause of the bill was vehemently opposed Walpole, fearing to further offend the members for Scotland, accepted amendments which changed both its name and character. Provided the Queen's action in granting the reprieve was justified and some punishment inflicted on the Provost and the city, he was not unwilling to depart from those penal clauses which had provoked so great hostility Accordingly, the imprisonment of the Lord Provost and the clauses touching the City Guard and the Nether Bow Port were dropped,[156] a fine of £2000 was imposed upon the city, to "be applied to and for the sole use and benefit of the widow of the said deceased Captain John Porteous", and the measure, considerably curtailed, became *An Act to disable Alexander Wilson, Esq., from taking, holding, or enjoying any Office or Place of Magistracy in the City of Edinburgh, or elsewhere in Great Britain, and for imposing a Fine upon the Corporation of the said City* [157] Even in this modified form, the bill was nearly lost on the motion for reporting it to the House The division was 130 for reporting and 130 against it; and Colonel Bladen, Chairman of the Committee, gave his casting vote in favour of the bill But for the absence of the Solicitor-General for Scotland and Erskine of Grange, who were engaged as counsel in an appeal case before the House of Lords, where, it was said, they were purposely detained by the Lord Chancellor, the bill would have been thrown out by a majority of two On 13th June the majority for the third reading was 128 to 101. The Commons' amendments were

---

156 This venerable structure, erected by James the Sixth in 1606, was demolished in 1764 by a Town Council with whom "there was no remembrance of former things " In the local poet Clandero's " Last Speech, Confession, and Dying Words, of the Nether Bow Porch of Edinburgh, which was exposed to roup and sale on Thursday, the 9th August, 1764," the doomed fabric is made to say—" My gates were shut by the exasperate inhabitants of the city against those who might have prolonged the inglorious life of Captain Porteous, which I have not, even to my dying hour, repented of, and though my ruin at that period seemed certain, yet the great Argyll, a powerful patriot, averted the blow."—*Miscellanies in Prose and Verse*, 1766, p 60

157 Appendix XIV

Captain Porteous.

accepted by the Lords, and the measure received the Royal assent on the last day of the session [158]

So inconsiderable was this result of the long labour of the Legislative mountain that "Honest Shippen" is reported to have said they had spent too much time in declaring a man incapable who was willing to declare himself so, and in providing for a cook-maid

While the Provost's bill was engrossing the attention of the Legislature a less conspicuous measure was placed upon the statute book [159] On 25th May 1737, Lord Ilay introduced, in the House of Lords, a bill entitled *An Act for the more effectually bringing to Justice any Persons concerned in the barbarous Murther of Captain John Porteous, and punishing such as shall knowingly conceal any of the Offenders,* which passed both Houses with but little opposition This Act provided, *inter alia,* that persons against whom sentence of fugitation was pronounced, on or before 1st May, 1738, by the High Court of Justiciary for not appearing to abide their trial, who did not render themselves up within twelve months from the date of such sentence, should be attainted of felony, and incur the pains of death; that any one knowingly concealing such persons should be similarly punished, that any concerned in the murder who disclosed their accomplices before 1st February, 1738, should not be liable to prosecution; that such informers should receive a reward of £200 sterling for every person so convicted, and should not thereby be disabled from appearing as witness against such person [160] The two last-mentioned clauses were added to the bill by the Commons What was to prove the most important provision, however, was that appointing the Act to be read on the first Sunday of every month for one whole year from 1st August, 1737, in every parish church in Scotland The effect of this enactment upon the feelings of the Scots people exceeded. as we shall shortly see, even that caused by the Provost's bill.

Meanwhile, on 28th June, the former Lord Provost returned, free and comparatively victorious, to the city he should rule no more The occasion was one of great public rejoicing. Thousands of enthusiastic citizens crowded the road by which

---

158 *Commons' Journals,* 21st June, 1737, 10 Geo II, cap 34
159 10 Geo II, cap 35
160 Appendix XV

The Provost's Bill.

he approached the town, the music-bells rang continuously from
four o'clock, and the great bells from seven till nine   It
had been arranged that he should make a triumphal progress
through the city with the great company that waited upon
him; and for that purpose barricades were erected along the
line of route.   "But, according to his wonted modesty, he
declined any such ostentation, and privately stepped out of
his coach and came in by Bristo Port "   His admirers, however, paraded the streets in his honour.   At night the city
was illuminated, and two bonfires blazed before his door.   The
general rejoicings were appropriately crowned by closing at
the usual hour the gates of the Nether Bow Port, which, since
the riot, had been ignominiously chained back.[161]   A local
bard, over the patriotic subscription SCOTICUS, voiced the
popular feeling on the occasion as follows —

"VERSES addressed to Alexander Wilson, Esq, late Lord
Provost of Edinburgh, on his arrival there from London."

> Hail to thy Land! hail to thy Friends return'd '
> Belov'd when present, and when absent mourn'd
> But, as when breaking thro' the Veil of Night
> The Morn to Mortals gives a cheerful Light,
> When you return, thus ev'ry Bosom glows,
> And from each Heart a warm Resentment flows
> See Crowds on Crowds with kind Affections meet,
> To hail thee thro' thy own Edina's Street
> But, WILSON, be those modest Virtues thine,
> That scorn Ambition and Applause decline.
> Let the brib'd Courtier sell his Country's Cause,
> And for curs'd Pelf devise oppressive Laws,
> But thine be Virtue ever calm and pure,
> And bravely bear those Ills you cannot cure 162

A somewhat different reception was given, a month later,
to the witness Bailly, who had stated in the Commons' inquiry
that the riot was fixed for Tuesday, 7th September   He
returned from London by sea to avoid observation, but the
news of his landing at Leith rapidly spread   Bells were rung
to collect the populace, and people rushed through the streets,
crying "Bloody Bailly is come!"   The unpopular hero,
however, flung himself into the Edinburgh stage-coach; in
which, protected by a lady passenger, he reached his home in
safety

One of the first acts of the magistrates on their return to

---

161 *Courant*, 28th and 30th June, 1737
162 *Ibid* 11th August, 1737

131

Captain Porteous.

town was the dismissal of Captain Lind, on 28th July, from the office of captain-lieutenant of the City Guard (which he had held since 31st May, 1732), presumably because his memory had proved unduly retentive   As a compensation for this treatment the Government immediately afterwards appointed him "Lieutenant in Tyrawley's regiment of South British Fusileers at Gibraltar "[163]

The Town Council next proceeded to the settlement of the expenses incurred by the city in connection with the Provost's bill, and a committee was appointed to examine the accounts. A question having arisen as to how far the city was liable in payment of the sums disbursed by the late Provost and magistrates in the course of the inquiry, a memorial on the subject was submitted for counsel's opinion   In their answers to this memorial the Solicitor-General, James Grahame, and William Grant were of opinion that the bailies were entitled to repayment of their expenses, seeing nothing personal was found against themselves nor any penalty inflicted upon them ", but with regard to the late Provost, " as he was found to be culpable in the execution of his office, and for that cause had a penalty enacted upon him," the expenses of his personal defence must be borne by himself   As only one solicitor was employed for all the parties, however, they were of opinion that the town should pay the whole of his fees, and also the fees of both Houses, the shorthand writers account (which amounted to no less than £69 sterling), the travelling expenses to and from London, " the house-keeping there " and all other charges which must have been incurred, " although the Provost had not been separately pointed at "   Accordingly, the committee having reported on the accounts, the Council ordered payment to be made to the ex-Provost of £211 16s 6d , and to the four bailies £1234 6s 1½d , being the amounts due to them in the premises, together with a further sum of £577 13s 5d disbursed by Bailie John Cochrane in opposing the bill   The Council also voted a honorarium of 200 guineas to Mr Irvine, the town-clerk, for his services to the city, which that gentleman generously declined to accept.   Apart from the fine of £2000, the total cost of the inquiry to the city of Edinburgh   as appears   from   the   Council   minutes,[164]

---

163 Chambers's *Domestic Annals of Scotland*, III 601
164 *Council Records.*

The Provost's Bill.

amounted to the sum of £2254 0s 10½d —a summation which
would have provoked the contempt of Mr Mantalini

Some of the minor charges in connection with the affair are
of interest.   One is the account due to James Cleland, keeper
of the Tolbooth, before mentioned, the first item of which is
as follows.—"Captain John Porteous from the 14th of Aprile
to the 7th of Septemr. 1736 Inclusive being 21 weeks at 5
shill Sterling pr week, he having had a Room for himself
and a great deall of Trouble is £5 . 5 · "   Other items refer to
the imprisonment of the soldiers of the Guard for the same
period, "being 146 nights att 3 sh. 4d Scots each pr night,"
amounting in all to £18 2s 6d   The Council repudiated
liability for these items, "but in regard the said James
Cleland was at considerable trouble and expense about Captain
Porteous and soldiers while in his prison, are of opinion that
the City should pay him a gratification of Five Guineas"[165]
Another interesting document preserved in the City Chambers
is an "Estimate of the Charges of Mending and Cleaning of
those Arms in the City Armory of the Good Town of Edinburgh
which was Damnadged at Porteous's Mobb," amounting to
£18 17s 5d

On 4th January, 1738, Isobel Gordon, having desired that
payment of the £2000 appropriated to her use " might be
adjusted in an amicable manner," the magistrates appointed
a committee to take the advice of counsel "how far Mrs
Porteous can make such demand, and, if the lawyers' opinion
shall be in the affirmative, to treat with Mrs Porteous concerning the same "   Nothing further appears to have been
done in the matter, for on 2nd August the magistrates were
served with a process of *distringas* from the Court of
Exchequer requiring them to make payment to His Majesty
of the fine out of their Common Good ; upon which they
were ordered by the Court to pay the money into the hands of
the Receiver-General of His Majesty's Land Rents and
Casualties for Scotland, for payment to Isobel Gordon or her
assigns.   On 16th August the lady "condescended to give to
this city an abatement of the sum of £500 stg " of the fine,[166]
and proposed to take £600 in cash and the city's bond for

---

165 Appendix I

166 Maitland states that Mrs Porteous did so " in consideration of
the numerous favours received by her from the Common Council "—
History of Edinburgh, p 123

Captain Porteous.

£900, "bearing annual rent at one-half per cent below the legal interest," in exchange for a discharge of the fine from the Receiver-General   The transaction was settled accordingly; £600 was borrowed from the Royal Bank of Scotland on a bill granted by the seven magistrates in behalf of the city, the £1500 was declared chargeable upon the profits accruing to the city from the duty of two pennies Scots per pint of ale, the widow renounced the pension of £12 formerly given her by the town, and the discharge of the fine by the Receiver-General was laid up in the city's Charter-house [167] On 24th December, 1740, the Council resolved to pay off the bond in her favour at Candlemas following, at which term Edinburgh was finally quit of Mrs Porteous

Meanwhile, however, her husband's unquiet spirit still troubled the peace of the good town   The anonymous author of a contemporary *jeu d'esprit*,[168] giving an account of the Captain's appearance in Parliament in connection with the bills and his subsequent dealings with the Scots clergy, "with many other pleasant Jests relating thereunto; all in Elegiack Verse," observes—

> He in his Life was a great pest,
> And ever since he went to Rest,
> He hath not ceas'd us to molest,
> But hath our Hearts and Stomachs vext,
>   And made us groan;
> In sacred things us sore opprest,
>   Which gars us moan

So far the affair had affected only the feelings and pockets of the community, the public conscience—a more vulnerable part of the body politic—was now to be involved We have seen what provision was made by the Legislature for publishing the Act against the murderers of Captain Porteous   The clause appointing it to be read from every parochial pulpit throughout Scotland on the first Sunday of every month, immediately after the sermon, enacted that any minister who neglected to do so should, for the first offence, be declared incapable of sitting or voting in any Church judicature; and, for the second offence be declared incapable of taking, holding, or enjoying any ecclesiastical benefice in Scotland   It was further provided

167 *Council Records*
168 *Captain Porteous's Ghost*, Edinburgh, 1738.

The Provost's Bill.

that such offenders might be prosecuted by summary complaint to the Court of Session, or by process before any Court of Justiciary, at the instance of His Majesty's advocate "Perverse ingenuity," says Mr Hill Burton, "could scarcely have devised a better means of dividing and breaking up the Presbyterian Establishment."[169] The spirit in which the High Flyers among the Scots clergy regarded the murder of Porteous has already been indicated, consequently they were averse to assist in punishing the human instruments of what they considered a providential event. Their consciences were further offended by the employment of themselves and their pulpits as agencies for the detection of crime, while the formal words of enactment, "by and with the consent of the Lords Spiritual and Temporal," contained in the obnoxious Act, raised the vexed questions of Episcopal and civil authority, upon which Presbyterians were ever peculiarly sensitive

"This preposterous order was greeted as blasphemous dese-cration of the Sabbath Every minister who read it was accused of celebrating the death of a murderer before the death of the Saviour People would not take communion with any man who put Cæsar before Christ, and many left the churches never to return."[170] "The dispute was the more violent," says Scott, "as it was immediately subsequent to a schism in the Church on the fruitful subject of Patronage, which had divided from the communion of the Established Church of Scotland that large class of dissenters generally called Seceders"[171] Dr Carlyle says the object of the clause was to purge the Church of fanatics, that these might, by disobedience, render themselves liable to deposition Some of the ministers, however, perceiving, "either by information or sagacity," this Parliamentary snare, "convened meetings of clergy at Edinburgh and formed resolutions, and carried on correspondence through the Church to persuade as many as possible to disobey the Act, that the greater number of offenders might secure the safety of the whole" This astute policy was, as we shall see, entirely successful Carlyle refers to the distress and perplexity caused by the dilemma to such

---

169 *History of Scotland*, viii 412
170 Graham's *Social Life of Scotland*, 1906, p 369
171 *Tales of a Grandfather*, Standard Edition, p 972.

Captain Porteous.

ministers as harboured strong scruples as well as large families His own father was "very scrupulous," being guided in the narrow path by that experienced wayfarer, Lord Grange, but his nine children "pulled him very hard on the side of obedience," and he read the Act [172]

Various devices were adopted in order to evade the detested law, such as preaching no sermon or holding no morning service on the first Sunday of the month One ingenious divine announced to his congregation that although he was required to read the Act they were not bound to listen to it, whereupon the kirk promptly "skailed," and the proclamation was read to empty pews

Meanwhile a pamphlet war—that favourite form of ecclesiastical strife—was waged with exceeding dust and heat, and the braying of the clerical trumpets filled the land   The virulence of the reverend combatants was only equalled by their verbosity   "The printer's presses," to borrow Fergusson's phrase,   graned unco sair " under a load of tracts, the modern reader of which still groans in sympathy   *Reasons, Memorials, Conversations, Queries, Answers, Observations, Remarks, Considerations, Addresses, Letters,* and *Replies* by anonymous and prolific prophets were bandied about with bewildering rapidity [173]

Some idea of the amenities with which the controversy was conducted may be gathered from the following excerpts from one of the more prominent pamphlets,[174] wherein the Act is described as being hatched either in Hell, Rome, or Lambeth. " 'Tis said in the title or preamble of the Act, ' the barbarous murder of John Porteous ', an affronted lie in the beginning, as a shrewd sign what the rest of the libel will be   Can it be murder, far less a barbarous murder, to put a condemned criminal to death, condemned both by the law of God and man, as said is, and that in the very same manner that the law directs?   Can an usurped power pardon a murderer or make void the law of God?"   And, again, with what Arthur Clennam called "such hiccupping reference," as *Num* chap xxxv , vers 31, 32, and 33, "That cuts off all at once all claim of prerogative to pardon murderers, and for any

---

172 *Autobiography*, pp 40-41
173 See Bibliography. Appendix XVII
174 *A Memorial for the People of Scotland*, &c , 1737

136

The Provost's Bill.

sinful worm to presume to dispense with the divine law and arrogantly to usurp the above prerogative of the great Jehovah, is robbery, sacrilege, and high treason against the majesty of heaven and earth, for which wicked attempt they will one day pay dear " This must have proved agreeable reading at the Court of St James's "As to the matter of the Act, 'tis said 'Be it enacted by the Lords Spiritual and Temporal,' &c How will this Ashdod speech sound in a Presbyterian minister's mouth at any time, but more especially on the holy Sabbath and in the time of divine worship to acknowledge and homologate the office and authority of the twenty-six anti-christian Knights of the Black Order of England (brats issuing from Antichrist's foul womb) to be their dictators, judges, and lawgivers, combined, no doubt, with Satan and the Pope to insnare the ministers of the Church of Scotland " This tasteful allusion to the bench of Bishops is characteristic of the spirit of the time

The murderers of Porteous, on the other hand, are described as 'these poor innocents," for whose blood the Government thirsts "like so many rapacious vultures,' and as persons "deserving rather a reward than such cruel and barbarous treatment for their duty to God and the whole land, by taking away a condemned, bloody wretch from the earth, when such a superlative transgressor could not but be ponderous and heavy upon it " Exception is taken, with more show of reason, to "making the ambassador of the King of Kings to do the drudgery-work of scoundrel messengers and heralds, pouring the utmost contempt upon the sacred office of the ministry "; and the Parliament of Great Britain is denounced as waging war with Heaven [175] This vigorous writer significantly concludes—"If any minister shall be found to give implicit faith and blind obedience to these unjust and sinful commands, flowing from an Erastian foundation, they can never after be held and reputed to be the ministers of Christ; but the ministers of men and Satan, and no better than Baal's priests, whom Elijah and the people of Israel made an example of to all generations afterwards to imitate "

---

[175] " This method of inquisition, by the aid of the clergy and the religion of the country," was cited as a precedent in support of the famous *monitoire* in the answers to the petition against same, presented to the Court of Session in the Douglas Cause —*Edinburgh Museum; or, North British Magazine*, November, 1763

Captain Porteous.

Following in the footsteps of their spiritual directors, it is little wonder that the people kept their knowledge of the murderers to themselves, and that not one attempt was ever made to earn the Government's reward.

The Act came into operation on Sunday, 7th August, 1737 The *Courant* next day records that there was no sermon in a great number of the country parishes, but in Edinburgh the proclamation was read in four of the churches. References to various texts of Scripture bearing on the subject were pasted on the church doors and other public places in the city, but were at once removed by order of the magistrates. On the 13th the Solicitor-General writes that many of the clergy have not given obedience to the Act of Parliament, "which at present is the subject of discourse here," and hopes they will conform on 1st September, 'but the motions of our churchmen on this and several other occasions have been so eccentric that it is not easy to calculate them." The newspapers of the day narrate some quaint incidents in connection with the matter. The *Courant* on 6th September excuses the fact that the Act was only read in three of the churches on the 1st, by remarking that it would have been read in others "had not the ministers belonging to them been out of town for their health." Doubtless many of the reverend brethren felt a change of air desirable in the beginning of the month. The same journal waxes wroth with its rival the *Mercury*, for stating that the congregation of the Old Church would not hear their pastor read the Act, and "offered to throw stools at him." This slander the *Courant* quaintly confutes as follows:—"Nor indeed did any person there attempt to throw stools, nor is it practicable, because there are none there." Among those who left the church on the occasion of this disturbance was "honest John Dalgleish, *alias* Jack Ketch, whose scruples possibly arose from this, that the publication warned offenders of their danger, and thus seemed to be calculated to disappoint him of his proper business and the emoluments arising from thence." On 11th October "A merry account" is reported from Angus of a young man who, having undergone the discipline of the church for a grievous but not infrequent fault, received absolution from the minister, when the penitent turned the tables by blaming his pastor for not reading the Act, and offered to do so himself, which he accordingly

The Provost's Bill.

did "This odd behaviour," says the *Courant*, "was received by the congregation with abundance of good humour" A month later the same journal states—"We hear that as a certain clergyman in the country was reading the Act anent Captain Porteous, a good old woman, who had conceived great prejudice against it, called out, 'Ah, Sir! you're cheating us, that's no' the Black Act! *it's muckle baudier than that!*'"

Writing to the Duke of Newcastle on 1st September, the Solicitor-General reports—'I do believe that one-half read the Act in some way or other, generally upon their entrance into the pulpit, when the meeting was full, some deserted their congregations upon diverse pretences, others took no manner of notice of it Many pamphlets have been published, upon this occasion, for and against reading of the Act, two of them scandalous and seditious beyond measure The most abominable of the two had disappeared before I returned from my election I have used all possible diligence to discover the vile authors, and shall not omit doing all in my power to bring them to justice, if happily I can come at the knowledge of them" The last letter on the subject in the Record Office contains an account, given by the Solicitor to the Duke on 5th November, of the results of the Act during the first three months of its operation—"In a former letter I took the liberty to mention to Your Grace the state of our clergy with regard to the reading the Act of Parliament for bringing to justice the murderers of Captain Porteous, and then undertook to inform myself, in the best manner I could think of, of what the numbers were of the readers, and of those who had given no obedience to the law As I had early transmitted copies of the Act to the several Sheriffs, to be delivered to the parish ministers within their jurisdiction, I wrote a second time to them to report to me their diligence, and at the same time inform me, as far as they had access to know, how the numbers stood of the readers and those who had not read, within their bounds I have had returns from the greatest part of them, and from them and the best accounts I can have from other hands, I may venture to say that not above two-thirds have read the Act in any shape, the rest have entirely omitted it I have done my utmost to prevail with the ministers with whom I had any intercourse, to give that obedience to the law which is incumbent on them as well as

Captain Porteous.

other subjects; but though the prosecutions against the
offenders are directed to be brought in the name of His
Majesty's Advocate, seeing so great a body of the Established
Church seems to have fallen under the penalties of the law,
and that there are so many remaining Sundays in which this
Act ought still to be read by them, I judged it improper for
me to take upon me the determination of the time and number
of prosecutions against the offenders, [it] appearing to me to
be a subject of a delicate consideration; and therefore chose
as the best for his Majesty's service, which I shall ever with zeal
pursue, to submit it to Your Grace's more discerning eyes, and
shall, to the best of my understanding, with fidelity and the
greatest care, follow such orders as Your Grace shall be pleased
to give me "

Apparently His Grace's "discerning eye" saw fit to wink
at these delinquencies, for none of the reverend lawbreakers
was brought to justice. The roll of the drums ecclesiastic
waned with the passing year, and the national conscience,
wearied by the violence of its vindication, slept again the
sleep of the just

Chronological Table.

1715 9 November—John Porteous appointed adjutant to the Edinburgh Train-bands

1718 9 April—Porteous elected ensign of the City Guard

1726 21 January—Porteous promoted Captain-Lieutenant of the City Guard

1730. 20 November—Porteous appointed provisor of coal and candle to the Guard

1735 23 July—Captains Porteous and Fergusson dismissed from their command on account of their quarrel in the Burgh Room

6 August—Porteous and Fergusson reinstated as Captains-Lieutenant of the Guard

1736 9 January—James Stark, Collector of Excise, robbed at Pittenweem by Andrew Wilson, William Hall, and George Robertson

2-11 March—Trial of Wilson, Hall and Robertson by the High Court of Justiciary at Edinburgh Verdict—guilty. Sentence, to be executed on 14th April

1 April—Hall's sentence commuted to transportation for life

9 April—Wilson and Robertson attempt unsuccessfully to break out of the Tolbooth Prison

11 April—Robertson escapes from the Tolbooth Church when attending service

12 April—Lord Provost Wilson requests a party of the King's troops to attend execution to preserve order

14 April—Execution of Wilson Mob attacks the soldiers of the Guard, who fire upon the people, killing six persons and wounding many others

14 April—After precognition by the Magistrates, Porteous committed to the Tolbooth by order of the Lord Provost, on the charge of firing and ordering his men to fire

15 April—Fifteen soldiers of the Guard imprisoned for having fired upon the people

21 April—Town Council dismiss Porteous from all his offices

12 May—Magistrates resolve to prosecute Porteous at the public expense before the High Court of Justiciary, Crown counsel having advised against the Lord Provost as High Sheriff conducting the trial

Captain Porteous.

1736 21 June—Indictment served on Porteous

5 July—Trial commences Debate upon the relevancy

12 July—Information for His Majesty's Advocate given in.

13 July—Information for John Porteous lodged

16 July—Libel found relevant

19 July—7 a m —Jury empannelled Trial proceeds without intermission till 9 a.m next morning

20 July—4 p m —Court resumes Verdict—guilty Sentence, to be executed on 8th September

26 August—Sentence on Porteous respited for six weeks by command of Queen Caroline

2 September—Reprieve reaches Edinburgh

3 September—High Court of Justiciary grants warrant to the Magistrates for delaying execution until 20th October.

4 September—Captain Lind, of the City Guard, reports to Provost Wilson the rumour that the mob intends to hang Porteous

7 September—6 p m —Lind again warns the Provost, who takes no action

7 September—9 30 p m —A mob assembles in Portsburgh, secures the city gates, captures the Guard-house, and besieges the Tolbooth.

7 September—10 p m —Patrick Lindsay despatched by the Provost to General Moyle with verbal message for aid

7 September—10 30 p m —Magistrates repulsed by rioters

7 September—11 30 p m —Tolbooth taken by the mob.

7 September—11 45 p m —Porteous hanged in the Grassmarket

18 September—The Solicitor-General (Erskine) arrives in Edinburgh to conduct an enquiry into the matter

25 September—Proclamation by the Queen offering pardon to rioters who disclose their accomplices and £200 reward to informers for every person convicted.

4 October—The Earl of Ilay, Lord Justice-General, arrives from London to take charge of the enquiry.

8 October—The Lord Advocate (Forbes) and General Wade come to Edinburgh to take part in the enquiry

10 November—Pension granted to Mrs. Porteous by the Town Council.

Chronological Table.

1736 27 November—The soldiers of the Guard, imprisoned in the Canongate Tolbooth, set at liberty

16 December—The Solicitor-General embodies result of the enquiry in a memorial to the Government, nine persons imprisoned for complicity in the murder, and warrants issued against seven who absconded

1737 19 January—List of one hundred servants and apprentices, who had left their masters' service since the riot, published by order of the Magistrates Thirty of these return and offer to stand their trial, the others are fugitated on 13th June

1 February—Reference to riot in King's Speech on the opening of Parliament

10 February—Debate in the House of Lords thereon Provost and four bailies of Edinburgh, and others, ordered to attend, and proceedings relating to the trial of Captain Porteous to be laid before the House

10 March—Examination of witnesses commenced before House of Lords Committee

11-22 March—Trial and acquittal of William MacLauchlane by the High Court of Justiciary, for accession to the murder of Captain Porteous

3 April—Provost taken into custody of Gentlemen Usher of the Black Rod, and Bill of Pains and Penalties brought in

4 April—Bill read a first time

19 April—Provost admitted to bail

26 April—Debate on Lord Carteret's motion to have verdict and sentence pronounced against Captain Porteous declared erroneous

29 April—Debate as to calling the Lords of Justiciary to the bar of the House

4-7 May—Hearing of counsel against the Bill upon its second reading

9 May—Bill passed in Committee

11 May—Bill read a third time and passed

16 May—Bill received in the Commons from the Lords and read a first time

25 May—Bill for bringing to justice the murderers of Captain Porteous introduced by Lord Ilay in the House of Lords

1-9 June—Provost's Bill read a second time; examination of witnesses and hearing of counsel against the Bill

12 June—Provost's Bill passed in Committee by casting vote of chairman

Captain Porteous.

1737 13 June—Provost's Bill as amended in Committee read a third time and passed

    16 June—Thomas Linnen tried and acquitted by the High Court of Justiciary for accession to the murder of Captain Porteous

    21 June—Both Acts receive the Royal assent

    28 June—Ex-Provost Wilson returns to Edinburgh

1738. 4 January—Mrs Porteous applies to the Magistrates for payment of the fine of £2000 in terms of the Act

    2 August—Process of *distringas* served on the Magistrates to make payment thereof out of the Common Good

    7 August—Act against the murderers of Porteous comes into operation, and falls to be read during service by every parish minister in Scotland

    16 August—Mrs Porteous consents to give the city an abatement of £500 of the fine

    5 November—The Solicitor-General reports to the Government the returns from the several Sheriffs as to the reading of the Act by ministers within their jurisdiction " not above two-thirds have read the Act in any shape "

Andrew Fletcher of Milton, Lord Justice-Clerk.

From an Engraving after Aikman.

AUTHENTIC EXTRACT

OF THE

PROCEEDINGS

IN THE

TRIAL OF
CAPTAIN JOHN PORTEOUS.

Die Veneris, 25 Martii, 1737

Ordered, by the Lords Spiritual and Temporal, in Parliament assembled, That the Authentic Extract of the Proceedings in the Trial of Captain JOHN PORTEOUS, laid before this House the 3rd day of this instant March, be printed

WM COWPER, *Cler' Parliamentor'*.

CURIA JUSTICIARIÆ, S D N Regis, tenta in Novo Sessionis Domo Burgi de Edinburgo, quinto die mensis Julii, Millesimo septingentesimo trigesimo sexto, per honorabiles viros, ANDREAM FLETCHER de Milton, Justiciarium, Clericum, Dominum JACOBUM MACKENZIE de Roystoun, Magistrum DAVIDEM ERSKINE de Dun, Dominos GUALTERUM PRINGLE de Newhall, et GILBERTUM ELLIOT de Minto, Commissionarios Justiciaiii, dictos S D N Regis.

Curia legitimé affirmata

Intran

JOHN PORTEOUS, lately one of the Captain-Lieutenants of the City Guard of Edinburgh, present prisoner in the Tolbooth of Edinburgh, pannel   INDICTED and ACCUSED at the instance of Duncan Forbes, Esquire, his Majesty's Advocate for his Highness's interest, for the crimes of murder and slaughter, and others, as is more fully mentioned in the indictment raised against him there annext.   Setting forth, THAT WHERE, by the law of God, the common law, the municipal law and practice of this kingdom, and the laws of all other well-governed

L   145

Captain Porteous.

realms, murder and slaughter, maiming and wounding with mortal weapons, any of the subjects of such realms, and the ordering, commanding, and causing any band, or number of men, aimed with firelocks, and other mortal weapons, to fall upon, wound, murder, and destroy numbers of his Majesty's subjects, innocently and lawfully assembled, by firing sharp shot amongst them, whereby multitudes are, or may be endangered, and many men, women, and innocent children are, or may be killed or wounded, without any just cause or occasion, and without lawful warrant, more especially when committed in the public streets of a city, by a person lawfully commissioned by the Magistrates thereof, to command such band of armed men, for the preservation of peace and order, and for the defence of the inhabitants, and others resorting thereto, are crimes of a high nature, and severely punishable · YET TRUE IT IS and of verity, That he, the said John Porteous, had presumed to commit, and was guilty and accessory, or art and part of all and every, or one or other of the foresaid crimes, aggravated as aforesaid IN SO FAR AS, upon the fourteenth day of April last, or one or other of the days of the said month, when the deceased Andrew Wilson, sentenced to be hanged to death by the High Court of Justiciary, was to be executed at the Grassmarket of the city of Edinburgh, he being at that time one of the captain-lieutenants of the town guard of the said city, lawfully commissioned by the Magistrates and town council thereof ; and in the ordinary course of rotation with the other officers of the said guard, being ordered to attend at the said execution, to preserve the peace and support the executioner in the discharge of his duty, having under his command a detachment of about seventy men. he did then attend in the said Grassmarket accordingly, and after the said Andrew Wilson had hung upon the gallows, erected for his execution, until he was dead, at least for a considerable time, and so long as there was ground to conclude he was dead , he, the said John Porteous, shaking off all fear of God, and respect to his Majesty's laws, and conceiving a most wicked and malicious purpose of destroying, wounding, and maiming numbers of his Majesty's subjects, the inhabitants of the said city of Edinburgh. and others there assembled at the said execution, without any just cause or necessary occasion, ordered the said detachment of the guard under his command to fire upon the people so assembled at the said execution · and the men, at least severals of them, having fired, as it seems he apprehended, over the heads of the multitude. so as to avoid doing them harm, he with threats and imprecations repeated his commands to fire, calling out to them to level their pieces, and be damned, or words to that purpose , and at or about the same time, he levelled the firelock that was

146

Indictment.

in his own hand, taking aim at Charles Husband, servant to Paul Husband, confectioner in the Abbey of Holyroodhouse, and most wickedly and murderously fired at him, whereupon he immediately dropped to the ground, having received a wound by a bullet, or large drop of lead, on the left side of his head, which pierced into his brain, and another large wound likewise by a bullet, or large drop of lead, on the left side of his neck, and a third wound in his body, and a fourth wound in his left hand, at least a mortal wound or wounds, whereof he died in some short space thereafter, AT LEAST he did so level his piece, and appeared to take his aim at some one of the innocent multitude, who happened to stand directly over against him, and he did fire, and upon his so firing, the said Charles Husband, at least one or other of the persons particularly after mentioned, or more of them, did immediately drop to the ground, having received a mortal wound or wounds, whereof they soon after died ; and by his said example and command, severals of the said guard, to the number of twenty, less or more, did at the same time with him, or soon after him, fire upon the innocent multitude, whereby all, or one or more of the following persons received mortal wounds, whereof they soon after died, viz , Archibald Ballantyne, son to John Ballantyne younger, dyster in Dalkeith, received several wounds, with bullets, or large drops of lead, which pierced into his body, at least a mortal wound or wounds in his head or body, whereof he died a few days thereafter ; and John Anderson, son to George Anderson in Craighead, drover, received a wound in the head with a bullet, or large drop of lead, at least a mortal wound or wounds in his head or body, so that he died in a few hours thereafter , and the following persons were grievously maimed, hurt, and wounded, to the great danger of their lives, viz , Margaret Arthur alias Airth, residenter in the Canongate, near the Watergate thereof, Jean Peal, servant to James Macdowal, merchant in Edinburgh, David Wallace, journeyman wright in Edinburgh, James Philip, late servant to   Lauder, Esq residenter in the Canongate, David Kidd, tailor in Edinburgh, Patrick Spalding, apprentice to David Mitchel, jeweller in Edinburgh, James Lyle and Alexander Wallace, both servants to James Wright, staymaker in Edinburgh, John Miller, tailor in Edinburgh, David Ogilvie, writer in Edinburgh, and James Nivan, late servant to William Sellars, writer in Edinburgh, residenter in the Potterrow AT LEAST the said persons were so killed, wounded, and maimed, by the firing in manner, and by the direction, as aforesaid, and by the second firing after mentioned ; for, not contented with the barbarities thus committed, after he had with the said company or detachment of the city-guard marched towards, or into the place or street called the West Bow, he, without just cause or occasion, again ordered

Captain Porteous.

the men under his command to face about and fire upon the people, and at or about the same time, he fired a musket or firelock that was in his own hand, having either reloaded, or caused to be reloaded his own piece, or taken another out of the hand of one of the guard, and severals of the said guard did, upon that second example and command of his, fire upon the multitude, whereby Alexander Macneil, son to Edward Macneil, indweller in Mortonhall, received a shot in the head with a bullet, or lead drop, which pierced into his brain, at least a mortal wound or wounds in his head or body, so that he died thereof in a few days thereafter, and Margaret Gordon, servant to William Ogilvie, tailor in St Mary Wynd, in Edinburgh, received a wound in the head above the left eye, with a bullet, or large drop of lead, which pierced into her brain, at least a mortal wound or wounds in her head or body, so that she died thereof in a short space thereafter, and Henry Grahame, tailor in Canongate, received a wound in the head, with a bullet, or large drop of lead, which pierced into his brain, at least a mortal wound or wounds in his head or body, of which he died in a few hours thereafter At least, by this and the other firings by him, and by his order and example above mentioned, all, or one or more of the persons particularly above recited as having been killed, received mortal wounds of which they soon after died, and all, or one or more of the persons above recited to have been wounded were grievously maimed, hurt, and wounded, to the great danger of their lives At least, at the time and place aforesaid, the said persons above named and mentioned to have been respectively killed and wounded, were all, or one or more of them, wickedly and maliciously slaughtered, murdered, and wounded, by wounds severally given them by mortal weapons And he was guilty art and part of the slaughter, murder, and wounding of all, or one or more of them; all which, or any part thereof, being found proven by the verdict of an assize, in presence of the Lords Justice-General, Justice-Clerk, and Commissioners of Justiciary, he ought to be most exemplary punished with the pains of law, to the terror of others to commit the like in time coming   *Sic Subscribitur,*

Ch Areskine, A D

Pursuers

Duncan Forbes, Esq his Majesty's Advocate
Mr Charles Erskine, his Majesty's Solicitor
Mr Hugh Forbes, his Majesty's Advocate-depute
Mr Patrick Haldan
Mr Hugh Murray Kinnymont
Sir James Elphingstoun

Interlocutor.

Prolocutors in Defence

Mr James Grahame, Jun
Mr Henry Home
Mr Alexander Lockhart
Mr James Lessly
Mr James Holburn   Advocates

The libel being openly read, and debate *viva voce*, in
presence of the judges, pannel, and jury, the Lords ordained
both parties to give in their informations to the Clerk of Court,
in order to be recorded, and the pursuers to give in theirs
against Friday next, at six o'clock at night, and the prolocutors
for the pannel to give in theirs against Tuesday thereafter,
and continued the cause till Friday, the 16th inst. and ordained
assizers and witnesses then to attend, and the pannel to be
carried back to prison

Captain Porteous.

July 12*th*, 1736

INFORMATION

FOR

His MAJESTY'S ADVOCATE, for His Highness's Interest,

AGAINST

JOHN PORTEOUS, late Captain-Lieutenant of the City Guard of Edinburgh,—*Pannel.*

THE pannel is charged by the indictment with murdering, slaughtering maiming, and wounding divers of his Majesty's subjects, by firing with his own hand, and causing and ordering a band of armed men, under his command to fire upon a multitude of innocent people, assembled to see an execution in the Grassmarket of the city of Edinburgh, without any just cause or provocation ; contrary not only to the laws of God and nature, and to the good and laudable laws of this and all other well-governed realms, but also contrary to the express duty of his office, who was one of the commanders of the City Guard, intended to preserve the peace of the city, and to protect the inhabitants thereof from all violence, and who was on that occasion entrusted with the command of a large detachment of the said guard, to preserve peace and order, to secure the execution of a sentence of the High Court of Justiciary, and to prevent all riots and tumults, whereby the execution of the said sentence might be disappointed, the laws might be violated, and the people assembled might be hurt or destroyed

The indictment sets forth, particularly, That, at the time and place libelled, where a great multitude of innocent persons, of all ages, and of different sexes, were lawfully assembled, to see the execution of Andrew Wilson, sentenced to be hanged by the High Court aforesaid, the pannel, having under his command a detachment of seventy armed men of the City Guard, and having conceived a most wicked and malicious purpose of destroying, maiming, and wounding, numbers of his Majesty's subjects, the inhabitants of the said city and others assembled at the said execution, without any just cause or necessary occasion, ordered the said detachment under his command to fire upon the people so assembled, that the men under his command, having probably, in his apprehension, fired over the heads of the people, he, with threats and impreca tions, repeated his commands to fire, calling out to them to

150

Duncan Forbes of Culloden, Lord Advocate.

From the Portrait by Davidson in the Parliament House.

Information for H.M. Advocate.

level their pieces, and be damn'd, that, at or about the same
time, he levelled the firelock that was in his own hand, taking
aim at one Charles Husband, and fired at him, whereupon he
immediately dropt to the ground, having received wounds
whereof he instantly died; at least, that he levelled his piece,
seeming to take aim at some one in the crowd, and fired it,
and that, upon his firing, the said Charles Husband, or one
or other of the persons in the indictment mentioned dropt,
having received wounds by bullets, of which they instantly
died, and that by his commands and example, several of the
City Guard under his command fired upon the innocent multitude, whereby the persons particularly mentioned in the indictment were killed, maimed, and wounded

The indictment further charges, That, not contented with
this barbarity, the pannel, after he had marched off his
detachment towards, or unto the place or street called the
West Bow, again ordered the men under his command to face
about and fire upon the people, and at or about the same
time, fired a musket or firelock that was in his own hand,
having either reloaded, or caused to be reloaded, the piece
formerly fired by him, or having taken another out of the
hand of one of the guard, and that several of the said guard
did, upon that second example and command, fire upon the
multitude, whereby the persons described in the indictment
were killed or mortally wounded And the indictment concludes,
in common form, that the pannel is guilty, or actor art and
part, of the crimes aforesaid, or one or other of them

The charge in this indictment is so heinous, that one should
have imagined it would have been decent in the pannel to
have made no objection to the relevancy, and to have founded
upon no defence for avoiding the effect of the libel, if true,
but to have contented himself with a flat denial thereof, reposing
himself upon his innocence, if he is truly not guilty of the facts
alleged, without any other desire but that of having a fair
examination of unbiassed witnesses, to be produced by him
as well as the prosecutor, in order to discover the real circumstances of the transaction

But his procurators, it seems, thought it their duty to move
every objection against the relevancy of the libel, and to offer
every defence that their invention could suggest, from a particular relation of the circumstances of the whole transaction,
which they laid before the Court upon the pannel's information,
and which they offered to prove, to make good their defence

They informed the Court, therefore, on behalf of the pannel,
That the Magistrates, apprehending that some violent attempt
might be made for rescuing Wilson, the offender sentenced to
be hanged, had ordered the pannel to attend the execution,
with the greatest part of the City Guard, to support and

151

Captain Porteous.

protect the executioner in the discharge of his office, with directions to repel force by force, that, to make those directions effectual, powder and ball were, by the town treasurer, delivered out of the town's magazine to the City Guard, the morning of the execution, with directions to load their pieces. That, besides this precaution, the danger of the rescue appeared to the Magistrates so great, that they desired of General Moyle, and obtained, a detachment of the regular troops, who were posted near to the place of execution, in order to support the City Guard, if there had been occasion : and whose commanders were told, that the Lord Provost would give them authority to fire, if it should prove necessary, that the pannel, with the Town Guard, attended accordingly the execution that when the offender was hung up on the gibbet, the magistrates retired from the scaffold, and repaired to a house over against it, in the Grassmarket, that after the offender had been hung up for some time, the multitude became unruly, and begun to fling stones of great size, and with great violence, that some of the guard were thereby hurt, one had his shoulder blade broke, others were bruised, and the timber of the drum was beat to pieces, that the insolence of the mob growing still greater, and they pressing from all sides upon the guard, the pannel, who apprehended they might have intended to carry off the criminal, who by this time was cut down, in order to attempt the recovering him to life found it necessary for him to keep off the multitude by threats and menaces; that to this end he presented his piece first to one quarter and then to another, calling to the people to stand off, and threatening that, if they did not, he would fire; that nevertheless, he neither fired himself, nor gave any orders to fire, but, on the contrary. when some of the guard, provoked by the hurts they received, had without his orders or authority, presumed to fire, whose example was followed by several others, he did all he could to prevent that mischief, by commanding them to desist, and actually did beat down the muzzle of one of the men's pieces. who was presenting it in order to fire, that finding he could not be obeyed, he endeavoured to march off his men, and prevailed with several of them to follow him some small way up the West Bow when again some of those men who followed him, provoked by what he did not know, faced about, and fired towards the Grassmarket, that the first notice he had of this firing was by hearing it, which made him turn about in order to stop it; that at this last place, he neither fired nor gave orders to fire, that he marched as many of his men as he could gather together back to the City Guard Room, that there he prevented the men's cleaning their pieces, that the guilty who fired might be distinguished from the innocent who did not fire, that his own piece had not at that time been

152

Information for H.M. Advocate.

at all fired; that, conscious of his innocence, and that he had, on this, as well as on every former occasion, done his duty with patience and temper, he presented himself before the magistrates, whereas nothing was easier for him than to have made his escape; and that in their presence the firelock which he had in his hand was presented, and appeared not to have been at all fired, and that therefore it was impossible the libel, as libelled could be true

From this, which was said to be the state of the case, the procurators for the pannel contended, First, That the libel was insufficient, as not describing with proper accuracy the particular part of the street, where the person supposed to be shot by the pannel stood, and his situation with respect to the pannel at the time, because thereby the pannel was deprived of the opportunity of making his defence, by founding it particularly on circumstances which he might avail himself of, if the position and situation had been distinctly described

To this it was, and is answered, That the libel is as particular as the law requires, describing the street where the execution was had, which is all that the utmost scrupulosity could expect in such a case. Minute circumstances cannot be known to the prosecutor, or certainly discovered, but by proof upon the trial, every circumstance of the pannel's own acting must be known to him, and, therefore, if, from the position or situation in which he was at the time of the firing, he can show that it was impossible he could have killed the person whom he is charged to have shot, describing and proving those circumstances, he may have advantage from them, but cannot object to the prosecutor, that he did not minutely describe a situation that was not known to him, and which describing perhaps erroneously, might minister an unjust occasion to a criminal to escape justice, wherefore this objection to the form of the indictment ought to be repelled

But, in the second place, the procurators for the pannel, very unnecessarily, one should think, if he is innocent of firing, or ordering to fire, and in some degree inconsistently with that plea, alleged, that the delivering out powder and ball to the city guard,—the ordering so great a detachment to attend,—the calling for the regular troops to support the town-guard,—the intimation to the commander of those troops, that they should have orders to fire in case of necessity,—and the direction to the pannel to support the execution of the sentence against Wilson, and in case of a violent rescue or deforcement to repel force by force, amounted to a flat order from the magistrates to fire when it became necessary, and that the violent assault made by the mob, as aforesaid, with stones, which were to be considered as lethal weapons, in order, as the pannel believed, to carry off the offender, in hopes of recovering him to life,

153

Captain Porteous.

made it necessary to repel force by force Wherefore these circumstances to infer the order, and the violent assault of the mob as mentioned, ought to be sustained and admitted to proof as a total defence against the indictment, at least as circumstances fit to mitigate the punishment, and restrain it from the *pœna ordinaria* since the pannel being *versans in licito*, and engaged in the discharge of a lawful piece of duty, if any excess was committed by him, it ought not to be attended with capital punishment, but ought to be corrected *extra ordinem*, according to the degree of the excess

To this it was answered, That though it were true, which is not at all upon the part of the prosecutor denied, that the magistrates, upon just apprehension of disorders, and an attempt for a violent rescue of the criminal, who was sentenced to die, had ordered powder and ball to be distributed to the guard, had increased their numbers, had obtained assistance from the commander of the regular troops, with assurance that in case of necessity they should be authorized to fire, had directed the pannel at all hazards to support the execution, and prevent a violent rescue, and had even told him, that, in case of necessity, he was to repel force by force, it will not in the least follow that those orders could in any degree justify him, except in case of necessity, except there had been an attempt towards a violent rescue, which could not otherwise have been prevented, and except all the proper precautions for dissipating otherwise the mob, and for legitimating the act of firing upon them, had been previously made use of

For, in the first place, no order from any civil magistrate whatever can justify a barbarity so horrid as that which is charged on the pannel. Had the provost and all the magistrates of Edinburgh been present on the spot, and had they ordered him to fire upon the innocent people when there was no just cause for so doing, those orders indeed might subject the magistrates, as well to the penal consequences that attend murder, but could not on the least acquit him, who was not at all bound to obey such illegal orders, and who therefore acted at his peril

In the second place, It is not at all pretended that the pannel had any orders expressed or implied to fire, except the violence of an attempt to rescue, not otherwise avoidable, made it necessary. Had that been truly the case, firing possibly might have been the pannel's duty, the reading the proclamation undoubtedly would have made it justifiable, and this the magistrates knew when they ordered ammunition to be distributed and invited the regular troops to their assistance But till it became necessary, when there was no hazard of a rescue, before any disorder was sought to be quelled by the legal precaution of reading the proclamation, which is intended to intimidate

Information for H.M. Advocate.

rioters, and to separate the innocent from the guilty, by giving
due notice to all thoughtless people, who, without any malevo-
lence, are mixed with the multitude, to separate from the ill
meaning, it was the most cruel, as well as most unjustifiable
act, that has at any time been heard of, to make use of the
weapons that were put in the hands of the guard for the
security of the peace and of the people, to destroy so many
innocents who had not in any degree offended

For, thirdly, Though the pannel mentioned the flinging of
stones, and the size of some of them, with some hurts received
therefrom, yet the libel charges, and he admits, that the
criminal was cut down before this trifling provocation prevailed
with any one to fire   His duty then, so far as concerned the
execution of the sentence, was over   He alleges no danger, nor
can he in those circumstances of a rescue, no invasion with fire
arms or other mortal weapons, fit to deforce or destroy a
detachment of seventy disciplined men with loaded pieces and
screwed bayonets   How then can the exigence of the orders
defend him?   If his act had been absolutely necessary, some
defence might have been founded on that necessity, joined
with his orders, but when his allegations, though they were
true, do not point out the least necessity, and are in reality
founded on nothing else than the customary impertinence, on
such occasions, of flinging dirt and stones at the executioner,
though the provocation thereby given might perhaps justify a
choleric man for drubbing any of the actors for their wantonness, yet to be sure it could not justify the slaughtering of the
offender, far less can such impertinence in a few boys, or other
idle people, excuse the firing sharp shot upon an innocent
multitude, whereby numbers of his Majesty's subjects were
destroyed   And therefore it seems to be beyond all doubt, the
pannel can find no shelter from those orders, or the duty he
imagines lay upon him to fire, and must therefore stand or
fall, upon his being or not being guilty of the facts charged
upon him

The procurators for the pannel endeavoured to find an argument for him in a late resolution of the Court, which suspended
a sentence of the Court of Admiralty, proceeding upon an inter-
loquitor that found it necessary for soldiers, who happened to
kill in the execution of their duty, when by order attending
customhouse officers, to prove, that the killing was necessary
for the defence of their lives, inferring from this resolution that
the Court did not think it necessary for the pannel to prove
that he was in danger of his life   And though all that their
observation necessarily implies were granted, they could have
no benefit by it, because, in this case the pannel neither does,
nor can aver, that the firing which he was personally guilty of,
and ordered, was necessary for securing the execution of that

155

Captain Porteous.

trust that was committed to him, or for preserving the rights of the Crown, or any subject

Where a man has by law weapons put in his hand, to be employed, not only in defence of his life when attacked, but in support of the execution of the laws, and in defence of the property of the Crown or liberty of any subject, he doubtless may use those weapons, not only when his own life is put so far in danger that he cannot probably escape without making use of them, but also when there is imminent danger, that he may by violence be disabled to execute his trust without resorting to the use of those weapons, but when the life of the officer is exposed to no danger, when his duty does not necessarily call upon him for the execution of his trust, or for the preservation of the property of the Crown, or the preservation of the property or liberty of the subject, to make use of mortal[1] weapons which may destroy his Majesty's subjects, especially numbers of them who may be innocent, it is impossible, from the resolution of the Court of Justiciary hinted at, to expect any countenance to, or shelter for the inhumane act

And upon a principle very nearly allied to this, the pannel's pretence, that, being *versans in licito*, and entrusted with the execution of legal orders, any excess that for lack of discretion he may have been guilty of. cannot be punished *pœna ordinaria*, ought to be repelled, for it is obvious, the trust reposed in him, and the duty expected from him, was no more than to see the execution perfected, and to resist any violent attempt to rescue which should disappoint the execution of the law Now, when the sentence of the Court of Justiciary was executed, when the criminal was hanged and cut down, before any person fired, the trust reposed in the pannel, and the duty expected from him, ceased, he was no longer an officer employed, to that end for which the fire-arms were loaded, and his actions came to be estimated of by the same rules, that would have made them lawful or unlawful upon every ordinary occasion, where no particular danger threatened, and where no necessary service was in view

And, therefore, as in such cases, the pannel must be convinced, that nothing short of being constituted in immediate danger of death without firing could justify him or his guard for making use of loaded fire-arms, he must in consequence acknowledge, that, in the case in question, no danger of life, which he could not have avoided, having threatened him and his guard, he was absolutely inexcusable for firing, and that, therefore, his mischievous and temerarious act must be attended with the highest penalty.

An armed man who assaults, and without just cause destroys another man though armed, and in no particular trust or confidence with him, the law considers and demeans as a murderer,

156

Information for H.M. Advocate.

but when the captain of a city guard, who has an armed force
committed to his care for the good and safety of the community,
thinks fit, upon any slight offence or provocation, to turn those
arms and that force upon a crowd of citizens lawfully as well
as innocently assembled, he is, in addition to the slaughter
and destruction that ensues, guilty of the most notorious breach
of trust, and for an example to others whom it may be necessary
for the good of the community to trust, ought to be punished
in the most severe manner Men so trusted are under double
ties, for, besides the general obligations of duty and humanity,
a particular confidence is reposed in them, which, at the peril
of their lives, they ought to answer

The procurators for the pannel complained, that in the
indictment he was charged with a wicked and malicious purpose
of destroying, wounding, and maiming numbers of his Majesty's
subjects, and by the pannel's sober and modest deportment on
former occasions, and the whole circumstances precedent to the
melancholy accident now in question, endeavoured to show that
he had no premeditated malicious design But this again was
to no purpose The prosecutor never heard, nor, so far as he
knows, did ever any man before this time complain of the
wickedness or inhumanity of the pannel, and he has received
no information by which he can be induced to think, that for
any considerable time before the fact complained of the pannel
had premeditated the destructive action of which he is accused
But then his procurators very well know, that firing and ordering to fire imply, and are proof of a wicked and malicious
purpose of destroying those that are fired at *Malitia* and
propositum præcedunt ictum, in the construction of reason as
well as law, and whoever wilfully murders and destroys his
Majesty's subjects must be demeaned as a murderer, if his
malicious purpose preceded the drawing of the tricker or giving
the orders one moment, as much as if it had been preconceived
a whole year

These shews of defence, rather than defences, being removed,
the next thing that comes to be considered, is the history of the
pannel's behaviour, during the melancholy transaction, which
his procurators offered to prove, and insisted, would, if proved,
be a sufficient defence against the facts charged in the libel

But in this the prosecutor can by no means agree, for he takes
it to be extremely plain, that every single circumstance alleged
by the pannel may be true, and yet it may also be true, that
he with his own hand fired, and killed one or more of the
innocent people, and that he ordered the men under his command to fire

It may, for example, possibly be true, that he, at some period
or another of the action, called out to the multitude to stand
off, or that he would fire , that he at some one point or another

Captain Porteous.

of time prohibited the men to fire, and struck down the pieces of such as were presenting them, and yet it may also be true, that he at some other point of time gave the precise word of command to fire, and actually fired the piece that was in his hand before he lost his temper he might have threatened only, before he took the resolution of annoying, as well as after he saw mischief done, he might have endeavoured to prevent a particular act of inhumanity; but his doing so at certain periods, is no conclusive evidence, that, at other points of time, his conduct might not have been very different

Were his giving orders, or actually firing dubious, the circumstances mentioned for the pannel might create a strong presumption for him. but if it shall be proved, as it is charged in the libel, that he actually fired the piece in his hand oftener than once, and gave positive orders to fire; what can it avail him, that, at some other periods of the fray, he behaved himself in a different manner? since both the one allegation and the other may be true

But the procurators for the pannel insisted, that though the proposition they undertook to prove was in some degree a negative, yet it was so circumstantiated as to be capable of a positive proof; for they said that credible witnesses could be produced, who would inform the Court and jury, that, during the whole fray, they kept their eyes upon the pannel, and were attentive to his actions, and that they could take upon them to say, that throughout the scuffle he did not fire his piece, nor order the guard to fire, but that he threatened to fire, which might by persons at a distance, who heard the word fire only pronounced, be mistaken for a command, and that he presented his piece only in a menacing posture, but without firing, which might have misled the spectators into an opinion that he did fire, though he really did not, if any one who was near him happened to discharge his shot about the same time

This reasoning, however, is manifestly defective. because the evidence of the witnesses, who shall say they did not see or hear, bears no proportion in point of weight to the testimony of those who shall upon oath positively say that they did hear or see

And besides the obvious reason for maintaining this distinction in the common case, there is a particular consideration that supports it, in the case of a fray or tumult, where shots are fired, murder ensues, and there is a general confusion and surprise No one could possibly be so interested in keeping his eyes upon the pannel, when it could not be foreseen there would be occasion to give evidence touching his behaviour, as not to be liable to be carried off from that object, upon any fresh surprise that happened in the tumult; the firing of a shot, the flinging of a stone, the extraordinary behaviour of

Information for H.M. Advocate.

any one of the multitude or of the guard, might imperceptibly have drawn the eyes and attention of any spectator from the pannel to that new object, and prevented his seeing or hearing what he said or did in the meantime, and, therefore, no witness, or number of witnesses, who should take upon him or them to say absolutely, that the pannel did not at any period of the fray fire or order to fire, would at all be credible, at least, most certainly they could not be credited against such witnesses as should positively say, that they saw or heard him fire or order to fire

If witnesses shall say against the pannel, that they saw him present his piece and fire, and for their *causa scientiæ* shall aver, that they observed fire and smoke issuing out of the muzzle of his piece, and a man drop down dead in the place towards which he pointed it, will that evidence be sufficiently contradicted by persons who may say they observed no such thing, or that others of the guard fired about the same time and at the same place? It is humbly thought it cannot, because this is setting up negative evidence only against positive, which neither law nor reason permits

And if credible witnesses shall aver, that the captain distinctly ordered the guard to fire, can it avail him that other witnesses heard him threaten the crowd, that, if they did not retire, he would fire, without hearing the positive orders for firing given? In a tumult, every individual cannot possibly hear every thing that passes, but then it is no evidence that particular words were not uttered in a fray, that some persons present at the fray did not hear or attend to them.

And the pannel, in framing his defence on this article, does not seem to have attended to what is expressly libelled against him, that in great anger he said to the men under his command, upon their firing over the heads of the multitude, level your pieces, and be damn'd! Will this circumstance, should it be proven, be at all consistent with that part of the defence, which tends to render the expression of fire dubious? If the pannel's passion moved him to utter the expression. level your pieces, and be damn'd! is it at all doubtful in what sense the word fire was pronounced? These things are, it is thought, too plain to be further insisted on

The only remaining circumstance, on which the procurators for the pannel seemed to lay stress was the condition of his firelock, when the action was over, and his voluntary presenting himself before the Magistrates, when he could have made his escape, from which they would have inferred an impossibility that he was guilty of actually firing, his firelock appearing not to have been discharged, and a strong improbability, that he was conscious of having given any criminal orders, since without necessity he freely presented himself to justice

Captain Porteous.

Now, as to these matters, it must be observed, first, that the condition in which the pannel's firelock appeared can yield no evidence for him   A piece that has been fired may be reloaded, and so cleaned and brushed up, as to leave no vestige or mark of the former firing; and the piece which the pannel made use of in firing might have been changed, and another produced to the Magistrates in the room thereof

But 2dly, The indictment nowhere avers, that the pannel made use of his own piece when he fired   Where he is first charged with firing, no more is said, than that he levelled the firelock that was in his hand, and fired it at Charles Husband Now, the firelock that was in his hand might have been that belonging to another man, as well as his own.   And in the other part of his indictment, where he is charged with firing, it is said that he made use of a musquet or firelock that was in his hand, having either reloaded, or caused to be reloaded, his own piece, or having taken another out of the hand of one of the guard; so that the libel in every article of it may be true, and proved; and yet it may be also true, that the pannel did not fire his own piece

And as to the article, that the pannel, conscious of no guilt, appeared voluntarily before the Magistrates, when he could easily made his escape, it can possibly infer no presumption for his innocence, if the facts charged in the indictment are made good   Whoever shall be satisfied by the proof, that the pannel acted in manner libelled, must be convinced that he was governed in his actions by no principle of discretion, and must therefore lay no weight upon an act of his, which can yield no inference, unless he is supposed to have been governed by discretion and prudence

Having thus run over the several circumstances of the pannel's narrative, the prosecutor apprehends he may safely conclude, that they cannot, jointly or separately, be sustained as a defence against the charge laid in the indictment; because, though every circumstance alleged were undeniably proved, the unhappy pannel might nevertheless be guilty, and a positive proof of the facts charged, must necessarily prevail with every unbiassed juryman, to join in a verdict against him

The prosecutor is nevertheless far from wishing that the unfortunate pannel should be deprived of an opportunity of laying every circumstance that may make for his defence before the jury by proof, though he humbly insists they cannot be sustained as a defence relevant to assoilzie from the indictment.   It is possible the fact may come out otherwise in the trial when witnesses are upon oath, than it did when the examination was taken in the precognition, and should the proof of the indictment be in material circumstances defective, the evidence offered for the pannel may have its weight;

Information for H.M. Advocate.

wherefore, so far as the forms of the Court will allow, the prosecutor makes no opposition to the indulging the pannel to bring what legal evidence he can, for the information of the jury

It is far from being the interest of the Crown, or of the public, that an innocent man should suffer ; but it is greatly the interest of both, that a fair and strict inquiry be made where the guilt lies, when a massacre so cruel and so dangerous happens, to the end that, if the officer, who has power put in his hand, for the preservation of the peace, and for the protection of the people, should, from any unjust motive whatever, make use of that power in breach of the laws, to the destruction of the people, he may be made an example to restrain others in the same circumstances, from the like monstrous and dangerous abuses in time coming

In respect whereof, &c ,

Sic subscribitur,

Dun. Forbes

Captain Porteous.

INFORMATION

FOR

JOHN PORTEOUS, late Captain-Lieutenant of the City Guard of Edinburgh,

AGAINST

HIS MAJESTY'S ADVOCATE

THE pannel stands indicted, at the instance of his Majesty's Advocate, for his Highness's interest, for the crimes of murder, and slaughter, maiming, and wounding, and the facts charged against him, from whence these crimes are pretended to be inferred, are these following That the pannel being one of the captain-lieutenants of the said city-guard, was by the magistrates of the city, ordered to attend, with a detachment of about seventy men of the said guard, at the execution of Andrew Wilson, sentenced to be hanged by the High Court of Justiciary, and that the said Andrew Wilson, having hung upon the gallows, erected for his execution, in the street called the Grassmarket, until he was dead, at least for a considerable time, and so long that there was ground to conclude he was dead, he the said pannel, conceiving a wicked and malicious purpose of destroying, wounding, and maiming the persons, inhabitants of the said city, and others, assembled at the said execution, did, without any just cause or necessary occasion, order the said detachment, under his command, to fire upon the people so assembled; and that some of the men having fired, as it would seem the pannel apprehended, over the heads of the multitude, with intention to avoid doing them harm, he the said pannel did with threats repeat his commands to fire, calling out to the men to level their pieces and be damned, or words to that purpose, and that, at the same time, he levelled the firelock that was in his own hand taking aim at one Charles Husband, and, having fired the said firelock, the said Charles Husband immediately dropped to the ground, having received a wound or wounds, by bullets or large drops of lead, whereof he died in a short space and that, by the pannel's said example and command, severals of the said guard, to the number of about twenty, did, at the same time, or soon thereafter, fire upon the innocent multitude, by which fire, two other persons were killed, and several others wounded,

Henry Home, afterwards Lord Kames.

From an Engraving after Martin.

Information for John Porteous.

maimed, or hurt, and that the said pannel having thereafter
marched off the said detachment of the guard into that part
of the street aforesaid called the West Bow, he did again,
without any just cause or occasion, order the men under his
command to face about and fire upon the people, and that,
at this time, the said pannel did fire a musket that was in his
own hand, having either reloaded, or caused to be reloaded,
his own piece or firelock, or taken another out of the hands
of one of the guard, and that severals of the said guard did,
upon that second example and command of the pannel's, fire
upon the multitude by which five three other persons were
killed at least that, by the said firings of the pannel, or of
the firings of the other men in the said detachment of the
guard proceeding from the pannel's order and example, the
several persons mentioned in the indictment to have been killed,
maimed, or wounded, were all respectively killed, wounded,
or maimed Whereby the pannel is guilty of the killing, wounding, or maiming of the said persons, at least is art and part
thereof, or accessory thereto, from whence the indictment
concludes, that the pannel ought to be punished with the pains
of law *i e*, capitally

To this indictment the pannel pleaded not guilty, for that
he had, at no time during the execution of Andrew Wilson
aforesaid, given any order, or shewed any example to the said
detachment of the guard then under, or that ought to have
been under his command, to fire upon the multitude so
assembled, and that he did, at no time, fire any piece or firelock himself upon the said crowd, that though it might be
true, that at or about the time of the said execution, several
persons were killed and wounded by the firings of that detachment of the guard, which indeed ought to have been under
the pannel's command, and which he does, with great grief
and sorrow, regret, yet that, as such firing proceeded wholly
from the men in the said detachment, without any order or
example from the pannel, so he could not be charged therewith, however fatal or tragical the consequences of such firing
may have proved

That though the pannel, as conscious of his own innocence,
could safely rest his trial upon the denial of the facts aforesaid, and upon such proof as he could bring, by the evidence
of multitudes of persons of undoubted credit who happened to
be present, close by him, during this unhappy scene, that he
was nowise instrumental in the killing or wounding the said
persons, but that, upon the contrary, he did all that was in
his power to prevent and restrain the said firing upon the
multitude, yet, that he was advised by his counsel, that they
could not, during the conducting of his trial, consistent with
their duty, suffer him, the pannel, to omit or abandon any

Captain Porteous.

defence that was competent to him in law, and that, therefore, as, by the law of Scotland, the pleading to an indictment, upon supposed facts, is no legal admission of such facts, the pannel was at liberty to plead any other exception that lay against the form of his indictment, or even to plead, that, though such firing had proceeded from his order or example, yet, even in that case, such firing, and the consequences wherewith it was attended, was not sufficient to support the charge against the pannel of the crimes of either murder, slaughter maiming, or wounding or to render him obnoxious to the pains libelled

And in the entry of the debate, the procurators for the pannel ask liberty to offer to the Court a full recital of the behaviour of the pannel, during the execution of the said Andrew Wilson, and for some short space previous and subsequent thereto, and also, to offer a short relation of what they apprehend was the cause that the execution of the said Andrew Wilson was attended with such an unusual confluence of people, and was ordered to be guarded and overseen by such a numerous and unaccustomed armed force

The said Andrew Wilson, along with one Robertson, and others, had been sentenced to death by your Lordships, for robbing one of the collectors of his Majesty's revenue of considerable sums of money of the public; and while they lay under this sentence, they were allowed, as usual, to go to the church adjoining to the prison, for the benefit of divine service, under the custody of a small detachment of the city-guard, and while the convicts were thus at church, Robertson, one of them, found means to escape from his keepers of the guard, by suddenly jumping over a pew, and getting out at the door of the church, his retreat apparently being favoured by the mob, or lowest sort of the people, he easily made his escape, without having been ever since overtaken

From this escape of Robertson's, so favoured by the mob, and from strong surmises and suggestions, that, at the execution of Wilson, a rescue was intended by the mob, which indeed there was a reasonable ground to apprehend, because the commons have imbibed a pernicious and absurd conceit, as if the robbing of the public money was a crime more pardonable than private robbery therefore it was, as the pannel apprehends, that the magistrates of the city, from a sense of their duty, to prevent the execution of the laws being any further defeated by the rescue of Wilson, took the strongest precautions that the execution of him should be made effectual

In consequence whereof, as would seem, the provost of the city sent for the pannel, in whom, he must take the liberty to say, confidence was generally put upon those difficult occasions, and told him, that there being great apprehensions of

Information for John Porteous.

a mob at Andrew Wilson's execution, that therefore there was
a necessity to be well prepared to prevent their designs, and
for that end, that he would have the whole city guard to
attend at the execution, he having given orders to the town-
treasurer to furnish the men with powder and shot, and such
other military ammunition as might be necessary for the use
of the men in maintaining the peace of the town, and supporting the execution of the laws   And this conference with the
provost happened upon the Monday preceding the execution
of Wilson, which followed on the Wednesday thereafter   But
it seems, the magistrates of the city, not thinking even this
precaution sufficient, upon the Tuesday thereafter, the provost
sent the pannel with a letter to General Moyle, residing near
the city, and chief commander of the forces in Scotland telling
the pannel, that the import of this letter was, desiring from the
general an order for a party of the regiment lying in the
Canongate to enter the city, (a thing very uncommon, except
in the case of urgent necessity,) in order to overawe the mob,
and thereby maintain the peace during the said execution
   It seems this letter to the general induced him to send a
verbal message in return thereto, by a person of known honour
and veracity, Major Pool, of that regiment now lying in the
Canongate, who told the provost that the general wanted to
know of him what part the King's troops were to act, and
what precautions had been taken for preventing any insult
or invasion that might be made upon the troops, or what
length these troops might go in the case of tumult or disturbance   To which the provost made answer, that there was no
reason to apprehend any inconveniency would happen to the
King's troops, because he would have them only to parade,
for a terror to the mob, in a street called the Lawnmarket,
removed from the sight of the execution, but at a small distance
only, where, nevertheless, they would be ready at a call in
case of necessity, but that he had ordered the whole band of
the city-guard to attend at the execution itself, with proper
arms and ammunition, namely, slug-shot, with orders to repel
force by force, and even to discharge their arms among the
mob in case of resistance
   On Wednesday, the day of the execution, in the forenoon,
the pannel attended the provost, and told him, that, in obedience to his commands, the men were all ordered to be in readiness, their arms put in order, and loaded; whereof the provost
approved, and told the pannel, that he was to be ready betwixt
two and three in the afternoon with his guard, and to draw
out until the party of the King's troops from the Canongate
past him, and that so soon as the King's troops were drawn
up in the Lawnmarket, the pannel, with the city guard, should
forthwith march to the prison, and conduct the prisoner to the

Captain Porteous.

place of execution, without allowing him first to go to the town's council-house, as usual, still with intention, as would seem, to prevent any opportunity of rescue, or disturbance upon that head, and at this time in the forenoon the pannel humbly proposed to the magistrates of the city, that they would send a proclamation through the town, as a caution to such innocent unwary people, as might by curiosity be drawn to the sight of the execution, warning them of their danger, in case any disturbance should happen, or attack be made upon the guard   And, accordingly, George Lindsey, one of their clerks, made a scroll of the said proclamation to be sent through the town, but for what reason it was not proclaimed the pannel knows not· and, at the same time, the pannel remembers some one or other of the common council of the city proposed, in case of disturbance, the reading ot the riot act, and for that purpose sent for a dozen of copies of the act to a bookseller's shop, in order to distribute them among the proper officers of the law authorised to read and proclaim such act, but it seems at no time either of those proposals were put in execution, nor at the time of the said execution, did any officer of the law, authorized to proclaim such act, attend with the pannel

A short space before the pannel marched with his men from the guard-house towards the place of execution, he was heard say, that he had no cartrages in his box, on which a corporal told him that he would get him some, and accordingly the corporal did, in presence of several of the men, open the pannel's cartrage-box, wherein it was observed there were no cartrages, and put three cartrages therein, with one ot which the pannel loaded his piece, and immediately marched away with his men

When the criminal was conducted to the scaffold erected for his execution, the detachment of the city-guard were posted on the street, in a circle surrounding the scaffold, in order to keep off the mob, but because of a certain building, called the Corn-market, nigh adjoining to the scaffold, part of the men did also encircle that building   And here it may not be improper for the Court to cast their eye upon a plan of the ground, and the posture of the men, in order to have a clearer view of the descriptions to be hereafter mentioned

So soon as the criminal was thrown over the ladder, and so left hanging upon the gibbet, the city bailies immediately withdrew nigh to, directly opposite, and in view of the scaffold, but without leaving any order or officer of the law to attend with the pannel, and it had happened, that some short space before the act of execution, while the minister was assisting the criminal by prayer, the pannel had gone up to join, leaving his piece with the serjeant, and so soon as public prayer was

Information for John Porteous.

ended, or some short time after, and the convict left to his own private devotion, the pannel took back his piece in his hand, and afterwards came off the scaffold, and posted himself at the west end of the detachment of the guard

So soon as the convict had been hung up as aforesaid, and that the city bailies had withdrawn from the scaffold, the mob became to be troublesome, intending, as would seem, to use this last shift, immediately to cut down the criminal, and endeavour to bring him to life by bleeding; an expedient which, when timeously applied, has, on many other occasions, been known to be attended with success ; and the mob fell a murmuring, that they would have him instantly cut down, and if it were not quickly done, they would do it themselves ; and at this time they pressed hard upon the guard, striking at them with sticks, seizing of their fire arms and bayonets, and throwing exceeding big stones at the guard, one whereof cut a drummer to the skull, another broke one of the men's shoulder bones, another wounded one of the men's legs, and several others of the men were wounded, whereby they are yet unable to do duty   The truth of all which can be attested by their common surgeon, who is by the city ordered to attend them upon all exigencies

This insolence in the mob alarmed the pannel, and still observing it to increase, he was apprehensive that the mob might obstruct the perfecting of the execution , for no criminal can be cut down from the gibbet but upon the order of a city bailiff upon a judgment that the criminal has hung up until he is completely dead, agreeable to the sentence which always commands such convict to be hanged until he be dead ; therefore it was that the pannel sent a message to the bailiffs to know if he should suffer the criminal to be cut down from the gibbet, who brought back an answer, that the convict was to hang there yet for a quarter of an hour

At this time the mob waxed exceeding bold, became very turbulent, and prest hard upon the guard, and while the pannel was endeavouring to keep off the crowd from pressing among the soldiers, at one end of the scaffold some of the convict's friends, assisted by the mob, catched an opportunity and cut him down without any order   And though the convict, being thus cut down, was in the possession and keeping of the mob, who were endeavouring to recover him to life, by causing the veins of both arms to be opened ; whether it was that they were apprehensive that the guard would recover him out of their hands, as having been cut down without order, or that the officers of the law were designed to see to his interment, and that he was executed to death , or that the convict's body was intended to be given to be anatomized by the surgeons, as is sometimes practised where persons

167

Captain Porteous.

of low degree, or notorious offenders, are sentenced to death; or from whatever motive it proceeded, the mob began to insult and attack the guard, and upon this attack it was, that the man aforesaid had his shoulder blade broken, and another so bruised, that he has been never able to do duty since; and the timber of the drum was broke by the force of an exceeding large stone that was thrown, and several others of the men were hurt and wounded

This violence in the mob so alarmed the pannel, that he made a step or two forwards to the westward of the scaffold, turning about his face towards the Westport, from whence the throwing of the stones mostly proceeded; and having put his piece to his shoulder, he levelled it at the mob, and pointing it around to them, threatening with an audible voice, that if they would not be at peace, and leave off throwing stones, and attacking the men, he would fire among them, but immediately recovered his piece without firing it; the threats being only intended to intimidate the mob.

But unfortunately upon this ensued the whole tragical scene; for no sooner had the pannel stept forward, threatening to fire as aforesaid, but one of the men came up from behind him, and running by him upon his right hand, instantly discharged his piece, upon which one of the crowd dropt down, supposed to be Charles Husband, and which Charles Husband will, upon proof, be found to have been the person who tumultuously stept in and cut down the criminal

Immediately upon this first fire, another of the guard came up to the pannel, with his piece presented and cocked, and asked if he should fire, to which the pannel answered with some vehemence. No, by no means, and struck up his piece, bidding him go to his rank, and actually thrust him thereto.

After the example of this first fire, several more of the men were heard to discharge their pieces, but upon what provocation the pannel cannot tell, these shots having been at a considerable distance from the pannel, proceeding, as is supposed, from such of the men as were standing at the south-west corner of the Cornmarket; whereas, as has been noticed, the pannel was still standing at his former station to the west of the scaffold and gibbet

The pannel not knowing the fatal consequences of those shots, but suspecting, however, that mischief would happen, seeing the men had been so rash as to fire without orders thought it was the best course he could take to lead off the men of the guard as soon as he could, and for that end he called aloud to them to follow him, and after having given orders to the serjeants to gather them together (for it was impossible to bring them into ranks by the confusion of the mob,) he marched off as many of them as he could find, by the north side of the

Information for John Porteous.

scaffold towards the foot of the West Bow, and towards a parcel of the men whom one of the serjeants had got together at the foot of the Bow, but as he was going to join that parcel of the men, he heard a piece fired near him, with which he was a good deal surprised, and yet more when he observed two or three people fall to the ground. and which observation was the first thing that greatly alarmed the pannel, as knowing from thence that certainly mischief was done ; but it is certain that this fatal shot did not proceed from the pannel but from a certain man in the guard that can be well proven, who, after having fired this shot, immediately retired amongst the crowd, and then got himself joined to the party And surely the magistrates of the city will remember, that when a precognition was taking of the several facts and occurrences upon this tragical day. that a certain person told them, that if they would be pleased to sist the whole band of the guard before them, he would point out the man who made this last fire, but the magistrates overlooked this offer

As soon as the pannel saw there was no restraining the men from irregularities, he marched off so many of them as he had got together, without taking time to form them into any order, giving orders at the same time to the serjeants to beat and press off the rest with all manner of dispatch Upon which he observed those that had straggled come off partly from about the scaffold, and partly from the east end of the Cornmarket, and fall into the rear and while the pannel was thus marching up the Bow upon the front of the foremost part of the men, and had come as far as the turn of the Bow, he heard some dropping shots firing in the rear, and about thirty or forty paces distant from him, which he supposes may have proceeded from those men who were straggling upon the east side of the Cornmarket. nigh to the head of the Cowgate, but upon what occasion the pannel knows not, but being alarmed with the shots, he looked back, supposing the men might be attacked by the mob, and observing no marks of any such attack. he thought the most prudent course he could take was forthwith to march off the men

It falls here to be noticed, that all this firing, from first to last, and whereby so much mischief has been done, lasted not above two or three minutes ; and, therefore, considering the violence of the mob, and the straggling situation of the men of the guard , and supposing the truth of the above narrative. which will be attested in proper time by the oaths of many gentlemen of undoubted veracity, and who had fair opportunity of observation at the time, it is left with the Court, and to every impartial bystander, whether the pannel could well have done more for the safety of the burgh , considering that it shall also be proved, that during these few minutes of firing,

Captain Porteous.

accompanied with great hurry and confusion, the pannel gave several repeated orders to the men to restrain from firing, but observing those orders prove ineffectual, he endeavoured to sweep them off the field with all manner of precipitation.

The pannel marched on with the men to the guard-house, and as he thinks with coolness and deliberation, passing by the King's troops in the Lawnmarket, (a thing generally esteemed somewhat inconsistent with guilt, especially such horrible guilt as he is charged with) Upon his arrival at the guard-house, he drew up his men there, sending a serjeant to the provost for orders, which were brought, that they should wait on their arms till the King's troops past, and some of the men in waiting, offering and attempting to clean their guns, but the pannel discharged it, and would not allow it to be done Meantime a certain person of credit came up to the pannel and asked if he had fired? To whom he made answer, he had not, but the person not being satisfied with the answer, put his finger into the muzzle of the pannels piece, and after having rubbed it about, and after having also viewed the lock, said to the pannel, I see you have not fired, and I am glad of it.

The King's troops having passed the guard, the pannel filed off the men into the guard, and ordered the serjeants to keep them close till further orders, and by all means not to suffer them to clean their pieces, and at the same time the pannel delivered his carabine, loaded as aforesaid, at the guard-door, to one of the guard, neither entering the guard himself, nor any other house, but went immediately to the provost, thus his own piece was brought back loaded, and apparently without having been fired, and the other two cartrages which he had got at the guard were found upon his return in his cartrage box

When the pannel went up to the provost, some person there present alleged he had seen the pannel fire, which he contradicted, and begged the provost to send for his piece, which he told he had delivered at the guard as aforesaid, and that it would appear from inspecting of her, that she had not been fired, and the piece being accordingly sent for, and brought up to the council chamber, and after being strictly inspected, it was agreed by all present that she had not been fired, and in this condition she still lies loaded, in the custody of the magistrates, along with the cartrage box, containing the two cartrages, as aforesaid

Though the pannel has a pretty important prize at stake, yet he rests in full security, that he will prove to the conviction of the Court every article above recited, and a good deal more on his behalf to be hereafter mentioned and if it should here be made matter of wonder how such different accounts

Information for John Porteous.

as are given of this matter can consist together, seeing numbers
of people are impressed with the guilt of the pannel, and that
even good, well-meaning people, who were present upon the
spot, persist in affirming that the pannel was guilty, by both
firing himself, and giving repeated orders to fire

The pannel can give no other account of this matter than
in this way A miserable slaughter was, somehow or other,
committed within the town The guilt must be laid to somebody's door, and whether any art might be used to lay the
heavy load upon the pannel, in order to draw the attention
of the multitude from another point in view, the pannel shall
not say, but entreats the Honourable Court, and every candid
reader, who may happen to take up this information, to look
into the *Caledonian Mercuries* of the fifteenth and nineteenth
of April last, papers supposed to be published by authority;
where will be found a most charitable account of the matter,
touching this misfortunate pannel, who was then lying in
close confinement, without anybody being allowed access to him,
and, of consequence, could have no opportunity of vindicating
himself, until once the prejudices were deep rooted and
rivetted so as even to catch the unwary, though well-meaning,
part of the people, and these beautiful relations of this transaction are adorned with some witty sarcasms, very proper to
this melancholy occasion, and painted out with ingenious
reflections and quaint rhetorical invectives, very suitable to
the authors of these historical relations

And indeed the authors of these accounts of the matter,
whoever they are, have the impudence to affirm, and the
wickedness to endeavour to fix it upon the pannel, as an
instance of premeditation and felony forethought, that the
pannel had ordered the detachment of the guard to load with
ball and slugshot, before they marched from the guard And
this worthy author affirms, that such doing was unprecedented,
and such as the pannel would not pretend orders for; notwithstanding that it is now, with his usual candour, admitted by
his Majesty's Advocate in his information against the pannel,
and dare not be denied, but that the pannel had orders to
see the whole men's pieces loaded with bullet and other shot,
and even to fire those pieces amongst the mob in case of
exigency

The prejudices against the pannel being once artfully rooted,
it was an easy matter to catch the giddy mob, who are not
able to look back and discern the true springs and causes
of things for such is the nature of human passions, that if
they are once artfully moved, they will be apt to misguide
the understandings, even of persons of observation, and thus
the speat having once been created against the pannel, it grew
into a torrent, and flew like a train of fire, everyone adding

Captain Porteous.

fuel to the flame, and sparks originally increase into a mighty combustion, and so, in like manner, things entirely of themselves innocent, may be multiplied into horrid cruelties and savage barbarity

It might also operate to the prejudice of the pannel, that this scene was acted in a very short space, attended with great commotion and confusion Words and actions might be misconstrued, (whereof more particular notice shall be taken hereafter,) whereby persons, even of judgment, might be deceived, and thereby fall into the vulgar notions And here it cannot be deemed an useless digression in the pannel to give a caution to all gentlemen, who may happen to be called in evidence upon this trial, (for it is feared the mob are not capable of this advice,) not to affirm things upon oath, except their observations have been accompanied with all that certainty which those sensations wherewith mankind is endued, can admit of, because any inconsiderate rashness to the prejudice of the life or fame of the pannel, cannot fail, for hereafter, to be attended with very painful stings of remorse

It was observed for the pannel, as a thing that could not be denied, that, upon many former occasions, he had been singled out as the fittest person to maintain the peace of the city, by quelling of mobs and tumults, and that he had never hithertofore, during all the many occasions on which he had been employed, ever discovered any imprudent rashness or cruel temper in the exercise of his command, but had exposed his person to very great danger, rather than involve the city in blood, or proceed to such extremities as the law even would have entirely justified

It was also observed in behalf of the pannel, that it was no new thing for the private men in the city guard, who, though they are tolerably acquainted with discipline, yet are not subject to the military law, to take upon them to fire upon the multitude, without any order from their commander, whereof the following instances are offered, and which cannot be denied, to wit

That at the settlement of Mr Wotherspoon as a minister in the West Church parish, a party of the city guard under the pannel's command did, one or more of them, in the rear ranks, within the west gate of Edinburgh, while the pannel was marching on their front, face about and fire upon the mob, without any order, and by which severals were dangerously wounded, and the like happened in a few years ago after the execution of one Campbell. when a detachment of the city guard were conducting the corpse of the person executed, which was delivered over to the surgeons of Edinburgh, by order of the magistrates And the same thing happened a few years ago at a race at Leith, where the party of the guard

Information for John Porteous.

was commanded by Captain Lind, whereby several persons
were wounded   And another instance was given, where the
same irregularity happened, within these few months, at the
execution of Brown the smith, when the detachment of the city
guard was commanded by both captains Lind and Ferguson
And, indeed, innumerable other instances might be given of
the rashness of the men in this particular, which it is needless
to condescend upon, because they are notourly known in the
city.

It may also deserve notice, that the private men of the
guard might be prompted to fire without orders, partly from
resentment, that Robertson before mentioned had escaped out
of their hands, and partly from being encouraged by the
general order they heard was given by the magistrates to fire
in case of resistance for it is now found, that severals of them
were heard say before they went out to the execution of
Wilson, that now they got arms and ammunition put into their
hands, and therefore would not fail to use them, in case they
were attacked, or any resistance made

These observations, it is thought, cannot fail to operate in
favours of the pannel, in case the proof of the libel shall be
attended with any uncertainty or dubiety and although the
pannel is not so weak of judgment as to imagine that such
presumptions can prevail against positive and certain proof,
yet he doubts not, that in due time, when the proof is led,
such observations must have weight with the candid jury.

One thing more we must observe in general, that as he has
been employed for these many years past as the scourge of the
mob, though never once known to proceed to extremities, yet
such station of his may be the cause of drawing resentment
from the lower sort of the people against him

The pannel has just reason to ask the forgiveness of the
Honourable Court for dwelling so long upon generals , but it
is hoped, from what is above noticed, and that this is the
first occasion he had of vindicating himself from the aspersions
and prejudice of his adversaries, he may merit the pardon
of the Court

And now to proceed to the particulars in the indictment ·
And whereas it sets forth That the pannel, conceiving a most
wicked and malicious purpose of destroying, wounding, and
maiming, numbers of his Majesty's subjects, inhabitants of
the city of Edinburgh, had acted the several matters and
things charged in the indictment: the pannel must observe,
that the circumstances of the case naturally exclude any sup-
position of premeditate malice and resentment in the pannel,
because it is impossible to conceive that the pannel should
have retained any malice against a multitude of persons, of
whom he neither had, nor can be supposed to have had any

173

acquaintance, and though it was admitted, that the circumstances of the case do exclude any supposed long premeditated malice, yet it was urged, that in law every wicked action does presume malice, though instantaneous to such wickedness committed

To which it was answered in behalf of the pannel, That the circumstances of the case, as laid in the indictment, do even exclude any presumption of malice accompanying the acts charged in the indictment, because every action must be construed in the most favourable sense, and therefore the actions charged against the pannel must even be construed to have proceeded from a principle of duty in the pannel in maintaining the peace of the place, and in supporting the authority of the laws, and the guarding of that execution of them, which was committed to him by lawful authority

In the next place, an exception was taken to the indictment, as not having been laid with sufficient certainty; the indictment nowhere expressing the particular places of that large street wherein the guilt is charged to have been committed, whereby the pannel was precluded from making his defences with certainty, for had it been laid in the indictment at what places in the street the particular persons, affirmed to have been killed and wounded, were so killed or wounded, the pannel might have had an opportunity of proving, from the circumstances of his situation at the several periods, that it was impossible that such wounds could have been received from his hands   And though it may be true, that such part of the indictment as charges the pannel's order to fire would be of universal influence, and reached over the whole circumstances of guilt charged in the indictment, yet as actual execution made by the pannel was charged separate from his order to fire, such proof of innocence, whereof the pannel pleaded an opportunity might have afforded him a defence against such part of the indictment as charges his own firing and killing

To this it was answered by his Majesty's Advocate, That the libel was as particular as the law required, describing the street where the execution was committed, which is all that the utmost scrupulosity could expect in this case, because minute circumstances, cannot be known to the prosecutor, or certainly discovered, but by proof upon trial, and that every circumstance of the pannel's own acting must be known to him   And, therefore, if, from the position or situation in which he was at the time of the firing, the pannel can show that it was impossible he could have killed the person whom he is charged to have shot, by describing and proving these circumstances he may have advantage from them, but cannot object to the prosecutor, that he did not minutely describe his situation, which was not known to him   and that, by the describing of which, perhaps

Information for John Porteous.

erroneously, the prosecutor might minister an unjust occasion to a criminal to escape justice.

To which it was replied for the pannel, That though it is true, that, in most cases, the describing the street where the guilt was committed would be a sufficient description, yet that, in the present case, where it was laid in the indictment, that in a crowd or multitude, various shots were fired by different hands, and thereby wounds given, it is even necessary to describe the particular place of the street where such wounds were received, in order to form a judgment from whose hands those wounds had proceeded The pannel might have fired elusory, or in the air, and the wounds received may have proceeded from the shots of others That though the pannel knows his own position and situation, and can prove them, yet such proof could not avail him, nor be received by the Court in the point of relevancy, because it would be a simple negative, which could not be admitted of, nor would not apply, unless the particular places of the street in which the wounds are said to have been received had been described to him, a situation which the pannel cannot be supposed to know; whereas the prosecutor must be supposed to have known it, seeing the same information that led him to know of the wounds received, must necessarily upon inquiry have certiorated him at what places of the street such wounds were received, seeing the matters and things laid in the indictment are charged to have been committed at high daylight, in presence of multitudes. And though the pannel is fully satisfied of the good disposition of the honourable prosecutor to lay a fair and certain indictment against every pannel, yet it must be admitted, that all indictments ought to be laid with all that accuracy and full description that the nature of the thing can admit of And, as to such part of the answer for his Majesty's Advocate, as saith, that such particular description of place, if perhaps erroneously described, might minister an unjust occasion to the pannel to escape justice, it is answered, that such erroneous description of place could in no sense affect the trial, because, though such description should not be proved, it would not vary the case, providing the act of killing were proved against the pannel, because such description of place is but a circumstance immaterial to be proven by the prosecutor, but, for the reasons above assigned, highly material for the pannel to know, in order to lay his defence before the Court

It was in the next place offered as a defence for the pannel, That the resistance of the mob was so great, and the attack of the city-guard so violent against them, in beating, bruising, and wounding the men, as has been above noticed, while they were in the lawful execution of that office, committed to them by lawful authority, that such resistance and attack must have

Captain Porteous.

justified the guard in repelling the violence of the mob, since such proceedings in the guard were acted in support of the due execution of the laws, which the mob were highly criminal in disturbing   That this argument, as pled for the pannel, was not only consonant to the rules of reason, but agreeably to sundry judgments and precedents of the Court, particularly that, in the year one thousand six hundred and ninety-two, it appears from the books of adjournal, that James Gordon, messenger, at the execution of a caption, did, with many others, his assistants, armed with guns, swords, and other hostile weapons, shoot several shots, whereby one Alexander Jack was killed dead upon the spot, amidst a numerous crowd, which the alarm of noise and tumult had drawn together, and whereof only part can be supposed to have come there with intention to resist the messenger, and the said James Gordon, and the others, his assistants, being indicted for murder, the Lords sustained this defence to him, relevant to elide the libel simply, viz   That he, in the execution of a caption, having his blazon displayed, was by force of arms hindered to enter the house of Loanmy, by the persons within that house, and that they did threaten and menace the messenger and his assistants, and that they threatened to raise the country, and that the country did accordingly rise, and beset and surround the messenger, either in the house, or without the house, the said country people being armed with guns, swords, and other invasive weapons

Here your Lordships perceive, that the Court justified the messenger in shooting amongst the mob, and killing, because the persons in the house forcibly hindered him from entering, and threatened and menaced him, being armed with invasive weapons, and the present case is more favourable in behalf of the pannel, who acted by lawful authority, as well as Gordon in the other case did, and who was supporting the execution of the laws as well as Gordon was, with this difference upon the side of the pannel, that he was not only hindered and menaced in the execution of his duty, but he and his guard invaded and assaulted, beat, bruised, and wounded, as has been above noticed, and whereof a strong proof shall be brought, and that the mob in the present case were not only armed with, but in their attack upon the guard, made use of big stones, of two or three pound weight, which must be allowed to be very invasive weapons, and therefore the pannel subsumes, that the defence offered for him in the present case is stronger, and ought rather to be allowed him, than that which was sustained to Gordon   Only the pannel must do the justice to his Majesty's Advocate as to acknowledge, that this precedent was not hitherto offered in the debate, but when the

176

Information for John Porteous.

record is inspected, will be found to stand in the precise terms as above mentioned

There was, in a former debate, a precedent of the Court offered, as against the pannel, which the pannel, with submission, apprehends makes for him, namely, Captain Wallace's case, sometime after the Revolution Captain Wallace was indicted in the one thousand six hundred and ninety-two, for having refused in the one thousand six hundred and eighty-eight, to deliver up himself, in obedience to an order of the president of the council, and several privy councillors, whereof two were officers of state, and the bailiffs of Edinburgh, having gone down to the Canongate, with a herald and pursuivant, with their coats of arms displayed, to put the order of privy council in execution, notwithstanding which, Captain Wallace would not deliver himself up, but retired with the men under his command to the Abbey, and defended himself, and fired upon the bailiffs, heralds, and pursuivants, shot several persons dead upon the spot, and wounded a great many others

The defence pled for Captain Wallace was, That the keeping of the Abbey was committed to him by order of the privy council, which he was obliged to maintain so long as the trust of it was committed to him That as to the order of privy council to deliver up his person, it was contrary to an act of parliament James the Sixth, whereby any general warrant for putting the person of any man in ward, except where such warrant was signed by four officers of state, whereof the chancellor, treasurer, or secretary of state to be one, which had not been practised in Wallace's case, was prohibited and discharged

The Lords, after a very learned debate, did sustain these defences to Captain Wallace, viz that on the Sabbath night, or shortly before, a rabble did meet in several places in great numbers, and that several of them did declare to John Paterson their resolution to trouble the pannel on his guard, and to pillage the Abbey, relevant to restrict to an arbitrary punishment

Here your Lordships perceive that the Court sustained a previous intention only declared, that they would trouble the pannel on his guard and pillage the Abbey, sufficient to moderate the punishment, so tender are the laws towards any person committing hostility in defence of his guard And then the Lords sustained the following defence relative to elide the libel altogether, to wit, that the rabble did, in a tumultuous manner, come down the Canongate with swords and fire-arms, and did beat some of the pannel's centinels, and being desired to stand, they notwithstanding advanced so near that the pannel could speak with them, and after he had desired them to remove or be

Captain Porteous.

at their hazard, they, notwithstanding thereof, still persisted to advance

The application in the present case is easy   The pannel many times exhorted the mob to stand off, notwithstanding of which they still pressed upon him, he many times advertised them of their hazard, threatened to fire upon them if they would not keep off   his centinels were not only beat, but bruised and wounded; all which is offered to be proved

Another case was mentioned in the debate to your Lordships, which strongly supported the plea of the pannel, because it was a judgment of your Lordships, pronounced but very lately after the most solemn declaration of the Court, and wherein, the pannel is informed, the Court, was unanimous, and which judgment seemed to be of that importance, as to induce the Court to reverse the proceedings of the High Court of Admiralty after a solemn trial by jury in that Court, a verdict returned, finding the libel proven and the defence not proven, and a sentence of death pronounced by the Judge of the High Court of Admiralty *

The case before the Admiralty was this   A corporal and a private centinel in Colonel Hamilton's regiment were indicted before the Admiral for murder, for that they had, upon the high seas, killed Hugh Fraser, younger of Belnain, by stabbing him with a bayonet in the breast, and afterwards throwing him into the sea, whereof he instantly died

The defence pled for the pannels was this, that the pannels were by military order appointed to attend the officers of the customs in seizing of goods by law made seizable, and that the pannels being in a boat upon the seas along with the customhouse officers in quest of such goods, the person killed did come up with them in another boat, with others in company with him, and that Fraser, the deceased, jumped into the boat where the pannels and the customhouse officers were, and endeavoured to take hold of their arms, which was both a resistance and an attack of the customhouse officers, while in the execution of their duty

Upon the other hand, it was pled against the pannels, that Fraser's jumping into the boat was with no intention to make resistance, but rather to save his own life from the thrusts of the pannels, their pieces having been aimed at him, that

---

* *Thomas Macadam and James Long*, 25th September, 1735   See Hume's *Commentaries*, 1819, 1 201-202   Extracts of the proceedings in this case before the Court of Admiralty in Scotland and the High Court of Justiciary were, on 19th April, 1737, ordered by the House of Lords to be printed, in connection with the Parliamentary enquiry regarding the Porteous affair; and these were printed accordingly by John Baskett, Printer to the King's Most Excellent Majesty (London, 1737) —Ed

Information for John Porteous.

those in the customhouse boat could have no just apprehension of being mastered by Mr Fraser, he having no invasive
weapon about him whatever, and being the only person who
offered to get into the customhouse boat, in which there
were several persons well armed

The Judge of the High Court of Admiralty admitted of the
pannels' plea, in this manner only—sustains the defence of
self-defence proponed by the pannels, that the killing of the
said Hugh Fraser by them, or either of them, was in the
necessary defence of their lives, and repelled the whole other
defences proponed for the pannels

The jury returned their verdict, finding the pannels both
guilty, art and part, of killing the said Mr Fraser, and finding
it not proven, that the killing of Mr Fraser was in the necessary
defence of the pannels' lives, upon which verdict returned,
the Judge sentenced both the pannels to be hanged

The proceedings of the Court of Admiralty were laid before
your Lordships for a review, which, it is believed, is the single
instance wherein it was ever contended, that the proceedings
of the High Court of Admiralty in matters criminal could be
reviewed by any other Court

Notwithstanding of which, your Lordships were pleased to
reverse the sentence of the Judge-Admiral, no doubt upon
supposed error in his proceedings; because the verdict of a
jury, pronounced upon evidence, cannot be reversed, and in
consequence of which judgment of your Lordships the pannels
were set at liberty

Now the pannel is advised, that such judgment in your
Lordships could stand upon no foundation other than this,
viz, that your Lordships had reversed the judgment of the
Admiral as erroneous, in not sustaining this defence to the
pannels that they were resisted by Mr Fraser deceased, while
they the pannels were in the execution of their duty

And as the degree of resistance offered by Mr Fraser to the
pannels was by the pannels themselves maintained to have
been no higher than what has been set forth to your Lordships,
the foresaid unanimous judgment of your Lordships, pronounced after many solemn deliberations, does by consequence
show, that it was your Lordships' unanimous opinion, that a
very small degree of resistance of persons in the execution
of their duty will justify the persons resisted in the act of
killing the resister

And if that was the solemn and unanimous opinion of the
Court in a case so recent, must not such judgment afford a strong
argument to the pannel, that he and his guard were resisted,
while in the undoubted execution of their duty, in being beat,
wounded, and bruised by an unruly mob, who, there was good

179

Captain Porteous.

reason to apprehend, intended to defeat the execution of the criminal?

To this last case the pannel met with no other answer from his Majesty's Advocate but this, that the pannel cannot plead the benefit of this case, because he neither does nor can aver that the firing proceeding from him or his order was necessary for securing of the execution of that trust that was committed to him. His Majesty's Advocate does admit, that where a person has by lawful authority weapons put into his hands, to be employed either in defence of his life when attacked, or in support of the execution of the laws, or of the property of the Crown, or property of the subject, such person may use those weapons, not only when his own life is so far in danger that he cannot probably escape without making use of them, but also where there is imminent danger, that he may by violence be disabled to execute his trust; but withal seems to contend, that the pannel was under none of those circumstances at the time he committed the guilt charged upon him in the indictment, for that the execution of the criminal was over before the scuffle began, or any resistance was made to the pannel and the guard under his command, and that being the case, the pannel can plead no other defence than such as might arise from his being put under the imminent danger of his life.

But with great submission, these positions of his Majesty's Advocate are assumed without any authority, and, as would appear, not only in plain opposition to the laws, but to the many precedents already offered in behalf of the pannel; for it is hoped it must be admitted, even by my Lord Advocate himself, and is indeed so admitted by him, that the pannel was once in the lawful execution of his duty, and was obliged at all hazards to support the execution of that criminal who was committed to his guard, surely then, the execution of the pannel's duty can never be said to have been at an end until once the criminal was fully executed to death, and as such, ordered to be cut down by lawful authority: unless it shall be said, that it was the pannel's duty, the moment the convict was hung up, to let him instantaneously be cut down, rescued by the mob, and brought to life again, which seems to have been their plain intention. For it seems to be confessed upon all hands, that there was danger of a rescue, which seems to have been the occasion of all this extraordinary apparatus: and for preventing of which it is admitted, that the whole guard was sent out with their pieces loaded, and even with orders to fire at all ventures in case of such rescue. Was it not then a necessary part of the pannel's duty to protect and support the execution of the convict, when hanging by the neck in the air, until such time as he was cut down by

Information for John Porteous.

lawful authority as supposed fully dead? And it is certain
that in answer to the pannel's message, orders were brought
him from the bailiffs that he should yet hang a quarter of
an hour, which surely it was the pannel's duty to see obeyed
and which orders of the bailiffs the mob nevertheless did
resist, and cut down the criminal long before that time was
elapsed, and which the pannel was in duty bound to oppose;
and from this contrast, it is offered to be proved, all the
violence in the mob proceeded   But can it be with any justice affirmed, but that the pannel was in the execution of his
duty, while he and his guard were standing upon the spot under
arms?   Is not every person in the execution of his duty while
he is either going to, or coming from any lawful expedition?
and, therefore, it seems impossible to maintain, but that the
pannel, and the detachment under his command, were in the
lawful execution of their duty, until they had once returned,
and were dispersed and dismissed from duty, at which time
only they were reduced under a private capacity

And even the protection of the hangman, who had actually
received several wounds and contusions, and was in danger
of being tore to pieces by the mob, was a part of the pannel's
duty   For though he is a minister of the law somewhat
odious, yet he is a necessary one for the society, and lies
under a greater necessity of being protected, from his being
so obnoxious to the resentment of the mob, and at least, in
humanity, must have such protection afforded him as to defend
him from having his brains knocked out

How then can it be said, in any sense, that the pannel was
in such situation that he could only plead the benefit of self-
defence?   It is a known rule in self-defence, that a person
invaded must retire as far as he can with safety   But if that
is the case of a city guard, (maintained at great expence,)
that so soon as they are invaded, they must immediately
betake themselves to their heels, it will be apparent, that they
are but kept up for very useless purposes.

At the same time the pannel can with great candour aver,
that he is far from being of that disposition of mind, as to be
ready to take the advantage which the law might afford
against an unruly, giddy mob, whereof he has given proof
upon many former occasions, as must be allowed him, and
whereof even the present case will be an instance in his
favours, if he meets with justice from the evidence   But
withal, he must be allowed to observe, that it would be a
dangerous position, that a guard kept up for the maintenance
of the peace of the capital city of this part of the nation,
when they are assembled together upon duty, should be
allowed to plead no higher privilege than that of self-defence
in the strictest sense

Captain Porteous.

And whereas my Lord Advocate seems only to admit, that a person who has weapons put in his hands by lawful authority for the defence of the property of the Crown, or liberty of the subject, may only use these weapons when he is in imminent danger of having the execution of his trust defeated by violence, if such is the case, the execution of duty will become a very ticklish point, and it is apprehended, that few folk will be fond of it if they can possibly live without it; and of consequence, such doctrine must very much discourage any persons from offering their service either to the Crown or commonwealth

And as the supreme executive power is by the constitution vested in his Sacred Majesty, our Sovereign, therefore, my Lord Advocate, who, by his office, is of counsel for his Majesty in all causes, will, no doubt, have due consideration, how far an argument is to be pressed against the pannel, which, by plain consequence, must tend to weaken, if not defeat, the execution of the laws.

One would rather be inclined to think, that, where a person has the trust of the execution of the laws committed to him, the smallest resistance to this trustee, as such, is a guilty aggression, and that every opposition of such aggression is lawful defence, because no man must be above the laws, and the life of the laws, in which the common good is employed, is of greater value than the lives of any one or number of the individuals, and so ought to be defended at all perils

His Majesty's Advocate, upon this head, in his information against the pannel, does assume this fact, that the mob, or multitude assembled at the execution, were behaving themselves peaceably, and from this seems to draw his inferences against the pannel, which, indeed will run high enough The pannel very well knows, that no order whatever will justify the person executing that order, if such order appears evidently to be unlawful and yet in cases which appear doubtful, an order from a superior will have its own weight, more especially in military matters, or such other things as resemble them

But, with submission, this reasoning upon the mob's being supposed quite peaceable and innocent is entirely out of the case For, as we are now upon relevancy, the facts must be supposed, and then the argument considered in that view, and as the pannel does aver, that he and his guard, while in the execution of their duty, did meet with strong resistance from the mob, in so much that many of the men were greatly hurt and bruised And if that was the case, it was an unlawful invasion of persons to whom the execution of the laws were committed and so might be by them in support of those laws resented to a pretty great length, except it shall be maintained, that, in the situation of the pannel and his men were

Information for John Porteous.

posted, they could plead no higher privilege than that of self-defence, which, with great respect, cannot be maintained, but rather seems to be a contradiction, because they had not only their own defence to take care of, but also the defence of the peace and quiet of this city, and of the execution of the laws, and that due obedience was given to them

In a word, upon this head, the pannel's argument is not only supported from the nature of the thing, because a man who fights with the laws upon his side, fights with great advantage against those who are fighting against the laws, and, for that reason, if a man were to fight a duel, the laws would be the best second; but also, it is believed, that no instance can be given in this country, or in any other of civilised policy and government, where a person, proceeding to what extremities whatever against persons who had assailed him, while in the due execution of the law, ever suffered the pains libelled

My Lord Advocate seems to insinuate, as if the reading of the riot act had been a duty incumbent upon the pannel, whereby the innocent part of the multitude would have had time to have taken care of their own safety, but then his Lordship will be pleased to consider, that no person is by law authorized to proclaim that act, other than a justice of the peace, sheriff, mayor, bailiff, or other head officer; and no person, under any of these characters, was left with the unfortunate pannel but he was abandoned and left to grapple with occurrences in the best manner his own discretion could suggest to him

But then the reading of that act could not answer the present exigency for, though the reading of that law may perhaps sometimes answer the end for which it was intended, namely, the preventing the demolition of any house or meeting-house, but if the pannel, in the present case, shall be supposed bound to have kept his hands across for the space of one hour after the reading of this act, then it is certain that the mob might have prevented the execution of the law in far less space And it is certain, that, by the act, the mob is not put in contempt, or exposed to the penalties of it, until once they continue together one hour after the reading thereof.

His Majesty's Advocate is also pleased to hint, as if the offering of this plea in behalf of the pannel, founded upon the resistance of the mob, was in some sort inconsistent with another to be hereafter mentioned for him, viz, his innocence of the facts But, no doubt, my Lord very well knows, that, by the laws of Scotland, there is no inconsistency in such different pleas. And this leads to the consideration of the exculpation offered for the pannel, arising from his innocence of the guilt, either of the action, command, or order, charged against him in the indictment

183

Captain Porteous.

And, in the first place, as to such part of the indictment as charges him with either having fired himself, or having given orders to fire, whereby Charles Husband was killed   Though it is indeed true, that it is impossible, from the nature of the thing, for the pannel to prove an absolute negative, because, as his Majesty's Advocate very justly argues, if the charge in the libel is proven, to wit, that the pannel either did fire, or gave orders to fire, at this time himself, no negative evidence can prevail against it, yet as to this point, the pannel offers to prove, what the lawyers call a circumstantiate negative, which in a good measure resolves into an affirmative, viz , that at this time, when Charles Husband fell, and got the wounds charged in the indictment, whereof it is supposed he died, the pannel, as has been above recited, was in the following situation . that is to say, he was pointing his piece with his face towards the West Port, threatening the mob, that if they would not keep off he would fire , and that immediately, upon this expression, a private centinel of the guard came up from behind him, and discharged his piece, by which it will be proven Charles Husband received his death wounds , because it shall be proven, by persons of undoubted veracity, that were hard by the pannel all the time, that they not only observed that he did not fire his own piece, and gave no order for firing, joined with this other circumstance, that no proof will appear, during the whole scuffle that ever the pannel made use of any firelock but his own , and that his piece, when returned to the guard, was found loaded, and in such condition, that it was even confessed by the magistrates themselves, and many others, not to have been fired . with this further addition, to exclude that further part of the charge in the indictment, of the pannel's having made use, at any time, of any other piece than his own, viz , that he carried his own piece in his hand the whole time, except during the space of prayer above mentioned, when he gave it to his serjeant   And it shall also be proved, that there was but one shot fired at this time, at which Charles Husband is supposed to have received his death wounds   And as to the other dropping shots that are charged in the indictment to have followed upon this first shot, if, from the evidence adduced, the pannel's proof shall appear to be most pregnant, that he gave no orders to fire at this time. then he is not chargeable with the consequence of such firings

And this further circumstance must strongly operate in favours of the pannel, to wit, that, at the time of this supposed orders to fire, the men were not drawn up in a regular line or band, but were either straggling, mixed with the mob, or in a circular form, surrounding the scaffold in the Grassmarket, which excludes all possibility of any supposed order to fire , unless it be supposed that the pannel was a madman, seeing

184

Information for John Porteous.

any compliance with such order must have led the men to fire each in his opposite neighbour's breast, and a great many into that of the pannel.

It is not altogether impossible that the pannel's expression of the word fire might have erroneously induced this fellow that came from behind his back (who of himself perhaps was too forward to embrace such order, had it been given) to discharge his piece and if the person firing was guilty of an error, or of a misconstruction of duty, the pannel is not chargeable therewith, seeing that every person that has the least knowledge of the exercise of arms must know, that he is not to receive an order to fire from implication, but from some known certain rule of discipline

And for this reason it is, that the pannel takes it to be a very wise part of the military institution, to avoid misconstructions, That no man receives orders to fire (especially when he is resting or shouldering his arms) but upon a precedent series of exercise, attended with some solemnity, to avoid mistakes greater or less, indeed, according to the nature of the occasion

Sometimes, indeed, as was observed in the debate on the side of his Majesty's Advocate, persons will, very justly, fire upon so short advertisement as the tuck of a drum, but it is believed that it is never practised but during the noise or tumult of battle, when it is supposed that the voice of verbal order cannot reach the men, and then this tuck of the drum, or any other signal of firing, must be previously advertised to be the signal of such action

Another thing falls also to be noticed here, touching this first charge in the indictment, and which may even be taken through the whole; that, when two or more persons are nigh together, levelling their pieces at the same time, it is not easy for the sharpest eye, especially if at any distance, to determine from what piece the fire proceeded; and of this point military men, best acquainted with the exercise of firearms, can give the best account

And lastly, upon this head, the best conjecture the pannel can make is this, that, upon this first fellow's firing, without either order or example from the pannel, his commander, the other dropping shots that ensued proceeded from other rash fellows of the guard, who, encouraged by this first example, directed and discharged their pieces against such part of the mob as they respectively supposed any injury or invasion upon them had proceeded

The next material circumstance charged in the indictment is that touching the pannel's behaviour at the West Bow, where it is charged, That he commanded the men to face about and fire upon the people; and that, at or about the same time,

Captain Porteous.

he fired a musket or firelock that was in his own hand; having either reloaded, or caused to be reloaded, his own piece, or taken another out of the hand of one of the guard, and that, upon this second example and command of the pannel's, several others of the guard under his command did fire, whereby the persons mentioned in the indictment were killed and wounded

As to which part of the charge, the pannel offers the following proof; and first, as to order, he shall prove, by multitudes of persons nigh him at the time, and who were narrowly observing him, (and orders are generally given with an audible voice,) they heard no such order given, nor heard no expression of the pannel that, by the most remote consequence, could have been interpreted an order to fire, and here the pannel's memory, upon the most serious reflection, cannot divine what could have given occasion to anybody's conjecturing that he gave an order to fire at this time   And here, also, the former observation falls to be noticed, touching the solemnity of an order for firing

2do As to the action of firing, charged against the pannel himself, for firing at this time, the pannel offers to prove the very centinel, at least that it was a centinel of the guard, who gave the first fire at this time, which was the shot at Robertson's Close head   And the pannel is informed, as has been above noticed, that, at the time of taking the precognition, an offer was made to the magistrates to single out the fellow, if they would suffer the guard to be drawn out, who fired that shot towards Robertson's Close head, by which the two or three people fell   And further, the pannel offers to prove, upon this head, not only that this fellow was the first person that fired without any order from the pannel, circumstantiated, as is above-noticed, but also by many persons of undoubted credit, that they could not observe the pannel fire, or discharge any piece himself, during the whole time that this firing is supposed to have continued   And here the pannel could evidently cast up many inconsistencies to your lordships, that must necessarily be implied, and many presumptions that strongly exclude any supposed order or example of the pannel at this time; but does not think it altogether so prudent to mention them at present

As to the taking a piece out of another man's hand, and firing of it, such action was a remarkable occurrence, and must have fallen out under observation, and so the pannel can say nothing about it, but leave it to evidence, with this only observation, that, as it was a notable event, it will operate almost as strong in the negative as in the positive.   And it must be left to the jury to balance the evidence, if a contrariety shall appear, and to lean to that side attended with the greatest credibility, taking the known rule of the law into the compass, namely,

186

Information for John Porteous.

favour to the pannel in case of dubiety   Only this observation falls to be made to your Lordships, that the circumstances of the case call aloud for the pannel's being allowed a proof upon this part of the indictment

The pannel does agree with his Majesty's Advocate, that no negative evidence can take away a positive proof, but the pannel humbly thinks he has offered a pretty circumstantiate one, and, as my Lord Advocate seems to admit the necessity of a proof on both sides, so the pannel will not labour that point with your Lordships, not doubting but you will allow him, in general, to prove what he can to exculpate him from the guilt laid in the indictment, and that your Lordships, by your interlocutor, will allow him as much scope in that particular as any precedent of your Lordship's Court can authorize. And there are several instances, and one very particular one, wherein great latitude was allowed, both as to the circumstances precedent, concomitant, and even subsequent to the acts charged in the indictment

Some general useful reflections might be made, but this paper is already drawn out into too great length, and as the pannel has learned Judges, and a discerning and candid jury, the less needs be said, because it is supposed they will naturally occur to those interested in the trial, and no doubt such will lay aside all prejudices and prepossessions, and will never once think of, but utterly despise, the consequences of popular rage, or vulgar clamour

If the pannel is guilty of the charge in the precise way and manner it is laid against him in the indictment, he is of opinion himself he deserves to suffer, but if, upon the other hand, it shall come out that he is entirely innocent of the blood of those men wherewith he is charged, he thinks his case deserves singular commiseration, because, if bonds and imprisonment, loss of employment and bread, obloquy, and reproach of blood-guilt and massacre, and, of consequence, loss of character, be calamities in human life, then he has had as great a share of them as ever attended innocence   *Sic subscribitur,*

JA GRAHAME, Jun

Captain Porteous.

CURIA JUSTICIARIÆ, S D N Regis, tenta in Prætorio Burgi de Edinburgo, decimo sexto die mensis Julii, Millesimo septingentesimo trigesimo sexto, per honorabiles viros, ANDREAM FLETCHER de Milton, Justiciarium Clericum, Dominum JACOBUM MACKENZIE de Roystoun, Magistrum DAVIDEM ERSKINE de Dun, Dominos GUALTERUM PRINGLE de Newhall, et GILBERTUM ELLIOT de Minto, Commissionarios Justiciarii dictos S D N Regis

Curia legitimè affirmata

Intran

JOHN PORTEOUS, lately one of the Captain-Lieutenants of the City Guard of Edinburgh, pannel,

INDICTED and ACCUSED as in the former sederunts

The Lord Justice-Clerk and Lords Commissioners of Justiciary, having considered the indictment pursued at the instance of Duncan Forbes, Esq his Majesty's Advocate, against John Porteous, pannel, with the foregoing debate thereupon, find, that the pannel having at any of the times and places libelled fired a gun among the people assembled at the execution libelled, or having given orders to the soldiers under his command to fire, and thereupon, they, the soldiers, or any of them, having accordingly fired, and upon the firing, either by himself or them, the persons mentioned in the indictment, or any of them, were killed or wounded, or the pannel's being art and part of any of the foresaid crimes; all *separatim* relevant to infer the pains of law, but allowed the pannel to adduce what evidence he could with respect to his behaviour, at the time of the foresaid crimes are libelled to have been committed, for taking off the circumstances which should be brought for inferring his being guilty, or art and part of the crimes libelled; and remitted the pannel and the indictment, as found relevant, to the knowledge of an assize   *Sic subscribitur*,

AND FLETCHER, I P D.

The Lord Justice-Clerk and Lords Commissioners of Justiciary continued the above diet, at the instance of his Majesty's Advocate against Captain John Porteous, till Monday next, at seven of the clock in the morning, and ordain assizers and witnesses then to attend, under the pain of law, and the pannel to be carried back to prison

Sir Walter Pringle, Lord Newhall.

From the Portrait in the Parliament House.

The Assize.

CURIA JUSTICIARLE, S D N Regis, tenta in Novo Sessionis
Domo Burgi de Edinburgo, decimo nono die mensis Julii,
Millesimo septingentesimo trigesimo sexto, per honorabiles
viros, ANDREAM FLETCHER de Milton, Justiciariium Clericum,
Dominum JACOBUM MACKENZIE de Roystoun, Magistrum
DAVIDEM ERSKINE de Dun, et Dominum GILBERTUM ELLIOT
de Minto, Commissionarios Justiciarii dict S D N
Regis

Curia legitimè affirmata

Intran

JOHN PORTEOUS, lately one of the Captain-Lieutenants of
the City Guard of Edinburgh pannel,

INDICTED and ACCUSED as in the former sederunts   Thereafter
the Lords proceeded to make choice of the following persons
to pass on the Assize of the said John Porteous

Assize.

Sir John Inglis of Cramond
Alexander Gibson of Pentland
George Halyburton of Fordell
James Baird of Chesterhall
John Hogg of Cambo
Thomas Dundas of Lethem
Alexander Bland of Blandsfield
John Jollie, vintner in Edinburgh
James Hunter, wright there
William Wight, baxter there.
John Bell, brewer there
James Davidson, bookseller there
David Inglis, merchant there.
Alexander Sharp, merchant there
Patrick Manderstoun, merchant there

The above Assize being all lawfully sworn, and no objection
of the law in the contrary;

The Pannel, JOHN PORTEOUS, judicially confessed, That, time   John P
and place libelled, the several persons mentioned in the indictment to have been killed and wounded, viz Archibald Ballantyne, son to John Ballantyne, younger, dyster in Dalkeith;
Margaret Arthur, *alias* Airth, residenter in the Canongate,
near the Watergate thereof, John Anderson, son to George
Anderson in Craighead, drover, Jean Peat, servant to James
M'Dowal, merchant in Edinburgh David Wallace, journeyman
wright in Edinburgh; James Philp, late servant to

Captain Porteous.

John Porteous Lauder, Esq , residenter in the Canongate; David Kidd, tailor in Edinburgh; Patrick Spaldan, apprentice to David Mitchell, jeweller in Edinburgh, James Lyle and Alexander Wallace, both servants to James Wright staymaker in Edinburgh, John Miller, tailor in Edinburgh, David Ogilvie, writer in Edinburgh, and James Nevin, late servant to William Sellars, writer in Edinburgh, now residenter in the Potterrow; Alexander M'Neil, son to Edward M'Neil, indweller in Mertounhall, Margaret Gordon, servant to William Ogilvie, tailor in Saint Mary Wynd in Edinburgh, and Henry Grahame, tailor in Canongate, and Charles Husband, servant to Paul Husband, confectioner in the Abbey of Holyroodhouse, were so killed or wounded by firing proceeding from the party of the city guard, then under his command, as mentioned in the indictment *Sic subscribitur*,

John Porteous.

And Fletcher, I P D.

His Majesty's Advocate, for proving his Libel, adduced the Witnesses after deponing, viz.

J. Drummond JAMES DRUMMOND, merchant and residenter in Edinburgh, aged thirty years or thereby, married, solemnly sworn, purged of malice, partial counsel, examined and interrogated, deponed, That, time and place libelled, and after Andrew Wilson had hung some time upon the gallows, about a quarter of an hour, as the deponent thinks he saw the executioner going up the ladder, as the deponent apprehended, to cut him down; upon which he saw some small stones thrown by the mob at the executioner, some whereof the deponent believes might have fallen upon the guard Upon which he saw the pannel advance from the guard westward, resting his firelock upon his thigh, as if he had been bending it, and thereafter saw him raise it to his breast, moving it from one point to another, and soon thereafter, the deponent heard a shot from the place where the pannel was standing, but did not observe whether the shot came from Captain Porteous's firelock; and, much about the same time, observed one of the soldiers go out of his rank westward, and upon the north side, and saw him go farther west than the place where Captain Porteous was . the side of the window where the deponent was standing in Robertson's house, covered the said soldier from the view of the deponent by the time the first shot was fired; and which soldier had a gun and a screwed bayonet in his hand, levelled with the butt end of it at his breast, and the deponent did apprehend at the time that Captain Porteous had fired, because he saw him in a firing posture, and immediately

Evidence for Prosecution.

heard a shot, and saw a man in a few minutes thereafter, as J. D soon as the mob dispersed, lying upon the street, upon a line whither the deponent saw Captain Porteous's piece directed; and that the above mentioned soldier came from the body of the guard which was behind Captain Porteous *Causa scientiæ patet* And this is the truth, as he shall answer to God *Sic subscribitur*,

J DRUMMOND
ANDREW FLETCHER

Sir WILLIAM FORBES, advocate, aged thirty years or thereby, W. married, solemnly sworn, purged of malice, partial counsel, examined and interrogated, deponed, That, time and place libelled, and after the deceased Andrew Wilson had hung about twenty or twenty-five minutes upon the gallows, the deponent, from a window in Orr the stabler's house, opposite, but a little to the westward of the gallows, saw the executioner go up some steps of the ladder, as the deponent believes, to cut down the said deceased, and saw thereupon stones thrown at the executioner, upon which the executioner immediately retired to the guard, and the mob continued throwing of stones, so that the deponent does believe some of the stones might have touched the guard, and, about this time, the guard were drawing together to the north and west of the gallows, where the captain was standing, and did soon thereafter see the pannel, advancing westward, fire his gun among the people assembled at the execution, and observed the fire and smoke issuing out at the muzzle of his piece, to the best of the deponent's observation, which he thought at the time very distinct, and that the said shot was the first which the deponent heard, and the deponent at the time did imagine, that the pannel had fired his shot high, but whether that proceeded from the situation his firelock was in, or from the appearance that the fire and smoke made that issued out of his piece, the deponent cannot now particularly charge his memory That thereafter the deponent heard several dropping shots about twenty, but cannot be positive as to the number That, when the foresaid facts happened, the deponent was upon the south side of the street, and the pannel to the north of the middle of the street, almost opposite to the window where the deponent was, and when the pannel so fired, the deponent did not observe any soldier so far advanced westward from the body of the guard as the pannel was *Causa scientiæ patet* And this is the truth, as he shall answer to God *Sic subscribitur*,

WILLIAM FORBES
ANDREW FLETCHER

Captain Porteous.

W. Fraser   Mr WILLIAM FRASER, son to the Lord Saltoun, aged twenty-four years or thereby, unmarried, solemnly sworn, purged of malice, partial counsel, examined and interrogated, deponed, That he was in a window in one Orr's house in the Grassmarket, the south side of the street, that day that Andrew Wilson was executed That, after Wilson had hung some time on the gallows, he saw the executioner go up some steps of the ladder, as he apprehended, to cut him down and then saw the mob throw stones and dirt at him; upon which the hangman came down, and went in among the soldiers that were standing at the foot of the scaffold. That soon after the hangman had come down, he saw the pannel present and level his gun, moving the muzzle to and fro, and then saw him fire, and to the best of his knowledge and apprehension, saw the smoke issue out of the mouth of the piece, that immediately thereafter within a second or two, he heard several dropping shots fired by the soldiers, who were there on their arms. That he thinks the dropping shots he then heard came from near the place where the pannel was standing And deponed, That at the time foresaid the pannel fired his gun, he did not observe any of the soldiers advance before him and present their guns   *Causa scientiæ patet*   And this is the truth, as he shall answer to God   *Sic subscribitur,*

WILL. FRASER

JA. MACKENZIE

W. Urquhart   Mr WILLIAM URQUHART of Meldrum, aged thirty-eight years or thereby, married, solemnly sworn, purged of malice, partial counsel, examined and interrogated, deponed, That he was present at Andrew Wilson's execution the time libelled, in the house of one Orr, on the south side of the street, in company with Sir William Forbes and Mr Fraser, the preceding witnesses That after Wilson had hung some time, he saw the executioner go up some steps of the ladder, in order to cut him down, as he apprehended, and saw the mob throw several stones at him, upon which he came down; therefore the mob continued to throw stones, some of which fell amongst the guard, whereupon he heard several dropping shots fired by the soldiers That he saw the pannel present his piece, immediately heard a shot, which he apprehended was shot by the pannel, but did not observe it so narrowly as to see the smoke or fire issue out of his piece   *Causa scientiæ patet*   And this is the truth, as he shall answer to God   *Sic subscribitur,*

WILLIAM URQUHART.

JA MACKENZIE

Evidence for Prosecution.

JAMES DEWAR of Vogrie, aged sixty-four years or thereby, James Dewar married, solemnly sworn, purged of malice, partial counsel, examined and interrogated, deponed, That, time and place libelled, at Andrew Wilson's execution, he was in a window in his own house at the foot of the West Bow, in the east side of the way That he saw the hangman go up some steps of the ladder, after Wilson had hung some time, and saw the mob throw some stones, one of which hurt the executioner on the face, upon which he came down the ladder, whereupon he saw the pannel present his piece, and fire, which was the first shot he heard or saw, That when he saw the pannel fire, his side was to the deponent, and that the pannel was then standing on the east side of the gibbet, and that he fired his piece to the west And deponed, he saw the fire of the powder from the pan, and heard the report of the shot Depones, That when the pannel fired as aforesaid, he was standing on the south-east side of the scaffold Deponed, That Wilson was cut down, not by the hangman, but by some that were standing at the foot of the gallows, and that Wilson was cut down before he heard any shots Deponed, That he stood at his own window before Wilson was thrown over, and continued looking at the place of execution till he was cut down, and heard the shots as before mentioned And being interrogated, what kind of clothes Captain Porteous had then on? declares, He cannot be positive, but believes they were red clothes, but is positive that he knew Captain Porteous's face when he saw him fire *Causa scientiæ patet* And this is the truth, as he shall answer to God *Sic subscribitur,*

JAMES DEWAR
JA MACKENZIE

GEORGE DRUMMOND, Esq one of the Commissioners of the G Drummond Customs, aged   years or thereby, married, solemnly sworn, purged of malice, partial counsel, examined and interrogated, deponed, That, at the time and place libelled, the deponent was in the house of Bailie Halyburton, on the right hand, on the north side of the corner of the Strait Bow, the third story, at the time of the execution of Andrew Wilson, and from a window of said house, after the criminal was thrown over, and had hung for fifteen or sixteen minutes, the executioner was about going up the ladder; and after he went up two or three steps, he observed several stones thrown at him, which made him return, and while he was on the ground, he observed his nose bleeding and at this time he observed one or two persons, or more, standing at the foot of the gallows, one of whom stretching up his arm with a knife, he observed cut the rope; the executioner having mixed with the soldiers,

Captain Porteous.

G. Drummond he did observe the throwing of stones to continue, and some of them fell among the soldiers. Deponed, That immediately thereafter, he observed one of the soldiers advance a little before Mr Porteous to the westward, with a gun in his hand, which he presented, and immediately thereupon, the deponent heard a shot, which he imagined to be from that soldier, but did not observe fire or smoke, though at the time he concluded it was from that soldier's gun, and is positive that that was the first shot that was fired, and the deponent did not think that the stones that were thrown did give any just cause for the firing Deponed, That about the time when he observed the soldier present his gun, as said is, he also observed the pannel holding his gun in his hand in a level, but is not sure of his putting the butt of it to his shoulder Deponed, That after the said first shot, within a minute he heard another, and so it continued till about the number of eighteen or twenty, and this was at the time of the firing observed by the deponent, but within some minutes thereafter, there was a second firing, which he did hear, and upon hearing, came to the window, and observed some lime fallen from an opposite house, which he judged to have been occasioned by the bullets and as to the eighteen or twenty dropping shots, in the first firing, were from the soldiers immediately behind the pannel, betwixt whom and them he observed no person interposed, and he observed, the time of the first shot, the pannel's face was looking westward, as was all the soldiers behind him Deponed, That the soldiers at that time who fired were, to the deponent's best remembrance, to the northward of the scaffold, and the pannel was then, to the best of his remembrance, either upon a line to the gibbet, or a little westward of it Further deponed, That the soldier who first fired, as said is, advanced from behind the pannel, and passed, upon his right hand, to the northward of him *Causa scientiæ patet* And this is the truth, as he shall answer to God. *Sic subscribitur* 1736,

G Drummond
Da Erskine

W. Johnston WILLIAM JOHNSTON, druggist in Edinburgh, aged forty years or thereby, married, solemnly sworn, purged of malice partial counsel, examined and interrogated, deponed, Time and place libelled, he, the deponent, being present at the execution of Andrew Wilson, he did observe the pannel take a gun out of a soldier's hand, at which time he was standing betwixt the Cornmarket and one Tod's shop, which is under Bailie Halyburton's house, thereupon he observed the pannel advance some steps westward, and did see him present and level his gun, that is to say, hold it out and fire amongst the multitude, and did observe the smoke come out of the gun And deponed

194

Evidence for Prosecution.

That this was the first shot he heard, which shot immediately **W Johnston** followed after the criminal was cut down by a hand standing at the foot of the gibbet, and the deponent at the time was standing in a window in the house of one Gairdner, horse-farrier, by the Meuse Well, and when the pannel was taking the gun out of the soldier's hand, he appeared to be in passion, and it was some short time before he was master of the gun Deponed, That, to the best of his remembrance, the pannel was clothed in red, but he being well acquainted with the pannel's face, he is positive that he was the person that took the gun and fired as aforesaid. And deponed, That he believes there was about thirty yards distance betwixt the window where the deponent was and the pannel at the first firing *Causa scientiæ patet.* And this is the truth, as he shall answer to God *Sic subscribitur,*

Wᴍ Johnston
Dᴀ Erskine.

Mᴀʀᴋ Sᴘʀᴏᴛ, skinner, and one of the constables of Edinburgh, **Mark Sprot** aged twenty-eight years or thereby, married, solemnly sworn, purged of malice, partial counsel, examined and interrogated, deponed, That, time and place libelled, as he stood on William Orr stabler's window, south side of the Grassmarket, he saw Wilson, the criminal, cut down from the gibbet, upon which occasion he did not observe that there was any greater disturbance than usual at executions That a very little while after the criminal was so cut down, he observed the pannel advance before the soldier, and upon the north side of the scaffold, over against the gibbet, he saw him fire his piece towards the west, and the smoke issue out of the mouth of his gun This, he says, was the first shot that was fired, but immediately on the back of that, a tall man with his own hair, about the third behind the pannel, as he thinks, fired off his piece like-wise towards the west, but up in the air over the heads of the multitude That very soon after, several other dropping shots followed, after which, when the people fell back and opened, he observed a young man lying on the ground as dead, directly opposite to the place where the pannel fired. *Causa scientiæ patet* And this is the truth, as he shall answer to God *Sic subscribitur,*

Mᴀʀᴋ Sᴘʀᴏᴛ
Gɪʟʙ Elliot

Geᴏʀɢe Cᴀᴍᴘʙeʟʟ, wright in Edinburgh, aged twenty-eight **G. Campbell** years or thereby, married, solemnly sworn, purged of malice, partial counsel, examined and interrogated deponed, That, time and place libelled, the deponent stood in the window of Mr Carmichael's house, in the south side of the Grassmarket,

Captain Porteous.

G. Campbell directly opposite to the gibbet That a very little after Wilson was cut down, he observed the pannel, with four or five of his men about him, and that, as he pointed his piece to and fro towards the multitude, he observed him receive a stroke by a stone thrown from behind the scaffold, off which it rebounded, and struck him, upon which he immediately fired his piece, but whether this was the first shot or not, the deponent cannot tell, for there were three or four fired much about the same time, but that the pannel fired he is sure, for he saw fire and smoke issue from his piece That upon these shots already mentioned, he saw a man fall down upon his back on the street That after this, he saw the pannel raise his musket, and put his hand to his cartridge box as if he intended to load again; but does not know what followed upon this because he immediately lost sight of him Deponed, That when the pannel fired his piece as above, he was standing towards the south-east corner of the scaffold, and pointed his piece towards the south-west That the pannel's fire, with the shots that went off at the same time, were the first that were made on that occasion *Causa scientiæ patet* And this is the truth, as he shall answer to God *Sic subscribitur,*

> GEO CAMPBELL
> GILB ELLIOT.

James Bald JAMES BALD, merchant in Edinburgh, aged thirty-two years or thereby, widower, solemnly sworn, purged of malice, partial counsel, examined and interrogated deponed, That, time and place libelled, the deponent stood in the same window with the immediately preceding witness, or at least in a window in the same room · That a little after Wilson was cut down from the gibbet, he saw the pannel advance a little westward from the Cornmarket, towards the south side of the gibbet, and fire off his piece westward, toward the Meuse Well That at this time he saw none of the soldiers near him, nor observed any other fire but his, and before there was any more firing, when the multitude fell back, he saw a man lying dead, towards the place that the pannel pointed his piece That he is sure the Captain fired, since he saw the fire and smoke issue from his piece *Causa scientiæ patet* And this is the truth, as he shall answer to God *Sic subscribitur,*

> JAMES BALD
> GILD ELLIOT.

Andrew Daw ANDREW DAW, servant to James Montgomery, brewer in Potterrow, aged twenty-two years or thereby, married, solemnly sworn, purged of malice, partial counsel, examined and interrogated, deponed, That, time and place libelled, the deponent was standing at the foot of Robertson the stabler's

196

Evidence for Prosecution.

close, when Wilson was cut down from the gibbet; immediately **Andrew Daw**
after which, the pannel, who was standing in the middle of the
street, between the deponent and the Cornmarket, fired his
piece toward the place where the deponent was standing, upon
which a baxter in the Abbey, called Charles Husband, dropt
just by the deponent, and his deponent's coat was torn in
the shoulder with the same shot· That he heard the report
of the Captain's piece, though he neither saw the fire nor the
smoke, yet he is sure the pannel fired, because he saw no
other piece presented at the same time That the pannel when
he fired as above, was as near to the deponent as the end
of the table, where he now stands, is to the west end of this
room Deponed, That the shot mentioned to be made by the
pannel was the first he heard that day Deponed, That during
the whole time of the execution he never came nearer the
scaffold than Robertson's Close-foot, (by Robertson's Close-foot
is meant the end nearest the Grassmarket) *Causa scientiæ
patet* And this is the truth, as he should answer to God And
declared he cannot write *Sic subscribitur,*

GILB ELLIOT

WALTER SHEARGOLD, indweller in Edinburgh, aged twenty- **W. Sheargold**
eight years or thereby, married, solemnly sworn, purged of
malice, partial counsel, examined and interrogated, deponed,
That he was present the time and place libelled , and after
the criminal Wilson was cut down, he saw Captain Porteous
fire his gun, holding the same straight out at the multitude ,
and that the deponent was then within three yards of the
Captain, when he saw him fire, and that after he had fired,
he heard him call fire , then heard some shots, but does not
know from what hands they came, for he immediately retired
to the Lawnmarket Deponed, That when the pannel fired,
his left hand was towards the scaffold, and he fired towards
the West Port Deponed, That the scaffold was nearer to the
West Port than the pannel was when he fired, that is, the pannel
was nearer to the Cornmarket Deponed, That this shot
by the pannel was the first that he heard at that time, and
that he was present all the time of the execution That he
was so near as to see the fire and the colsin fly out of the
pannel's gun *Causa scientiæ patet* And this is the truth,
as he should answer to God *Sic subscribitur ,*

WALTER SHEARGOLD
WA. PRINGLE.

JOHN RITCHIE, servant to Mr. Archibald Murray, advocate, **John Ritchie**
aged seventeen years or thereby, unmarried, solemnly sworn,
purged of malice, partial counsel, examined and interrogated,
deponed, That, the time and place libelled, the deponent was

197

Captain Porteous.

John Ritchie present at the execution of Andrew Wilson, and after the criminal was cut down, he saw and heard about three shots fired, and then he heard a fourth shot, which was by Captain Porteous, and that he saw a man fall down, but the deponent imagined it was from the pressure of the crowd That there was very short time betwixt the shots, but that which was by Captain Porteous was the last in order That after the criminal was cut down, the guard drew towards the north side of the scaffold That the deponent was standing within two or three yards of the foot of Robertson's Close, when he saw and heard the firing Deponed, He heard the pannel mention the word fire, before the firing Deponed, That the pannel was, to the best of the deponent's remembrance, standing as far west as the gallows, but he cannot be very positive the mob and crowd was such, that he could not very distinctly discern Deponed, That the shots mentioned by the deponent, first three, and then a fourth, was the first he heard that time *Causa scientiæ patet* And this is the truth, as he should answer to God *Sic subscribitur,*

JOHN RITCHIE
WA. PRINGLE

Thomas Crookshanks THOMAS CROOKSHANKS, servant to Thomas Trotter, brewer in Edinburgh, aged twenty-two years or thereby, unmarried solemnly sworn, purged of malice partial counsel examined and interrogated, deponed, That, the time and place libelled, the deponent being upon the causeway on the south side of the scaffold, saw the pannel, who was then standing upon the north side of the scaffold, fire the gun that was in his hand upon the multitude, the point of the piece being directed westward, and saw the fire and smoke issue out of the muzzle of the gun that was in the pannel's hand And further, deponed, That the pannel was standing at the north side of the scaffold, and at that end of it which is next the Bow *Causa scientiæ patet* And this is the truth, as he should answer to God *Sic subscribitur,* THOMAS CROOKSHANKS And being further interrogate, If the said shot that the pannel fired was the first shot? deponed, That it was the first shot, but that several other shots followed immediately thereafter And this is likewise the truth, as he shall answer to God *Sic subscribitur,*

THOMAS CROOKSHANKS
ANDR FLETCHER

James Neilson JAMES NEILSON, gardener in the Bull Close of Edinburgh, aged thirty-one years or thereby, married, solemnly sworn, purged of malice, partial counsel, examined and interrogated, deponed, Time and place libelled, the deponent being standing

198

Evidence for Prosecution.

within the foot of a turnpike near the Meuse Well, saw the pannel, who was then standing upon the north side of the scaffold, a little to the eastward, where the gallows was, and saw the pannel advance, westwards, towards the multitude, with his firelock in his hand, moving it to and again, as if he had been beating back the people, and at the third or fourth motion, saw the pannel fire the piece that was in his hand upon the multitude, pointing it westward, and saw the smoke issue out at the muzzle of the said piece. That this was the first shot which the deponent heard, which was soon followed by others, for the deponent observed the pannel, after he had fired his piece, retire some yards to the soldiers, and saw five or six of these soldiers advance and fire upon the multitude, and soon thereafter, when the multitude were beat off, the deponent saw a boy with black hair lying within ten yards of the turnpike where the deponent was standing, and saw four other persons lying at different places upon the street, and saw the first mentioned boy bleeding at the ear *Causa scientiæ patet* And this is the truth, as he should answer to God *Sic subscribitur*,

JAMES NEILSON
ANDR FLETCHER

WILLIAM GORDON, baxter, and servant in the common bake house in Hastie's Close in Edinburgh, aged twenty-one years or thereby, unmarried, solemnly sworn, purged of malice, partial counsel, examined and interrogated, deponed, That, the time and place libelled, the deponent being at the head of the turnpike at the back of the Meuse Well, did from thence see Captain Porteous, pannel, who was then upon the north-west corner of the gibbet, wave his firelock to and again, and thereafter saw the said firelock while in his hand go off, and saw the fire and smoke go out at the muzzle of it, and this was the first shot which the deponent heard that day, but heard several shots thereafter, and that the shot which the pannel fired was soon after the deceased Andrew Wilson was cut down *Causa scientiæ patet* And this is the truth, as he should answer to God *Sic subscribitur*,

WILLIAM GORDON
ANDR FLETCHER

JAMES NASMITH, servant to Colin Ahson, wright in Edinburgh, aged twenty-six years or thereby, married, solemnly sworn, purged of malice, partial counsel, examined and interrogated, deponed, That, time and place libelled, and soon after the deceased Andrew Wilson was cut down from the gibbet, the deponent being upon the causeway of the north-

Captain Porteous.

J. Nasmith east end of the scaffold, beginning to take down the scaffold, and did then hear the pannel, who was towards the north end of the scaffold, say several times to the soldiers under his command, Fire, and be damned! and at the same time saw the pannel advancing westward, with his piece presented in his hand, and immediately after hearing the foresaid words, he heard several shots go off, and when the foresaid words were spoken by the pannel, he was passing by the deponent westward about a yard or two distant from him *Causa scientiæ patet* And this is the truth, as he should answer to God *Sic subscribitur,*

JAMES NASMITH
ANDR FLETCHER

David Brown DAVID BROWN, servant to Colin Alison, wright in Edinburgh, aged twenty-eight years or thereby, unmarried, solemnly sworn, purged of malice, partial counsel, examined and interrogated, deponed, That time and place libelled, and after the deceased Andrew Wilson was cut down from the gibbet, the deponent being standing at the east end of the scaffold, assisting to pull it down, and then saw the pannel, going along the north side of the scaffold westward, and heard him give orders to the soldiers under his command to fire, but does not remember the particular expression, and immediately upon the orders being given as aforesaid, he heard several shots, and when the deponent heard the pannel give the foresaid orders, he was about the distance of the breadth of the scaffold from him *Causa scientiæ patet* And this is the truth, as he should answer to God. *Sic subscribitur,*

DAVID BROWN.
ANDR FLETCHER

M Kidd MATTHEW KIDD, servant to Thomas Miln, deacon of the masons in Edinburgh, aged thirty-three years or thereby, married, solemnly sworn, purged of malice, and partial counsel, examined and interrogated, deponed, Time and place libelled, and soon after the deceased Andrew Wilson was cut down from the gibbet, the deponent being standing upon the plainstones near Captain Todd's shop, he saw the pannel going from the well at the Bow-foot westward, and saw him fire the gun that was in his hand, and thereafter give orders to the soldiers under his command to fire; thereafter heard him call to the said soldiers to level their pieces, and saw the said soldiers fire; and that the shot fired by the pannel as aforesaid, was either the first or second shot, which shot he fired standing to the north-east of the scaffold, half way betwixt that and the Bow-foot Well, and that when the pannel

200

Evidence for Prosecution.

ordered the soldiers to level their pieces, he was some yards ^{M.} nearer the foot of the Bow *Causa scientiæ patet* And this is the truth, as he should answer to God *Sic subscribitur,*

> MATTHEW KIDD
> ANDR FLETCHER

JAMES MAXWELL, servant to Colin Alison, wright in Edin- ^{J.} burgh, aged thirty-two years or thereby, married, solemnly sworn, purged of malice, partial counsel, examined and interrogated, deponed, That, the time and place libelled, after Wilson was cut down and put in his coffin, there were some stones thrown by the mob amongst the guard, upon which he heard the pannel order the soldiers to turn in; and immediately heard him give the soldiers orders to fire, and be damned, and then saw him advance two or three paces, and saw his gun cocked, and his thumb upon the doghead, and saw him fire the gun, and immediately before he heard any other shot, he saw a boy fall near a coppersmith's shop, to the northwest of the place from which the pannel fired his gun There were six or seven shot after the orders were given, and then he saw three men and a woman fall, one of which had a wound in his forehead, and another in the side of his head: That after the soldiers fired as aforesaid, he heard the pannel say to one of the soldiers, that, if he did not fire, he would take his piece from him Deponed, That he the deponent was then standing on the south side of the scaffold helping to pull it down, when he heard and saw what is above deponed upon, and that the pannel was upon the north side of the scaffold about ten yards from it, over against the middle of the scaffold, and deponed, That the pannel's shot at that time was the first he heard then shot Deponed, That he was present at the time, from Wilson's coming down to his execution, till after he was cut down and carried away, during which time he heard no shot fired, until that fired by the pannel *Causa scientiæ patet* And this is the truth, as he should answer to God. *Sic subscribitur,*

> JAMES MAXWELL.
> JA. MACKENZIE

WILLIAM DOUGLAS, one of the soldiers in the City Guard, Edin- ^W burgh, aged forty-seven years or thereby, married, solemnly sworn, purged of malice, partial counsel, examined and interrogated, deponed, That, the time and place libelled, as the executioner was going up the ladder to cut down Wilson, there were several stones thrown at him, which obliged him to come down the ladder, at the same time, there were several stones thrown amongst the guard, before Wilson was cut down, at

Captain Porteous.

W. Douglas which time he heard the pannel say to the soldiers, be damned to you, bougars, fire, after which he heard several shots fired by the men, but knows nothing of the pannel's having fired, and that these were the first shots he heard fired that day, to the best of his knowledge   Deponed, That the pannel, when he uttered the words before mentioned, was standing at the south side of the gallows   Deponed, That the first shots were fired before Wilson was cut down, and likewise some of them thereafter   *Causa scientiæ patet*   And this is the truth, as he should answer to God, and declares he cannot write   *Sic subscribitur,*

JA MACKENZIE

A. Yetts   ARCHIBALD YETTS, litster in the Abbey of Holyroodhouse, aged forty-eight years or thereby, married, solemnly sworn, purged of malice, partial counsel, examined and interrogated, deponed, That, the time and place libelled, a little after Wilson was cut down from the gallows, he saw the pannel fire his piece among the multitude, and immediately heard him say to his men, level your pieces, and fire, and be dam'd ! whereupon there were a great many shots fired by them, and saw the pannel take a gun from one of the men, which he the pannel fired   Deponed, That he the deponent was within six yards of the pannel when he fired, and spoke the words before mentioned   Deponed, That at the time when the pannel took the gun from the soldier, he laid his own upon the scaffold, and that there were some persons, but very few, then standing upon the scaffold.   Deponed, That betwixt the time that the pannel fired his own piece, and his taking the gun from the soldier, as aforesaid, it might be about eight or nine minutes   And deponed, That at the time he fired the second gun, there were several other guns fired at the same time   Depones, That there was no shot fired before the first fired by the pannel, and that the second shot fired by the pannel was near the same place where he fired the first ; and that he had not moved above six or seven yards betwixt the first firing and the second, and that some of the soldiers followed the pannel in that space, and returned with him again to the place where he fired first   *Causa scientiæ patet*   And this is the truth, as he shall answer to God   *Sic subscribitur,*

ARCHIBALD YETTS
JA MACKENZIE

W Murray   WILLIAM MURRAY, barrowman and indweller in Edinburgh, aged twenty-seven years or thereby, married, solemnly sworn, purged of malice, partial counsel, examined and interrogated, deponed, Time and place libelled, the deponent being present at the execution of Andrew Wilson, he did observe two of the

Evidence for Prosecution.

soldiers, under the pannel s command, fire their guns, but their w. Murray guns were fired up in the air, thereafter he observed the pannel fire his gun amongst the multitude, whereupon he observed a boy drop down, and did hear the pannel call out to the soldiers, damn them for bougars, why did they not fire even forward and clean the street? At which time the deponent was standing about the south pillar of the Cornmarket, about twenty yards distance from the pannel, as he apprehends Further deponed, That after the said first firing, he observed the pannel take a gun out of a soldier's hand, and fire again, directing it towards a man he was pursuing, which he did thirty or forty yards, and upon firing, he observed the person so pursued fall down And being interrogated, How long his present dulness of hearing remained with him? deponed, He has been as dull of hearing these seven years past Deponed, That the two shots from the two soldiers were the first firing he heard upon that occasion *Causa scientiæ patet* And this is the truth, as he shall answer to God *Sic subscribitur*

> WILLIAM MURRAY
> DA ERSKINE

JAMES NICOLL, watchmaker in Canongate, aged thirty-six James Nicoll years or thereby, married, solemnly sworn, purged of malice, partial counsel, examined and interrogated, deponed, That he was present, time and place libelled, at the execution of Andrew Wilson, and then he did observe the pannel fire his gun, holding it out straight before him, amongst the multitude there assembled, and as he heard the report of the gun, so he observed the smoke of the powder coming from the gun, and this shot was the first he heard upon that occasion, and the pannel, when he thus fired, was standing betwixt the gibbet and one Mr Cunningham's shop, on the north side of the street, near the north-east end of the scaffold *Causa scientiæ patet* And this is the truth, as he shall answer to God *Sic subscribitur*,

> JAMES NICOLL
> DA ERSKINE

WILLIAM JAMESON, merchant in Edinburgh, aged twenty-four w. Jameson years, married, solemnly sworn, purged of malice, partial counsel, examined and interrogated, deponed, That he was present, time and place libelled, at the execution of Andrew Wilson, and about the time when they were cutting down the criminal, the deponent then standing within three or four yards of the pannel, did hear him give orders to the soldiers that were behind him to fire, and immediately thereafter he did hear the pannel fire the gun that was in his own hand, and upon his firing, observed the smoke of the powder come

Captain Porteous.

W. Jameson from it, thereafter he observed the pannel take a gun from one of the soldiers, but what use he made thereof, he knows not, and it was very short time betwixt the pannel's firing and his taking the gun from the soldier, as also a very short distance betwixt the place where he fired, and where he took the said gun, the place of his firing, to the deponent's memory, being near to Robertson's Close-head, and where he took the gun, was a very little way up the street from it; and the shot he heard from the pannel s gun was the first he heard that day. *Causa scientiæ patet* And this is the truth, as he shall answer to God *Sic subscribitur*,

WILLIAM JAMESON
DA ERSKINE

John Moffat JOHN MOFFAT, baxter, and servant in the common bakehouse in Hastie's Close in Edinburgh, aged twenty-six years or thereby, married, solemnly sworn, purged of malice, partial counsel, examined and interrogated, deponed, That, at the time and place libelled, the deponent was standing in Mr Orr's door, on the south side of the Grassmarket, and some short time after Wilson was cut down, he saw the pannel take a gun out of one of the soldiers hand, before Mr Todd's shop-door, which he immediately fired off towards the north-west, a little before which, the deponent saw him fire his own gun from the same place; That upon the captain's firing, the deponent saw some of the soldiers, who stood behind the Corn-market, fire their guns up in the air *Causa scientiæ patet* And this is the truth, as he shall answer to God *Sic subscribitur*,

JOHN MOFFAT
GILB ELLIOT

John Stewart JOHN STEWART, merchant in Edinburgh, aged thirty years or thereby, unmarried, solemnly sworn, purged of malice, partial counsel, examined and interrogated, deponed, That, at the time and place libelled, the deponent was standing in a window of Wine Garden's house, on the south side of the scaffold That some short time before Wilson was cut down, upon some stones being thrown at the hangman, he observed the pannel jump down from the south side of the scaffold, and walk up briskly towards the place where the disturbance was, but nothing in his hand but a cane, immediately after this, Wilson was cut down, upon which the guard that attended the execution began to march up the Bow, and that, at the north-west corner of the gallows, he observed the pannel take a gun out of a soldier's hand, with which he pushed back the multitude; and that, when the pannel came the length of the Bow-foot, being upon the rear of his men, he saw him receive a stroke

204

Evidence for Defence.

with a stone, upon which he suddenly turned about, and waved ^{John} his piece to and again towards the multitude, but without firing, but a very little after that, he turned about all at once, and stepped some steps forward, and fired off his piece towards the crowd westward, That this was the first shot which the deponent either heard or saw made that day *Causa scientiæ patet* And this is the truth, as he should answer to God *Sic subscribitur*,

JOHN STEWART
GILB ELLIOT

JOHN GIBB, cowfeeder in Canongate, aged forty-four years ^{John} or thereby, married, solemnly sworn, purged of malice partial counsel, examined and interrogated, deponed, That, time and place libelled, he was standing at Mr Robertson's Close-head, in the Grassmarket That a very little after the hangman had been on the ladder, as he thought to cut down Wilson, he observed the pannel with his gun in his hand, advance towards the crowd, where the disturbance was, and present his piece three times, the last of which times. the deponent thought he fired her off, for he saw the priming burn in the pan, but could not see the fiery smoke at the muzzle, because of the crowd. neither could he with certainty distinguish the report, because several other pieces were fired off at the same time That upon these pieces being so fired, he saw one Mr. Niel drop down at the Meuse Well: That before the firing above mentioned, he neither heard nor saw a shot made that day *Causa scientiæ patet* And this is the truth, as he should answer to God *Sic subscribitur,*

JOHN GIBB.
GILB ELLIOT

Follow the Witnesses adduced for the Pannel

GEORGE SMEITON, writer in Edinburgh, aged thirty years or ^{Geo.} thereby, married, solemnly sworn, purged of malice partial counsel, examined and interrogated, deponed, That, time and place libelled, he was present at the execution of Wilson. That when the executioner was doing his duty, he saw Captain Porteous come off the scaffold. because the mob was crowding upon the guard, and while the pannel was endeavouring to keep off the mob, he saw a man with a silk napkin about his neck press upon the pannel, and seem to endeavour to grasp at, but that a young gentleman there, in green clothes, kept him off; and then the pannel returned to the scaffold, but about the time the criminal was cutting down, or to be cut down, the pannel went off the scaffold again, and about that time

205

Captain Porteous.

Geo. Smeiton there were stones thrown by the mob at the hangman and the guard, and some of them fell amongst the guard That, so far as the deponent could observe, being upon a baitizan, upon the south side of the scaffold, five story high, the stones seemed to be pretty large, but the deponent cannot tell the dimensions; and then he soon observed a shot, which was the first that he observed, and came from one of the soldiers, and this shot was after the criminal was cut down, and after this shot, in a very little followed three or four other shots, and at this time the pannel had his piece presented towards the multitude, and that he saw the flash of the pan of the soldier's gun that fired the first shot Deponed, That the pannel was pretty near the soldier that fired the first gun *Causa scientiæ patet* And this is the truth, as he should answer to God *Sic subscribitur*,

GEO SMEITON
WA PRINGLE

T. Harton THOMAS HARTON, doctor in the regiment of Welsh Fusiliers, in the Canongate, aged thirty-nine years or thereby, unmarried, solemnly sworn, purged of malice, partial counsel, examined and interrogated deponed, Time and place libelled, he was present at the execution of Wilson, when he saw several stones thrown by the mob at the guard, of such bigness that was sufficient to have killed them, in case they had hit them in a proper place, which continued some little time Deponed, That while the criminal was hanging upon the gallows, the deponent saw a man press towards the pannel, and being come near him, he held up his hand to him in a threatening manner, but the deponent did not hear what words he uttered Deponed, That when the pannel was upon the scaffold, he had no gun in his hand; but when he came off again, he took a gun from a soldier Deponed, That when the pannel came off the scaffold, he went about to the west side and turned about towards the north, endeavouring to get his men together, which he could not well do, they being so much interspersed with the mob and they continuing still to throw the stones, the pannel turned about with his face towards the west; and having his fusee in such a manner in his hand, as if he had not designed to fire, but waving it from side to side, rather seeming to intimidate them and at this time there was a soldier came upon his right hand, and fired close by the pannel, and this was the first shot the deponent observed : and deponed, That he had his eyes fixed upon the pannel all this time. Deponed, He did not see the pannel fire; and he is very well assured, that he did not fire at that time Deponed, That this shot was immediately after the criminal was cut down. Deponed, That after this, the pannel endeavoured to carry

206

Evidence for Defence.

off his men   Deponed, That the soldier that came up by the ^{T. Harton} pannel's right side, came up from behind him   *Causa scientiæ patet.*   And this is the truth, as he should answer to God   *Sic subscribitur,*

Tho Harton
Wa Pringle

David Rannie, merchant in Edinburgh, aged forty years or ^{David Rannie} thereby, married, solemnly sworn, purged of malice, partial counsel, examined and interrogated, deponed, That after the first firings were over, the deponent, from his own window in the land above Bailie Dewar's, at the foot of the Bow, saw the pannel draw off his men, and marching up the Bow, halt at Bailie Crocket's shop, at which time the deponent heard some soldiers fire, which the deponent apprehended was in the rear. the deponent looking upwards, and they that fired not being under his eye   *Causa scientiæ patet*   And this is the truth, as he should answer to God   *Sic subscribitur,*

David Rannie
Andr Fletcher.

John Clark, serjeant in the regiment of Welsh Fusiliers, ^{John Clark} aged thirty-three years or thereby, unmarried, solemnly sworn, purged of malice, partial counsel, examined and interrogated, deponed, That, the time libelled, the deponent was sent by the Captain who commanded the detachment of the King's forces in the Lawnmarket to the place of execution to get orders from the Magistrates or the pannel, and having gone up to the scaffold, and while the deponent was conversing with the pannel, he saw a stone thrown at the executioner, which cut him in the nose so that he bled, and about the same time there was a stone about the bigness of the deponent's two fists, hit the calf of the deponent's leg, upon which the deponent with the pannel came down from the scaffold, and thereafter saw the pannel moving his fusee in order to keep off the crowd, who had by that time pressed upon the guard, and drove them about four or five yards from the place where they were posted at first, and thereafter the deponent saw Captain Porteous endeavouring to keep off the mob with his fusee, waving it to and again, telling them to keep off, or he would fire, but that there was no fire at that time, and the deponent then walking towards the West Bow, saw four or five of the soldiers presenting their pieces, and saw one of them advance to the right where the deponent was standing, and fire upon the crowd; which was the first shot the deponent heard; at which time the deponent saw the pannel upon his left hand, about seven yards from him: and then the deponent saw two other of the soldiers come up betwixt the pannel and

Captain Porteous.

John Clark the deponent, and fire in the air, and thereafter heard four or five more shots, which the deponent thinks were fired betwixt the place where the deponent was standing and the pannel, and the deponent during that time had his eye fixed upon those who fired, and did not observe Captain Porteous fire or give orders to fire; and upon the first shot as aforesaid, the deponent observed a man drop at the entry of Robertson's Close. *Causa scientiæ patet* And this is the truth, as he shall answer to God *Sic subscribitur*,

JOHN CLARK
ANDR FLETCHER

C. Campbell COLIN CAMPBELL of Ardonnick, aged forty-four years or thereby, married, solemnly sworn, purged of malice, partial counsel, examined and interrogated, deponed, That at the time and place libelled the deponent, in a window from Mrs Carmichael's, opposite to the scaffold, observed no disturbance, till once the executioner was going up the ladder to cut down the deceased Wilson, and then saw some stones thrown at the executioner, upon which he retired, and as he was passing the Cornmarket, the deponent observed one of the stones hit him, and saw some stones thrown at the guard who were upon the north side of the scaffold, and saw the pannel making motion with his fusee to keep off the mob; and afterwards turned towards the foot of the Bow very civilly, and then saw a stone hit one of the soldiers and which soldier the deponent saw present his firelock, and saw another stone hit the same soldier, and thereupon the said soldier pointed his firelock westward, and fired immediately; and another soldier fired immediately after him, which firings took the deponent's eyes from the pannel; and which two firings the deponent thinks were the first that were fired by the said two soldiers who had advanced among the crowd from their party. *Causa scientiæ patet* And this is the truth, as he should answer to God *Sic subscribitur*,

COLIN CAMPBELL
ANDR. FLETCHER

Wm Meanie WILLIAM MEANIE, serjeant in the City Guard of Edinburgh, aged forty-eight years or thereby, married, solemnly sworn, purged of malice, partial counsel, examined and interrogated, deponed, That, time and place libelled, and about the time the deceased Andrew Wilson was cut down, there were showers of stones thrown at the guard, and particularly one big stone lighted betwixt the deponent and Serjeant Finlay, above three pound weight and that the drummer was cut in the head with a stone, and the drum struck with a stone; and that Alexander Mushet sentinel, one of the guard, had his shoulder-blade broke with a stone; and that, before these

208

Evidence for Defence.

strokes were given, the deponent, by order of the pannel, was drawing off, and forming his men in the foot of the Bow · That the pannel gave the deponent his fusee, which was the fusee the pannel ordinarily carried, to keep, while he attended the execution and the prayers; which the deponent returned to the pannel again, upon the sign being given to cut down Wilson, and before the pannel came down from the scaffold. *Causa scientiæ patet.* And this is the truth, as he shall answer to God   *Sic subscribitur,*

WILLIAM MEANIE
JA. MACKENZIE

Wm. Meanie

ALEXANDER CAMPBELL, apprentice to George Young, surgeon in Edinburgh, aged eighteen years or thereby, unmarried, solemnly sworn, purged of malice, partial counsel, examined and interrogated, deponed, That, at the time and place libelled, he saw several stones thrown among the guard, after Wilson was cut down; and saw two of the soldiers of the guard step aside from among the rest and fire; and these were the two first shots that he heard   *Causa scientiæ patet*   And this is the truth, as he should answer to God. *Sic subscribitur,* A. Campbell

ALEXR CAMPBELL.
JA. MACKENZIE

MATTHEW HOWERT, soldier in the City Guard of Edinburgh, aged forty years or thereby, married, solemnly sworn, purged of malice, partial counsel, examined and interrogated, deponed, That he was present at Wilson's execution, at the time libelled; and that, before and after Wilson was cut down, there was a great many stones, both great and small, thrown among the guard by the mob   That after the pannel came down from the scaffold, he saw him wave his piece he had in his hand, but did not offer to present it; then he saw a soldier step out from the rest, and fire his piece in the air, as likewise two or three soldiers, that fired thereafter, did likewise fire their pieces in the air, and that these who fired first were standing close by the pannel and the deponent, and these were the first shots he heard that day; and he heard the soldiers say, one to another, Fire, or we shall all be knocked down; and upon more stones being thrown among them, several of them did fire; but, before that time, he heard the pannel say to the soldiers twice, Do not fire   After these shots were fired, the Captain marched up towards the Bow, and the men followed him   That, at the time that the shots were fired, as aforesaid, the pannel was standing at the foot of the steps of the scaffold, with his face towards the Castle   And deponed, He was one of those that followed the Captain, nor did he see the Captain fire as he was going up the Bow: That, when the Captain was marching on the head of the men up the Bow, he heard a M. Howert

Captain Porteous.

M. Howert dropping shot or two fired from the rear, nor did he see the Captain return again towards the scaffold, but marched straight on up to the town   *Causa scientiæ patet*   And this is the truth, as he shall answer to God   And declared he cannot write   *Sic subscribitur,*

JA. MACKENZIE.

D. Martine   DAVID MARTINE, soldier in the City Guard of Edinburgh, aged forty years or thereby, married, solemnly sworn, purged of malice, partial counsel, examined and interrogated, deponed, That he, the deponent, was one of the party of the City Guard who attended the execution of Andrew Wilson, and, before there was any firing, he did hear the pannel call to them, Not to fire, and, before that, the deponent had his shoulder-blade disjointed with a stroke he received upon it with a stone   *Causa scientiæ patet*   And this is the truth, as he shall answer to God   And declared he cannot write. *Sic subscribitur,*

DA. ERSKINE

Wm. Byres   WILLIAM BYRES, soldier in the City Guard of Edinburgh, aged fifty-one years or thereby, married, solemnly sworn, purged of malice, partial counsel examined and interrogated, deponed, That he was one of the City Guard who attended the execution of Andrew Wilson, and that he did not hear Captain Porteous give any orders to fire, but, when the firing happened, he was at some distance from the pannel, after the firing of several shots, the pannel called unto the soldiers, To fall into their ranks, and follow him, which, accordingly, the deponent and the rest did, falling in gradually, as they were able, and followed him to the guard-house, till they were dismissed; and, in their march up the Bow, did hear one shot, that came from the rear, but by whom he knows not   *Causa scientiæ patet.* And this is the truth, as he should answer to God   *Sic subscribitur,*

WILLIAM BYRES
DA. ERSKINE

J. Armour   JAMES ARMOUR, Writer to the Signet, aged fifty years and upwards, married, solemnly sworn, purged of malice, partial counsel, examined and interrogated, deponed, That he was looking over a window to see the execution of Andrew Wilson; after the criminal was thrown over and cut down, he observed the crowd of people throwing stones of considerable bigness, but against whom they were directed he knew not, but they fell among the soldiers; upon which he heard two or three shots, but from whose hands he did not observe   Thereupon there was an intermission for two or three minutes; but thereafter, when the pannel, with his party, were retiring,

Evidence for Defence.

which they did in great confusion and disorder, the crowd pur- ^{J. Armour} sued after them, renewed the throwing of great stones, and in great number, upon which some of the soldiers turned about, and marched back, some eight or ten paces, still in disorder; and then heard a good number of more shots fired, which, to his grief, he saw did great execution *Causa scientiæ patet* And this is the truth, as he should answer to God   *Sic subscribitur,*

JAMES ARMOUR
DA. ERSKINE.

JOHN ROBERTSON, stabler in the Grassmarket of Edinburgh, ^{J. Robertson} aged thirty years or thereby, married, solemnly sworn, purged of malice, partial counsel, examined and interrogated, deponed, That, at the time libelled, as he stood in his own window, in the Grassmarket, he saw the pannel, with his piece in his hand, moving it to and again, keeping off the mob; and heard him say, Fire, or I will fire, does not know which of the two   That immediately after this, he saw a single man step out, three or four paces before Captain Porteous, and fire his piece, and the deponent verily believed, that the people who fell near his Close got their wounds by that shot, because they were lying that place towards which the man seemed to point Deponed, That he heard some firing towards the foot of the Bow, before the last-mentioned shot *Causa scientiæ patet* And this is the truth, as he should answer to God   *Sic subscribitur,*

JOHN ROBERTSON
GILB ELLIOT

GEORGE VINT, coal-grieve to Sir William Baird of Newbyth, ^{George Vint} aged forty-six years or thereby, married, solemnly sworn, purged of malice, partial counsel, examined and interrogated, deponed, That, at the time libelled, he was in John Robertson's window, in the Grassmarket, when he observed the pannel moving his piece to and again, as if keeping off the mob; and at the same time, he saw one of the soldiers, a black haired man, step forward before the pannel, and fire his piece, upon which the pannel turned about to him and pushed him into his rank   Deponed, That he did not see the pannel fire at that time, or any other. and that the mentioned shot was the first he heard or saw that day *Causa scientiæ patet* And this is the truth, as he should answer to God   *Sic subscribitur,*

GEORGE VINT
GILB ELLIOT.

ALEXANDER THOMSON, town-officer in Edinburgh, aged forty ^{A. Thomson} years or thereby, married, solemnly sworn, purged of malice, partial counsel, examined and interrogated, deponed, That,

211

Captain Porteous.

A. Thomson being upon the scaffold on the 14th of April last, when Wilson was executed, the pannel sent him to the Magistrates, who were in William Orr's house, to know of them how long the criminal should yet hang upon the gallows: That he returned to the pannel with the Magistrates' direction, which was, that he should still hang a quarter of an hour; but, before the half of that time was expired, Wilson was cut down   *Causa scientiæ patet*   And this is the truth, as he should answer to God. *Sic subscribitur,*

ALEX. THOMSON.
GILB ELLIOT

P. Colstoun PETER COLSTOUN, merchant in Edinburgh, aged twenty-five years or thereby, married, solemnly sworn, purged of malice, partial counsel, examined and interrogated, deponed, That, time and place libelled, and after the first firing, the deponent, being standing under the north-west corner of the Cornmarket, saw the pannel march the guard under his command up the West Bow, and saw several of the rear of that guard fire upon the people assembled at the execution. and, at the same time, observed, that the pannel was within the first turn of the West Bow, and so out of the deponent's view   *Causa scientiæ patet.* And this is the truth, as he should answer to God.   *Sic subscribitur,*

PETER COLSTOUN
ANDR FLETCHER

John Kennedy JOHN KENNEDY, surgeon in Edinburgh, aged fifty years or thereby, married, solemnly sworn, purged of malice, partial counsel, examined and interrogated, deponed, That, some short time after the execution of Andrew Wilson, in April last, the deponent attended the persons of the Town Guard after-mentioned, viz Alexander Mushet, soldier, the spine of whose shoulder-bone was crushed, and Alexander Braid, soldier, who had a contusion in his right foot, both which persons informed the deponent, that they received these hurts at the execution of the said Andrew Wilson; and that the last-mentioned person is lame to this day   *Causa scientiæ patet.*   The deponent was employed to wait upon the said persons   And this is truth, as he should answer to God   *Sic subscribitur,*

JO KENNEDY.
ANDR FLETCHER

The Lords Justice-Clerk and Commissioners of Justiciary ordained the assize to inclose instantly, in a room prepared for them in the Exchequer, and return their verdict in the Old Court-House to-morrow, at four o'clock at night, and the whole fifteen to be then present, each person under the pain of law, and the pannel to be carried back to prison

212

Verdict and Sentence.

CURIA JUSTICIARIÆ, S. D. N. Regis, tenta in Prætorio Burgi de Edinburgo, vigesimo die mensis Julii, Millesimo septingentesimo trigesimo sexto, per honorabiles viros, ANDREAM FLETCHER de Milton, Justiciariium Clericum, Dominum JACOBUM MACKENZIE de Roystoun, Magistrum DAVIDEM ERSKINE de Dun, Dominos GUALTERUM PRINGLE de Newhall, et GILBERTUM ELLIOT de Minto, Commissionarios Justiciarii, dict S. D. N. Regis

Curia legitimè affirmata.

Intran.

JOHN PORTEOUS, lately one of the Captain-Lieutenants of the City Guard, pannel

INDICTED and ACCUSED as in the former sederunts.

The persons who past upon the assize of the said John Porteous returned their verdict in presence of the said Lords, whereof the tenor follows

Edinburgh, July 20, 1736

The above assize having inclosed, did choice Sir John Inglis of Cramond to be their Chancellor, and James Davidson, bookseller in Edinburgh, to be their Clerk, and having considered the indictment at the instance of Duncan Forbes of Culloden, Esq his Majesty's Advocate for his Highness's interest, against John Porteous, late one of the Captain-Lieutenants of the City Guard of Edinburgh, pannel, with the Lord Justice-Clerk and Lords Commissioners of Justiciary their interlocutor thereupon, and depositions of the witnesses adduced for proving thereof, the pannel's own judicial confession, and depositions of the witnesses adduced for the said John Porteous, pannel, his exculpation, they all in one voice found it proven, that the said John Porteous, pannel, fired a gun among the people assembled at the place of execution, and time libelled, as also, that he gave orders to the soldiers under his command to fire, and upon his and their so firing, the persons mentioned in the indictment were killed and wounded, and found it proven, that the pannel and his guard were attacked and beat by several stones of a considerable bigness, thrown amongst them by the multitude, whereby several of the soldiers were bruised and wounded.   In witness whereof, our said Chancellor and Clerk, in our name, have subscribed these presents, day and place foresaid   *Sic subscribitur,*

JO. INGLIS, Chancellor.
JAMES DAVIDSON, Clerk.

The Lord Justice-Clerk and Lords Commissioners of Justiciary, having considered the verdict of assize returned against

Captain Porteous.

John Porteous, pannel, of this date, they, in respect thereof, by the mouth of John Dalgleish, dempster of Court, decerned and adjudged the said John Porteous to be taken from the Tolbooth of Edinburgh upon Wednesday the eighth day of September next to come, to the Grassmarket of Edinburgh, the common place of execution of the said burgh, betwixt the hours of two and four of the clock of the afternoon of the said day, and there to be hanged by the neck upon a gibbet, by the hands of the executioner, until he be dead, and ordained all his moveable goods and gear to be escheat and inbrought to his Majesty's use, which was pronounced for doom *Sic subscribitur,*

And Fletcher.
Ja Mackenzie
Da Erskine
Wa Pringle
Gilb Elliot

The Respite.

CURIA JUSTICIARIÆ, S. D N Regis, tenta in Novo Sessionis
Domo Burgi de Edinburgo, tertio die mensis Septembris,
Millesimo septingentesimo trigesimo sexto, per honorabiles
viros, ANDREAM FLETCHER de Milton, Justiciarium Clericum,
Dominos JACOBUM MACKENZIE de Roystoun, et GUALTERUM
PRINGLE de Newhall, Commissionarios Justiciarii, dict.
S D N Regis

Curia legitimè affirmata.

The said day the Lord Justice-Clerk delivered a letter from
his Grace the Duke of Newcastle, one of his Majesty's Principal
Secretaries of State, whereof the tenor follows:

Whitehall, August 26, 1736.

MY LORDS,—Application having been made to her Majesty
in the behalf of John Porteous, late Captain-Lieutenant of the
City Guard of Edinburgh, a prisoner under sentence of death
in the gaol of that city, I am commanded to signify to your
Lordships her Majesty's pleasure, that the execution of the
sentence pronounced against the said John Porteous be respited
for six weeks from the time appointed for his execution   I
am, my Lords, your Lordship's most obedient humble servant
Sic subscribitur,

HOLLES NEWCASTLE

Directed on the back thus, "To the Right Honourable the
Lord Justice-General, Justice-Clerk, and other Lords of the
Justiciary at Edinburgh "

Thereafter, the said Lords gave their warrant to the Magistrates of Edinburgh for stopping the said execution, whereof
the tenor follows —By the Right Honourable the Lord Justice-
Clerk, and Lords Commissioners of Justiciary: Whereas her
Majesty, guardian of the kingdom, has been graciously pleased,
by a letter signed by his Grace the Duke of Newcastle, one of
his Majesty's Principal Secretaries of State, to signify her
pleasure to us, that the sentence of death pronounced against
John Porteous, late Captain-Lieutenant of the City Guard of
Edinburgh, present prisoner in the Tolbooth of Edinburgh,
which was to have been executed upon him upon the 8th
day of September instant, be respited for six weeks from the
time appointed for his execution   These, therefore, in
obedience to her Majesty's commands, discharge and prohibit
the Magistrates of Edinburgh, and all other officers of the
law, from putting the foresaid sentence of death in execution
upon the said John Porteous till the 20th of October next to

215

Captain Porteous.

come ; on which day, the said Magistrates of Edinburgh are hereby required and ordained to put the former sentence of death in execution upon the said John Porteous, in all points, as they will be answerable   Given at Edinburgh, the third day of September, 1736 years   *Sic subscribitur,*

ANDR FLETCHER.

JA MACKENZIE.

WA PRINGLE.

Extracted furth of the Books of Adjournal, upon this and the preceding one hundred and twenty-four pages, by me, John Davidson, Clerk to the Court of Justiciary

Jo. DAVIDSON, *Clk.*

APPENDICES.

APPENDIX I

DOCUMENTS RELATING TO CAPTAIN PORTEOUS, HITHERTO UNPUBLISHED

(From the original MSS in the possession of Edinburgh Town Council)

I.—PETITION OF JOHN PORTEOUS, 1716

Unto the Right Honourable the Lord Provost, Honourable Baillies, and Remnant Town Councill of Edinburgh,

The Petition of John Porteous, Adjutant to the Honourable Trainbands of Edinburgh,

Humbly Sheweth,

That when the Honourable Councill was Pleased by their Act, Dated the 9th and 11th days of November 1715, to nominat, appoint, and Install me to be Adjutant to the said Honourable Trainbands, under which Character I have exerc'd myselfe to the satisfactione and Approbatione of all concern'd, having neglected no Oportunity in serving the Good Town's Interest during the late Rebellion, By Imploying my Wholl tyme in Teatching the Military Exercises even before and after my Instalment. Notwithstanding of which services and my being still Capable, to my surprise the said Act in my favois is Rescinded. I therefore in all humility Demean myselfe to your Lordship and Honour's Justice and Goodnesse, Humbly Craving the Honourable Councill would be pleased to Reconsider the matter with the Honourable Captains of the said Trainbands, their Recommendatione in my favors herewith produced, And thereupon to Repon me to the said post, Especially considering the Great Pains and Charges I have been put to this year and your Petitioners willingness to serve the Good Towne.

May it therffor please your Lordship and Honours In Consideration of the premises and the said Honourable Captains Recommendation, to Repon me to my said post for what tyme your Lorp and the Honourable Councill shall think fitt and your Petitioner shall ever pray

JOHN PORTEOUS

II.—PETITION OF JOHN PORTEOUS, 1723

To the Right Honble The Lord Provost, Bailies, and Town Councill of Edinburgh,

The Petition of John Porteous, Ensigne in the City Guard,

Humbly Sheweth,

That your Petitioner was, in Anno 1715, Elected Adjutant to the City Trainbands which I Officiate and Receav'd Sallary £25 Starg per Annum till the year 1719, att which time The then Honble Magistrats and Councill thought fitt to withdraw my said Sallary: which your Petior rested satisfy'd with, In regard that the Watch-money out of which the said Sallary is payble was lookt upon as burdensome to the Neighbourhood att that time, And your Petitioner was then also appointed to pay to Arthurston's Lady One hundred pounds Scots yearly, which I have ever since punctually pay'd by the hands of John Hogg, Collector, And continues so to doe out of my subsistance

Your Petitor has continu'd to Officiate as Adjutant ever since that year 1719 without any allowance and seeing that the Fund of Watchmoney is now in a better condition than formerly,

It's Humbly Expected the Honble Magistrats will appoint such a Sallary to the said Office as they shall see just and suitable, And your Petior shall ever pray   JOHN PORTEOUS

Edinburgh, 5th May, 1724 The Comittee having considered the within Petition are of Opinion that in Reguard Ensign John Porteous officiates as Adjt to the City Train Bands and has no allowance for the same, he should be Eased of the One hundred pounds Scots he Pays yearly to Mrs Murray, and that sum be appointed to be paid her by John Hogg out of the Guard money

Robt Lindsay.	Archibald Wallace, Baillie
Tho Crockatt	J Nimmo, Baillie
James Mitchelson, Convr	Ro Fergusson, Baillie.
John Keir.	Alexr Wilson, Baillie
	Jo Drummond, D.G.
	Will Hutton, Treasr

III —PETITION OF JOHN PORTEOUS, 1726

Unto The Right Honble The Lord Provost, Baillies, and Councill of the Good Town of Edinburgh,

The Petition of John Porteous, Ensign to the City guard,

Humbly Sheweth,

That your Petitioner has served in that Station and as Adjutant to the Trainbands to the satisfaction of the Honourable Magistrates and Captain of the Trainbands ever since the year 1715, And now there being a vacancy of Liewtenant in the City guard by the decease of Liewt Andrew Johnstone, and the Councill being in use to reward the Good service of their Officers with Promotion when a Superior vaccancy does happen,

Your Petitioner therefor Humbly Expects the Council will prefer him to be Liewtenant to the City guard in the place of the said Liewt Andrew Johnstone Deceast, And your Petitioner shall ever pray   JOHN PORTEOUS.

IV —PETITION OF JOHN PORTEOUS AND JOHN FERGUSSON, 1735

To the Right Honourable The Lord Provost, Magistrates, and Town Councill of Edinburgh,

The petition of Captains John Porteous and John Fergusson, late of the City Guard of Edinburgh,

Humbly Sheweth,

That on account of a late Difference that happened betwixt your petitioners in the burrow Room in presence of some of the Honble

Facsimile of Petition of John Porteous, 1735.

From the original MS. in possession of Edinburgh Town Council.

Appendix I.

magistrats and members of the Council your Lop and Honours was pleased to Dismiss us from our severall Stations and Service aforesaid   And now that these Differences are most amicably Removed and a good understanding betwixt us, Wee humbly hope your Lop and honours will be pleased to Remove the foresaid Sentence and Repone us to our severall Stations as formerly

And your Petitioners shall ever pray,

JOHN PORTEOUS
JO FERGUSSONE

V —MEMORIALL & QUAERYS TOUCHING THE JURISDICTION OF THE PROVOST AND MAGISTRATS OF EDENBR , TO TAKE TRYALL OF THE MURTHERS COMMITTED BY CAPTAIN PORTEOUS, AND PART OF THE CITY GUARD UNDER HIS COMMAND ON THE 14TH APRILE 1736, AT THE EXECUTION OF ANDR. WILSON

From a precognition taken of the Conduct and proceedings of Captain Porteous, and of a party of the Guard of the City of Edenburgh under his Command on the 14 of Aprile 1736 at the Execution of Andrew Wilson by virtue of a warrand from the High Court of Justiciary There is little reason to doubt of its being proved to the Satisfaction of a Jury if the Captain shall be brought to a Tryall, that he was guilty of a most atrocious and bloody Murder, by discharging several shott himself of one or more firelocks, loaded with large drops of lead or swan-hail, amongst the crowd of the Spectators, and by ordering the Soldiers under his Command to do the like, which they did, and thereby killed dead and mortally wounded Seven or Eight Innocent persons, and gave dangerous wounds to ten or eleven more of the Spectators, and that after the execution was over, and the Criminal cutt down without any just cause or provocation, other then the throwing of a few stones by some of the spectators at the Execution, part of which lighted amongst the soldiers of the Guard, so that one of them lighted on the Capt and several others of them hitt some of the soldiers of the guard, as may more fully appear from an abstract of the Precognition formerly laid before his Majesty's Advocate and Solicitor

The detestableness of the Crime, as well as the peace and quiet of the minds of the Burgesses and Inhabitants of the City of Edenbr seem to require the proceeding to the Tryall of the Capt and such of his Guard as appear to have been guilty, with all the speed & expedition that the Rules of Law can admitt of.

The absence of the Lords of the High Court of Justiciary by their goeing to the Circuits about this time will occasion a very Considerable delay in case it should be carried on before them, and My Lord Provost and Magistrats of Edenburgh are desirous to have the oppinion of His Majesty's Advocate and Solicitor, whither or not they have sufficient Jurisdiction to bring the Captain and his Guard to a Tryall before themselves which may be finished in a shorter time, and at less expense, than if the Tryall be carryed on before the high Court of Justiciary   The grounds upon which the Jurisdiction of the Lord Provost and Magistrats in the above point stands, is as follows —

By a Charter under the great Seal from King James the 3 of that name, bearing date 16 Decemr 1482, and reciting very eminent Services, then recently done by the Provost, Magistrats, Clerk, & Community of Edenburgh, An ample Criminal Jurisdiction is granted to them in the following words

.   .   .

In perswance of this Jurisdiction the Provost and Magistrats of

Captain Porteous.

Edenbr have been in use as appears from their Records to take tryall of Mutthers and Slaughters Committed within their bounds, particularly in the Case of John Cheesly of Dalrye, for the Murder of Sir George Lockhart President of the Session where a power was granted to them, by a particular act of the Convention of Estates then mett at Edenbr to use Tortuie and some assessors were adjoined to them by the states, under protestation by the provost and Magistrats, that same should not prejudge the ancient libertys of the good town

Severall other Tryalls for Murther, upon which Capital punishment ensued appear from the said Records, but such of them as were antecedent to the year 1700 have been finished, and sentence executed on or before the third day

In that year John Bryce was try'd on the 20 & execute the 27 of September for a Murder Committed on the 17th said month, but before that year the time for executing sentences of death, pronounced within three days after the Crime, was extended to nine days, by a Clause in the end of the 4 act of Parliat anno 1695

In the year 1732, James Henderson & David Hamilton were try'd on the 3d Novr 1732 for the Murder of John Campbell Committed on the 5th of October said year, But on a petition for transportation their tryall ceased

And in the year 1733 John Christie was try'd on the 17 August for a Murder Committed on the 14 June said year

In which last case the following Interloqr was pronounced, by the advice of the best Lawyers of all Caracters in this place, " Repells the Declinator, that the Sheriff is not Judge competent to the Murder, where the murder is prosecuted within fourty days of the commission of the Crime, But sustains that seperat declinator, That this Indictment was not raised nor executed against the pannel within fourty days of the alleadged Murder, nor of the pannels being apprehended for the same, and therefore refuse to sustain process, and desert the dyet against the pannel, reserving to the prors ffiscal, or any other persons having interest, to prosecute the pannel for the said Crimes as accords of the Law "

Then it seems to appear that the provost and Magistrats, have by the words of their Charter and by the practice following thereupon, a Clear Jurisdiction for taking Tryall of Murtherers of the most atrocious nature

And that this jurisdiction in the provost and Magistrats of Edenbr is founded on the particular extent of their priveledges, granted by their said Charter so as to withdraw their case from the objections which may be laid against the Jurisdiction of Ordinary Sheriffs and Burrows as to the point of trying Muiders seems to be evident from the words of Sir George Mackenzie, Book 2 Tit 5

.   .

But the doubt is, if Sir George has adverted fully when he wrote what is above to the Import of the said Act 28 Ja 4 which doubt may be excused since Sir George in his Institutions delivers a very different oppinion Lib 1st tit 4 S2 in fine, in these words, " The Sheriff is Judge in all crimes, except Treason, and the four pleas of the Crown, To witt, Murder, fire-raising, Robery & Ravishing of women, but Murder he can only Judge, if the Murtherei was taken with Red-hand, That is to say immediately Committing the Murder, in which case, he must proceed against him within three Suns."

Besides the above objections against the Provost and Magistrats proceedings to Try Capt Porteous after the three Days are elapsed, taken from the above state of our Laws and practise, There is a seperat objection arising from the attrocious Circumstances under which the facts in this case were Committed which are alleadged to

Appendix I.

make this murder fall under that species, which in all the ages and periods of our Law, was reackoned one of the four pleas of the Crown, Cognizable only by the High Court of Justiciary, because of the great danger of Elusory Tryalls in such attrocious cases, The most ancient of our Laws & Law books, take notice of this specialty, with respect to Murder, wilfull fire-raising and Ravishing of women viz Laws of Malcom 2d Cap 11 or Alexr 2 Cap 14 S2 *Leges Burg* Cap 6 & 7 &c Skeen *de verb signiss verbis Murthrum* and *plaistum* Sir George Mackenzie *Dictis locis*

And it is Contended that the said acts of Ja Ist & 4 touched only Slaughters of a less attrocious nature, tho' Capitall, but not such Murders as were Committed, where the partys slain were (as is alleadged to have been in the Case here) under the trust Credit assurance and power of the slayer And it is contended that this distinction subsisted even after the said act 89 Ja Ist and that the difficulty of distinguishing in many cases, whither the Slaughter fell under the Sheriffs Jurisdiction or the pleas of the Crown Occasioned the 51 act anno 1587, whereby to avoid further doubts, such Murder as fell under the pleas of the Crown is particularly defined, and declared to be Treason.

From what is above, the following Quærys arise —

1mo Does not the said Charter and act of Parliament containing rescisiory clause foresaid give to the Provost and Magistrats of the City of Edenbr a more extensive Jurisdiction with respect to the murder then belongs to all Sheriffs, in vertue of their offices, within their own territorys, at least over the officers & soldiers of their City guard, Or at least does not the said recisory clause, being in an act of Parliat posterior to the 28 Act Ja 4 remove any limitation which may be supposed to have affected the Jurisdiction of the Magistrats of Edr granted to them as to the Tryall of Crimes by their Gift antecedent to the said 28 Act and whilst the 89 Act Ja 1st was in full force, tho' the said 28 act should be thought to derogat, as to other Sheriffs from the said 89 Act Ja 1st

2o Have not all Sheriffs by vertue of the said acts 29 Ja 1st and 28 Ja 4 a Jurisdiction to try Murders or Slaughter within fourty days after the Murder or Slaughter is Committed

3o Is the distinction between more and less attrocious murders to be observed, so as to subject Murders, falling under the description in the said 51 act, anno 1587 only to the Cognizance of the High Court of Justiciary as pleas of the Crown and to admitt of the Sheriffs Jurisdiction in less attrocious Slaughters tho' Capitall

4o Do the Murders Committed by Capt Porteous and his guard in the Circumstances Contained in the Abstract of the precognition formerly sent, fall under the description of the said act 51 anno 1507 So as to make it one of the pleas of the Crown Cognizable only by the High Court of Justiciary, Or may the Provost & Magistrats of Edenr by vertue of the Jurisdiction granted to them by their foresaid Charter proceed to take tryall of Capt Porteous and his Guard or either of them at any time within fourty days after the Murders were Committed, or at any time without regard to the fourty days

It is also sudgested that Capt Porteous may, in order to gain time and preplex his Tryall, be advised by his Lawyers to pretend, and offer to prove, as a defense or Exculpation, or Mitigation, tho' it be most false and groundless, That he had orders from My Lord Provost and the other Magistrats, or some of them, to fire upon the spectators, or possibly he may offer a Declinator of the Magistrats to be his Judges under that pretense, As to which it is to be observed, that two of the Baillys were out of the Town, and at a distance from it on the day of the Murder, and for some days before and by the Charter the Lord Provost is Sheriff but the Baillys are his Deputes, conjunctly

223

Captain Porteous.

& severally, so that any one, or two of them may act as Judges in the Tryall

Io If a Declinator be offered on the above ground Ought it to be sustain'd, and admitted to probation by the Magistrats, or ought it to be repelled

: 2o May the Provost & other Magistrats, who may be named in the Declinator, Join in pronouncing Interlocr upon it, and taking the proof of it, if sustain'd, or ought only the two, who were absent to act as Judges in such case

. 3o If orders from the Magistrats be proponed by way of Defense, Exculpation or Mitigation Ought it to be sustain'd as Revelant, and admitted to probation, or Repelled as being rather a ground for accusing such of the Magistrats, who shall be pretended to have given the orders, then as any Defence or Mitigation of the pannels Crime.

. 4o In Judging or taking the proof of such Defense if sustained, May the Magistrats named as givers of the orders act, or only those who were absent

5o Is the above Circumstance of pretended orders from the Magistrats, or some of them, which probably will be proponed (tho most falsely) for the Captain in case the Tryall be before the Magistrats, any good Reason for prosecuting the Captain and his guard directly before the Lords of the High Court of Justiciary

It is also sudgested, that the soldiers who were under Capt Porteous's Command, will plead in Exculpation, or at least for mitigation, The Captains orders to fire, which they will clearly prove as to those who fired, Together at the first and Second firings which by the precognition appears to have been made, but as to dropping shotts made by single soldiers, after they had marched a Considerable way up the Bow, which will also be proved to have been shott by particular soldiers, It is thought the soldiers who fired them will not be able to prove orders for the said dropping Shotts

. Io Will the defense of orders by the Captain be Relevant to Exculpat or mitigat the penalty of the Soldiers, and to what extent may it mitigat

. 2o Will the Generall orders to fire, be relevant to Exculpat those who fired the dropping shotts at some distance of place and time after the Generall order had been obeyed

: 3o Will such defenses of the soldiers be more proper to be Judged of by the Court of Justiciary then by the Magistrats

---

VI —Answers to the Queries touching the Jurisdiction of the Magistrat's of Edinburgh in the case of Captain Porteous.

We have considered the Memoriall with the Laws and authorities therein referred to, and answer to the 1st Querie That, we are of opinion, Sherriffs after the Act 28th par 4th James 4 had no jurisdiction in the crime of Slaughter but where the offender was taken red-hand, and judged within three Suns, And as this Statute seems plain so had it been doubtfull the constant practice for several centuries of Sheriffs judging Criminalls taken red hand within three Suns, and never attempting to proceed in any other case, demonstrates that it was the received opinion of the Nation. And as to authorities, Hope is plain and positive, and tho' Sir George Mackenzie in his Criminalls Seems to lean the other way, yet in his Institutes, a book which is wrote with greater exactness, he agrees with Hope.

To the 2d We would answer That the charter do's not seem to us to give greater powers to the Magistrat's of Edinburgh than what belong to the jurisdiction of Sherriff, the clauses therein contained·

Appendix I.

being executive of the grant of Sherriffship Excepting the prohibition upon other Judges to interfere with the jurisdiction thereby granted, which however do's not extent the powers, Neither do we apprehend the Criminal's being Captain of the City guard can make any difference in the point of Law

To the 3d That no distinction between Murders more or less atrocious can raise a jurisdiction to the Sherriff

To the 4th That the crime is atrocious if the whole circumstances of the fact are justly set forth in the Abstract laid before us

As to the 2d Set of Queries

To the 1st We cannot possibly conceive how the allegance suggested, could be a cause of Declinator upon the part of the Prisoner For supposing the alledgance true and capable of proof, it would be of all others the strongest reason why he ought not to decline being tryed by them, and therefore supposing the tryall carried on before the Magistrats, which we think ought not to be, and such a declinator offered, we look upon it to be so absurd that it ought to be repelled.

As to the 2d it Seems to be answered by the first

To the 3d Supposing the tryall before the Magistrats as it might have been if prosecuted within three Suns, and supposing such a defence offered before them, we cannot see how they would repell it, because without considering how far the order of the Magistrats would be found a relevant Defence by the Court of Justiciary, which as this case is said to be circumstanced we think it would not, Yet in a tryall before themselves, we cannot see how they could avoid sustaining orders given by themselves as Magistrates to exculpate from any guilt consequent upon the exact execution of those orders But this very consideration, appears to us to be a very urgent Motive for trying this crime before the Court of Justiciary, rather than the Magistrats, tho' these last had, as we think they have not, jurisdiction after three Suns

To the 4th If by the Charter, the Provost is constituted Sherriff and the Baillies conjunctly and severally Deputes, if the Provost choise to act, he must we think act by himself, because we do not see how his Deputes can act in conjunction with him But if the Baillies were to judge, they might all join in the act to give it the greater weight.

To the 5th We need in our opinion say little after having declared we think the Magistrates have now no jurisdiction, But cannot help thinking it. as we have already said, an additional reason why they ought not at this time to attempt raising a jurisdiction contrary to the words of a Statute and inveterate practice

As to the last Set of Queries

To the 1st The question is very delicate and cannot possibly be answered but as it arises upon particular circumstances In general no order from the Captain of the Town-guard can justify the Men under his command for fireing upon an innocent Multitude so as to kill, where the defence of their lives or the execution of some very important piece of their duty do's not evidently call for it, and yet circumstances may appear that shall alleviate the crime in obeying their order, and make their case a very compassionate one, Especially where it cannot be distinguished, who the unhappy Persons were, whose fire took place.

To the 2d The general order cannot in our opinion yeeld any excuse for those who fired the dropping Shots as mentioned in the Querie, Especially if it can be discovered that those dropping Shots did any mischief, so that the act of killing can in those instances be brought home to the individual offenders.

Q   225

Captain Porteous.

As to the last We repeat the Answer given to the last of the 2d Set of Queries
London, 6th May 1736
This is the humble opinion of

Dun Forbes
Ch Areskine

VII.—Execution of Arrestment for Debt due by Captain Porteous, 1736

I David Simpson Sheriff officer by virtue of an Decreet of furth-coming att the instance of Thomas Young, Brewer at Fountain-Bridge Agt John Porteous Captain in the City Guard of Edinr and George Kinghorn vintner att the Cowgate port there, common Debitor for his interest, containing Arrestment obtained before the Sherriffs of Edinr the nineteenth day of March last, In his Majesty's name and authority and in name and authority of the sds Sherriffs of Edinburgh lawfully fence and arrest in the hands of each of you Alexander Wilson, Provost, Thomas Crockatt, James Colhoun, Alexander Blackwood, and Gavin Hamilton, Baillies, Mr Thomas Herriot, Dean of Gild, and Thomas Young, Treasurer of the City of Edinr All and Haill the sum of Five pounds Sterling money, less or more, due and addebted by you each of you and as representing the said Community of Er by Bond, Bill, Ticket, Accompt, Word, Write, Promise, Paction, Condition, Contract, Agreement, Decreet, by gone sallary or any other manner of way whatsoever Together with all goods, gear, debts, and sumes of money in each of your hands, custody and Keeping belonging to the sd John Porteous All to remain in each of your hands under sure fence and arrestment att the sd persuers instance ay and while he be fully satisfied and paid the sume of Three pounds ten shilings Sterling contained in the sd Decreet, conforme to the same in all parts This I do upon the Twenty first day of April seventeen hundred and thirty six years betwixt the hours of Ten and Eleven forenoon before these witnesses James Willeson and John Selkrig, vintner Edr and indwellr there, with certification by me

David Simpson, officer

VIII —Account due to the Keeper of the Tolbooth, 1736

Accompt The Good Town of Edinr to James Cleland, Keeper of the Tolbooth for the prison dues of the persons following Incarcerat by Warrand of my Lord Provost

Captain John Porteous from the 14th of Aprile to the 7th of Septemr 1736 Inclusive being 21 weeks at 5 shill Sterling pr week, he having had a Room for himself and a great deall of Trouble is - - - - -	£5	5	0
John Paterson, John Kettle, Andrew Tod, David Gilchrist Matthew Buckles, John Lesly, and Robert Brown, all Souldiers in the City Guard, from the 15th of Aprile to the said 7th Septemr 1736 being 146 nights att 3 sh 4d Scots each pr night is - - - - - -	14	3	10¾
James ffala, Souldier in the said Guard, from the 19th Aprile to the said 7th Septemr. 1736 Inclusive being 142 nights att 3 sh 4d Scots pr night is - - - -	1	19	5½
George Mitchell, also Souldier in the said Guard, from the 20 Aprile to the said 7th Septemr 1736 Inclusive being 141 nights att 3 sh. 4d Scots pr night is - - -	1	19	2
	£23	7	6

Appendix I.

Brought forward, - - - - - -					£23	7	6

To bread, ale and brandy to John Dalgleish [the Hangman]
when in the Tolbooth before Andrew Willson's
Execution - - - - - - - - - 0 1 6½

To bread, ale and candle to four shoulders when guarding
Andrew Willson in the Tolbooth - - - - - 0 4 6

To the Masons and Smiths when mending the window in the
Gentleman's chamber and building up the window in
the Iron house - - - - - - £0 11 6½   0 5 6

£23 19 0½

Edinburgh, 27th November, 1738. The Committee hereunto sub-
scriving having examined the within Accompt and having had under
their consideration the Councils Act, dated 18th August, 1736 declaring that noe Wairand to be granted thereafter for liberating prisoners
shall subject the city in payment to the keeper of any prison fees,
do find that there is no part of the within Accompt due by the City
except eleven shillings sixpence halfpenny Sterling of furnishings to
John Dalgleish four soldiers, masons and smiths But in regard the
said James Clelland was at considerable trouble and expense about
Captain Porteous and soldiers while in his prison, are of opinion
that the city should pay him a gratification of Five guineas, and that
upon payment thereof and of the said article of eleven shillings sixpence half penny and of twelve pounds seventeen shillings and four
pence Sterling due to him by the above in part recitd Act of Council
dated sd 18th August 1736, making in all eighteen pounds thirteen
shillings ten pence half penny sterling, the said James Clelland should
grant to this City a receipt of the same in ful and compleat satisfaction to him from the City of all fees, dues, and emoluments due to him
(by this City) as the principal jaylour and keeper of their prison and
in full satisfaction to him of all clams and demands competent to him
against this City for aliment to prisoners and every other cause hereto
proceeding

Will M'Vey	George Loch	Tho Crockat, Baillie.
Thomas Simpson.	Willm Mitchaill.	Geo. Haliburton, D.D.
	Saml Neilson	Alex Sharp, Treas^r
		J. Balfour, O B.

IX.—Declarations by John Ure and others regarding Captain Porteous, 1737.

John Ure, Writer in Edinr, being Examined Declairs that he Dined
with John Porteous, Late Capt Lieut of the City guard that Day he
was hanged That a son of George Gordon Wryter in Edinr and one
Haswell, a Mercht Dined with them That in the forenoon of that
Day the declarant happen'd to meet with Capt John Ferguson, also
of the City Guard, and told him that he the declarant had heard there
was a Mob to be in town that Day on accot of Capt Porteous, to
which Capt Fergusson answer'd that there would be no mob that
Day, no more than there had been for the eight days preceeding.
That when he the Declarant was at Dinner with Capt Porteous he
acquainted him with what had passed betwixt him and Capt Ferguson,
To which Capt Porteous answered That he was no manner of Way
affraid of any mob, and that if the Door was open'd to him he would
venture to goe to the Cross with his Cane alone in his hand, and at
the same time he told the declarant that on the morrow thereafter,

227

Captain Porteous.

which was the day appointed for his publick Execution, The Lord Drummore's son was to dine with him, and he invited the Declarant to come and take part of his next Days dinnar to bear Company with Mr Dalrymple

JOHN URE.

Eoe die

Willm Ure, Goldsmyth in Edinr, being Examined Declairs that Mr Robt Yetts, preacher of the Gospel in Edr, Carryed the Declarant alongst with him to the Tolbooth of Edinr to visit Capt John Porteous in the afternoon of that Day, on the evening of which he was hanged, That they stay'd with Capt Porteous from betwixt four and five in the afternoon till about seven a Cloak at night, During which time he heard Mr Robert Yetts insinuat to Capt Porteous that he should take Care of whom he gave Access to come in to him, for that he was affraid some evil might come over him Upon which the Capt said, that he understood what he meant was, untill the next day should be over, but that he was in no Apprehension of Danger that way, and that it he were set at Liberty, he would not be affraid to walk on the street at the Cross

WILLIAM URE

Edr 14th Aprile 1737

Dishingtoun declars that on tuesday the 7th of Septr between the hours of twelve and one he went to see Mr Porteous in the Tolbooth and said to him he Wished he were in the Castle That the Capt answered him that he might have been in the Castle if he pleased, but that he did not desire it for that he had undergone a Great Change in his Constitution upon being committed to the Tolbooth and dureing his Stay in it and that he was affraid he might have run the Risque of another Change if had been sent to the Castle That the Declarant asked him if he would not have been affraid of being insulted by the Mob if he were going out upon a Remission from the King to which Capt Porteous answered that if he had the King's remission in his pocket he would not be affraid to go along with the declarant to the Cross of Edr that moment Declars att that time Mr Gordon, a Gentleman in Company, Told Mr Porteous that he was going in a few days to the West Country But Mr Porteous desired him to stay a Week or so and he would go along with him

Appendix II.

APPENDIX II

PETITIONS TO QUEEN CAROLINE FOR REPRIEVE OF CAPTAIN PORTEOUS.

(State Papers, Scotland (George II), vol xxiii No 4)

I —Petition of John Porteous.

To the Queen's Most Excellent Majesty. The Humble Prayer
and Supplication of John Porteous, late Captain Lieutenant
of the City Guard of Edinburgh

Shewith

That I, your Majesty's unhappy Supplicant Lye now under
Sentence of Death to be Executed upon me the Eighth day of September next; as having been convicted of being Accessary to the
Killing and Wounding severall persons assembled at the Execution
of Andrew Wilson

That, as I stand convicted according to the usuall method of Tryall,
I shall not adventure to make any Declaration To Your Royall Majesty
of my Innocence, Because such Declarations from a person under my
Circumstances cannot be supposed to have great Weight with Your
Royall Wisdom, and that I trust my case may be laid before Your
Majesty by persons of Great Honour & Dignity, who may have the
Generosity and Goodness to appear in my behalf

That I beg leave, With the most Profound Humility and Reverence
To lay before Your Majesty, That my Behaviour (whatever it may be
thought to have been) upon that Melancholly Occasion, which gave
Rise to the Prosecution against me, cannot possibly be supposed To
have proceeded from any Felonious Intention in me to Shed the blood
of those persons, who were unfortunately killed or Wounded at that
time

That I do, in the most Humble Manner, throw myself At the Feet
of Your Royall Majesty, Imploring the Benefit of that Clemency,
which is known to be the Darling attribute of the Brittish Crown, and
which is ever Exerted upon all Occasions, where the Circumstances of
the Case can admitt of it

May it therefore please Your Most Excellent Majesty, To take my
unfortunate Condition Under Your Royall Consideration, and to give
such Relieff, as to Your Majesty in Your Royall Wisdom may seem
meet

JOHN PORTEOUS

[Endorsed]   Petition of John Porteous
in the Ld Justice Clerk's of Aug 25th, 1736

II —Petition of John Porteous

To Her Most Excellent Majesty Queen Caroline, Guardian of
these Realms,

The most humble Petition of John Porteous, late Captain-
Lieutenant of the City-Guard of Edinburgh, now under
Sentence of Death

Sheweth

That a certain Person named Andrew Wilson, being convicted
in the High Court of Justiciary of Scotland, for a Robbery of the
Publick Money, committed on the High-Way, was sentenced to death

Captain Porteous.

for that offence, and it being apprehended the Populace would
rescue the said Offender, or commit some Outrage at his Execution,
your Petitioner was appointed by the Magistrates of the said City, to
attend such Execution with a Detachment of the City-Guard, with
Orders to see the same duly executed, and to suppress any Tumults
that might happen upon that Occasion And, for that end, the said
Detachment had Powder and Ball delivered to them out of the City-
Magazine

That, while the said Offender was hanging upon the Gibbet, the
Populace began to insist to have his Body cut down, before the
Magistrates had given Orders for that purpose, and your Petitioner
having no Authority to consent thereto, without such Orders, they
threatened to cut him down by Force, and, in order so to do, crouded
in great Numbers upon your Petitioner and his Men, and did actually
assault them with large Stones by which several of the Detachment
were hurt and wounded.

That, during this Tumult, divers of the said Detachment, without
Order from your Petitioner, unfortunately fired upon the Multitude,
whereby several Persons were killed, and others wounded

That your Petitioner, after having used his utmost Endeavours to
restrain such Firing by his Men, perceiving them to run into Confusion, and to act without Orders, drew them off as fast as possible
to the Guard; and committed such as he suspected to have fired, to
the Custody of the Guard, together with their Pieces, which he
ordered to be kept for Inspection, in the same Condition as they were
then in

That your Petitioner being accused of having himself fired upon the
Multitude on this Occasion, and also of having ordered the Detachment to fire, without any just or reasonable Cause, your Petitioner
was put upon his Trial in the High Court of Justiciary aforesaid, for
the said supposed Offence and the Jury empannell'd to try your
Petitioner, by their Verdict, found, *That it was proved, that your
Petitioner had fired a Gun, and also had given Orders to the Detachment of Guard under his Command, to fire upon the Multitude so
assembled, from which firing, either of your Petitioner, or of the
Detachment of Guard under his Command, by his Order, the several
Persons specified in the Indictment against him, were respectively
killed and wounded And also found it proved, That the Mob
assembled at the Execution aforesaid, did invade and attack your Petitioner,
and the Detachment of Guard under his Command, with Stones, of a
considerable Bigness, whereby several of the Men of the Guard were bruised
and wounded*

Upon which Verdict returned by the Jury, the Court decerned
and adjudged your Petitioner to be hanged upon a Gibbet, upon
the Eighth Day of September next

That tho' your Petitioner is sensible of that Deference and Respect
that's due to the Verdict of a British Jury yet he humbly begs leave
to represent to your most EXCELLENT MAJESTY, the following Circumstances as they appeared upon his Trial To wit, That the Evidence against your Petitioner, as to his having fired, or given Orders
to fire, was very contradictory and inconsistent, for tho' some of the
Witnesses deposed that your Petitioner fired the first Shot, yet they
differed extremely as to your Petitioner's Situation, at the time he is
alleged to have so fired, as well as in other Circumstances, some
placing him at one Corner, and others at a quite opposite Corner of
the Scaffold; Some alledging, that none of the Soldiers were then near
your Petitioner, and that no other Shots were fired at that time,
while others describe your Petitioner as encompassed with Soldiers,
and say, that several Shots were fired instantly upon your Petitioner's
firing such first Shot, and some agree, that the first Shot was not
fired by your Petitioner, but by a Centinel of the Guard, who was

230

Appendix II.

close by your Petitioner. Whereas a great many Persons of undoubted Credit and Veracity, produced on the Part of your Petitioner, expressly swore, That, during the whole time of the Firing, (which continued about four or five Minutes) they took exact Notice of your Petitioner's Behaviour and Conduct, and could not observe that he fired at all, but that, upon the Mob's pressing severely upon your Petitioner and his Men, and pelting them with large Stones, your Petitioner called aloud to keep off, otherwise he would fire, and that, upon your Petitioner's pointing his Piece, in order to intimidate the Mob, a Centinel of the Guard, (unknown to the Witnesses) advanced from behind your Petitioner, and fired the first Shot, upon which one of the Multitude fell to the ground. From which Example, they supposed, several others fired, by means whereof, the several Persons, in the Indictment mentioned, were either killed or wounded

And as a further Circumstance, to shew that your Petitioner did not fire, it was proved, that upon his Return from the Execution, your Petitioner went directly of his own Accord to the Magistrates, who examined his Piece, and found the same loaded, and in such condition, that they agreed and were satisfied, it had not been fired, and the Serjeant of the Detachment attested, that your Petitioner having delivered his Piece (being that which he usually carryed), to the Deponent to Keep while your Petitioner attended the Devotions at the Execution, the Deponent restored the same again to your Petitioner, just before your Petitioner descended from the Scaffold, which is a strong circumstance to shew that your Petitioner must have fired his own Piece if he had fired at all

Your Petitioner also begs leave humbly to observe, that when a Band of armed Men are together, and some of them fire, it is very difficult, especially for those at a distance, to discriminate the Persons that actually fired, and your Petitioner is in Charity led to believe, that the Circumstance of your Petitioner's levelling his Piece, and threatening to fire attended with that of the Centinel's having fired just behind your Petitioner may have induced some unwary Persons, in the heat of popular Fury and Resentment, to be too positive in the Assertion of Facts, in their nature dubious and uncertain

And as to your Petitioner's having given Orders to the Men to fire, though two or three Persons gave Evidence against your Petitioner as to that Fact, yet neither did they agree touching the Place where your Petitioner was standing, nor in the Form of Words pretended to be used by your Petitioner in the giving thereof. Whereas it was deposed by a great number, particularly of the Soldiers, who were close by your Petitioner during the whole time of the Fray, that they could not observe that your Petitioner gave any such Orders, but on the contrary, that he called aloud to the Men, *Don't fire*, and that he pushed back the Man that fired the first Shot into his Rank, (which shews that your Petitioner did not approve thereof) that he drew off the Men as fast as he could, and that being pursued and pelted by the Populace, divers in the Rear turned about and fired when your Petitioner was at such distance, that he could not possibly be privy or consenting thereto

It was likewise observed at the Trial, and not contradicted That upon many former Occasions of Tumult, when your Petitioner with the Guard hath been ordered to quell the same, your Petitioner had bore great Insults from the Populace, even to the danger of his Life, without firing, or ordering his Men to fire, and that in Cases where he would have been well justified by the law in doing either

So that upon the whole, as your Petitioner hath the inward Satisfaction of being conscious to himself of his innocence of the Facts charged against him, so he humbly apprehends, that the Evidence adduced to prove the same, when compared with your Petitioner's Defence, will not appear to be certain or conclusive

Captain Porteous.

But in case your Petitioner had been guilty either of firing, or ordering his Men to fire, upon the Occasion aforesaid, your Petitioner most
humbly entreats your Majesty to consider, that your Petitioner was in
the Exercise of a Trust delegated to him by the lawful civil Authority,
that he and his Detachment were first unlawfully assaulted and invaded
by the Populace, and divers of his men bruised and hurt, and if, in
the Case of such an Insult upon the Laws, your Petitioner had pro
ceeded to repel Force by Force, your Petitioner humbly begs leave
to observe, That tho' he shou'd look back with the utmost Sorrow
upon so fatal an Event, yet he humbly hopes, that the Provocation and
and Agression aforesaid, wou'd be considered by your most Excellent
Majesty, in your profound Wisdom, as a great Extenuation of an
Offence, which could not be supposed to be attended with any propense
Malice of your Petitioner against Persons of whom he had no Knowledge; and that your Petitioner would be deemed a proper Object of
the Royal Clemency

Your Petitioner therefore most humbly prays Your most Excellent
Majesty, to take your Petitioner's unfortunate Case into Your Royal
Consideration, and to extend that Mercy and Compassion to your
Petitioner, by which your Majesty, adorned with all Excellent and
Princely Qualities, is so remarkably distinguished, and that Your
Majesty will be graciously pleased to issue Your Royal Warrant for
your Petitioner's Pardon And your Petitioner, whose duty hath
hitherto rendered him, on all Occasions, most zealously attached to
His Majesty, and Our happy Constitution, will, from the additional
Bond of the most powerful Gratitude, devote that Life to the Service
of His most excellent Majesty, and His Illustrious House, which he
shall enjoy as the Fruit of Your Majesty's Clemency and Grace

---

III —Petition of Noblemen and Gentlemen of Scotland

To the Queens Most Excellent Majesty   The humble supplication of the Noblemen and others underwritten

Sheweth
That we his Majesty's most dutyful and Loyall subjects hereto
subscribeing Doe with the most profound reverence and submission
Beg leave in humble Manner to lay before your Majesty
That John Porteous late Captain Lieutenant of the City Guard of
Edinburgh was indited by his Majesty's Advocat Generall ffor having
while he the said John Porteous was attending the Execution of
Andrew Wilson with a Detatchment of the Guard of the said City
under his command ffired himself and given orders to the men of the
Guard to ffire upon the Multitude assembled at the said Execution
Whereby severall persons were killed and wounded
That the Jury sett upon him after Evidence adduced Did ffind
speciall in Manner ffollowing viz " Found it proven That the said
" John Porteous ffiied a Gun among the People assembled at the
" place of Execution and tyme lybelled, As Also That he Gave orders
" to the soldiers under his Command to ffire, And upon his and their
" so ffireing The persons mentioned in the Inditement were killed,
" and wounded And ffound It proven that the Pannell i e John
" Porteous and his Guard were attacked and Beat with several stones
" of a Considerable bigness, Whereby severalls of the soldiers were
" Bruised and Wounded "
That upon the return of this Verdict the high Court of Justiciary
Did Condemn the said John Porteous to be Hanged upon the Eight
day of September next
That We Doe with the outmost humility and Reverence Beg leave

Appendix II.

to submitt it to your Royall Wisdom Whether there are not some Circumstances, attending the Case of the said John Porteous That may plead our Excuse ffor thus presenting him to your Majesty as a proper object of the Royall Clemency? And Whether if the said Sentence shall be executed to the rigour, It may not Encourage wicked and evill disposed persons to adventure upon resisting the just Execution of the Laws? And Therefor If in Respect of the Attack upon the Guard so found proven by the Jury The said John Porteous may not Merit some Mitigation or Commutation of the Sentence pronounced against him

> May it therefor please your most Excellent Majesty to take the premises under your Royall Consideration and to give such Releiff as to your Majesty in your Royall Wisdom may seem Meet

pet. Walkerr Barronett.

Rd Somers, Comʳ Ex
Gr Burnet, Comʳ Ex.
Ch Cockrane, Comʳ Ex.
Pet Wedderburn, Secʸ Ex
Ja. Campbell, Comʳ Cu
W. Westby
John Campbell
Jo Murray of Philiphaugh.
Cha Leslie of Newton
Ld George Ilay
Tho. Lockhart of Castlehill
Richd Cockburne, of Chikingtoun
Normand MacLeod of MacLeod.
John Drummond, M of P
Walt Sandilands, Sheriff of Edibʳ
Alex Lind, Sheriff of Edinʳ
A Marjoribanks, one of the Comisʳˢ Edinburgh
Home for E, Cassillis
Ja Leslie, one of the Comsʳˢ of Edʳ
    Buccleuch.
    Morton
    Home
    Balcarres
Ld Edward Murray.

John Whitefoord, Baronet.
William Nicolson, Baronett.
Ja Spital of Lovehat
Joⁿ Cant. of Grainge
R. Moubray of Cockairny.
Robert Colvile of Ochiltree.
Peter Halket, M. of P
Thomas Dundas of Fingask.
John Moyle, M Genˡ
S Duroure, Lᵗ Col of Whethams.
N. Peers, Lᵗ Col of Genˡ Sabines
G Lockhart of Carnwath
Arch Primrose, Barᵗ
    Elphinstone
    Napier.
Alex Home.
Torphichen for E Lauderdale
    Torphichen
    Primerose
    Moray
    Lindores.
    Doune.
    Aberdour
Ld Charles Hay.
    Wigtoune.

IV —Petition of Noblemen and Gentlemen of Scotland

(From the original MS in the possession of the Society of Antiquaries of Scotland.)

> To the Queens Most Excellent Majesty, The Humble Supplication of the Noblemen and others underwritten,

Sweweth,
    That Wee, his Majesty's most dutyfull and loyall Subjects hereto subscribing, doe with the most profound reverence and submission beg leave in humble manner to lay before your Majesty,
    That John Porteous, late Captain Lieutenant of the City Guard of

Captain Porteous.

Edinburgh, was indited by His Majesty's Advocate-Generall, ffor having, while he the said John Porteous was attending the execution of Andrew Wilson, with a detachment of the guard of the said City under his command, ffired himself, and given orders to the men of the guard to fire upon the multitude assembled at the said execution, whereby severall persons were killed and wounded

That the Jury sett upon him after evidence adduced, did find speciall in manner following, viz FOUND IT PROVEN that the said John Porteous fired a gun among the people assembled at the place of execution and time libelled, As also that he gave orders to the soldiers under his command to fire, and upon his and their so fireing, the persons mentioned in the Inditement were killed and wounded AND FOUND IT PROVEN, That the pannell, i e John Porteous and his guard, were ATTACKED AND BEAT with several stones of considerable bigness, whereby severalls of the soldiers were bruised and wounded

That upon the return of this verdict the High Court of Justiciary did condemn the said John Porteous to be hanged upon the eight day of September nixt

That Wee doe with the utmost humility and reverence beg leave to submitt it to your Royall wisdom, whither there are not some circumstances attending the case of the said John Porteous that may plead our excuse for thus presenting him to your Majesty, as a proper object of the Royal Clemency, and whither, if the sentence aforesaid shall be executed to the rigour, it may not encourage wicked and evill disposed persons to adventure upon resisting the just execution of the laws And THEREFORE, if in respect of the attack upon the guard so found proven by the Jury the said John Porteous may not merit some mitigation or commutation of the sentence pronounced against him

   MAY IT THEREFORE please your Majesty to take the pre-
    mises under your Royall consideration, and to give such
    relief as to your Majesty in your Royal wisdom may seem
    meet

               SALTOUN

    Hew Dalrymple of Drummore
    Cha Fraser of Inveralachie
    Alexander Fraser, Master of Saltoun .
    Geo Skene of that Ilk
    Alexander Udny of Udny
    A Burnett of Leyes
    Tho Forbes of Echt
    Arch Grant of Monymuske
    Rot Burnett of Sauchen
    Geo Burnett of Kemnay
    Jo Arbuthnott of Fordound
    Phil Foulerton of Philpshal
    A Fraser of Powis
    John Irvine of Drum
    J Foulerton of Cowie
    Arthur Forbes of Craigievar
    Al Gordon of Pitlurg
    Will Forbes of Desblair

Appendix III.

APPENDIX III.

EXCERPTS FROM THE *Caledonian Mercury*, REFERRED TO IN THE INTRODUCTION TO THE TRIAL OF CAPTAIN PORTEOUS

(Caledonian Mercury, 15th April, 1736)

Yesterday being the day fixed for the execution of Andrew Wilson, for the robbery of Collector Stark, and it being strongly surmised, that plots were laid for favouring his escape also, from a sympathy the populace had generally conceived with him, preferably to his associates in that ugly scrape, the Magistrates, to defeat all hopes of whatever attempt that way, put the executioner the day before into the Tolbooth, to prevent his being carried off, the centinels were doubled on the prison without, besides those posted within, the officers of the trained bands were ordered to attend the execution, also the constables with long batons, the whole city guard had ammunition distributed to them, and marched to the place of execution, bayonets screwed on their pieces, intermixed with the town officers, and to make the work very sure, a small battalion of the Welsh Fuziliers (headed by six Captains or other commission officers) marched up the streets of the city, and drew up on each side of the Lawnmarket, upon application of the Right Honourable the Lord Provost, whilst another body of that corps stood under arms at the Canongate guard At two o'clock Wilson was carried from prison to the Grassmarket, manacled, where he died very penitent, but expressing more sorrow on account of the common frailties of life, than the crimes for which he suffered He was a stout young man, a bachelor, and his body was delivered to his friends, who carried it over to Fife

Nor was there, during the whole procession or after he had hanged till he was dead, the remotest appearance of a riot, or the least disturbance on the part of a vast crowd of people; till after the Magistrates had retired from the scaffold to a house hard by, reasonably concluding there could now no disturbance happen, and the executioner was actually on the top of the ladder cutting Wilson down, when a few idle boys, or rather children, began to throw some pebbles or garbage at him, as is (very foolishly) practised at all executions, and the rather now, that he was treating the affair ludicrously, which was so highly resented by Mr Captain Porteous, who commanded the City Guard, that, without the least authority from the Magistrates, or offering to read the proclamation, as is directed, the guard, at his precept and example, fired sharp dropping shots among the crowd, whereby about twenty persons were killed or wounded Among the slain are,

1. Henry Graham, tailor in Canongate, shot through the head while looking out at a window two stairs up

2 Alexander Macneal in Monktonhall

3. John Anderson, son to George Anderson of Craighead, Esq

4 Charles Husband, relation and servant to Paul Husband, confectioner   The three last were killed on the street with slug shot

Among the wounded are,

1 Archibald Ballandine, a young gentleman at the school of Dalkeith, so mortally wounded that he cannot live

2 James Niven, brewer, shot in two places of the head, and in the arm

Captain Porteous.

3 Patrick Spalden, son of   Spalden of Ashintully, Esq and
apprentice to Mr David Mitchell, jeweller twice shot in the head,
and twice in the right shoulder, lies dangerously ill

4 Jean Peat, servant to James Macdowal in Deanhaugh, shot in
the head, side, and arm, and will not recover

5 David Kid, tailor, wounded in the breast

6 James Philip, servant to Captain Lauder, mortally wounded in
the breast and arm

7 David Wallace, wright, servant to Mrs Allison, shot through
the upper jaw and right side

8 Margaret Gordon (of Elgin,) servant to David Ogilvie, tailor,
mortally wounded

9 Margaret Arthur, residenter at the Watergate, shot in the left
shoulder, and twice in the right arm, lies dangerously ill

10 and 11. Alexander Wallace, and James Lyel, servants to Mr.
Wright, staymaker, the one shot in the arm, the other in the belly

The Magistrates (after ordering the killed and wounded to be buried
and looked after at the city's expence) immediately convened in
council, and after taking a precognition touching this unhappy event,
the Lord Provost, as High Sheriff, ordered Mr Porteous to close prison
for eight days, and to be afterwards detained in custody till liberate
in course of law   He was accordingly carried to prison by his own
guard, without which the mob had unquestionably *finished* him,
so exasperated were they on seeing their innocent fellow citizens
wallowing in their blood, and that the same should have been shed
by those nursed up in our own bosom, while, on the other hand, both
officers and soldiers of the military detachment behaved with all
honour

———

(*Caledonian Mercury*, 19th April, 1736)

BY ORDER OF THE MAGISTRATES OF EDINBURGH

Various accounts having been given of the melancholy event that
happened at the execution of Andrew Wilson upon Wednesday last,
the 14th of April instant, in order to satisfy the world as far as we can,
we thought proper to publish the following account of it, part of
which we had access to witness, and partly what clearly appears by
declarations emitted before us

When the criminal was thrown over, the Magistrates (according to
custom) retired to a public house near the place of execution   Hitherto
there was no appearance of any tumult, nor till the executioner was
about to cut him down, when some idle persons threw a few stones at
him, some of which falling among the city guard, that day commanded
by Captain Porteous, whereupon he, in an unwarrantable and barbarous manner, first discharged his own piece among the spectators,
and at the same time ordered his guard to fire in like manner, using
these words, *Fire Buggars, and be damned !* without the least orders
from the Magistrates, who were then attending, and from whom he
should have received his orders   The Magistrates, ministers, and constables, were stationed in the first storey of a house to the street, were
themselves in danger of being killed, a ball having grazed on the side
of the window where they stood, (but this was not known till some
time after)   A dropping fire continued for some time, but the firing
being over, the Magistrates were put into a great consternation, upon
some persons coming to them, and informing that several dead bodies
lay on the streets   Upon this, one of the magistrates flying to the
window, found it but too true, and instantly calling for his officers to
give the necessary orders for immediate assistance, to his great surprise

Appendix III.

they were all removed, and the guard was now marching off   One
of the magistrates immediately repaired to a tavern in the Lawnmarket, where the Lord Provost and some of the council were attending, to give proper orders to the detachment of the Royal Welsh
Fuziliers posted before them, to whom he gave accounts of this dismal
scene   Hereupon Captain Porteous was ordered forthwith to attend
the magistrates in the burgh room, when they proceeded to an examination of what had passed, and have ever since been closely employed
in taking the precognition, in order to do all justice to the injured,
so far as is in their power   That night, upon the declarations emitted
before them, the Lord Provost committed the Captain to close prison,
(though he denied he had either fired himself, or given orders to his
guard to fire,) until his trial for life in due course of law   Next day
15 centinels of the guard were committed to the same effect   it appearing clearly, after a careful examination of all the firelocks of the party,
that they were the persons who discharged their pieces   The above
narration is attested by T. Crockat, B Gavin Hamilton, B
     The following persons in this city were wounded on that occasion
besides those in our last.
     12 John Millar, taylor in Niddery's Wynd, the bone of his right
arm broken with a ball
     13 William Philp, wheelwright in Cowgate, shot in the legs
     14 John Ferrier, indweller in Grange-gateside, shot in the arm
     15 David Ogilvie, writer, shot in the foot.
     16 George Ballantine, servant to Andrew Orrock, cutler in Leith
wynd shot in the hand
     And it being market day many people, who were in the town about
business, had the curiosity to go to see the execution, several of whom
having shared in the unlucky fate retired or were carried off by
friends and we are informed two or three of them have died in
the country   There are also others in town wounded who rather
incline to put up with their misfortunes than, by publishing the same,
alarm their friends
     The names of those of the City Guard committed in the city jail are
Matthew Buckles, John Lesly, Robert Brown, John Kettle, David
Gilchrist, Andrew Tod, and John Paterson for prevarication   Sent to
the Canongate Tolbooth, Frank Wilhams William Hunter, James
Allan, Andrew Macklefreish, George Robison Archibald Campbell,
William Gun,—most of whom we hear have declared they had not the
word of command to fire and indeed, if upon the proof it should
come out that the word was *G d   why don't ye fire!* it might be
pled for them that their declaration is in some measure true, there
being no such word of command authorised by the martial law, and it
will at the same time serve to show what vast improvements our
captain had made in that discipline   What excess of brotherly love
have we here!   These creatures, it seems to screen their captain will
expose themselves to the punishment he justly deserves
     And indeed for what has been said on this dismal subject, there is
but too good ground to affirm that Captain Porteous did nothing on
this occasion but what he had premeditated, for to what good purpose
else was this so early precaution in ordering his detachment to load
with ball and slug shot before they marched from the Guard   This
was unprecedented and for which he will not pretend orders   At the
same time the body of General Sabine's regiment had no such orders;
nor was one of their pieces loaded till after hearing repeated firings,
and that several dead bodies lay on the spot, *then* indeed their officers
ordered them to load, which they did in sight of some thousand
spectators
     'Tis pity our noble captain was not at Rome with his instruments of
death when the above fray happened there, he'd soon have tam'd the

Captain Porteous.

Romans, there indeed a riot happened which, the cause still subsisting lasted several days here again there was no appearance of a riot nor the least ground to occasion one, Wilson being already hung and dead; yet our noble captain did more execution on a multitude of innocent people (to whom he stood indebted for his daily bread these twenty years past) in less than three minutes, than all the Roman officers put together could effectuate in the space of three days among actual rioters

None of the wounded persons, as in our last, were dead yesterday, though most of them are in such agony that their death would be a great satisfaction to their concerns

P S —Mr Ballantine died this morning, he had left the school of Dalkeith some time and was about to be bound apprentice to a joiner, nor were any of that seminary at the execution

---

(*Caledonian Mercury*, 9th September, 1736)

Tuesday night last, a most outrageous and violent insult to the laws and constitution of the nation was made in this city, that perhaps ever happened in any civilized country, viz

A few minutes before ten at night a multitude of people, most of them from the country, rushed in upon the City Guard on a sudden, turned out the whole soldiers, and seized all the fire-arms, &c in the guard   At the same instant of time others, having posted themselves near the several gates of the city   made themselves masters of the same, and then attacked the prison   The Magistrates, with several members of the council, and burghers, attempted to suppress them, but they threw stones in so violent a manner, and wounded several of those that attended the magistrates with Lochaber-axes and butts of muskets   and at the same time threatened to fire, that they were forced to retire   The mob   now finding themselves absolute masters, immediately set fire to the prison door, and in less than an hour forced their way up stairs; they then dismissed all the prisoners, seized Captain Porteous, dragged him down stairs, and hurried him through the streets to the Grassmarket, where they broke open a shop, and took out a coil of ropes, tied it by one end about Mr Porteous's neck, and throwing the other end over a dyer's cross-trees, close by the common place of execution, hoisted him up and hanged him   The body was taken down about break of day, and put into a church hard by

This forenoon his corpse was interred in the Grayfriars church-yard.

Last night, about 50 of the Welsh Fusileers commanded by proper officers, reinforced the garrison of the Castle, two companies of the City Trained Bands mounted guard in the borough-room and council-house, and there was a guard at the Netherbow   But there was not the remotest appearance of disturbance all night, nor, indeed, have we heard of any other mischief done the night the riot happened, but what is above narrated

No less than seventeen criminals escaped from the city jail on this occasion, among whom are the dragoon who was indicted for the murder of the butcher's wife in Dunse   the two Newhaven men lately brought in from Blackness Castle for smuggling, seven centinels of the City Guard, &c   The prisoners in the City Guard were in like manner set at liberty.

About fourteen tradesmen, or others, were taken up the morning after the riot   and committed to the Canongate prison, eleven of whom are since discharged; but the other three, not giving so good account of themselves, remain in custody

Appendix III.

(*Caledonian Mercury*, 13th September, 1736.)

The narrative in our last with relation to the surprising and unparalleled riot that happened in this city the 7th instant not having been so particular as the world might expect, from an event so uncommon in all its circumstances, we have thought proper, by way of supplement, to give the following disinterested relation thereof, as from the best information could be collected, willing always, if what is here related shall at any time appear to have proceeded from misinformation, to retract either facts or circumstances. And it is reported,

1. That a body of strangers entered the West Port betwixt nine and ten at night, who having seized the Portsburgh drummer by the way, brought along his drum, and some of them advancing up into the Grassmarket, beat a call to arms, then called out, *Here! all those who dare avenge innocent blood!* This probably was a signal for their associates to fall on, in regard it was followed by instantly shutting up the gates of the city, posting guards at each, and flying centinels at all places whence a surprise might be expected. while a separate detachment threw themselves upon and disarmed the City Guard, and, seizing the drum, beat about the High Street, to notify, (it is thought) their success so far. At that instant, a body of them advancing to the Tolbooth, called for the keeper, and, finding he was gone, fell a-breaking the door with fore-hammers, but, making no great advances that way, they got together a parcel of broom, furze, (or whins,) with other combustibles, and heaps of timber, placed over a barrell of pitch, they set fire to the latter with the flambeaux they had taken from the city officers, when they repulsed the magistrates with showers of stones, and threats to discharge platoons of fire-arms among them, if they offered to appear in the streets at night, and it is even said they placed centinels to eye the motions of the magistrates. It is reported,

2. That upon the prison door taking fire, several citizens, particularly two gentlemen made up to the rioters, and expostulated touching the imminent danger of setting the whole neighbourhood on fire, insinuating that this outrage might come to be highly resented; but they were answered, that they'd take care no prejudice should happen to the city, and that, for the rest, they knew their business, and that they (the gentlemen) might go about their's. It is reported,

3. That, before the prison door was near burnt down severals rushed through the flames, up the stairs, demanded the keys from the keepers, and though they could scarce see one another for the smoke, got into Captain Porteous's apartment, calling, *Where is the Buggar?* He is said to have answered, Gentlemen I am here, but what are you to do with me? And that they answered, We are to carry you to the place where you shed so much innocent blood, and hang you. That he begged mercy, but finding none at their hands, requested some time to prepare himself, but that they instantly seized and pulled him to the door, in his night-gown, cap, and breeches, but he struggling, they caught him by the legs, and dragged him to the stairs-foot, while others set the whole prisoners at liberty. That he was set upon his legs how soon he was brought to the street some seizing him by the breast and arms, while others pushed behind, thus conducting him to the Bow head, where they stopped a little, at the pressing solicitations of some citizens, that so he might die peaceably, but whose real view was to gain time expecting every moment the Welsh Fuziliers from the Canongate, who, it was said were to enter the city by the Trinity Hospital, or that the garrison of the Castle should come to his relief. Here he is said to have addressed some of the citizens who appeared in his behalf, and gave one of them 23 guineas, &c.,

Captain Porteous.

for his brother's use   By this time, some who appeared to be in the
direction ordering a march, he was hurried down the Bow, and to the
gallows stone, where he was desired to kneel, confess his sins, particularly the havoc he had committed in that place, and to offer up
his petitions to God   In a few minutes after, he was led to the fatal
tree; but, on seeing the rope, made remonstrances, and caught hold
of the tree, but, being disengaged, they set him down, and as the
noose was about to be put over his head, he appeared to gather fresh
spirit, struggled, wrenching his head and body   Here, again, some
citizens appeared for him, telling, that the troops being now in full
march, they must all expect to be sacrificed, and that the artillery of
the Castle would doubtless be discharged among them, and that they
answered, No man will die till his day comes   It is reported,

4 That, a quarter of an hour before twelve they put the rope about
his neck, and ordered him to be pulled up, which done, observing his
hands loose, he was let down again, after tying his hands, he was
hauled up a second time, but, after a short space, having wrought one
of his hands loose, he was let down once more, in order to tie it up,
and cover his face   Stripping him of one of the shirts he had on,
they wrapped it about his head, and got him up for a third time, with
loud huzzas, and a ruff of the drum   After he had hung a long time,
they nailed the rope to the tree   then formally saluting one another,
grounding their arms, and the other ruff of the drum, they separated,
retired out of town, and severals of them were seen riding off, in
bodies, to all quarters, leaving him hanging till near five in the
morning   It is also reported,

5 That neither the gentlemen who conversed them at the tolbooth,
nor those who were sent out by the magistrates to see if they knew
any of the rioters, could say they had ever seen any one of them
before, though the flames rendered it as light as at noon   So that it
is generally believed no citizen acted any principal part in this tragedy,
though, indeed, it is certain that many of the inhabitants, led by
curiosity, stept out to behold the surprising boldness and incredible
extravagance of this scene

Upon the whole, it would seem their plot was concerted with judgment, conducted with secrecy, enterprised with resolution, and execute
in the space of two hours, with unexpected success

Ever since the riot   an officer's command of the Welsh Fuziliers
mounts daily in the Castle, the Canongate guard is reinforced all night,
besides their picquet guard; the city company has a guard at the
Netherbow, the gate whereof is locked back on both sides, that passage
may be open at all times, two companies of trained bands mount
guard each night, a troop of Lieutenant-General Gore's Dragoons
arrived last Friday in Canongate, and another of the same at Leith.

Appendix IV.

APPENDIX IV.

LETTER GIVING A CONTEMPORARY ACCOUNT OF THE MURDER OF CAPTAIN
JOHN PORTEOUS, HITHERTO UNPUBLISHED

(From the original in the possession of John A. Fairley, Esq)

Sepr 11th, 1736

My Dr Charles,
  I receivd yours the day you left Stirling, & shall keep the Snuff
till you give me directions as to the disposall of it, I was glad to
hear from your Sister, that you had got the length of Carlisle well;
Ld Islay is expected every hour, & Ld Bute & his Lady, but this is
no news, to what I have to send you, for last tuesday the most barbarous, wicked & Insolent Murther was Committed on poor, (I say,
& most people now say, Innocent) Porteous, that ever was heard of;
the very day or two after the petition for him went up, a Reprieve
came down from her Majesty for Six weeks, who doubtless had been
well informd of the hard Circumstances of his case, by the Reprieve's
comming so long before She Coud receive the petition. Now as it was
not doubted that a pardon woud follow the Reprieve, the Mob, whose
Resentments had always ran high against him (for having, you know,
been their Standing terror by reason of his Courage, Strength, &
Vigilance, which he really possessed in a very Eminent degree, tho
but a Mean Man) & who had the Spirit of Revenge kept strongly alive
in them by those true Trumpeters of Sedition & Cruelty in all
Countries, the damnd Priests, the Mob, I say, dropd some threatning
Letters, & many reports were Spread, of what they would do, if
Porteous was not Executed on Wednesday the 8th inst, according to
the Tenor of the Sentence, this, any one woud have thought shoud
have alarmd the Magistrates, & put 'em upon their Guard, so as to
have taken all the proper Precautions, not only for the Security of
the unhappy Man, but for that of the Constitution, the Laws & the
preservation of every individual of the Society, who is now liable to
be taken out of his bed, & murthered, whenever the mob please to
take a Spight against him, however whether the Magistrates did not
Credit those reports, or did not believe the Mob durst make any
attempt on the Life of the Prisoner, or for what other reasons I don't
pretend to know, but every thing was very Quiet till tuesday, till about
three Quarters after Nine at night, when instantaneously, at one & the
very same Moment of time, the Town Guard commanded by Lynn was
disaimd and dismissd, all the whole Ports of the City seizd & Lock'd,
& numbers left to Guard 'em, then the rest of the Mob marched away
to the Tolbooth, huzzaing, & Drums beating, where they were above
an hour trying to force the Outward Door, which not being Able to
do they set fire to it & burnd it down, but as there was a few paces
within that, a much stronger door than the outward one, viz a huge
Massy Iron one, they must necessarily have been detaind above an
hour more there, as Bailie Colquhon ownd to me himself next
Day, if unhappily thro' Stupidity, or rather worse, the Keeper had
not staid in the Way, & him they obligd to unlock the Door, then
they draggd poor Porteous down Stairs, who having nothing to
make resistance with begd for Mercy, but alas! the Mercies of a
Mob, like those of Church men, are barbarities & Cruelties, for as
they Carried him to the Grassmarket, they run torches in his face,
which they had with 'em, tho' the moon made it as light as day,

Captain Porteous.

& beat & punchd him most unmercifully, when he was Come to the
Grassmarket, they broke open a Shop, & took out a whole Coil of
rope, & tied one end of it immediately about his Neck then he begd
for mercy again which being with imprecations denied, he Entreated
they woud allow him half an hour to pray, while they were debating
this among themselves for about two minutes, he spied John Carmichael, the Merchant (from whom I had it) who had followd the
Mob to see if he Coud do him any Service in Mollifying them, &
beckoning him up to him, he Slippd a purse with 23 Guineas into
his hand, & twice whisperd him to give it his Bror, which as he knew
it would be of Service to him, as being a poor Man was surely an
astonishing instance of presence of Mind, the Mob then Calld out to
Mr Carmichael, & askd him what Porteous said, to which he readily
replied he had only been taking leave of him, upon this the Monsters
threw the Rope over a Dyers trees, which happend to be Close by,
& is, you know, in the form of a Gallows, about 15 foot high, on
which they dry their Worsteds & Cloaths, & immediately hauld him
up; after he had hung about three Minutes, the barbarians let him down
again (Quite alive) & Strippd off his Night Gown & Shirt, which last
they tied about his head, but not his face, & then with huzzas pulld
him up again, but as his hands were not bound, he struggled poor
creature, very much, upon which one of the villains up with a
Lochaber Ax, & Broke his right Arm & Shoulder, & then they kept
Jerking him up & down about an hour, when they were sure he was
dead, they wound the rope as it was very long, about one of the Supporters of the Gallows, & nailing the end of it with Several great
Nails, left him hanging till five in the Morning, when the Mob being
Separated, the Magistrates BOLDLY venturd to send some people
to take him down, & Carry his body to the Grey Friars Church, in
the Yard of which it was buried the day following; I Shoud have
told you that when they forcd the prison Doors, or rather had 'em
opened to 'em, they made a Jail delivery of about Seventeen
Robbers, Murtherers, horse Stealers, & Smugglers, which last had
been brought in a few days before from Newhaven, for a most daring
Violation of the Late Act of Parliament having deforcd & beat some
Customhouse Officers there most Cruelly, and what plainly Shews
that the fury of the Mob was kept up & directed solely against the
person of poor Porteous, & not against the Action of firing at Wilsons
Execution, is, that tho' nine of the Town Guard were in the Tolbooth for firing that day, & killing the Several people, which one
woud naturally Suppose shoud equally have made 'em Objects of the
Mobs resentment, yet so far were they from receiving any Injury,
or even abuse, that they were Every one Set at Liberty with the
other Prisoners, & are gone off with 'em, besides the barbarity &
Circumstances of this Murther, I believe it is the most daring insult
upon a Government & the Justice of a Nation that was ever either
heard or read of, as I heard my Ld Justice Clerk say, with whom I
was very Late in Company at a Tavern the next night, and who, I
dare say, will both as a Minister & a Judge Exert himself to have
some of these Monsters discoverd and brought to punishment, for
otherwise no man knows whose turn it will be next to show the
Insolence of these Devils to the Government, when they were
murthering the poor man, they cried out, the Queen might wipe her
b—— now with her bonny Reprieve.

The Regt was under arms all night from a Quarter after ten,
but the Genll told Peter Lindsay, (who some way or other got out)
that he woud not attempt to force the City gates, without a Warrant
from Ld Justice Clerk, or some other Ld of the Justiciary, for that
he had a very strong instance before his Eyes, in the very case of
poor Porteous, of the Danger of firing or giving orders to fire, with-

Appendix V.

out a Sanction that was undoubtedly Legal, this is much debated now pro & Con, tho My Ld Advocate certainly laid this down for Law in his information against Porteous, It is very astonishing that since Mr Lindsay coud get out, no one Baillie shoud have gone down to authorize the Troops, & still more astonishing that the Proclamation was never read

I am very tird with Writing, so after making Madams Compliments to you, must Conclude with assuring you of being Ever yrs

[Indecipherable initials]

There is a troop of Goies come into the Cannongate & another to Leith, & the Regt sends every day an Officers Guard to the Castle

---

APPENDIX V

A Brief Account of the Riotous Proceedings at Edinburgh relating to the Murther of Captain Porteous

(Newcastle Papers, B M Add MS. 33,049, f 17)

Collector Stark of Kinghorn, having been robb'd of the Publick Money and narrowly escaped himself by leaping out of a Window, one Wilson was Tryed and Condemn'd for the said Robbery and three of his accomplices made their Escapes

The day before the Execution of Wilson upon a bare Surmise that a Mobb of Smuglers & their Associates (who thought it had that a man should be hang'd as they said for taking his own) intended to rescue Wilson at the place of Execution   The Provost of Edinburgh wrote a letter to General Moyle acquainting him therewith, and desiring him to send two Companys of the Regiment quartered in the Canongate to assist the Magistrates in dispersing the Mobb, in case any such attempt should be made, which General Moyle order'd accordingly, they were drawn up at some distance from the place of Execution to be at hand in case their Assistance had been requii'd

After the Condemnation of Porteous several persons of Rank and Condition believing him to be Innocent of the crimes he was charged with and for which he was condemn'd, signed a Petition in his favour at which the Populace were much displeas'd, and said altho that Petition should procure his Pardon he should notwithstanding be hang'd on the day he was sentenc'd to dye

Her Majesty having been Graciously pleas'd to send a Reprieve for Porteous, It arriv'd at Edinburgh a week before the day appointed for his Execution, which was receiv'd with so much Indignation by the generality of the People, That it was publickly said in all conversation both in Town and Country, that Porteous would be hang'd the day he was Sentenced to dye without any regard to her Majesty's Reprieve, and this was industriously spread through the Country, Fifty miles round Edinburgh to Induce them to come and assist in that Execrable Murther   It is likewise confidently said, that the Provost received several letters from different hands, acquainting him with the Intentions of the Mobb, and some threatening him, that if he did any Act or thing that should defeat their design of hanging Porteous he might expect to be hang'd in his place

Captain Porteous.

It is likewise said that the Captain of the City Guard not knowing how to act went to the Provost about six of the Clock the same night the Mobb got together in order to hang Porteous (as he had done three days before) for his directions how he should proceed, But he only gave him the Word without any other Orders, or delivering out Powder and Ball, which cannot be done but by order of the Provost, and which was done at the Execution of Wilson

About nine the Provost sent for him, and told him he heard there was a Mobb in the Grass market, ordering him to go there & see what they were doing, But he chose to go to his Guard & sent a man who brought him word they were marching to seize the City Gates, of which he went and acquainted the Magistrates and returning to his Guard Room found it seiz'd by the Mobb, and all the Arms above 100 in number in their Possession   The Provost and Magistrates were at this time at a Tavern near the Prison, and continued there from seven that afternoon 'till 4 the next morning after Porteous was hang'd, except an excursion they made for a few minutes towards the Mobb, when they had invested the Prison, but return'd without Reading or attempting to Read the Proclamation

From the time when the Messenger arrived with the Queen's Reprieve, to the day of the Murther of Porteous, General Moyle, who was no Stranger to the Rumour that was spread of this intended Villainy, was in daily expectation of a letter or Message from the Provost requiring the Assistance of the Troops to defeat a design that was so publickly known and the common Topick of all Conversation but receiv'd no Message 'till after the City Gates were seiz'd on and Lock'd, & Porteous in the power of the Mobb, tho' there were many ways of preventing that Barbarous Murther, Viz by sending the Prisoner to the Castle of Edinburgh, by placing a Guard of Soldiers at the Gate that leads to the Canongate, By Posting a Guard about or within the Prison where Porteous was confined, and even after the City Gates were seiz'd and the communication of the Regular Troops cut off, they might have sent to the Castle of Edinburgh which is but a small distance from the Prison, where Major Roberton who commanded in the Castle, was with his Garrison of one hundred men under Arms from the time he heard the Mobb were assembled   Fifty of which he immediately march't down to the Castle Gate with a Basket of hand Granades ready loaded & prim'd, and waited there above three hours, & 'till after the Murther was committed in expectation of the Magistrates requiring his Assistance, during which time he had the mortification from the Works of the Castle to hear the hammers striking against the Prison Gate and of seeing the Fire that was plac'd against it in order to Burn it   And it was near an hour & half from the time they Invested the Prison before they got Porteous into their hands   Whereas the Major could easily have march't from the Castle to the Prison in five or six minutes had his Assistance been requir'd by the Provost or any other Civil Magistrate, but no such Assistance ever was requir'd, Altho it is confidently said that Bailiff Cohoon propos'd it more than once to the Provost   All which makes it more than probable, that the Provost & Majority of the Magistrates wilfully & knowingly permitted this outrage to be Committed in breach of their Trust & in Contempt of Her Majesty's Authority

But as great Artifices have been used to throw the Blame of this their Ill conduct on General Moyle suggesting as if he had refus'd the Assistance of the Troops when Mr Lindsey came to him from the Provost, General Moyle does averr, that the first and only Message he had from the Provost or any other Civil Magistrate was not 'till a quarter of an hour before eleven at night, and an hour and half after the Mobb had seiz'd & lock'd the Gates of the City, Although before Mr.

Appendix V.

Lindsey came he had notice that the Mobb was up, and the City Gates seiz'd, upon which he immediately ordered the Companys in the Canongate to assemble under Arms and those from Leith to join them. And the message which was brought him by Mr Lindsey was in the words or to the Effect following, Sir, I am come from the Provost & Magistrates to acquaint you, that there is a great Mobb in the City and that they have seiz'd the City Gates, and then said, I was forc'd to get out at a private door, and to give six pence to the person that let me out, I expect my house will be pull'd down before I can return & I believe their Intention is to seize Porteous To which General Moyle answered that he had already order'd the Troops to assemble with the utmost expedition, but his hands were Tyed up and that he could not break open the Gates of the City without authority from the Civil Power, or an Order in writing from one of the Lords of the Justiciary, and then asked, If Lord Justice Clerk was in town, he answer'd, he was at his Country house, which is about two Miles distant from the City, he then was ask'd If any other of the Lords of the Justiciary were in Town? his answer was Lord Newhall was in Town but not to be come at Upon which the General desired him, to write to Lord Justice Clerk for an order to break open the City Gates, and sent his own servant with the letter who gallop'd all the way going and coming, But was detain'd there above an hour, so that the answer did not come 'till near two of the Clock, which was above an hour & half after the Murther was committed The letter being directed to Mr Lindsey & not coming 'till after the man was dead, the General did not open it, but sent it to Mr Lindsey who had promis'd to wait for him at the Canongate Guard, and Altho the General Immediately got on horseback & follow'd him there, he found Mr Lindsey had not stop't for him at the Guard but was gone directly to the City, The General continued for near three hours at the head of the Regiment who were drawn up under Arms before the Guard house, in expectation either of an answer to the said Letter, or that a Civil Magistrate would have been sent to require his Assistance, & Authorise him to force his way into the City, but during all that time no Magistrate came, nor was he any ways applyed to by the Civil Authority

Some days after when the General sent Col Peers & Capt Bendish to desire a sight of Lord Justice Clerks letter it was refus'd by Mr Lindsey. The General was afterwards credibly Inform'd the contents of it were to the following effect That he could not take upon him to give the General an Order to break open the Gates of the Town not knowing what the consequences might be

The General asked the Lord Justice Clerk the morning after the Murther of Porteous, if he could have been justified in breaking open the Gates of the Town without the Authority of the Civil power, he said, if he had, he must have answered for the consequences that might have followed on his giving such an Order General Moyle then said, That if Porteous had been sent to the Castle his Life might have been saved, the Justice Clerk answered, That it had been propos'd to the Magistrates but that they would not consent to it

Some days after the General ask'd the Lord Justice Clerk the purport of his letter to Mr Lindsey who answer'd it was of no consequence

Had Mr Lindsey brought a letter from the Provost Impowering the General to force open the Gates or had a proper Magistrate been sent that would have gone with the troops and authoris'd them to have done it, he would without any hesitation have Marcht the Troops and forced open the Gates

But Mr Lindsey's verbal Message could not be a sufficient Authority, not being one of the Magistrates or a Justice of the Peace, neither did he offer to go with the troops.

Captain Porteous.

Memorandums

It was so clear a Moonlight when Porteous was murthered That the face of any Person could be known from one side of the street to the other

The Grassmarket where the Murther was committed was filled with people, and is large enough to contain 4 or 5000 in number

Captain Lort of General Sabines (who is now in Town) was told by the Turnkey of the Prison, that he had notice given him the 7th September in the morning that the Prison would be Attack't that night which he told to the headkeeper desiring him to acquaint the Provost of it

The usual Town Guard is an Officer and 30 men But that night there was no more than a Sergeant & ten men (besides Centinels) who deliver'd their arms to the Mobb without making any resistance

It is confidently said, that before the Murther of Porteous, some of the Clergy from their Pulpits said that the Land was defiled with Blood, and that the Judgements of God would hang over their heads, 'till the Bloodshedders were deliver'd into the hands of the Avenger And afterwards some of them said, that God often made use of mean Instruments to bring about his Blessed Will and Purpose

General Moyle was told by one of the Writers of the Edinburgh News Papers, That having prepared a Paragraph giving an account that the Troops were ready & the General at the head of them waiting for an Order from the Civil Power to force open the Gates, he was threatened to be sent to prison If he did not strike it out

No persons were apprehended or Committed to Prison 'till the arrival of the Justice General which was a month after the Murther of Porteous And of six that were then Committed, Four have been admitted to Bail, and since the house of Lords have summon'd the Magistrates to appear before them William McLauchlan has been order'd to be brought to a Tryal

What they call the City Guard consists of near 100 men Officers included, They are cloth'd, Arm'd and Accoutred like the Regular Troops, and the Provost for the time being is their Captain, who never will permit the Regular Troops either for the Relief of the Castle or on any other Emergency to enter the Gates of the City without his leave

How far are they authoris'd by Law to keep a Body of Regular Troops in pay, Independent of His Majesty's Authority is a question

Appendix VI.

PROCLAMATION BY QUEEN CAROLINE FOR DISCOVERING THE MURDERERS OF CAPTAIN PORTEOUS

(From the *London Gazette*, Saturday, 25th September 1736)

By the QUEEN'S most Excellent Majesty, Guardian of the Realm of Great Britain, &c.

A PROCLAMATION,

For discovering, apprehending and bringing to Justice the Persons concerned in the barbarous Murder of Captain John Porteous, and the wicked, violent, and audacious Outrages, committed at EDINBURGH on the SEVENTH DAY of this Instant September

CAROLINE, R C R

Whereas it hath been represented unto us, That on the Seventh Day of this Instant September, a great Number of wicked, dissolute and disorderly Persons did, in a most tumultuous, riotous, and Outragious Manner, and in open Breach and Violation of the Peace, and in Contempt and Defiance of the Laws of the Realm, assemble and conveen themselves together in the City of Edinburgh, and seize the Arms of the Guard of the said City, and drive them from the Guard Room, where they had been posted for the Safety and Security of the said City, and did by Force possess themselves of the Gates thereof, and did likewise break open the Tolbooth or Prison of the said City, by setting Fire to the Gates thereof, and thereby set at large the several Prisoners therein confined for divers Crimes, and did thereout in a most cruel Manner, drag JOHN PORTEOUS, commonly called Captain John Porteous, there also confined under a Judgment and Sentence of Death, the Execution whereof had been by a Reprive granted by us respited, and did most barbariously and inhumanly Murder the said John Porteous, by hanging him up by the Neck until he was dead, without any legal Warrant or Authority for so doing And whereas it is highly necessary that the Persons concerned in such unparalleled Cruelties and Violences should not escape without speedy and exemplary Punishment; We therefore, being moved with a just Indignation and Abhorrence of such outragious and detestable Practices, and to deter all others from committing the like for the future, have thought fit, by and with the Advice of his Majesty's Privy Council, to issue this Proclamation And we do strictly charge and command all Magistrates and other civil Officers whatsoever, and all other his Majesty's Subjects, that they do make strict and diligent Search and Inquiry after the Persons concerned in the said barbarous Murder, Tumult, and Riot, and the Authors, Actors, and Abettors, thereof, and that they do apprehend and seize or cause to be apprehended or seized, the said Offenders, that they may be punished with the utmost Rigour of the Law; And we do hereby strictly charge and command all his Majesty's loving Subjects, that they do use their utmost Endeavours to discover and apprehend the said Offenders And for the Encouragement of all Persons to be diligent and industrious in their Endeavours to make such Discovery, and for the better and more effectual bringing the Offenders

247

Captain Porteous.

to Justice, and to prevent such wicked, detestable, and abominable Practices for the future, We do hereby promise and declare, That if any Person or Persons, concerned in any of the Offences before mentioned, shall, before the Twentieth Day of November next, discover any other Person or Persons, who hath or have been guilty of any of the said Offences, so as the Person or Persons so discovered may be apprehended and convicted of the said Offences, such Discoverer or Discoverers shall have his Majesty's most gracious Pardon; and as a further Encouragement to the Discovery of the said Offenders, We do hereby promise and declare, that any Person or Persons, who shall before the said 20th Day of November, discover and apprehend, or cause to be discovered and apprehended, any of the Persons concerned in the said heinous Offences, so as he, she, or they may be convicted thereof, shall have and receive for every Person so discovered, apprehended, and convicted, the Sum of Two Hundred Pounds Sterling, which said Sum of Two Hundred Pounds Sterling, for every such Offender so discovered and convicted, The Commissioners of his Majesty's Treasury, or the Lord High Treasurer of Great Britain for the Time being, are hereby directed to pay accordingly, without any further or other Warrant in that Behalf And lastly We do hereby strictly charge and command all his Majesty's loving Subjects, that they do use their utmost Diligence and Endeavours, in their Several Places and Stations to find out, discover and apprehend all such Offenders, as aforesaid, upon Pain of his Majesty's highest Displeasure.

> Given at the Court at Kensington the Twenty third Day of September 1736, in the tenth year of his Majesty's Reign.
> GOD save the King

APPENDIX VII

MEMORIAL CONCERNING THE MURDER OF CAPTAIN PORTEOUS, DELIVERED BY THE SOLICITOR-GENERAL (ERSKINE) TO GENERAL WADE ON 16TH DECEMBER, 1736

(State Papers, Scotland (George II), vol xxiii No 4)

14th December 1736

Upon the 7th of September last, when the unhappy wicked murder of Captain Porteous was committed, His Majesty's Advocate and Solicitor were out of town, the first beyond Inverness, and the other in Annandale, not far from Carlyle, neither of them knew any thing of the reprieve, nor did they in the least suspect that any disorder was to happen

When the disorder happened, the magistrates and other persons concerned in the management of the town, seemed to be all struck of a heap, and whether from the great terror that had seized all the inhabitants, they thought ane immediate enquiry would be fruitless, or whether being a direct insult upon the prerogative of the Crown, they did not care to intermeddle, but no proceedings was had by them Only soon after, ane express was sent to his Majesties Solicitor, who came to town as soon as was possible for him, but, in the meantime, the persons who had been most guilty had either

248

Appendix VII.

run off, or, at least, kept themselves upon the wing until they should see what steps were taken by the Government

When the Solicitor arrived, he perceived the whole inhabitants under a consternation   He had no materials furnished him, nay, the inhabitants were so much afraid of being reputed informers, that very few people had so much as the courage to speak with him on the streets   However, having received her Majesties orders, by a letter from the Duke of Newcastle, he resolved to sett about the matter in earnest, and entered upone ane enquiry, groping in the dark   He had no assistance from the magistrates worth mentioning, but called witness after witness in the privatest manner, before himself in his own house, and for six weeks time, from morning to evening, went on in the enquiry without taking the least diversion, or turning his thoughts to any other business

He tried at first what he could do by declarations, by engaging secresy, so that those who told the truth should never be discovered, made use of no clerk, but wrote all the declarations with his own hand, to encourage them to speak out.   After all, for some time, he could get nothing but ends of stories which, when pursued, broke off, and those who appeared and knew any thing of the matter were under the utmost terror, lest it should take air that they had mentioned any one man as guilty

During the course of the enquiry, the run of the town, which was strong for the villanous actors, begun to alter a little, and when they saw the King's servants in earnest to do their best, the generality, who before had spoken very warmly in defence of the wickedness, begun to be silent, and at that period more of the criminals begun to abscond

At length the enquiry began to open a little, and the Solicitor was under some difficulty how to proceed   He very well saw that the first warrand that was issued out would start the whole gang, and as he had not come at any one of the most notorious offenders, he was unwilling, upon the slight evidence he had, to begin   However upon notice given him by Generall Moyle, that one King, a butcher in the Canongate, had boasted in presence of Bridget Knell, a soldier's wife, the morning after Captain Porteous was hang'd, that he had a very active hand in the mob, a warrand was issued out, and King was apprehended and imprisoned in the Canongate tolbooth

This obliged the Solicitor immediateely to proceed to take up those against whom he had any information   By a signed declaration, William Stirling, apprentice to James Stirling, merchant in Edinburgh, was charged with haveing been at the Nether-Bow after the gates were shutt, with a Lochaber ax or halbert in his hand, and haveing begun a huzza, marched upon the head of the mob towards the Guard

James Braidwood, son to a candlemaker in town, was, by a signed declaration charged as haveing been at the Tolbooth door, giveing directions to the mob about setting fire to the door and that the mob named him by his name, and asked his advice

By another declaration one Stoddart, a journeyman smith, was charged of having boasted publicly, in a smith's shop at Leith, that he had assisted in breaking open the Tolbooth door

Peter Traill, a journeyman wright, by one of the declarations, was also accused of having lockt the Nether-Bow Port when it was shutt by the mob

His Majesties Sollicitor haveing these informations, imployed privately such persons as he could best rely on, and the truth was, there were very few in whom he could repose confidence   But he was, indeed, faithfully served by one Webster, a soldier in the Welsh fuzileers, recommended to him by Lieutenant Alshton, who, with

Captain Porteous.

very great addiess, informed himself, and really run some risque in, getting infoimation, conceining the places wheie the persons informed against used to haunt, and how they might be seized   In consequence of which, a paity of the Guard fiom the Cannongate was agreed on, to march up at a certain hour, when a message should be sent   The Solicitoi wrote a letter and gave it to one of the town officers, oideied to attend Captain Maitland, one of the town Captains, promoted to that command since the unhappy accident, who indeed, was extremely diligent and active thioughout the whole, and haveing got Stirling and Braidwood appiehended, dispatched the officer with the letter to the military in the Cannongate, who immediately begun their march, and by the time the Sollicitor had half examined the said two persons in the Buriow-ioom, where the magistrates weie present, a paity of fifty men, with drums beating, marched into the Parliament Close, and drew up, which was the first thing that struck a teiroi, and fiom that time foiward, the insolence was succeeded by feai

Stirling and Biaidwood were immediately sent to the Castle and imprisoned   That same night Stoddait the smith was seized, and he was committed to the Castle also, as was likewise Tiaill the journeyman wiight, who were all severally examined, and denied the least accession

In the meantime, the enquiry was going on, and it haveing cast up in one of the declarations, that a hump'd-backed creature maiched with a gun as one ot the guaids to Poiteous when he went up the Lawn Markett   the person who emitted this declaration, was employed to walk the streets to see if he could find him out, at last he came to the Sollicitor and told him he had found him, and that he was in a ceitain house   Whereupon a warrand was issued out against him, and he was apprehended and sent to the Castle, and he pioved to be one Buinie, a helper to the Countess of Weemys's coachman

Thereafter, aie infoimation was given in against Wilham M'Lauchlan, ffootman to the said Countess, he haveing been very active in the mob, ffoi sometime he kept himself out of the way, but at last he was appiehended and likewise committed to the Castle

And these were all the prisoners wio weie putt under confinement in that place

Theie were other persons imprisoned in the Tolbooth of Edinburgh, and severalls against whom waiiands were issued, but could not be appiehended, whose names and cases shall afterwards be moie particulaily taken notice of

The ffiiends of Stiiling made an application to the Earl of Islay, Loid Justice-Generall, setting fuith, that he was seized with a bloody fflux, that his life was in danger   and that upon ane examination of witnesses whose names were given in, it would appear to conviction, that he had not the least access to any of the riotous proceedings of that wicked mob

This petition was by his Lordship putt in the hands of his Majesties Solicitoi, who examined the witnesses, and by theii testimonies it appeaied, that the young man, who was not above eighteen years of age, was that night in company with about half a dozen companions, in a public house in Stephen Law's closs, neai the back of the Guard, where they all remained until the noise came to the house, that the mob had shut the gates and seized the Guaid, upon which the company broke up, and he, and one of his companions went towards his master's house, and, in the course of the after examination   there was a witness who declared   nay, indeed swore, (for the Sollicitor by this time saw it necessary to put those he examined upon oath,) that he met him [Stirling] after he entered into the alley where his master lives, going towaids his house, and another witness, fellow-

Appendix VII.

prentice with Stirling, declares, that after the mob had seized the Guard, he went home, where he found Stirling before him, and that his master lockt the door, and kept them both at home till after twelve at night upon weighing of which testimonies, and upon consideration had, That he was charged by the declaration only of one person, who really did not appear to be a witness of the greatest weight, and that his life was in danger from the imprisonment, he was admitted to baill by the Lord Justice-Generall, by whose warrand he was committed

Braidwood's friends applied in the same manner, but as he stood charged by more than one witness, he was not released—tho' indeed, the witnesses adduced for him say somewhat in his exculpation—that he does not seem to have been upon any original concert, and one of the witnesses says he was along with him at the Tolbooth door, and refuses what is said against him, with regard to his having advised the burning of the Tolbooth door But he remains still in prison

As to Traill, the journeyman wright, he is charged by the same witness who declared against Stirling, and there is none concurs with him, and to say the truth concerning him, he seemed to be the most ingenuous of any of them whom the Sollicitor examined, and pointed out a witness by whom one of the first accomplices was discovered, and who escaped when the warrand was to be putt in execution against them He positively denys his having shutt the gate, and 'tis thought Traill ought to be admitted to baill

As to Birnie, he is charged only by one witness, who had never seen him before, nor knew his name, so, tho' I dare say the witness honestly mentioned him, 'tis possible he may be mistaken, and in the examination of above 200 witnesses, there is nobody concurs with him, and he is ane insignificant little creature

With regard to M'Lauchlan, the proof is strong against him by one witness, that he acted as a sergeant or sort of commander, for some time, of a Guard, that stood cross between the upper end of the Luckenbooths and the north side of the street, to stop all but friends from going towards the Tolbooth; and by other witnesses that he was at the Tolbooth door with a link in his hand, while the operation of beating and burning it was going on that he went along with the mob with a halbert in his hand, untill he came to the gallows stone in the Grassmarket, and that he stuck the halbert into the hole of the gallows stone that afterwards he went in amongst the mob when Captain Porteous was carried to the dyer's tree, so that the proof seems very heavy against him

To sum up this matter with regard to the prisoners in the Castle, 'tis believed there is strong proof against M'Lauchlan, there is also proof against Braidwood But as it consists only in emission of words said to have been had by him while at the Tolbooth door, and that he is ane insignificant creature, and will find people to swear heartily in his favours 'tis at best doubtful whether a jury will be got to condemn him.

As to those in the Tolbooth of Edinburgh, John Crawford, who had for some time been employed to ring the bells in the steeple of the new Church of Edinburgh, being in company with a soldier accidentally, the discourse falling concerning Captain Porteous and his murder as he appears to be a light-headed fellow, he said, that he knew people that were more guilty than any that were putt in prison Upon this information, Crawford was seized, and being examined, it appeared than when the mob began as he was coming down from the steeple, the mob took the keys from him, that he was that night in several corners, and did indeed delate severall persons whom he saw there, and immediately warrands were dispatched, and it was

251

Captain Porteous.

found they had absconded and fled But there was no evidence against him of any kind Nay, on the contrary, it appeared that he had been with the magistrates in Clerk's the vintner's, relating to them what he had seen in the streets Therefore, after haveing detained him in prison ffor a very considerable time, his Majesties Advocate and Sollicitor signed a warrand for his liberation

There was also one James Wilson incarcerated in the said Tolbooth, upon the declaration of one witness, who said he saw him on the streets with a gun, and there he remained for some time, in order to try if a concurring witness could be found, or that he acted any part in the tragedy and wickedness But nothing further appeared against him; and being seized with a severe sickness, he is by a warrand signed by his Majesties Advocate and Sollicitor, liberated upon giveing sufficient baill

As to King, enquiry was made, and the ffact comes out beyond all exception, that he was in the lodge at the Nether-Bow with Lindsay the waiter, and several other people, not at all concerned in the mob But after the affair was over he went up towards the Guard, and having met with Sandie the Turk and his wife, who escaped out of prison, they returned to his house at the Abbey, and then 'tis very possible he may have thought fitt in his beer to boast of villany, in which he could not possibly have any share, for that reason he was desired to find baill and he should be sett at liberty. But he is a stranger and a fellow of very indifferent character, and 'tis believed it won't be easy for him to find baill Wherefore 'tis thought he must be sett at liberty without it Because he is a burden upon the Government while kept in confinement, not being able to maintain himself

What is above is all that relates to persons in custody But there are warrants out against a great many other persons who have fled, particularly against one William White, a journeyman-baxter, who, by the evidence, appears to have been at the beginning of the mob, and to have gone along with the drum, from the West-Port to the Nether-Bow, and is said to have been one of those who attacked the guard, and probably was as deep as any one there.

Information was given that he was lurking at Falkirk, where he was born. Whereupon directions were sent to the Sheriff of the County, and a warrand from his Excellency General Wade, to the commanding officers at Stirling and Linlithgow, to assist, and all possible endeavours were used to catch hold of him, and 'tis said he escaped very narrowly, having been concealed in some outhouse; and the misfortune was that those who were employed in the search did not know him personally Nor, indeed was it easy to trust any of the acquaintances of so low obscure a fellow with the secret of the warrand to be putt in execution

There was also strong evidence found against Robert Taylor, servant to William and Charles Thomsons, periwig-makers, that he acted as ane officer among the mob, and he was traced from the guard to the well at the head of Forrester's Wynd, where he stood and had the appellation of Captain from the mob and from that walking down the Bow before Captain Porteous, with his Lochaber-axe, and by the description given, of one who hawl'd the rope by which Captain Porteous was pulled up, 'tis believed Taylor was the person, and 'tis further probable, that the witness who delated Stirling had mistaken Taylor for him, their stature and age (so far as can be gathered from the description) being much the same

A great deal of pains were taken, and no charge was saved in order to have catched hold of this Taylor, and warrands were sent to the country where he was born, but it appears he had slipt himself off for Holland, where it is said he row is

Appendix VII.

There is strong evidence also against Thomas Burns, butcher, that he was an active person from the beginning of the mob to the end of it. He lurkt for some time amongst those of his trade, and artfully enough a train was laid to catch him, under pretence of a message that had come from his father in Ireland so that he came to a blind alehouse in the Flesh-market closs, and a party being ready, was by Webster the soldier, who was upon this exploit, advertised to come down. However, Burns escaped out of a back window, and hid himself in some of the houses which were heaped together upon one another in that place, so that it was not possible to catch him. 'Tis now said he has gone to Ireland to his father, who lives there.

There is evidence also against Robert Anderson, journeyman and servant to Colin Alison, wright, and against Thomas Linnen, and James Maxwell, both servants also to the said Colin Alison, who all seem to have been deeply concerned in the matter. Anderson is one of those who putt the rope upon Porteous's neck. Linnen seems also to have been very active, and Maxwell (which is pretty remarkable) is proven to have come to a shop upon the Friday before, and charged the journeymen and prentices there to attend in the Parliament closs on Tuesday night, to assist to hang Porteous. These three did early abscond, and though warrands had been issued out against them, and all endeavours used to apprehend them, could not be found.

One Waldie, a servant to George Campbell, wright, has also absconded and many others, and 'tis informed that numbers of them have slipt themselves off ffor the Plantations, and upon an information that a ship was going off ffrom Glasgow, in which severall of the rogues were to transport themselves beyond seas, proper warrands were obtained, and persons dispatched to search the said ship, and seize any that can be found.

The like warrands had been issued with regard to ships from Leith. But whether they had been scar'd, or whether the information had been groundless, they had no effect.

This is a summary of the enquiry, ffrom which it appears there is no prooff on which one can rely but against M'Lauchlan. There is prooff also against Braidwood, but more exceptionable. His Majesties Advocate, since he came to town has join'd with the Solicitor and has done his utmost to gett at the bottom of this matter, but hitherto it stands, as is above represented. They are resolved to have their eyes and their ears open, and to do what they can. But they labour'd exceedingly against the stream, and it may be truly said, that nothing was wanting on their part. Nor have they declined any labour to answer the commands laid upon them to search the matter to the bottom.

Captain Porteous.

ACCOUNT OF MOBBS AT EDINBG IN 1701, & 1734

(Newcastle Papers, B M. Add MS 33,049, f 21)

About the year 1701 The Mob rose in Edinburgh, burnt open the Door of the Tolbooth, & released what Prisoners they thought fit This is commonly called the Darien Mob

In 1705, when Green & 2 others were condemned for Piracy, the Privy Council sat in order to consider of their Petition for mercy; the Mob rose upon this, & with one common cry, declared, that the Prisoners should be hanged, The Privy Council influenced, as it was then thought, by the danger they were in, gave way to the Execution, but the Mob imagining that the Criminals were reprieved by the Privy Council's sitting so long, did attack the Lord Chancellor in his Coach' with stones and stickes, who with great difficulty escaped, his Coach being broke to pieces, & My Lord run up the stairs of a house, This hapned close by the Guard Room, & the Guard gave no manner of Assistance

During the Union Parliament there were almost daily mobs in Edenburg, & stones thrown frequently at the Coaches of the Nobility going through the Street to the Parliament House, the Lord High Commissioners coach not excepted The Town Guard at that time neither prevented these insults or seized the Criminals The Mob were so insolent at that time as to beat with stickes and clubs at the very Door of the Room where the Parliament was actually sitting, which the Town Guard did not attempt to prevent It happened one night at that time, while 7 or 8 Lords of the Privy Council were at supper at the Earl of Loudons then Secretary of State, the Mob rose armed with Stickes & Stones, & filled the whole Street before the Earl of Loudons House, & upon the High Commissioner sending for these Lords to attend him in his Majesties Palace at the other end of the Town, the Lords found themselves in the greatest danger, They durst not go in their coaches, but were forced at the hazzard of their lives to walk with their servants through the streets where the mob was so assembled, without the least assistance from the Town Guard

In 1734 Two Apprentices were put in prison for a misdemeaner by the Magistrates, Upon which the Mob rose and marched towards the Nether Bow Port where Major Leighton met them with the Cannongate Guard, the Mob attacked the Troops with great stones & wounded the Major The Deacon Conveener went to the Mob & ordered them to disperse upon which they seized him & held him up in the air, telling him that he came in good time, for they knew the soldiers would not fire upon him At last they were pacified by the Earl of Crauford & the Lord Justice Clerk, The Deacon Conveener offering himself as Bail for the Prisoners The Town Guard all this while, though so near as to be in sight gave no manner of Assistance

A few days before the Execution of Andrew Wilson, he & one Robertson who were condemned to be hanged were (according to a very bad custom) brought out of Prison by some of the Town Guard to hear a Sermon : Robertson in time of divine service broke from the Soldiers of the Town Guard & by stepping over the Tops of the Pews made his escape, and has never since been heard of

Appendix IX.

APPENDIX IX.

The Provost's Bill.

An Act to disable Alexander Wilson, Esq , from taking, holding, or enjoying any Office or Place of Magistracy in the City of Edinburgh, or elsewhere, in Great Britain, and for imprisoning the said Alexander Wilson and for abolishing the Guard kept up in the said City, commonly called The Town Guard , and for taking away the Gates of the Nether-Bow Port of the said City, and keeping open the same

Whereas upon Tuesday the 7th Day of September, in the Year of our Lord 1736, there was a most seditious and outragious Riot in the City of Edinburgh, in that Part of Great Britain called Scotland notoriously concerted and carried on by great Numbers of wicked, disorderly, and blood-thirsty Persons who did, with open Force and Violence, seize the Arms of the City Guard possess themselves of the City Gates, and, by setting fire to and breaking open the Door of the Tolbooth of the said City, did unlawfully and audaciously rescue and set at large several Criminals therein confined And whereas Captain John Porteous, then a Prisoner there under Sentence of Death, but graciously reprieved by the Queen's most Excellent Majesty, as Guardian of the Realm, was by the said Rioters in a cruel Manner dragged from the said Prison, and most barbarously hanged by the Neck, and murdered, in manifest Violation of the publick Peace, in Defiance and Subversion of legal Government, in high Contempt of our Sovereign Lord the King and his Laws, and to the most presumptuous and unparallel'd obstruction of the Royal Mercy And whereas for some time before the committing of the said Murder and Riot, it was commonly reported in the said City of Edinburgh, that some such atrocious Fact would be attempted which, by proper Care in the Magistrates Citizens, and Inhabitants of the said City, might have been prevented , notwithstanding which Alexander Wilson, Esq , then and now Provost of the said City, and fully apprised of the said wicked Design, did not take any Precautions to prevent the said Murder and Riot, nor use the proper or necessary Means to suppress the same, or to preserve the Peace of the said City , or, after the Perpetration of the said Fact, to discover, apprehend, or secure the Authors, Actors or Abettors thereof, in manifest Violation of the Truth and Duty of his Office of chief Magistrate of the said City ; nor were any Means or Endeavours used by the Citizens and Inhabitants of the said City, to prevent or suppress the said notorious Riot or to hinder the said inhuman and barbarous Murder, or to discover the Persons concerned therein, in order to bring them to Justice Now in order to express the highest detestation and Abhorrence of the said Murder and Riot, and to the End that the said enormous Misbehaviours and Neglects of Duty herein before mentioned may not go unpunished, and that other Persons may not presume, through Hopes of Impunity, to be guilty of the like for the future: Be it enacted by the King's most Excellent Majesty, by and with the Advice and Consent of the Lords Spiritual and Temporal, and Commons, in this present Parliament assembled, and by the Authority of the same, That the said Alexander Wilson be, and he is hereby, from and immediately after the passing this Act, disabled, and made incapable to have, hold, exercise, or enjoy

255

Captain Porteous.

the said Office of Provost of the said City of Edinburgh And that the said Alexander Wilson be, and he is hereby forever hereafter, disabled, and rendered incapable to have, hold, exercise, or enjoy any Office or Place of Magistracy in the said City of Edinburgh, or elsewhere in Great Britain

And it is further enacted by the Authority aforesaid, That a new Provost be immediately chosen in the room of the said Alexander Wilson, in the same Manner as if the said Alexander Wilson was naturally dead, and that he, the said Alexander Wilson shall be detained and kept in close and safe Custody, without Bail or Mainprize, during the Space of (One whole Year) to be accounted from the Day of passing this Act, in any Goal or Prison within the Kingdom of Great Britain, to the Custody of the Goaler or Keeper whereof the said Alexander Wilson shall from time to time be committed, in Pursuance of this Act, by any Warrant under the Hand and Seal of any Secretary of State, of His Majesty, His Heirs, or Successors, which Warrant or Warrants any Secretary of State for the time being is hereby authorised and empowered to make

And whereas the said City of Edinburgh hath, for many years past, kept up a Military Guard, called the Town Guard, which upon the said late unhappy Occasion has appeared to be of no Use And whereas for want of an open Communication between the said City, and a Place called the Cannongate, adjoining thereto, wicked and disorderly Persons are the more encouraged (especially in the night, when the Gates of the Nether-Bow Port of the said City are shut) to attempt to commit Disorders and Riots in the said City And whereas, it is just and necessary, that the Power of keeping up the said Guard should be taken away and that the said Nether-Bow Port should be kept open, Be it further enacted by the Authority aforesaid, That from and after the first Day of July 1737, the said Military Guard, commonly called the Town Guard be taken away, and abolished, and no longer kept up, any Law, Statute, Prescription, or Usage to the contrary in any wise notwithstanding And that the then Provost and Bailiffs of Edinburgh, on or before the said first Day of July 1737, shall cause the said Gates of the Nether-Bow Port to be taken down, and that the Communication between the said City and the Cannongate, be for ever hereafter kept open, both by Night and by Day, any Law or Usage to the contrary notwithstanding

---

APPENDIX X.

EXTRACTS FROM LETTERS OF GEORGE, EARL OF MORTON, TO HIS SON JAMES, LORD ABERDOUR, AS TO THE PROCEEDINGS IN PARLIAMENT RELATIVE TO THE PORTEOUS MOB.

(From the Miscellany of the Maitland Club)

London, 10th February 1736-7

James,
     This day being appointed to take the Kings Speech under consideration, the Lord Carthret moved that the house might be adjourned and turn'd into a Committee of the whole house, and then he made a long speech upon the ryots and mobs that had been committed at sundry turnpyiks in the West and at Spitlefields; and then his Lordship expatiate upon the horrid mob and murder that was committed

256

Appendix X.

at Edinburgh, and even said that it might take away the privileges of the City, and proposed that the Provost and Majestrates that were in place at that time should be ordered to appear at the barr of the House of Lords to give an account of their behaviour on that occasion He was answered by the Duke of Newcastle, who spoke as modestly as that horrid subject could bear, and the Lord Batters spoke and seconded Lord Carthret's; then the Earl of Ilay (who has not as yet recovered his late ilness) spoke in a very hansom manner, and tho' he condemned the horridness of that mob and the cruelty which they had committed, yet he spoke very strongly against taking away the priviledges of the city, or removing the Court of Justice to another place, which was proposed by the Lord that opened the debate, and then Lord Carthret made the motion that the Provost and Majestrates that were in office at that time, and the officer that commanded the Town Guaird, should be ordered to appear at the barr of the House of Lords to answer such questions as shall be asked at them, and that General Miles should be ordered to appear at the same time, and a true copy of Captain Porteous's tryal, and the orders that were sent down after that mob should be laid before the house, which was seconded by Lord Batters, and was carryed, and they are appointed to appear this day moneth   By this you'l see what a dilemma that vilanous mob has brought upon our nation, and the City of Edinburgh in particular, and God knows what length it will be carryed   I wish to God the Majestrates may be able to make a discovery of the ring-leaders, which I perceive will be the only thing that can obtain them and that ancient City favour   I give you all my blessing, and am

Your affectionate Father,
MORTON

London, 15th February 1736-7

James,
I believe before this time that the warrand for ordering the Provost, Baillies, and Captain of the Town Guaird of Edinburgh, (to appear at the bar of the House of Lords) will be arrived, which I suppose will lay the courage of your mob vindicators and encouragers, for the Peers are resolved to be at the bottom of it

I am sorry to have it to tell you that yesterday morning my Lord Chancellor dyed, of five days ilness, of an inflammation in his stomach, which is as great a loss to this nation as could come by the death of any subject, for there is not a man in England that can supply his place for a learned, upright, honest, and just Judge, and who is lamented by every body   The King is much better this day, and the Duke of Newcastle, Sir Robert Walpole, my Lord Herrington, and his Secretary of War, were with him this forenoon

I give you all my blessing, and am

Your affectionate Father,
MORTON

London, 5th March 1736-7.

James,
I had yours of the 26th ultimo, and hear that Captain Linn came to town two or three days agoe and Mr Irvin and some others came since but the Majestrates were not come this afternoon, but am told they will be here to morrow, and I suppose the ministers will forgive them for traveling on Sunday, being a case of necessity, but how they will mannage their matters it's more than I know, but you may believe that a sett speech will not do their business, for there

Captain Porteous.

are some Lords designs to have them examined very strictly, but I hop that nothing will appear that can hurt the priviledge of the City and I realy believe it will not appear that the Majestrates have been anywise concerned in encourageing the mob, and that their only crime is being deficient in their duty, in not exerting themselves in time to supress that mob, which I realy think was occasioned from ignorance and fear; as for Linn, I doubt not but he will vindicat himself, tho' it is not doubted but he must certainly know some of those that were active among the mob, but a litle time will clear us of this.

    I give you all my blessing, and am

Your affectionate Father,
MORTON

London, 8th March 1736-7

James,

    I have yours of the 1st by yesterday's post, with an account of the Master of Ross's ilness, which I am heartly sorry for, and wish him a good recovery, for I have reason to believe that one will succeed him that will not fill his place   I suppose you have heard that Lord Bute is to stand for the 16 Peer in room of the Earl of Orkney   Yesterday the house of Peers were upon the Duke of Athole's claim, to the tytle of Lord Barron Strange, as the next heir to it, which he carryed unanimously so that he and his successors will sit as a Peer for England in the House of Lords for ever

I hear our Majestrates are all come to town, and must make their appearance on Thursday next   I give you all my blessing, and am

Your affectionate Father,
MORTON

London, 10th March 1736-7

James,

    Yesterday I received yours of the 3d, &c

This day the Majestrates of Edinburgh, and others that were sent for, were called to the bar of the House of Lords, and swore, and afterwards were ordered to withdraw, and the house went into a Committee of the whole house, the Provost was called to the bar and examined upon several queries given in by the Lord Carthret, and several questions asked him by other Peers, the examination continued till near 7 o'clock, and realy he behaved very well, and much better than was expected, the debeat is adjourn'd till Wedensday next, and then the rest will be taken to task, and I doubt not but they will behave as well as the Provost did, so I hop they will come much better off than was expected, but there was a motion made that Lieut.-General Wade, and Provost Linsay, should ask leve from the House of Commons to be examined I reckon it will be a pretty tedious business before we end it.

I give you all my blessing, and am

Your affectionate Father,
MORTON

London, 17th March 1736-7

James,

    I have been laid up with the gout since Saturday last, and was not able to goe and hear the Majestrates examined yesterday, but this day (tho' very lame) I went in my clok to the house, and

Appendix X.

heard Captain Lind examined, who answered very distinctly and very pointedly, but differed in several questions from the Provost, and I am affraid that the poor Provost does not stand in so good a light as he did, others are to be examined to-morrow, and if I am able I'll venture out   I give you all my blessing, and am
Your affectionate Father,
MORTON

London, 19th March 1736-7

James,
Yesterday Provost Lindsay was examined at the bar, who gave very distinct answers, which were as favourable for the conduct of the Magistrates and himself as the nature of the thing would bear, but it still appeared they were very negligent and difficient in their duty in not suppressing that vile mob   General Miles was examined next, who said very much for his own vindication, and bleamed the Majestrates and Mr Lindsay for not bringing a written order to him, and certainly they were to bleam, seeing he had all the sogers about the town in readyness at the Canongate Guard to march, before Mr Lindsay came to him, but these two differed in some respects, General Wade is not yet examined, but will on Tuesday first, but I think it seems to be agreed on all hands that the Majestrates have been very deficient, and I am affraid the Provost will not come off so well as I would wish him   A little after the Commitee was up and the house resumed, to our great surprize Lord Lovel moved, that the Lord Justice Clerk should be sent for, which occasioned long debeats, it being an unprecedented thing to send for a Judge without giveing a reason, and the Lord Chancellor himselfe spoke against it, and shew'd the unreasonableness of it, then it was proposed to delay it at that time, and that it might be taken up afterwards, but this they would not yield to; and severals of the Court party disserted us, but at the division we caryed it, but I believe that it will be moved again to send for him   I give you all my blessing, and am
Your affectionate Father,
MORTON

London, 22d March 1736-7

James,
I have yours of the 15th   I cannot tell you what to think of the Duke of Athol's being made an English Peer, seeing I don't hear of any Scots Peer being to be elected in his room at this time, but I cannot give you the reasons, I not haveing heard as yet what they are that are given for it   I have been pretty much out of order of late by a fit of the gout, and pains in my shoulders, tho' I was oblidged to goe to the House of Peers this day, where I heard Colonel Durure, Major Pool, and General Wade examined, which continued near five hours; they do not make for the Majestrates   I suppose you'l soon hear that Lord Milton, Lord Royston, and Lord Dun are ordered to attend the house, which motion was made yesterday by the Duke of Newcastle, which if it had not, I believe the other party wou'd have moved this day to have brought Lord Milton by himself; and as the house was riseing it was moved to send for Mr James Graham, Jun, which was occasioned by something that Major Pool told of a discourse that happened betwixt him and Mr Graham, upon Captain Porteous's wryting a letter to the Major, to stay till his tryal was over, which Mr Graham said he would speak to the Advocat about, and that the Advocat told him he might goe, and that he would allow the evidence he gave to be admitted in the tryal, which

Captain Porteous.

I can hardly believe, and upon this Mr Graham is ordered to attend Monday comes three weeks, which I think is very hard upon him
.   I give you all my blessing, Is all I have time to say to-night, but am

Your affectionate Father
MORTON

___

London, 24th March 1737

James,
I have yours of the 17th   I fancy by this time the Jury has brought in their verdick against M'Lauchline, tho' he is indicted for high Treason, as well as other crimes, To morrow all the evidence that was given at the bar is to be read to the house, and then the consideration will be adjourned for some time, and I believe till the lords of Justiciary come up   I give you all my blessing, and am

Your affectionate Father,
MORTON

___

London, 26th March 1737

James,
I have no news to write you to-night, but that on Thursday last the depositions of the Majestrates of Edinburgh, Colonel Durure, Major Pool, and General Wade, were read before the house, and the consideration of them is to be taken upon Thursday next, which realy comes out pretty strong, and it was moved by a Lord, that the Provost should be sent to Newgate, for prevaricating in his examination, but the consideration of the whole having been put off till Thursday, it was let drop 'till the whole was before them, and then I am affraid they will be heavy on his lordship and some of the Magistrates I heartly wish we may have the account of M'Lachline's being condemn'd before that day come, otherways, we shall be all affronted, and make good the paragraph of General Mile's letter, wherein he asserts to the Duke of Newcastle that no Jury will condemn any of Porteous s murderers that are tryed in Scotland I shall bring you down a coppie of the heall afidavats, which I have been at the expence to cause write out
I give you all my blessing, and am

Your affectionate Father,
MORTON

___

London, 29th March 1737

James,
That unhappy affair of Porteous's is like to keep us long togither It was indeed surprizing to every body to hear that M'Lauchlean has got off for want of evidence against him, and I am affraid it will be of ill consequence to the Majestrates, whose affair is to be before the House of Lords Thursday next, I admire they should have tryed this fellow without haveing clear evidence against him, for it has brought a scandall upon the whole nation, and God knows what the consequence may be, it has made good what General Wade and Miles wrote to the Duke of Newcastle, that no Jury in Scotland would condemn any that were conceined in the murder of Porteous, and I now make no doubt but all England believes it
I give you all my blessing, and tell Sholto that I hear he is a very good child I am

Your affectionate Father
MORTON

260

Appendix X.

London, 2d April 1737

James,
    Yesterday the Edinburgh affair came before the House of Lords,
and I herewith send you a coppie, (which I had from one of the Clerks
of Parliament) of the motions and resolves which past yesterday,
which occasioned long debates and speeches; and M'Lauchlan's being
assoilzied has occasioned a great spight against the provost   it
seems some days agoe it was resolved to punish the Provost, and not
to medle with the rest of the Magistrates, and it was agreed by the
whole house that he should be punished, but they differed in the
method of doing of it The Duke of Argile spoke twice extraordinary
well, and exprest his indignation against the horrid mob, and neglect
of the Provost for not useing proper means to prevent it, but was not
for having the punishment by a bill, he thinking bills of that nature
might be of ill consequence to the priviledges of the House of Peers,
but said, he thought it might be done after another manner, but as
a bill was thought the best method, it was carryed as you'l see by
the inclosed, and the Duke of Argile voted against that method, as
did the Duke of Athole, Earl Islay withdrew, Earl Selkirk was absent,
Earls Crawfoord, Findlater, Dunmore, Breadalbean, Laudan, Cath-
cart, and myself were for the bill The Duke of Buckleuch and Port
more were in the country   All those that voted against the bill,
except the two Scots Peers, seem'd to be for having the punishment
higher, and Earl Strafoord proposed to have the Provost sent to
Newgate This will occasion the Parliament to sit a long time, for it
must be all tryed of new, and witnesses examined, and its probable
the House of Commons may desire to have witnesses examined before
them, so the Provost may have a chance, for the Lords will not allow
the Commons to make the punishment greater, as some Lords would
have been at   I understand John Drummond writes to his brother
William, but I doubt if he will get a coppie of this which I send you,
therefore may shew it to him, or any other of your friends you please,
and if Wilyy Martin fall in your way, may shew it to him likeways, if
you find that he has not seen any other of them   I give you all my
blessing, and am

                    Your affectionate Father,
                            MORTON

London, 5th April 1737

James,
    Last night I had yours of the 29th ultimo, and likewise yours
of the 22d, wherein you mention something of M'Lauchlan's being
acquitted, which came safe to hand, and I don't doubt but Pitcur
may have likewise received his letter before this time, for letters will
fall by sometimes for a post, and yet come by the next   .
This day the Provost's bill was read the first time, and is appointed
to be read the second time on the 3d of May, when the tryal will
begin of new; the Provost is allowed to summond witnesses, and will
also be allowed council, and it's possible that the Commons may
either reject it, or make some amendments, which the House of Peers
won't agree to
I give you all my blessing, and am

                    Your affectionate Father,
                            MORTON

London, 16th Aprile 1737

James,
    Yesterday I was visiting our three Judges, who have made
a safe journey, and seems to be in very good health and spirit   I

Captain Porteous.

don't see how the House of Peers can trouble them, but am affraid the House of Commons will be very hard on poor Lord Milton, on account of imprisoning some of the Majestrates of Haddington at the last election   I give you all my blessing, and am
Your affectionate Father,
MORTON

London, 19th April 1737

James,
. I am afraid it will be the midle of June before I reach Edinburgh Our three Scots Judges are to make their appearance in the House of Lords upon Thursday 7 night, and I am told they are to do it by a write from the King, and will sit upon the Wool-Sacks with the English Judges, which will be the most honourable way of bringing them there, and I suppose they will appear in their gowns, I wish they may come off with as much honour at last, as I hop they will Upon Thursday next Porteous's tryal (which is printed) is ordered to be read to the house, and is to be taken to consideration upon this day 7 night, where it will be debeated, this day our Lord Provost was admitted to beal, and Mr Blackwood and Mr Claud Johnston are his two beals, each of them is bound in £1000, and the Provost himself is bound for £2000   .   I give you all my blessing, and am
Your affectionate Father,
MORTON

London, 26th April 1737

James,
I have yours of the 19th, with one inclosed for Colonel Charles, which I sent to him   I am still troubled with the pain at my stomack, tho' I am easier than when I wrote you last, and likeways I am troubled with rheumatick pains in my shoulders and arms which I have had less or more since before I came from Scotland which I was in hopes to have got carryed off by drinking goat-whey, but I have now given over hopes of it, it being thought that the Parliament wont rise till the latter end of June, or beginning of July and all this is owing to your cursed mob   This day the House of Peers was upon the consideration of Porteous's tryal, which occasioned many and long debates, and continued till 8 at night, and then the furder consideration of it was adjourned to Friday Our Judges have not as yet been called to appear before the house, nor do I hear that it is as yet determined in what manner they are to appear   I am very fatigued, and can say no more, but my blessing to you all   I am
Your affectionate Father,
MORTON

London, 3d May 1737

James,
Yesterday we had a long debate about the manner our Judges should appear and it being found by the Records of Parliament that never any Judges that were called by the Peers had been alowed to sit among English Judges, but one single instance of two that had been Judges who were called by the Convention at the Revolution, and afterwards were dismissed, and never allowed to come to the house again ∙ but it appeared upon many occasions that the Keepers of the Great Seall the Chancellor of Exchequer, always appeared at the bar, and even the great Lord Chief Justice Holt being once called

Appendix X.

appeared likeways at the bar, so it was put to the vote, and it carryed that they should come to the bar, 48 against 37, so they were ushered in by the Keeper of the black rod, and chairs set for them, tho' they had no occasion to sit down, and every question that was asked at them were put in writing, and joining their heads together Lord Dun, who was appointed to answer first as being youngest, gave his answer, and next Lord Royston, and then the Justice Clerk and they all answered very exactly to every question as they were put to them, so they were ordered to withdraw, upon Lord Carthret's moveing that some of our laws might be altered, and further proposed that English Judges and our Judges should conferr together, and prepare a bill against next year, to be brought in for that purpose, and I don't hear that they will be called again   This day being appointed to read the Provost's bill a second time, he was brought to the bar of the house, and the council for the King opened the case against him, and proposed to call witnesses, but it being late the house adjourn's till to-morrow at 11 of the clock, and then we shall have a pretty long day of it · The Duke of Argile moved three different questions in relation to what part the officers of the army were to act upon being commanded with a party to see the sentence of the law put in execution when a criminal was ordered to be hanged at Stocksmercat, or any other town in England, in case a mob attacked them, and likeways how they were to behave in case a mob drew themselves up in a narrow place to stop them from getting forward to the place of execution; and the third question was much to the same purpose, and the Judges were ordered to give their opinion, and then it was moved by some English Peer, that the Scots Judges that are here should give their opinion how the laws of Scotland stood in relation to these questions that were moved by Duke of Argile, but Earl Hay moved that the Judges should goe first to Scotland, that they might consult their law books, and discourse their brother Judges upon it, and then to return their opinion in writing; so with a good deall of debate this was yielded to, and I hop you'l get our Judges soon home

I send you all my blessing, and am

Your affectionate Father,
MORTON

London, 10th May 1737

James,

The Provost's bill was read a second time yesterday, which Lord Craoord made a speech against, and it is to be in the Committee to-morrow, and you may depend it will pass our house in spite of us all, but that which concerns me most is, that we cannot prevent the guards being taken away, and the Natherbow ports pull'd down, and I am affraid it will likeways pass the House of Commons, tho' some people will have, that they will throw it out I give you all my blessing, and am

Your affectionate Father,
MORTON

London, 12th May 1737.

James,

Yesterday the Provost's bill passed the Committee, and is to be read a third time to-morrow, where we will have a full division, and I doubt if there will be anybody against it but the Scots   I give you all my blessing, and am

Your affectionate Father,
MORTON

263

Captain Porteous.

London, 24th May 1737

James,

The Provost's bill (as they call it) is appointed to be read a second time to-morrow, and then the fate of it will be known, 'tho I make no manner of doubt but it will pass, and I am told they design to lay a fine on the town or the Provost for the behoof of Porteous's widow. At present it seems to be very uncertain when the Parliament rises, for the midle of June is reckon'd to be the soonest, so I don't expect to have the pleasure of drinking goat-whey this year

I give you all my blessing, and am

Your affectionate Father,
MORTON

London, 26th May 1737

James,

Last night I had yours of the 19th. Yesterday being appointed for reading of the Provost's bill a second time in the House of Commons, after some debate, it carryed to be read by 146 against 99, and the house is to goe into a Committee upon it next week, so you need make no doubt but it will pass the house; and I believe with some more clauses added to it than it had when it passed the House of Lords. I believe there will be a provision made for appointing a method to keep the peace of the town, 'tho not by a guard of souldiers with red coats and guns

I think of nothing else to say at present, but my blessing to you all. I am

Your affectionate Father,
MORTON

P S   I almost forgot to tell you that all the Scots Members voted against the reading the bill a second time, except Brigadier Anstruther, and Brigadier Robert Murray, who represents an English Burgh

---

APPENDIX XI.

LETTER TO A GENTLEMAN, CONTAINING A SUMMARY ACCOUNT OF THE PROCEEDINGS ON THE LORDS BILL FOR PUNISHING PROVOST WILSON, &c

(From *The Gentleman's Magazine*, June, 1737.)

The attention of the world having for some months been turned to the Parliamentary enquiry against the Lord Provost and citizens of Edinburgh, and their case being of so unusual a nature, I can't blame your curiosity in desiring an account of it. This request I shall the more readily comply with, as my curiosity led me to be present at all the material examinations and debates. The affair having been canvassed before both Houses of Parliament, I shall not set down the particulars of every evidence, because, as most of them appeared to the same points, they, of course, repeated the same things

It was agreed upon by the counsel for and against the bill that the Lord Provost's behaviour should be considered at three different

Appendix XI.

periods, viz. before, during, and after the riot in which Porteous was murdered The counsel for the bill, who were Serjeant Eyre, one of the King's Serjeants and Mr Pauncefort, by their witnesses endeavoured to prove, as to the first period, that there was a report spread about the town of Edinburgh (long before the riot happened) that it would be perpetrated; that the Provost had received information of this, and that he had done nothing, in consequence of this information to prevent it

The principal evidence they adduced for this was Mr Lin, captain of the City Guard the night of the riot, who declared that on the Friday before he waited on the Provost, and, finding him in company with Mr Lindsay, member for the city, and several other magistrates, called him aside and acquainted him with the report, who desired the said Captain Lin to repeat the same things before the company, which he did, and they were all of opinion there was no foundation for the report however, desired him to enquire into the grounds of it That he (Captain Lin) was out of town till the Monday evening, and after he came to town heard of the report again, and repaired to Munhead's Coffee-house to talk with the Provost, and, sending his name in, had for answer that the Provost was busy, but that he would be in the Council Chamber about four o'clock, when he accordingly went to receive his orders for next day but had none in particular as to the preventing of the riot This was the substance of Lin's evidence, but one thing remarkable, and what was laid hold of by the counsel against the bill, is that Captain Lin being asked when before the Commons whether in another place (viz, the House of Peers) he had not declared his disbelief of any foundation for the said report, he answered he had Then why, said the counsel against the bill, do you declare here that you did believe the same to be true? To which he replied that by what he said before he meant that he did not believe the mob would succeed in an attempt so unlikely to succeed

The other witnesses as to this fact were one Bailly and one Din, who both declared that they had heard of such a report and that they believed it, long before the riot One thing is observable—that they were the only witnesses who said that they heard the riot was to happen on the Tuesday All the other witnesses said that when they heard such a report, they always heard that the mob intended to wait till Wednesday, and then, in case the sentence was not then put in execution they were to hang Porteous themselves; and they unanimously declared that they never heard of it but from women and children, and they always treated it as a foolish surmise Bailie Hamilton, being examined about a conversation he had with Din upon the Monday, declared that Din spoke to him of it as a foolish story, and that he did not himself believe it

Din's evidence before the Commons was likewise suggested to be inconsistent with what he had said when upon oath before the Peers, viz, that if he did not come up as an evidence he would be removed from his post which he held and that this was told him by commission from the Provost and magistrates The counsel against the bill likewise brought the following members against his character, which was bad viz, Sir James Campbell, Mr. Hamilton, and Mr Lindsay The last member declared the present magistracy would not enter upon their offices till he (Din) was removed upon account of the infamy of his character The evidence against the bill endeavoured to prove that although the report went of such a design for some time before, yet there was nobody believed it, that the day given out was Wednesday, the day upon which Porteous was to have been executed, that the Lord Provost had thereupon determined in Council that the whole three companies of the Town Guard should mount upon that day, and that both he and

Captain Porteous.

the other magistrates, with the members of the Town Council, should be ready to attend, with the badges of their respective offices, in quelling the mob, should any happen

It was on the other side proved that there was no order given for that purpose to the captain of the guard upon the Tuesday, neither was there any ammunition distributed, which precautions had been used at the time of Wilson's execution, and that it appeared there was not a flask of powder nor a pound of shot amongst all the Town Guard To this it was suggested that if the Provost had made any such preparations before the riot, it would have been the readiest way to have created one, that if the Guard wanted ammunition it was their captain's fault, because he always, when his men wanted ammunition got an order from the treasurer, empowering the store-keeper to deliver out what was necessary for that purpose Young, the treasurer, and Hislop, the storekeeper's, evidence confirmed this

It was then objected to the Provost that there were two ways by which Porteous might have been secured from the mob The first was to have sent him to the Castle the other that he might have been sent to the Canongate Tolbooth In answer to this it was said that the sentence pronounced upon Porteous by the Lords of Justiciary run, "That he should be sent back to the Tolbooth of Edinburgh, there to remain till the execution of the sentence," and that it was not in the Provost's power to have sent him to the Castle, there being no instance of such a power having been exerted since the Union; and that, even before the Union, it could only have been done by a warrant from the Privy Council of Scotland, and, as for sending him to the Canongate, he had as little power, because the Canongate was a regality, and governed by its own magistrates

Duncan Forbes, Esq, Lord Advocate for Scotland, Patrick Lindsay, Esq, late Lord Provost, and the above Mr Young were examined on this point (before the Lords) The first declined giving any positive opinion as to the Canongate, but thought that the Provost could not have sent the prisoner to the Castle, and doubted, when asked, if the Lords of Justiciary themselves had that power The others spoke to the same effect, and all agreed that there was no precedent of any such removal A Scots clergyman, Mr Yates, was adduced to prove that the report was current before the riot. He declared that, being appointed to preach in the church where Porteous was allowed to hear sermon on the Sunday before his murder, he afterwards waited on Porteous, and took occasion to acquaint him with the report he had heard, desiring him at the same time to take care whom he admitted into his room Mr Yates added that Porteous slighted his informa-tion, and said "Were he once at liberty he was so little apprehensive of the people that he would not fear to walk at the Cross of Edin-burgh, with only his cane in his hand as usual" The King's counsel urged that the Provost had not so much as made the least attempt to transport Porteous to the Castle, and when one Walker a city officer, was examined, he declared that upon hearing the rioters' drum beat, happening to ask the reason, he was answered by his maid "that she fancied it was the guard transporting Porteous to the Castle" The former answer was made to this evidence viz, that the Provost was ignorant of such a report, or at least had no reason to believe it so far as to take such a step, and that his station prevented his coming to the knowledge of what the sentiments of the mob were about his removal But the most material evidence against the Provost was the aforesaid Bailly, who insisted that he heard it in every company that the design was to be put in execution on the Tuesday, and that he drank with several who had openly approved of it. To which it was answered that if Bailly kept such company, there was little stress to be had on his evidence, especially as he did

Appendix XI.

not pretend to affirm that he had ever once acquainted the Provost with either the report of the persons' names who approved the design These were the material charges and defences of that part of the Provost's behaviour that related to the first period, viz , before the riot

As for the second period, there were a great many witnesses produced, viz , Mr Lindsay, member for the city , the other magistrates, Din, Bailly, Stewart, a Common Council man, one Mr Bur, a midshipman, Mr Cochrane, Bailie of the Canongate, Mr Keir, Deacon of the Trades and Common Council man, Mr Baird, a merchant; Mr Hunter, a shoemaker, Walker, the town's officer, Sutherland, sergeant of the City Guard, Major-General Moyle, Captain Bendish, Lieutenant Ashton, Hislop, the storekeeper, Captain Lin, and Major Robertson, fort-major of the Castle of Edinburgh

Captain Lin said that, being informed that the mob was gathering, he went to Clerk's Tavern, where the Provost was drinking with the said Mr Bur, and other officers of His Majesty's ship, the *Dreadnought*, then stationed in the road of Leith, and upon acquainting him of the danger, the Provost desired him to go immediately back and draw out his men, and that he would instantly follow him, and put himself at the head of the Guard to face the mob That he accordingly went to the Guard, but found that the mob was already in possession of the Guard-house, having disarmed them, and that they were distributing the arms of the Guard out of the window, whereupon he instantly returned and met the Provost coming towards the Guard, that they immediately resolved to send Mr Lindsay to General Moyle, who went accordingly, that they marched again out of the tavern, to which they were obliged to retire, in order to quell the mob, and, after a fruitless attack upon the mob, in which some of the Provost's company were wounded, they were beat back He likewise said that there were but ten or twelve men besides the sergeant, corporal, and drummer upon Guard that night, there being eight or nine in prison on account of Wilson's execution, and as many absent with or without leave, that when he appeared first to the mob they desired him to be gone, for they had nothing to say to him

The Hon Patrick Lindsay, on his examination, said that after Captain Lin went out to his Guard the Provost and his company immediately followed, but, upon seeing how things went, they found they had no method left but to apply for the assistance of the regular forces, that some mentioning that a letter must be writ to General Moyle for that purpose, it was replied, "God's mercy ! what do you talk of a letter, if we stay till one is written, we shall all be in the hands of the mob Here is Mr Lindsay, our representative in Parliament, and personally acquainted with General Moyle, let him go directly and send us relief " Another of the company upon this applied to Mr Lindsay, who said he would go, if my Lord Provost would desire him Upon which the Provost said, "Go by all means, and lose no time " Mr Young said that he set out at the same time, in order that if Mr Lindsay was intercepted by the mob, he might escape to the General, but that having on his velvet coat, he was known to be a magistrate, and, when he came near the Nether-Bow, was obliged for safety to run down Chalmers' Close, where he was pursued, but that he escaped to the tavern where the Provost and the rest were He then proposed that the Act against riots might be read, but there was not a copy of it in the company, and, recollecting he had one at home, went for it I must here inform you, from all the evidence in general, that in the meantime the magistrates made another attempt to quell the mob, and advanced among them from the tavern, but were repulsed by a volley of stones and some of the Provost's company were wounded ; nay, some heard the mob call

Captain Porteous.

out to fire, and one or two witnesses said they saw the fire flash in the pan of a gun which was levelled at them. Stewart said that he, one Mr Clauson, and one or two more attacked them with Lochaber axes, which they wrested from the hands of some of the mob, and actually drove them to some distance, and said that if they had been vigorously supported by the Provost and his company, he did not doubt but that they would have driven them entirely from the prison. But all the other witnesses concurred that the Provost stayed as long as a man of prudence or courage ought to have done, and omitted nothing. One witness said that, if he remembered right, Captain Lin himself advised him to retreat. That after they returned to the tavern, Mr Band was dispatched to get on the wall and speak with Mr Lindsay on his way to the General to desire the General to make no scruple of breaking or blowing up the Nether-Bow Port, because the mob were masters of the town, but that Mr Band, after a fruitless attempt, was obliged to return. In the meantime Mr Lindsay, by going a great way round, and with vast hazard, got to General Moyle's, where he found him with his lady, who told him that he had been of late in a very bad state of health. Upon Mr Lindsay telling him the danger they were in within the town, he was answered that his orders from General Wade, his superior, were such that he could not march any of his troops to quell any riot except by a written order from the civil magistrate, or in cases where immediate bloodshed was apprehended; that he should be ready to assist him with his men, whom he would draw out for that purpose, in case he had a warrant from the Lord Justice-Clerk. Mr Lindsay represented to him the imminency of the danger, for he could not be prevailed upon till there was actually a letter written to that purpose to the Lord Justice-Clerk, whose answer, it seems came too late. It will not be amiss to mention some particulars here of the evidence as to the attempt and execution. One Hunter declared, in a very distinct manner, that when the mob began to gather at the Nether-Bow, he was coming by the Guard, and told the sergeant, or the sentry, the mob was gathered, and seemed resolved to have their will, and bade them take care of themselves; and that Captain Lin in the meantime came down from the Provost, and that he neither heard nor saw him give any orders to the Guard, only when he saw the mob gathered towards the head of Blackfriars Wynd, he clapped his hand to his sword and cried, " God's mercy, what's this? " and away he ran as fast as his feet could carry him. Sutherland, the sergeant, said that when the captain was gone, a fellow with a blue cap came up and asked the sentry what it was a clock. This, it seems, was the signal agreed on by the conspirators, for in a trice the same fellow, backed by ten or twelve more, beat the sentry on his back, rushed in, and made themselves masters of the Guard and their arms, being followed by many more. However, it appears by Lin's evidence that they were moderate enough in the use of power, at least at that juncture for when he came they very civilly desired him to be gone, for they wanted nothing with him, and warned him of his danger if he offered to insist. Sutherland, the sergeant, agreed with Hunter in the main, only that Hunter's words to the sentry were " The mob is up, I advise you to give them good words, for they will have their will." He said that indeed Captain Lin desired him to take care of the Guard, but that availed little for not one of the soldiers would have minded him nay, they were so intimidated by what had happened to those under Porteous's command that he believed, except himself, scarce any would have obeyed the captain himself, had he stayed; yet all agreed that had the captain been present, and assembled all the soldiers, who for the most part lived within a stone's throw of the Guard-house, they might have easily prevented the mob's

Appendix XI.

taking possession of the Guard-house The captain said in his defence that he had orders from the Provost to return the first time, and that he thought no messenger so proper as himself But how far, in the circumstances affairs were then in, the captain might warrantably have used a discretionary power, I shall leave you to judge.

In the meantime we shall return to the magistrates' whose next expedient was to raise the trained bands, to this purpose they despatched one, Hallyburton their commander, to Mr Rollo, at whose house were the books which contained the names and places of abode of every captain of a company, but when he came there he was denied access by Mr Rollo's wife, who desired him to be gone They then proposed to ring the alarm bell, but found the mob had taken the precaution to secure the tower in which it hangs They then sent to the magazine for arms, but it appeared, by the evidence of Hislop, the storekeeper, and others, that the mob had likewise secured that Great stress was laid upon the negligence of the Provost in not putting a guard of men in the Justiciary or Tolbooth Rooms, which, it seems, are but a short distance from one another, but it appeared by all the evidence that, in the situation affairs were then in, it was impracticable In the meantime, unfortunate Porteous was hurried away, after they had broke open the Prison, which probably must have been burnt down had not the mob prepared water to quench the fire they were obliged to make use of for gaining admission There was little came out on the examination as to the treatment of that unfortunate person more than was published before only Walker, the town officer, whom the mob had pelted so that he was obliged to throw off his livery coat declared he was by when they murdered him, and that one more forward than the rest, was checked by the others, and desired to wait for orders, that he thereupon quitted the end of the rope, which by this time, being about Porteous's neck, he was ready to have hoisted up, and went down to another, who very composedly gave him orders, and that he returned and drew the rope up which hanged Porteous

It further appeared that the magistrates were all this time getting what information they could by sending people who might mix in the mob and endeavour to know some of their faces, but all in vain, only one man returned who said he knew one person there The magistrates desired him to name him, which it seems he did, and was desired to be in readiness to give in what evidence he could against him when called upon

In the morning about five Mr Lindsay returned and with several who had been with the Provost all night, went to the Grass-Market, where the body of Porteous yet hung, and several people, to the number of twenty or thirty, as they thought, in a body, standing about Most of the evidence seemed to think these were some of the rioters, and said they advised them to depart. One was seized upon, but besides that they could make nothing out of him, they had no prison in which they could confine him, so thought it the most prudent method to dismiss him, for, being but a few of themselves, and the mob seeming resolute, they had no reason to doubt but they would rescue him, and, perhaps, as they had committed such outrages already, would not stick at greater The King's counsel laid great hold of this circumstance to prove the negligence both of the Provost and of the town But it was observed by Mr Murray, counsel for the Provost that he was not then present, consequently, admitting it to be a neglect, not answerable for it

Thus I have, in as distinct a manner as I could, run through the behaviour of the Provost in the three periods above mentioned I shall now give you an account of the evidence with respect to that of

Captain Porteous.

the city   It was attempted to be proved that upon this occasion
the burghers had not done their duties, that the Guard was of no
service, and that the Nether Bow Port would be a hindrance to the
King's troops upon any future exigency   As to the behaviour of the
burghers, it was mostly determined by that of the Provost and other
magistrates

I must observe to you again that all the witnesses agreed, except
Bailly and Din, that though there was a report of such a horrid
design, yet that it was fixed for the Wednesday, that not one of the
inhabitants of Edinburgh was known to be there, except one apprentice
boy   Mr Lindsay declared that, when he arrived from Major-General
Moyle's, the mob was pouring in vast shoals out of the town into the
country, and that he did not remember any one face of the many
hundreds he met with, though he had lived and borne the highest
offices in the city for several years   Another of the witnesses
declared that, being at Dalkeith, a little village about five miles
from Edinburgh, ten or twelve days before the riot, he there heard
a report that a conspiracy to murder Porteous if reprieved, was
formed by the friends of one Ballantyne, a youth of that town, who
went thence to see Wilson's execution, and was one of them killed
by Porteous, but that nobody believed it

There was produced, and admitted in evidence, an Act made in
the ninth of Queen Mary of Scotland, anno 1563, by which it was
enacted that all the citizens who assembled to suppress any riot
within the town of Edinburgh, without authority from the Provost
incurred the pain of death   There likewise was admitted in evidence
another Act of James the Third of Scotland, anno 1457, by which no
corporation was liable to punishment for the Provost's or any of its
magistrates' faults   The Articles of the Union were likewise insisted
on, by which the privileges of the burghs are to remain inviolable;
and Mr Hamilton, counsel for the town offered in evidence an
extract of the minutes and debates of the session of Parliament in
Scotland, in which the article anent the privileges of the Royal burghs
are settled, whereby it appears that upon a motion made to submit
them to the alterations of a British Parliament, a debate arose, and
it was resolved in the negative   But this extract could not be
admitted in evidence   It was proved against the city that Porteous
was insulted going to his trial by the mob   This was confirmed by
the testimony of my Lord Advocate, who said he believed that had
it not been for the Guard, he would have been torn in pieces between
the Tolbooth and Justiciary Room, though not forty paces distant
from one another   The case was admitted   but evidence was given
that the mob who so insulted Porteous had no interest in the Corporation who was to suffer by the present bill, being either the lowest
dregs of the inhabitants or people from the country, whose relations
had been killed on the day of Wilson's execution   It was likewise
proved that almost all they who were killed were people from the
country

Mr Lindsay, Mr Young, and several more were examined to prove
the usefulness of the Town Guard particularly in two respects, viz ,
that of extinguishing fires and quelling former mobs   It was plainly
made out that in a city so populous and so closely built,
where forty or fifty families live under one roof, as in
Edinburgh, it would be impossible to quench fires or to preserve the goods during fires, without such an armed force   That as to
the quelling of mobs, many instances might be adduced, particularly
one in the year 1725, when the common people had conceived a prejudice against the surgeons for raising dead bodies, and a mob had
arose thereupon, when the Guard was of singular use in suppressing
them, and that in the same year, upon the commencement of the

Appendix XI.

Malt Tax, there having been a contract signed by the brewers in the city not to brew any more, the paper containing the said contract was ordered to be burnt by the common hangman at the Cross of Edinburgh, which, by the assistance of the said Guards was effected accordingly, and one of the brewer's servants, concerned in the riot for rescuing a fellow who was set on the pillory upon the surgeons' account, was whipped through the town, notwithstanding the threatenings of the mob who were overawed by the Guard All the evidence produced confirmed that this Guard had always been of the greatest consequence for the safety and peace of the town till the late unhappy affair It will, perhaps, not be amiss to take notice here of a question put to one of the evidences in the House of Commons by Mr Winnington, member for Droitwich, viz, whether the said evidence believed that any officer, or any body of military men, would think himself safe to fire upon a mob, whatever the exigence were, while the sentence against Porteous stood unreversed? I shall let you make your own reflections upon the question, and the answer that might have been made to it I had almost forgot to tell you that an Act of Parliament in 1693 was admitted in evidence, by which Act it appears the town of Edinburgh had the old custom of watching and warding abolished as being a grievance upon the citizens, and the present Guard confirmed to them for their services at that Revolution

My Lord Advocate and Patrick Lindsay, Esq, were asked when upon examination whether, if the Town Guard had been under arms, and not surprised, they did believe the Guards would have been able to have quelled the mob? They answered they did, and most of the evidence declared that they believed that had the Guard been properly armed and commanded the rioters would not have attempted what they did

As to what related to the taking away of the Nether-Bow gate, it was proved unanimously that the said gate was of absolute consequence to collecting the city revenue, and that it prevented smuggling One of the honourable gentlemen above mentioned said that he did not think its being demolished would answer the intentions of the bill, because it was easy for a small body to defend the pass where it was built against a much larger, even though the gate was open Several evidences were produced, particularly the Act of Parliament by which the city collected two pennies Scots upon every Scots pint of ale vended within the town, to prove the loyalty of the citizens on former occasions, particularly in the year 1715, when they raised some companies, and, by their zeal and conduct, prevented the surprising the Castle by the rebels Mr Irvine, the town-clerk, said they had, during that period, and upon other occasions, manifested their loyalty much to the prejudice of their revenue, which is scarce able to defray the necessary exigencies of their town Mr Young declared that he found a bond for some hundreds of Scots marks, granted by the city of Edinburgh to one, Wightman, who was obliged to advance that money for the payment of the ministers' salaries, the revenue of the town having been so exhausted, and all agreed to its having always shown the most sincere attachment to the Protestant succession in the present Royal Family

Thus, sir, have I laid before you the sum of the evidence in this affair, by which you may the better judge of the motives which induced the Legislature to make so considerable an alteration as they have done in the above bill and of the reasons upon which the several speeches (I send you the substance of) are founded —Yours, &c

Captain Porteous.

EXAMINATIONS OF THE WITNESSES BEFORE THE HOUSE OF LORDS IN THE INQUIRY INTO THE MURDER OF CAPTAIN PORTEOUS

I.—The Lord Provost of Edinburgh's Examination

(Newcastle Papers, B M Add MS 33,049, f 27)

Question 1 —What Orders the Magistrates gave to Captain Porteous at the Execution of Andrew Wilson?—He had only the usual Orders to take care to keep the peace

What are the usual orders?—The usual Orders are, That he is to take care to keep his men together and in a Body, and two of the Magistrates go with him; and in case of necessity, they give the proper Directions

What Magistrates?—The Bailiffs

Who are they?—Mr Crokat and Mr Hamilton

Who gives the Orders to the Captain upon these Occasions?—He has Orders from the Provost, but he is under the direction of the Magistrates that go along with him

Question 2 —How they ordered the Captain to charge the Firelocks, whether with Ball, Swan Shot or Slugs?—He was ordered to charge the Muskets with Powder and small shot, as usual.

What do you mean by small shot?—The small shot which they make use of at Fowling

Whether any of them attended at the Time of the Execution, and whether they went away before it was over?—That is what I cannot answer because I was not there

[Four questions concerning Wilson's execution follow, to which the witness makes a similar reply]

Question 8 —Whether any of the Town Guard, who fired at the Execution, were discharged without Tryal, and why they were discharged?—They were not discharged by us, they run their letters, after a man has been so long in Prison he applies to the Lords of Justiciary and takes a Writ, and if the Indictment is not entered in a certain number of days, he gets a Warrant from the Justiciary to liberate him

Were they comitted and by whom?—They were comitted by warrant of the Justice of Peace, Those of the Canongate who had run their letters

Who was the Justice of Peace?—One Mr Cochran

Why they were not prosecuted and whether any body was bound over to prosecute them?—As to the Prosecution, after we had advised with our Lawyers, we found it difficult to get proofs against them, and therefore the bringing them to Tryal was delayed

Whether you know that the soldiers so discharged confessed they had no orders to fire?—All of 'em said, They had orders from the Commanding Officer

Whether Captain Porteous brought his Gun to him and how it was charged?—He brought his Gun to me, and it was charged , It was not examined then, it was sealed up and laid by till the Tryal came on

Appendix XII.

Whether he made any Inquiry of the Persons that were wounded, what charges they were wounded by?—It was with Swan Shot they were wounded, by the big Drops

Were there any signs on Porteous's Gun, that it had been discharged that day?—It was looked into by People, and they said, It might have been shot that day, and cleaned and charged again

Did you yourself see any signs that it had been discharged?—I saw no signs that it had been discharged, for I could not judge of that

How long was it before Porteous brought his Gun to you after the Riot?—Near to an Hour

Whether the Magistrates gave any written Orders, or other Orders to the Treasurer of the Town of Edinburgh to deliver out Shot that day, or the preceding Day?—The Magistrates gave no orders that I know of. There was no Shot delivered out that Day by the Treasurer, I was informed that Captain Porteous went to a Shop in the Town, and bought the Shot he made use of that day

Whether when they give the usual Orders, the Officer of the Guard comonly buys shot for himself?—No, they never did till that Day

Whether when they give the usual Orders the Magistrates used to deliver out Powder and Shot?—No, they always have it in the Guard Room

By whose Order does it come into the Guard Room?—By the Treasurer's Order

Have you heard that those Soldiers who fired at that time did likewise buy the Shot themselves?—No I never heard any such thing

Have you heard where they had the shot?—I was informed, That after Captain Porteous bought it, he delivered it to the Serjeants and the Serjeants to the Soldiers

Do you know whether there was a want of shot in the Guard Room?—I was informed, That there was small Shot in the Guard Room

Whether or no, previous to that Day's Riot, you did ever see any of the Shot that was there, or know what it was?—No, I saw none of it

How do you know then, that it was such shot as is made use of for Fowling?—I called the Day after the Execution of Wilson and saw the small Shot that is usually given out, and saw the big Shot that was bought by Captain Porteous out of the shop

What size is that shot which you call shot for Fowling?—The ordinary shot that Fowlers make use of for Partridge shooting

Question 9.—Whether any of the Magistrates had previous information given them, That a surmise run, that a Mob to murther Captain Porteous, or to make an attempt upon the Prison, was intended upon?—Upon Saturday the 4th Sept John Lyn, Captain of the Guard, came to my house in the evening, and told me he heard a rumour going about, That if Captain Porteous was not executed upon the 8th, in the afternoon there would be a Mob that would take him out, and hang him Upon which I desired Mr Lyn to make Inquiry, and see if there was any truth in it I did not see him again till Tuesday and then I asked him about it, and he told me he had been making Inquiry, and he understood it to be only a comon Clatter among comon servants and Children

Question 10.—Whether Mr Lindesay was sent by the magistrates to General Moyle, during the time of the outrage, and with what Orders and Instructions?—Mr Lindesay was in the Street with me about Ten o'Clock that night, the whole Street was in Confusion, the Guard was surprized, and their arms seized, and Mr Lindesay was desired by the Magistrates to go with all speed to General Moyle and tell him what a situation the Town was in, and to desire the Assistance of His Majesty's Troops under his command

What answer did General Moyle send to that message?—Mr Linde-

T   273

Captain Porteous.

say informed me, that he said, As the Ports were shut and barricaded, he would not give any assistance with his troops

Whether this was all the answer that Mr Lindesay brought?—Mr Lindesay said, That he had wrote to the Lord Justice Clerk to give him an account of the situation of the Town, and that the General had refused the Assistance of the Troops, and that his letter was forwarded by a servant of the General's

Whether the Demand made by Mr Lindesay was verbal?—It was verbal only

Whether the General did not insist upon an Order in writing?—He refused to grant the assistance of his Troops without a written Order from the Lord Justice Clerk, or one of the Lords of the Justiciary, and Mr Lindesay said, He informed the General that the Lord Justice Clerk was not in Town, nor any of the Lords of the Justiciary

Do you know whether the Lord Newhall was in Town at that time?— Lord Newhall lives just on the other side of the Town Wall, he was not within the City

Whether upon other occasions General Moyle had not furnished Troops upon a Letter from the Lord Provost?—Yes he has, I wrote a Letter to General Moyle the Day before the Execution of Wilson, desiring the Assistance of some of his Troops, because I was informed there was to be an Outrage and an Attempt to rescue the Criminal from our Guard, and he sent 150 men under the Comand of Six Officers

How came it then, that when you sent Mr Lindesay, you did not send a letter to the General?—We were all in such hurry and confusion, Mr Lindesay was very well known to the General, and we had not time to write

Whether at the time that Mr Lindesay was sent to General Moyle, the Magistrates were then assembled?—There were only three of us in the High Street at the Cross in Edinburgh when we sent him away

Whether it has not been usual for the Lord Provost and the Magistrates for the Time being to send a letter to the Comanding Officer of the Troops for his assistance when a Riot and Tumult has been apprehended?—To my knowledge we never had occasion, but at the Execution of Wilson, and then I sent a letter

How near were the Rioters and what was doing when you sent Mr Lindesay to General Moyle?—The Guard was surprised and their arms seized and taken from them and the whole street in confusion when Mr Lindesay was sent off, and they were as near to us as the length of this House

Don't you believe, that when you sent Mr Lindesay, if you had sent a letter signed by yourself, or any of the Magistrates, desiring General Moyle to assist with the Troops, he would have come with them to your Assistance?—That is what I cannot answer, I do not know, but he has answered our letter before, That one time

How long was the Riot begun before Mr Lindesay went to General Moyle?—I did not hear of it above 15 minutes before he went off It had been begun about 20 minutes before he went away

Question 11—Whether tho' the Gates were shut, the Walls could not have been scaled, or the Town entred at Leith Wind or any other place, or whereat other ways there are whereby Persons may come into the Town, without coming through the Gates?—The Wall at Leith Wind can easily be scaled and then there is an entry through the Old People's Hospital by which any Person may come into the City

Were these Passages seized by the Mob?—They were not seized, for there was one Mr John Beard a merchant in our Company when they had set fire to the Prison Gate, he went over the Wall at Leith Wind, and met Mr Lindesay near the Canongate coming from the General

Appendix XII.

Since they could get out by these passages, how came you not to send a Letter to the General then?—We expected Mr Lindesay's desire would have been granted, and only sent Mr Beard to tell Mr Lindesay the situation we were in, that he might forward the sending of the Troops

Question 12 —Whether that night the Captain was murthered, the City Guard had any Powder or Ball delivered to them?—I cannot answer that question, for I do not know

Who was Captain of the City Guard?—Mr. Lyn was Captain of the City Guard that night

Who is Comander in Chief of the City Guard?—The Provost for the time

What Officers are next under the Provost in the Comand of the City Guard?—We have three Officers in the City Guard, there were then two only, Captain Ferguson and Captain Lyn

Whether the Officers under the Lord Provost do not receive their orders from the Lord Provost?—They do receive their orders from the Provost when he is present, or from the Bailiffs when he is absent, because they are elected by the Magistrates and the City Council

Were you present in the City, and what Orders did you give to these Officers?—The Orders that I gave about 6 or 7 that Evening were to take care of the Guard, and I gave them the Parole as usual

Question 13 —Whether, upon the Provost's being informed that the Mob were assembling in the Grass Market, he gave any Orders to Increase the City Guard, or ordered them any Ammunition?—When I got the Account, I happened to be at a Tavern, I sent to the Captain of the Guard imediately, he came to me, and he brought me word, there was a great Tumult at the Netherbow, and I ordered him back to his Guard forthwith, to draw out his men under Arms; and before he could get there the Guard was surprized, and their Arms seized, and he himself was beat by the Mob

Whether the whole number of the City Guard was upon Duty, or only a part of them?—We have three Squads in the City Guard, there was only one of the three Squads there A Squad consists of thirty men, and they were all there, except those that were out upon Centry Post, for any thing I know

When that part of the Guard was surprised and their Arms seized, did you give any orders to the other Officers to assemble the rest of the Guard?—We gave all the Orders we could, I sent for the Captain of the Trained Bands to come, but the Drums were seized, and the Entry to the high steeple was seized so that the Bells could not be rung to alarm the Town

Question 14 —Whether the Magistrates believed, that if a few soldiers had been imediately placed in the Outward Justiciary Court Room, or in the Tolbooth, the Mob could have forced the Tolbooth Door?—I cannot answer as to that

Question 15 —Whether any of the Magistrates know of any person having advised either with the Provost or them to remove Captain Porteous to the Castle?—No

Upon the Information you received on Saturday the 4th September, of a design to murther Captain Porteous what precautions were used, or what Orders were taken by you or any other of the Magistrates to prevent it?—The Precautions which the Magistrates had taken were to have had the whole three Squads upon Duty upon Wednesday, and the Magistrates to attend themselves for the keeping of the Peace

Were any Orders actually given for that purpose, or only intended to be given?—The Orders were intended to be given upon the Wednesday morning

Whether on the night of the Riot you went to the Captain of the

Captain Porteous.

Guard, or whether you sent for him to come to you?—I sent to the Captain to acquaint him with the Uproar and Tumult in the Grass Market, and he came to me

Did you send for him, or did he come to you voluntarily?—He came to me voluntarily, upon my sending to acquaint him with the Tumult.

When the Captain was with you, did you send him to the Grass Market to inquire of the Tumult?—No, I bad him go to his Guard, and desired him to send to see what the Tumult was

Whether on the Information the Captain of the Guard gave you on Saturday, you imployed any other person besides that Captain to inquire into it?—No other person spoke to me about it, and I imployed nobody else but him

At what time on the Tuesday were you first informed of the Riot?—It was within 15 minutes of Ten at Night

Whether during the Tuesday you had any Information of a Design to make a Riot that night?—No, I had none

Did you see Captain Lyn at any time betwixt the Saturday and Tuesday?—I saw him on the Tuesday six o'Clock at night in the Council Chamber, and I asked him whether he had informed himself about the Rumour, and he said He had, and he looked upon it to be groundless

When the Mob was assembled that night, did you or any of the Magistrates do any thing to disperse them?—We went out of the Tavern into the Street, and about 26 men of us attempted to disperse the Mob, but we were beat back with stones, and they snapped their Firelocks at us, and some of the Firelocks flashed in the pan

Was the Intention to take Precautions for Wednesday the Effect of a Consultation with the Magistrates, or only your own private Intention?—It was upon Consultation with the Magistrates upon Tuesday afternoon

Did Porteous present any Petition to you or any of the Magistrates, Desiring to be removed to the Castle or the Canongate Guard?—No, I never heard of any

Whether the Guns that flashed in the pan, were the guns that were seized from the City Guard?—I cannot say as to that, The Mob had Guns of their own

[Endorsed]   Examination of the Provost of Edinburgh
March 10th, 1736-7.

— —

II —Examination of Bailie Crockat

(B M Add MS 33,049, f 46)

Mercury 16⁰ Martij 1736

Mr Thomas Croquhat the 1st Bailiff called in and asked

Question 1 —What Orders the Magistrates gave to Captain Porteous at the Execution of Andrew Wilson?—The Provost as oldest Magistrate, gives the Directions, he has the principal Comand of the Guard

What are the Orders?—I cannot tell what orders the Provost gave

Do you know what orders are usually given by the Provost to the Captain of the Guard when he attends at an Execution, or on like occasions, or how the Guard are usually furnished with Amunition in such Cases?—The Guard are ordinarily furnished with Amunition from the City Treasurer   The usual orders to the Captain are to take care to keep the Peace and keep his Men together

276

Appendix XII.

Question 2 —How they ordered the Captain to charge the Firelocks, whether with Ball, small Shot, or Slugs?—I know nothing about it

Question 3 —Whether any of them attended at the time of the Execution and whether they went away before it was over?—Mr Hamilton and I were the Two that went to attend the Execution, and we staid upon the scaffold till he was thrown off, and we went off in the usual Manner along with the Ministers to a House hard by the Gibbet, and we were to give a signal when he was to be cut down

What was that signal, and was the signal given?—There was no Signal given, The Executioner went up the Ladder, and was beat back by two Stones that were thrown, and upon a mistake that it was a signal, in putting down the sash window, a Friend of his own (as I apprehended) reached up from the street, and cut him down

What do you mean by reaching up from the Street?—The Rope was very long, He was within a foot of the ground, or there abouts

Question 4 —Whether the Criminal Wilson was cut down by their Order?—He was cut down by a mistake by putting down the sash window, as I apprehend

What reason have you to apprehend a Friend of the Criminal's cut him down by a mistake of the signal?—I can tell no reason for it at all, I apprehend it to be a mistake for there was no Disturbance at all at that Time

What is the usual Signal which the Magistrates give when the Criminal is to be cut down?—The usual Signal is the Rod which the Magistrates have at the Execution, a white rod

How is the signal given?—By pointing the Rod out at the Window

Question 5 —Whether they know by whom he was cut down, by the Executioner, or any of the Rioters?—I apprehend it was by a Friend of his own that was standing by the whole time

Question 6 —Whether they know or believe, that any Methods were used by Bleeding, or otherwise to recover Wilson to Life?—I know nothing about that

Question 7 —Whether they know, if the Tumult began on the Part of the Rioters, by assaulting the Guard, or whether the Firing was antecedent to it?—The Criminal was cut down, he was put into his Coffin, he was put on a Cart, and out of our View, a part of the Scaffold was carried off by the Porters before there was any Firing

Was the throwing of Stones and the attack by the Mob before the Firing?—I did not observe throwing the whole time (as far as I could perceive) six Stones, which I think were thrown before the Firing

How long did the Man hang before he was cut down?—Betwixt three and four and Twenty Minutes

How long was it designed he should have hung?—Half an hour

Question 8 —Whether any of the Soldiers of the Town Guard, who fired at the Execution, were discharged without Tryal, and why they were discharged?—There were fifteen soldiers, seven of which were put into the Edinburgh Prison, and eight in the Canongate Prison The seven that were in Edinburgh Prison got out at the breaking open of the Prison; One of those that were in the Canongate Prison got out in Women's Cloathes, The other seven applied according to an old Statute, either to be tryed or set at Liberty; and accordingly after the Days had run, they applied to the Lords of the Justiciary and got a Warrant for their Liberation, and were set at Liberty accordingly

Question 9 —Whether any of the Magistrates had previous Information given them, that a Surmise run that a Mob to murder Captain Porteous, or to make an attempt to break open the Prison was intended?—I never heard the least surmise of it

Question 10 —Whether Mr Lindsay was sent by the Magistrates to General Moyle during the time of the Outrage and with what Orders

Captain Porteous.

and Instructions?—I know nothing at all about that, for I was in my own House, from seven of the Clock at Night, all night

How came you to be at your own House, when there was such a Tumult?—I did not hear of the Tumult till it was very late, and put myself in Order to go out, and by the time I heard of it, according to the situation where I dwelt, it was impossible for me to go out but with the greatest Danger

Do you know, or were you informed when the Lord Provost had the first notice of the Mob, or whether it was to be on Tuesday the 7th or any other day?—I never heard anything at all of that

By what means had you the first Information of it?—The first Information I had of it was by a Message from the Lord Provost, but at that time, before I could get myself in Order, it was impracticable for me to go abroad, as I was situated, without putting myself in the utmost danger

What Hour was it when you received that Information from the Lord Provost?—About Ten of the Clock at Night

Was every body in your House as ignorant of the Fact as you were?—I know nothing at all of that.

Do you know, or have you been informed whether any Precautions were taken by the Lord Provost and Magistrates after the Notice the Lord Provost received?—I was informed the next day, That Provost Lindsay upon the first notice of the Mob, was sent down to General Moyle, in order to get the Troops imediately, and that he was in due Time, had they been granted

Was Mr Lindsay at that Time a Magistrate, or not?—He was a Member of the Town Council, but not Provost of Edinburgh

Was Mr Lindsay a Justice of Peace at that time?—I do not know

Was Mr Lindsay a Magistrate at that Time?—He was not a Magistrate of the Town of Edinburgh at that time

Have you been informed, whether the Message sent by the Lord Provost to Mr Moyle was in writing, or if not, how it came not to be in writing?—According to my Information, they had not time in the Hurry, It would have taken as much time to have wrote the letter, as to have brought up the Forces

How long was it from the Time they began to attack the Prison, before they got out Porteous?—I can make no answer to that I do not know

Have you heard how long it was from the attack upon the Prison door, till they got out Captain Porteous?—According to my Information, it was Two Hours I have been informed it was two hours and a half betwixt the beginning of breaking open the Prison Door, and Porteous's being murdered

Have you been informed whether any means were used by the Lord Provost to prevent the breaking open the Prison Door, other than sending for the Troops?—According to my Information, the Provost and the rest of the Magistrates that were there, with a few other Company, went out with Lights in order to beat them off, but they were beat back with stones, and the Mob offered to fire and snapp'd their pieces, and some of them flashed in the pan, and some of the Company were sore hurt, particularly the Lord Provost as he informed me

Were you informed how long the Mob continued in a Body after the Murder was over?—There was a part of the Mob continued together till about Four, or half an Hour after Four in the morning

Question 11 —Whether tho' the Gates were shut, the Wall could not have been scaled, or the Town entered at Leith Wind or any other place, or what other ways there are, whereby Persons may come into the Town without coming through the Gates?—There are three places

278

Appendix XII.

the Wall can be scaled at Leith Wind; There is Trinity Hospital where they can have easy access, 100 men may go through in two minutes, and there is the East End of the North Loch

Do you know whether communication betwixt the Castle and the Town was cut off at that time?—I know nothing at all about that

Do you know, or have you heard since, That any Message was sent to the Commander of the Castle for any assistance with his Troops?—I know nothing at all of that

Do you think in the Two hours from the breaking open the Prison Gate, to the taking out Captain Porteous there was time enough to write a letter to the Commanding Officer in the Castle?—There would have been time in Two Hours to write a Letter, there is no Doubt of that

Do you know or have you been informed at what time the Lord Provost sent notice to General Moyle of the Mischief that had happened, and what answer the General made to that?—According to my Information, it was before Two a Clock in the morning that Mr Hamilton was sent down to the General, and the Answer that he made to Mr Hamilton was, That had they sent to him in time, he would have given the Troops and see how the Magistrates would answer it, and the General seemed to be in a great Fright and Consternation

Have you heard that any of those Passages were seized by the Rioters before the Murther was comitted?—I cannot tell anything about that

Question 12—Whether that night the Captain was murthered, the City Guard had any Powder or Ball delivered to them?—I know nothing about it

Do you know whether Mr Young the Treasurer is in Town or not?—I do not know whether he be in Town or not

Question 13—Whether upon the Provosts being informed that the Mob were assembling in the Grass Market, he gave any orders to Increase the City Guard, or ordered them any Amunition?—I know nothing about it

Question 14.—Whether the Magistrates believed, That if a few Soldiers had been imediately placed in the outward Justiciary Court Room, or in the Tolbooth, the Mob could have forced the Tolbooth Door?—I cannot tell anything about that, what the consequence might have been

Did Mr Young set out from Edinburgh in Company with you?—Mr Young was not of our Company, I have not seen him these four weeks.

Question 15—Whether any of the Magistrates know of any Person having advised either with the Provost or them, to remove Captain Porteous to the Castle?—I never heard of it till I got to London

Who told you in London?—I heard it just of our own Folks

Who were they, do you know their names?—I do not remember, I heard a great many, but I do not remember the particular Persons names

What do you mean by our own Folk?—It was in my own Quarters; I cannot condescend upon a particular person

Who was with you at your own Quarters?—I cannot tell that

Will you tell, or will you not?—As far as I know, it was spoke by all the People that are in the House, by my Lord Provost and the other Magistrates

Did the Lord Provost or any of the other Magistrates tell you, That they had been advised to remove Porteous to the Castle?—No, they were telling that such a thing was going abroad, but they never heard of it till they came to London

He withdrew

Captain Porteous.

III.—*Examination of Bailie Colquhoun*

Then Mr Colquhoun the 2nd Bailiff was called in and asked

[To the first seven questions the witness replies that he knows nothing, having been out of town.]

Question 8.—Whether any of the soldiers of the Town Guard, who fired at the Execution, were discharged without Tryal, and why they were discharged?—Our Lawyers advised us not to carry on the Prosecution against the Soldiers till such time as the Event of the Tryal of Captain Porteous was known. In that Tryal it did appear, by many Witnesses, that Captain Porteous had both fired and given Orders to fire, upon which our Lawyers were of opinion then, that they could not prosecute the Soldiers, and upon that, such of the Soldiers as had not made their escapes, did Petition the Lords of Justiciary that they might either be brought to their Tryal, or Dismissed (This was founded upon a Law of our Country agt wrongous Imprisonment) On which Petition they were liberate by a warrant from the Lords of Justiciary There were imprisoned in all fifteen, seven in the City Prison, and eight in the Canongate The seven in the City Prison made their escape, in disguise, the night the City Prison was broke open by the Mob, and we have never heard of 'em since, so that it was the Soldiers that were in the Canongate Prison that did thus petition the Lords of Justiciary

Who were those Lawyers that gave that opinion?—The City Lawyers, Mr Haldane, Sir James Elphinstoun, Mr Hugh Murray and Mr Hugh Forbes, I cannot positively say that all the four were present at the consultation, I think Mr Solicitor was likewise advised with, but I cannot positively tell

Question 9.—Whether any of the Magistrates had previous Information given them, that a surmise run, that a Mob to murder Captain Porteous, or to make an attempt to break open the Prison, was intended?—What the other Magistrates had, I cannot tell, I can only answer for myself, I had no particular Information of a Mob being intended upon Tuesday the 7th Sept till within two or three minutes that it happened, further than a vague surmise, That there would be a Mob on Wednesday the 8th of Sept in the Evening, in Case Captain Porteous was not executed that day This was given no Credit to by any Mortal, I never heard any Body that gave the least Credit to it, It was among the Low sort of People only, The thing did appear both improbable and impracticable, as our Prison was very strong, We had our Guard at hand, and we had the Reason to expect the Assistance of His Majesty's Troops, if they had been demanded, which were just at the Gates of our City

Was not the general Talk and Discourse at that Time, That such an attempt would be made?—It was only among the lower sort of People, the better sort gave no Credit to it All the Foundation I could learn of it was, One said, my Boy brought it from School, and another, my servant brought it from Market, even the surmise was always mentioned to be on the 8th, but never upon the 7th

Do you know whether Captain Lyn came to the Council Chamber on Tuesday morning to know whether he should double his Guard that night upon account of the Information he had, that there would be a Riot?—No, I never heard it, nor do I know that Captain Lyn had given an Information

Were you at the Council Chamber that Morning?—We had no Council that day, I was in the Country that morning, It was 11 or 12 of the Clock before I came to Town

Appendix XII.

Were you at the Council Chamber that Day, after you came to Town?
—Yes, I was at the Council Chamber

Did you see Captain Lyn there?—I do not remember that I did, I think I did not.

Did you yourself at any time, after you heard the Riot was begun, propose to the Provost to send for the Guard to the Castle?—After Mr. Lindsay was sent to General Moyle, I do think that I did mention the Garrison in the Castle, but the Gentlemen were of opinion, that the Comanding Officer in the Castle could not give the assistance of the Soldiers that were there unless he had had a Warrant from General Moyle for so doing

Who were the Gentlemen that gave that opinion?—There were besides the Provost, Bailiff Hamilton Mr Harriot the present Dean of Guild, Mr Ronald Dunbar, Mr Beard, and several others that I do not particularly remember

Don't you know that the Comanding Officer of the Castle had actually marched out with part of his Guard in Expectation of being sent for?—I knew nothing of all that that night; The next day he told me, he had his men in readiness, but at the same time told me, That he apprehended, he could not have marched out his men without an Order from the General

Do you know, or were you informed that Captain Porteous, or any of his Friends or Relations had any suspicion that there was a Mob intended on Tuesday the 7th or Wednesday the 8th of September?—Both Captain Porteous and a good many of his Friends and well wishers did hear the surmise, as well as every body else, but they gave as little Credit to it as any body, That Evening 6 or 7 of them were in Company with him in the Prison (as I was Informed) and in a jocular way said to him, "Porteous take care of yourself to-morrow, for there is a surmise that there will be a Mob in the Evening" His answer was "That he was under no concern about that, for had he his Pardon, he could walk at the Cross with as little Concern about him as ever"

Have you heard or do you believe That the Lord Provost, or any of the Magistrates had a letter sent to them before the Riot, To acquaint them that there would be a Riot?—No, I never heard of such a thing

Have you not been informed, That the Lord Provost was acquainted by Capt Lyn, That there was a Riot to be on the Tuesday or Wednesday?—Since the thing happened, I have heard of such Information, but at the Time it happened I never heard of it

Do you know whether any Information by letter or Message was given by any body else to the Lord Provost or any of the Magistrates?—I was that night in Company with the Provost and several others, and about 20 minutes before [ten], so far as I could judge, the Lord Provost was called out of the Company and with him Mr Lindsay, They staid out about three minutes, and came in without mentioning any Thing what they had been called out for which I apprehend was occasioned by the numerousness of the Company we were with, I afterwards understood that the Message which the Lord Provost was called out upon, was from his Niece at Home, to acquaint him there was a Mob in the Grass Market, Upon which it seems, he had sent for Captain Lyn, and given him Directions to make Inquiry about it, and to report to him about Ten minutes after, the Lord Provost was called out a 2nd Time with Mr Lindsay, and they immediately came into the Room with Capt Lyn, who told us, There was a Mob not only in the Grass Market, but another part of them within the Netherbow This was the first Information I had of the Mob

What Precautions were taken by the Lord Provost and Magistrates betwixt their Knowledge of the Surmise and the Time of the Riot?—As the Surmise was always said to be for the 8th and not for the 7th

Captain Porteous.

My Lord Provost had taken Precaution that all the Guard should be upon Duty on Wednesday the 8th and that the whole Magistrates should attend

When Captain Lyn came to the Lord Provost, how long was he kept, before he was sent to the Town Guard?—As soon as Captain Lyn came into our Company and acquainted us with the Mob's being within the Netherbow Gate he was ordered immediately to his Guard to have his men under Arms, and that My Lord Provost, Mr Lindsay and myself with one or two more would follow immediately to give Orders, wch we did imediately

At what Time did the Mob take Possession of the Town Guard?— As I was informed, the Mob took possession as the Clock struck Ten, and it could not be a minute before

Question 10.—Whether Mr Lindsay was sent by the Magistrates to General Moyle during the Time of the Outrage, and with what Orders and Instructions?—Immediately upon our being acquainted of the Guard's being seized, we stepped aside to consider what was proper to be done, and we agreed imediately to send Mr Lindsay to General Moyle to acquaint him of the present Situation of the Town and to desire the imediate Assistance of the Troops, which was done by the Lord Provost's Order

Where were you when you sent Mr Lindsay to General Moyle?—We were near the Market Cross when we got the first notice of the Guard's being seized, We imediately retired towards the Tavern where we had been, I cannot say positively, whether we were got to the length of the Tavern before Mr Lindsay went off, he went off without loss of time, within two minutes after we got the notice

Did any Dispute arise among the Magistrates in relation to the sending Mr Lindsay with a verbal or a written message?—There was a dispute at first whether to send Mr Lindsay, because we were of opinion that Mr Lindsay would be very useful to be with us in Directing; But as the Mob were pouring out in Swarms, we were apprehensive it would be dangerous to lose time, and therefore agreed to send a verbal message by Mr Lindsay, who was very well known to the General which at that time we thought would have equal credit with a Letter from the Lord Provost, sent by an indifferent Hand

How many and which of the Magistrates were there at that time?— There were no other come at that time except the Provost and myself, the other two Gentlemen Mr Blackwood and Mr Hamilton came to us about Ten minutes after Ten

As there were but two of the Magistrates there, which was for the Verbal Message and which was for the Letter?—There was Company there, the present Dean of Guild was there, the Treasurer was there, and five or six more, I did not mind who was for the Letter, I believe I was for the Verbal Message, because I was apprehensive, that if Time had been taken to write a Letter, Mr Lindsay had not got out of the Town

Did the Lord Provost or any of the Magistrates read or attempt to read the Proclamation?—Upon Mr Lindsay's being sent away, we used all possible means to get as many of the neighbourhood together, and the Officers of the Trained Bands, as we could; But most of them had secured their Doors for fear of the Mob, so that we could not get access to them, In 20 minutes Time we got about 26, and about 20 minutes after, we went out with Intention to read the Proclamation, but we had not got to the North East End of the Prison, when the Mob did violently attack us with throwing big stones; They also threatened to Fire, and I heard one of their Pieces snap, There were several of the Company that was with us, that were bruised and hurt with the Stones

282

Appendix XII.

What is the Treasurer's name?—Thomas Younge

Had you or any of the Magistrates the Proclamation with you?—Before we went out, the Treasurer went to his House, which was in the same Close, in Order to bring the Proclamation, but before he got to us, and before we could get any thing done, we were obliged to retire

Do you know whether Mr Young is in this Town?—I do not know that he is in town, nor do I believe it, I left him at Edinburgh

How came you not to put people in the Prison, or how came you not to go with the 26 men into the Prison to defend it?—Tho our number was 26 when we came out of the Tavern, yet when we got to the North-West End of the Prison, it was much smaller, and we were under a necessity of retiring we were not able to quell the Mob

Do you know at what time the Prison Door was broke open and what Time Captain Porteous was murthered?—So far as I was informed, the Prison Door was broke much about half an hour past eleven, and as I was informed, Capt Porteous was murder'd but a very few minutes before twelve

Question 11 —Whether tho the Gates were shut, the Wall could not have been scaled, or the Town entered at Leith Wind, or any other place, or what other ways there are whereby Persons may come into the Town without coming through the Gates?—The Wall was scaled that night by a Gentleman at Leith-wind, it is about 15 foot high, but on the Inside the Earth is parallell with the Top of the Wall like a Terras, There is likewise access by Trinity Hospital at the foot of Leith Wind, and access likewise by the foot of the North Loch, and I believe it is likewise accessible by the back of the Castle

Do you know or were you informed, that the Mob did shew, or intended to shew their Resentment agt. any particular Person, if Captain Porteous was not executed?—No, I never heard any such thing, not the least surmise of any thing of that kind

Question 12 —Whether that night the Captain was murdered, the City Guard had any powder or Ball deliver'd to them?—I believe not, for the City Guard was surprized before we could get time to give any Directions of any kind

Question 13 —Whether upon the Provost's being informed, that the Mob were assembling in the Grass Market, he gave any Orders to increase the City Guard, or Ordered them any Amunition?—I believe not, for we did not know that he had got the Information, but I believe he gave no Orders till he had certain Information

Question 14 —[Answer of no importance]

Question 15 —[Do]

Whether or no since the Provost was examined before this Comittee, you have seen a copy of the Questions directed to be asked by the Comittee?—I have heard of most of them and I believe I have seen most of them

He withdrew

IV —Examination of Bailie Blackwood

[The evidence of Mr Alexander Blackwood, the 3rd Bailiff comes next, his answers are to much the same effect as what has gone before]

Captain Porteous.

Mr Gavin Hamilton the 4th Bailiff was called in and asked
Question 1 —What, etc [*sic* in MSS]?—I do not know any orders
my Lord Provost gave
Question 2 —How, etc ?—I do not know, but upon examining the
Pieces, I found they were charged with lead Drops of a pretty large
size
Question 3 —Whether, etc ?—Mr Croquhat and I attended, we
went from the Scaffold when the Man was hung up, and retired to a
Tavern at a little Distance, which was the constant Custom, and
waited there to give the signal for the cutting down
Question 4 —Whether, etc ?—He was cut down upon a Mistake,
we pulled down the sash, meaning that he should not be cut down,
but the Executioner and Officers attending upon the Scaffold took
it as a signal, and he was cut down upon it upon which I moved
that some officers might be sent over to the place of Execution,
that we might be satisfied the man was dead , but the Company
took notice that he had hung so long, that he was past all recovery,
he had hung about 24 minutes
Question 5 —Whether etc ?—He was not cut down by the Executioner, but a person from the Street, who called himself his Brother-
in-Law The same Person that cut him down had applied the day
before for his body to have him buried
Question 6 —Whether, etc ?—I do not know, I heard it reported,
that they endeavoured to bleed him at Leith and likewise endeavoured
to pour a Dram of Brandy down his throat
Question 7 —Whether, etc ?—The throwing stones was before any
Firing, very little after we heard the firing of the Pieces
Question 8 —Were you present when Captain Porteous brought his
Gun to the Provost?—Yes I was
Did you observe any marks upon Porteous's Gun, that it had been
fired?—I did examine it, and it appeared to me to be clean, I tryed
the Ram Rod and found it loaded.
Question 9 —Whether, etc ?—Etc , etc
Were not you yourself informed that a number of country people
called at a Publick House on the Monday, and desired the Landlord
to join with them in coming in order to take Porteous out and hang
him?—No, I never did hear of it

[Endorsed] Examination of the four Bailiffs of Edinburgh
March 16th, 1736-7

VI —Examination of Captain Lind.

(B M Add MS 33,049, f 62)

Jovis 17 Die Martij, 1736

Capn [John] Lynn Capn of the City Guard at Edinburgh was
called in and asked as follows (viz)
What Commission have you from the City of Edinburgh?—Captain
Lieutenant, I have my Commission here
Who is Captain?—The Lord Provost
Question 1 —Whether you had any Information or Notice of the
intended Riot before it happened? and what time you received that

Appendix XII.

notice?—It was a thing that was the common talk over the whole town about eight days before it happened, there was a Man who informed me of it upon Friday the 3rd of September.

Question 2—Whether you gave the Magistrates? or to all or any of them An Account of the Notice you had of the Design, and at what time did you acquaint them with the Notice you had received?—I went on Saturday betwixt Eight and Nine in the Evening and desired to speak with the Provost in private, he came into the next Room to me, Then I told him I was informed by a Man, that there was an Intention of carrying off Porteous next Wednesday, in case he was not hanged upon the Wednesday, but I was not at Liberty to name my Informer

Who was with the Provost at the time you gave him that Information?—After I told the Provost he desired me to walk into the next Room where were present, Mr Lindesay Member of Parliament for the Town, Mr Young the Town Treasurer, and Mr Harriot Dean of Guild, then I repeated the same that I had before told the Lord Provost, upon which Mr Lindesay said, that matter ought to be enquired into

In what manner did you receive that Information? From one person or from more?—I had it particularly from one, besides it was a thing that was commonly talked in all Coffee Houses upon the Street

Was the Report credited, or was it only among the meaner sort of people?—It was mostly talked among the meaner sort, most part of Folkes were of opinion they never would attempt such a thing

Had you no Conversation with ye Provost about it? betwixt Saturday and Tuesday?—No, I did not see him to the best of my knowledge, from Saturday till Tuesday six of the Clock at night

At the time you acquainted the Lord Provost with the designed Tumult, did you address yourself to the Provost only, or to the whole Company?—I think it was to my Lord Provost only

Did you speak wth. so audible a voice that the rest of the Company could hear you?—Yes, they all heard very well

When you gave the Provost the first Information on Saturday what did then pass betwixt you and the Provost, and what orders did he give you?—I proposed carrying him to the Castle Mr Young the Treasurer said that was a thing Impracticable, and could not be done without an Order from the Privy Council I afterwards proposed that the Provost, Magistrates, Constables and Officers of the Train Bands should meet together on Wednesday evening at one Bruce's, a Tavern hard by the Prison, but I got no Answer

Did you think the Rumour so well grounded that it was necessary to remove Capn Porteous to the Castle?—Yes, My Lords, I did

Did you tell the Provost on the Tuesday that you thought the Rumour was groundless?—I never did my Lords

Did you on the Tuesday tell the Provost that you understood the Rumours to be only a common clatter among comon servants and Children?—I'm very positive I never did

What was meant by Privy Council? a Council of the town of Edinburgh, or any other Privy Council?—It was Mr Young's Expression, I suppose it was ye Privy Council here he meant

Did you go to the Council Chamber on Tuesday morning? or any where else at any time? between Saturday or Tuesday, to seek for the Provost or Magistrates?—Not till the Tuesday I went two or three times to seek for the Provost, twice in the forenoon and once in the afternoon to the Council Chamber, I afterwards heard about five in the afternoon, that he was at Mureds Coffee House, and sent my name into the Provost by the Servt, and that I wanted to speak

Captain Porteous.

with him, the servant brought me word that he was busy, but was to be at the Council Chamber at six

Did not you send somebody to wait at the Council Chamber Door, to bring you word when ye Provost came?—Yes, after I came from Mnreds Coffee House, I went to Johns Coffee House, within a few yards, where I met three Gentlemen of my acquaintance, We agreed to go to one Clarkes a Tavern hardby one of the Gentlemen went along with me to the Guard where I left word with the Serjt and Centry at the Door where I was to be found, in case I should be wanted (according to our Instructions from the Magistrates) and at the same time sent a Soldier to the Council Chamber to wait the Provost's coming, and bring me word the moment he came there, which accordingly he did

Why were you so desirous to see the Provost on Tuesday? had you any fresh Information to give him?—Only the Report was a great deal stronger, there was more talk of it than there had been for three days before, and Wednesday the next day being my Guard day, I wanted to have the Lord Provost's orders for that Day

Is it not always customary when there is to be an Augmentation of the Guard to give out the Orders the night preceding?—Always, my Lords

Question 3 —Did you propose to the Magistrates—etc ?

Not put having been answered before [*Sic*]

Question 4 —Did not you upon mounting the Guard or at no other time, apply to the Provost or Magistrates, for orders what to do in case of any Disturbance?—Not, but upon the Tuesday night, I asked his Orders for the next day

Question 5 —What orders did you receive from the Provost or Magistrates?—None at all but the Parole of that Night, and then I told the Provost I would come back to him next forenoon to receive his Orders

What is the Parole? What is the Word?—I do not remember

Did you on Tuesday Night tell the Provost that you were under the same apprehensions that you had been before, that some disturbance would happen?—No, my Lords, I believe I spoke nothing of it to him that night

Was there any Notion that the Mob were to rise on the Tuesday night?—No, my Lords, I never heard of the Tuesday

Had you any Orders from any of the Magistrates besides the Provost? or from Mr Lindesay on the Tuesday Night?—None at all my Lords

After you had spoke with the Provost & receed the Parole did you receive any Order or Message from the Provost, & what was it?—I had no Message, 'till about half an hour after Nine, as I can judge, a Servt of the same Tavern came in and told me the Lord Provost wanted to speak with me in the next Room I immediately went to him, where was Mr Lindesay Member of Parliamt , the Provost asked, if I had heard any thing of a Mob gathering in the Grass Market, I made answer that I had heard nothing of it, upon which the Provost said, I wish you would go see, I said I wou'd I went first to the Guard, called for the Serjt told him I was informed there was a Mob gathering in the Grass Market, asked him if he had heard any thing of it. at the same time ordered him to get his men in Readiness in case it was so, and keep them together, And in the Officers Guard Room I over heard People upon the Street talking that there was a Mob gathering at the Nether Bow, I comeing to the Guard Room met one Mr Hunter, who confirmed what I had heard and said there was a great Mob at the Nether Bow, to the best of

286

Appendix XII.

my knowledge he said 4 or 5000 in Number, and bad us take care of ourselves upon which I came out of the Guard, I heard a Drum beat, I immediately run as hard as I could to the Provost, I acquainted him with what I had learned, he was still in the same Room with Mr Lindesay, where I had left him, upon which Mr Lindesay desired me to go and turn out my Guard, I desired that the Lord Provost or some of the Magistrates wou'd come to the Guard themselves to give Orders, and the Provost said he would follow me, I should have said when I came first to the Guard, I dispatched a Man to the Grass Market to bring me Intelligence, after Mr Lindesay desired me to go & turn out my Guard and the Provost said he would follow me, a little below the Cross, between the Cross and the Guard, I met twenty or thirty people with fire arms, which surprized me very much, I passed tho' them, upon which one of them struck at me as I was very near the Guard Door, I looked over my shoulder to see who it was, some of their number cryed spare him, we have nothing to do with him, I afterwards was going into the Guard Room, looking & seeing the Guard full of the Mob, & distributing the Arms of the City out of the Windows, I left the Guard & returned to the Provost & Magistrates whom I met upon the Street coming down to ye Guard and told them what had happened, upon which they returned to the same Tavern they came from, and then Mr Lindesay was sent to Genl Moyle To the best of my knowledge from the Time that I left the Guard to acquaint the Provost with the situation the Town was in, to the Time I returned was not above two minutes, as near as I can Judge

Was Mr Lindesay sent to Genl Moyle, from the Tavern or from the Street?—I cannot be positive of that, I think it was from the Tavern, I think he came into the House

Who was the Messenger that you dispatched to the Grass Market for Intelligence, & what intelligence did he bring you?—A soldier of the Guard, he never returned, the Guard was surprized before he came back

How came it when you were satisfied that there were a great number of people in a Tumultuous manner assembled not to put your Guard under arms the first thing you did?—I thought it was my Duty to go first & acquaint the Provost as I had been sent out to give him Intelligence, the House where the Provost was, was not above a hundred yards from the Guard I wanted that either the Provost or some of the Magistrates shou'd come themselves and give Orders, by whose Order I thought I could act more safely in case I was obliged to attack the Mob

Do you know whether the persons you saw in the Guard were Inhabitants of the Town or of the Country about?—I did not know one of them

How long did the Magistrates stay in the Tavern after they sent Mr Lindesay, before they came into the Street to attempt to disperse the Mob, or give any orders for dispersing them?—Mr Lindesay went away before ten and they came out about an hour after

Question 6 —How did the Mob make themselves Masters of your Guard?

Not put having been ansd before

Question 7 —What Number of them usually mount the Guard, and what number of men had you that night with you upon the Guard? —The Number of men we generally mount with is thirty, or twenty-nine more properly because we muster one for a Servt I mounted Guard that Day with twenty one men of my Company, there were seven that were put there on Acct of suspicion of their firing at

Captain Porteous.

Wilson's Execution, one sick that died a little after, there was one other man that fell sick that night and had gone home and one that was hurt at Wilson's Execution, who did his Duty in the day time & had liberty to go to his bed at night

How many were in the Guard Room when the Guard was seized? —I did not know till the next day. I was informed by the Serjt there were just ten men and the Centry at the door, ten private Men besides the Corporal Serjt & Drum. there was one at the Guard Room Door, one was at the Prison Door, one was at the Parliament Close, & one was sent to the Grass Market to bring Intelligence & there were three sick

Have you been informed that there was any Message sent by the Mob to the Centry at the Guard Room Door to tell him that he and the Guard had best get out of the way?—I never heard of any except Mr Hunter who I'm sure did not come from the Mob

Question 8 —Whether it is usual upon extraordinary occasions to double the City Guard?—Always my Lords

Do you not usually reinforce the Guard at a certain hour of the Night?—Yes, at ten o'Clock

With how many men do you generally reinforce it?—With ten since the Riot happened, but before we used to have only eight

Question 9 —Whether your men had Powder and Ball or any and what sort Shot delivered to them?—We had none at all, neither Powder nor Ball in the Guard

Did you ever inform the Magistrates that there was no Powder and Ball in the Guard Room? or did you ever make any request to them for it?—I never did

Whether you and the Men of the like Rank are of such as live upon the profession of Arms in General, or whether when you are not upon Guard, you have any other Profession?—Sometimes we do, one of the Gentlemen has a Shop in the Town

Whether the Provost as Capn of the Guard did not know of the want of Amunition in the Guard Room, and whether it was not his Duty to enquire into it?—I cannot tell whether he knew or not, We never have any but what is given out by the Provost's Orders, he orders the Treasurer to give it out

Question 10 —By whose Order is the powder and shot given out to the Men that Mount Guard?

Not put having been answered before

Do you know if at the Execution of Wilson Powder and Ball were delivered out to the Guard?—Yes, I know it was delivered out to them by the Serjt Major

Was it delivered out from the Town Store & by whose Order?—I cannot tell indeed my Lords

Do you know what sort of shot it was that was delivered out at that Execution?—Yes, I have seen a great deal of it, it was Swan shot

What kind of shot do the Magistrates usually order the Commander of the Guard to charge with?—I do not know I never had any Order of that kind

Did you hear that Capn Porteous bought the shot himself? or from whom it was that the Serjt receed it?—I never heard

Do you know whether the communication betwixt the Town and the Castle was cut off?—No my Lords I never did hear it

Did you ever hear any proposal made by any of the Magistrates or others to send to the Commanding Officer in the Castle for any assistance from him?—No I never did.

Appendix XII.

Did you ever hear any Instance in which the Guard was ordered to fire on the Mob before?—No, not to my knowledge

Question 11 —Whether all the arms of the City Guard are usually kept in the Guard Room?—Yes, it was always customary to keep them there except since the late Riot

Were you with the Provost & ye Magistrates when they went out to quell the Mob and wt did you Act at that time?--I went out with the Provost & Magistrates, at that time I had a Flambeaux in one hand and my cane in the other hand, I walked before the Magistrates to the Prison, where we were attacked with a shower of stones, One Mr Clarkson, Mr Stuart & I drove several of the Mob before us 'till we came near to the Prison Door, when I had the Flambeaux taken out of my hand and was obliged to retire on account of the number of stones that were thrown, which hurt us, Mr Clarkson had one stroak on the breast with a Stone, Mr Stuart likewise was hurt, after that we were obliged to retire

Were those arms that were taken away by the Mob ever returned? if they were, how came to have them again and from whom? [*Sic*] —They were mostly found upon the street the next Morning, several of them broke, I believe there was not above three or four that were lost

Were they all found again, if they were not, was any search made for those that were missing?—I cannot positively say how many were lost, I believe there were three or four, but as to any search, I never heard of any

Upon the first information you gave the Lord Provost on the Saturday, of the supposed Tumult, did the Lord Provost give you any Orders to make enquiry, and what enquiry did you make?—The Lord Provost gave me no Orders to make any Enquiry

Do you know whether the day after the Murder, or any other time or at what other time the Magistrates used any Endeavours to apprehend any of the Rioters, and what those Endeavours were?— To the best of my knowledge there was no search made after any body for some days, I believe not till they had a Return from London after that there were Warrants issued out for apprehending some of them

Did you ever hear of any Instance where the Guard fired with or without Orders?—Yes without Orders twice where I had the Command

How were their arms charged at that time, when they did fire?— That is what I cannot tell

Upon what occasion was it?—One time was at a Race at Leith, there was a Quarrel happened betwixt some Gentlns Servants & the Sailors, upon which I made two or three of the Sailors Prisoners, upon which the Mob became very Insolent, and I was obliged to take Bail for them I afterwards ordered the Drum to beat, to gather the men together, marched them off, & ordered ym to load, although I'm sure there was not above seven or eight of them, that had either powder or Ball, which was more for show than any thing else, & marching off the Guard the Mob attacked the Rear upon which two or three of the Soldiers turned about & fired & wounded two men in the legs, the other time was at the Execution of one Brown

Do you know with what kind of shot the wounds appeared to be given?—No, indeed I do not

He withdrew

The Lord Provost called in Asked,
Whether the day after the murder of Porteous, or at any other time & when, the Magistrates used any Endeavours to apprehend any of

Captain Porteous.

the Rioters?—We endeavoured all we could to get information who they were

What were those Endeavours?—We made all the Enquiry if any person could possibly inform us who they were

What Information did you get upon that Enquiry, and in what manner did you Enquire?—We could get no Information at all, the Sollr was sent for, & came to town & he made the Stricktest enquiry he could, as privately as possible

Whether the next morning the City Gates were kept shut? or whether they opened as usual, or if they were kept shut? how long they were kept shut?—Some of them were kept shut till about seven or eight in the morning

Has it not been usual when a Tumult & Riot has happened in the City of Edinburgh for the Magistrates to keep their Gates shut all the next day?—I do not remember anything of that

Whether the Magistrates gave any Orders that the City Gates should be kept shut?—Not that I know of

Did you hear of any Peoples absconding [sic] after this Riot & when?—I heard some days after that Sevl People had left the City

Did not one Mr Beard offer to carry a letter to Genl Moyle, if you would write one?—No my Lords

(He Withdrew)

[Endorsed]   Captn Lyn's Examination
17 March 1736

VII —Examination of Patrick Lindsay, M P.

(B M Add MS 33,049, f 69)

Veneris 18 Die Martij 1736

Mr Lindesay was called in & Asked.

Were you sent by the Magistrates to Genl Moyle during the time of the Outrage & with what Orders & Instructions?—I was in Company with the Provost, one other Magistrate, and some other Gentn, when they went out in order to join Mr Lyn, upon the first notice that there was a Mob gathering about the Nether Bow and beating the Drum I went along with the Provost and other Gentlemen and when we got near the Cross, We met Mr Lyn who told us, that a Mob had surprized his men, Drove them from the Guard, seized their Arms, beat himself and he was obliged to fly for his Life, After this some called out get away for the Mob are moving this way, and we step'd to the side of the Street, a little above the Coffee House Stairs, where it was proposed what is to be done, they all agreed there were no hopes of Relief, but by assistance from the Kings Troops, and one of the Company said let us go back to the House and contrive a Letter to the General, upon this Mr Colquhoon said with great Energy and Concern, Gods Mercy if we stay 'till you write three Lines We shall be all of us in the hands of the Mob, and then we shall have no hopes of Relief, And said, why may not Mr Lindesay go, he is known to the General, and acquaint him of our situation Upon this I turned & said, Lord Provost if you desire me I will go, he answered, By all means, make what haste you can, for there is no time to be lost

How long were you with the Magistrates, before you were sent to

Appendix XII.

General Moyle, after the first Notice of the Riot?—I do not believe it was three or four minutes, from Mr Lyn's going out, to our following him

How long was it from the first Notice the Magistrates had of the Riot, to the time of your being sent to Genl Moyle?—I had been in Company with the Magistrates from Eight o'clock, and the first Notice I had, the Provost called me out into another Room, I think it was about half an hour after nine o'clock and told me there was a Boy (pointing to the Boy) who had come in from his Niece to acquaint him that there were a few Boys beating a Drum in the Grass Market, he then sent the same Messenger to the Guard to know if the Officer was there, and to find him if he was not in five or six minutes thereafter The Boy returned & Mr Lyn along with him

Who was the Person that proposed writing the letter to General Moyle?—I really cannot tell, I believe two or three of them spoke at the same time, being all in a hurry by the surprize, but they said Let us go back and contrive a Letter

How long after that was it before you went to General Moyle?—I believe it might be near half an hour. because as I remember, just as Mr Lyn was giving us Notice near the Cross, the Town Clock struck ten.

What Directions did you Receive from the Provost or Magistrates, all or any of them, when you were sent to General Moyle?—I received no other than what I have told your Lordships in answer to the first question

By what time did you get to Genl Moyle?—The moment the Provost desired me to go, I walked down the Street as fast as I could till I came to the Nether Bow Gate, which I found was shut, and a very Great Number of Mob at it, And some few of them with Fire Arms, when I came near amongst them, I observed some of them begin to look me in the Face As I was afraid they might have known me and suspected my Message, I step'd aside into the Head of a little Close (a Lane without a thorough Fare) and immediately thereafter I walked back to the Street again, 'till I came near as far as the Guard, and there I step'd into another Close Head, to listen what the Mob were saying, and then it struck me in the head, that they might have neglected the Potters Row Port, and I immediately crossed the street, went down Marlins Wind, crossed the Cow Gate, went up the College Wind and came to the Potter's Row Gate; which I found lock'd & no body near it, but the Keeper who opened the Wicked & let me out, from thence I was obliged to go in my way to the Abbey Hill (where the General's House was) round by the Kings Park Wall

What did you say to General Moyle when you came to him?—As soon as I had access to the General, I made an Apology for disturbing him at so unseasonable an hour, I told him the present unhappy situation of affairs in Edinburgh made it necessary, That a Mob had surprized the City Guard, drove away the Soldiers and seiz'd their Arms, And I was come from the Magistrates, to acquaint him of it, and to desire his Assistance The General upon this told me. that he had notice of the thing before I came, but no such particular Account of it, That on the first Notice he had ordered all his men in Canon Gate to be under Arms, and likewise all his Men quartered in Potters Row and Westport, to be got under Arms least the Mob should also surprize them, and Seize their Arms, and then he said, Sir, I will do more, and immediately called for a servant and ordered him to take horse and go to Leith, and to acquaint the Commanding Officer there, that it was his Orders that he should get his men together with the Greatest Secrecy, get them under arms, and march

Captain Porteous.

them up to join the Canon Gate Guard   Upon this I said if we wait till these three Companies come from Leith, I am afraid it will be too late, The Mob are now absolute Masters, They are acting without controul, and no Mortal can Answer for the Mischief they may do, unless they are speedily checked and dispersed   Upon this the General made Answer, that he could not allow one Man to March from the Canon Gate Guard, without a Warrant from the Lord Justice Clarke or a Lord of Justiciary, I do not remember which, upon this I was very much at a loss, the nearest Judge of that Court, to the place where I was, was the Justice Clark   I told the General that if I knew any way of sending to him, I would write a letter and acquaint him what had happened, and what he had done   Upon this Mrs Moyle (who was in the Room) desired me to walk into the next Room, and gave me paper, Pen & Ink and told me there would be a servant & a Horse ready to carry the Letter to him, by that time it was wrote   I wrote a short Note to the Justice Clarke to acquaint him what had happened what the Genl had already done, but that he would proceed no further, without a Warrant from his Lordship, this is the substance of all that passed   The moment I had wrote the Letter & before I folded up I brought it towards the General, but he did not read it, but Mrs Moyle look'd on it while I read it and said it was very well

In what order did you find the Troops when you came to General Moyle's or were they preparing to get in Order?—The way that I was obliged to go as I told your Lordships before, was a long Circuit, & out of the way where any Troops were, but I returned directly towards the town from the General's, by Canon Gate, and when I came to Canon Gate, I saw about ten or twelve of the Officers standing at the Head of their Men, I talked a little with them, I said they had been very Expeditious, for as near as I could judge by my Eye, they had about an hundred File (three Men to a File) standing in close order   One of the Officers answered, Sir, There's a good deal above an hundred File   It was then about Eleven o'Clock   For just after I passed them I met a Messenger, who had come over the Town Wall, from the Provost to know if the Troops were coming, and to acquaint me that they had made an attempt to disperse the Mob and were beat back that the Mob had set fire to the Prison Door, and unless the Troops came within forty minutes, it was their opinion that they would get into the Prison in that time   After I had acquainted this Gentleman what had passed with the General and that no Troops could be expected till there came a Return from Lord Justice Clarke, I desired him if he could return by the Way he came, and get at the Magistrates, he would give them this notice, When I parted with him I looked at my watch & it was then five Minutes past Eleven

Did General Moyle ask you whether you had any Written Order or Authority from the Provost, or any of the Magistrates for Demanding the Assistance of the Troops?—He did not

Did General Moyle ask you whether you could get such a Written Order and if you could get such a one that then he would let the Troops march?—There was no such thing mentioned

Did you ask Genl Moyle that if you could have a written Order from the Provost, whether then he would march the Troops?—No, my Lords, after the General had said that he would not allow them to march, without a Warrt from a Lord of the Justiciary, and that I had wrote a letter to the Justice Clarke (which was sent away by his Servant) I thought it in vain to propose any other Authority, but took my leave of the General & returned to the Town

How came you not to send Word to the Lord Provost in an Hour's

Appendix XII.

time, of what had passed between you and the General?—I could send no notice to him, the Mob were Masters of all the Gates, the Gentleman that met me came over the Wall, by a Rope tyed to a Growing Tree in a Gentleman's Garden, and I walked round the Wall from Gate to Gate, till the Westport was opened by the Mob, and then I got in

What difference was there in the condition of the Potters Row Gate, betwixt your going out, and the time a Messenger could have Returned?—I cannot answer that question from my own proper Knowledge I was told afterwards that the Keeper said, that I had not been gone above two Minutes when a Number of the Mob seized that Gate and took the Keys of it

As you did not know when you were out, that that Gate was seized, how came you not to try?—I came out of the Town just as the Mob was begun, and I apprehended that by the time I got to the Generals, they would be up in all the Suburbs as well as in the Town, & that was the reason why I did not think of applying to ye Lord Newhall, whose house is just without that Gate

Did not the General tell you, that an order from you, who were no Magistrate, was not an Authority that he could act by, or whether he did not say something to that effect?—He did not, To the best of my Remembrance there was nothing more passed than what I have already told your Lordships

What time did you get to General Moyle's?—I believe it was about three quarters after ten The next day the General told me yt it wanted fourteen minutes of Eleven when I came to him

How far is it from Genl Moyle's to the Lord Justice Clarke's?—It is about three computed Miles

How far is it from the Genls to the Lord Newhalls?—I believe by the nearest way it is about a measured mile

How came you not to try to send a Letter to the Lord Newhall?—I can give no other reason than I have already given, that I apprehended the Mob would be up there, because the Soldiers from that Quarter were drawn up to the Canon Gate

At the time you went to Genl Moyle's, did not you know? that upon other occasions, the Genl had furnished Troops, when requested by Letter from the Lord Provost?—I cannot answer that question from my own proper knowledge, I have heard a good deal of talk of that, since Porteous's affair happened, with Relation to the Execution of Wilson, but then I was at London, and did not return to Edinburgh 'till the latter end of July last

Did you ever hear of any Precedent, where the Troops had been granted to the Magistrates without a Request in Writing?—I remember in the year 1725, when I was Eldest Bailiff of Edinburgh, and the Gentleman who was then Provost, was at London, attending the Service of Parliament, (his Authority then Descended by the usuage of the Town upon the Eldest Bailiff) there was then a Mob lasted Two Days, and we had a great many different Skirmishes betwixt them, and our Guard, and a good Number of Men Wounded on both sides, One night when we apprehended they were to attack us with their greatest Strength, We sent a Messenger to the Commanding Officer in Canon Gate, to acquaint him of our Situation, and desire of him in case the Mob should prove too many for our Guard, that he would sustain us, he sent back to acquaint us, that he mount that Night a double Guard And likewise order a Picquet and as soon as we sent him Notice that we had Occasion for them, he would order one of his Guards to march to our Assistance But we had no Occasion for it

Did you get any Answer from Lord Justice Clarke, and what was

Captain Porteous.

—The Answer came to me about two o'Clock in the morning, I have it in my pocket

> Then the Lord Justice Clarke's Ansr to Mr Lindesay was delivered in and read.

When you went from the Magistrates to General Moyle, Did you go back with them to the Tavern, or did you go from the Street?— It was from the Street, as I mentioned in a former Answer

In the Letter you wrote to Lord Justice Clarke, did you say that the General would not march any of his Troops, unless he had an order from the Lord Justice Clarke, or some Lord of Justiciary?— As near as I can remember, I expressed it in the words I have already said, which was, Recounting what preparations the General had made, but that he would proceed no further, without directions from his Lordship

Did Genll Moyle say to you, that he was willing to march his Troops, to appease the Tumult, if there was any Magistrate would go with him?—He did not so far as I can remember, I'm pretty sure he did not

Do you know, or were you informed, that any methods were used by the Magistrates to make a Discovery of the Rioters, and at what time such methods were used?—A little after I reced the Justice Clarke's Answr and read it to the Magistrates, we found there was no Authority for the Assistance of the King's Troops, & that we could not expect any unless we had it from Court, they then sent down some of their Company and a Dozen Porters to take down the body of Mr Porteous, but the Mob fell upon them and beat them, after this I with four or five of the Company went out into the Street and went down as far as the Nether Bow Gate, which we found locked, and the Keeper told us the Mob had Carryed away the Keys with ym We then went to the Cow Gate Port. which we found open, and the Keeper told us that he had hid himself with the Keys when he had heard of the seizing of the Nether Bow, But that the Mob had secured it with great Stones, and kept a Guard at it 'till the Murder was over, and then they opened it themselves As we were then nearer to the Canon Gate Guard than to the Mob, We examined every person we met in that Street, and seized three fellows who could not give a sufficient account of themselves, and Carried them prisoners to the Canon Gate Guard, where the officers told us, that their men had observed three fellows pass by a little before, and heard one of them boasting what part he had acted in the hanging of Porteous, we said we wished they had secured them, but they answered they could not do that having no orders, then we desired them that they might seize every one that they suspected and detain them upon their Guard 'till the morning, when we would send a Magistrate to examine them, in order to their being committed or acquitted, they accordingly seized nine besides the three we carryed there, after this we returned to the Town, and when we came near the place where Porteous was hanging our number was then increased to about twenty, by several of the Inhabitants having joined us, we walked up in a Body into the Middle of the Mob and got them dispersed, took down the Body and sent it into a Church just by, it was then just break of Day Between five and six in the Morning the Magistrates and Common Council then met in the Council Chamber, and sent for all the officers of the Train Band, and then ordered two Company's to mount that night, one in the low Council House under the Justiciary Hall, and another in the Borough Room Then they sent for all the Masters of the several Incorporations & ordered them forthwith to give in a List, of all their servants that

Appendix XII.

were abroad that night after ten o'clock, in order to make an enquiry how many of them had any Accession to the Riot When the Lord Justice Clarke came to Town that forenoon, the Magistrates told him, that one Campbell a Joiner had been among the Mob, and knew two who were very active in putting ye Rope about Porteous's Neck, they immediately sent for him to Justice Clarke, who examined him, and I believe he made a discovery, but their Enquirys were kept very secret for we heard that very day, that several tradesmens Servants left the Town and fled Mr Colquoon & I were sent to one Mr Nesbit who lived just over the Place where Porteous was murdered, to know if he could make any discoveries, he told us he looked on all the while, and took such marks of several of them, that he should know them again if he saw them, but was a Stranger to all their faces There was another Gentleman, one Mr. Carmichael a Mercht to whom Porteous had Delivered his Purse just as the Mob were putting the Rope about his Neck, he was likewise Examined by the Magistrates the same day, and likewise one Mr Renton Mr Colquoon and I, with one of the Common Clerks having heard of one Mr Bucannon that had been among the Mob at the Prison Door, and was the next day going to London, We took his Declaration & I remember he told us, that he was within sight of the Prison Door all the while the Mob were breaking and burning it, that he looked in many of their faces but knew none of them, that they were all Dressed like Tradesmen's Servants, but in his opinion by their Linen and the Colour of their hands some of them seemed to be persons of better condition, he said when the Magistrates attempted to Disperse them, they were at first in a great fright, and cryed out, the Magistrates are coming with the Canon Gate Guard, Some of them threw down their arms, & several of them run away, but they were soon told, the Magistrates were coming but nobody with them but a few of the Inhabitants, & that then Friends had gone in sufficient numbers to drive them back The Magistrates did not think it prudent to take up any person 'till they were sure of being assisted by the King's Forces, and a full discovery made, because on the first seizure every one who was conscious of his Guilt, wou'd probably run away, All the Examinations and informations which the Magistrates took, were put into the Solicitor's hands when he came to Town, which was about ten days after, and then he went on with the Examination, and has (as I believe) all the papers that relate to it

What Orders are commonly given on the Occasion of an Execution?—The Town Guard of Edinburgh were formerly furnished with the same kind of Amunition the King's Troops have, but in the year 1725 when that Mob happened, which I told your Lordships of before, We were apprehensive if we had been reduced to a necessity of Fireing, that such heavy shot might have passed thro' the Mob and killed innocent people at a great distance, and therefore we then provided them with a kind of small shot, I believe it is what they call Number one, they call it Hail, ever since that time the Officer whose turn it is to mount the Guard when an Execution is to be, Mounts the Guard with the usual Number, and another Officer with a detachment attends the Execution with fire Arms loaded with that kind of shot

Had you any Meeting with the Provost or Magistrates upon the Saturday before the Riot?—Upon the Saturday night before the Riot, I was at the Provost's House in Company with Mr Harriot Dean of Guild & Mr Young the Town Treasurer

Did you concert any measures upon the Saturday or the Tuesday to prevent it?—It was at that time, that Saturday night, that Mr

Captain Porteous.

Lyn gave the Provost Information that he had heard a Mob was intended to destroy Porteous, on Wednesday Night if he was not executed according to his Sentence, when the Provost brought Mr Lyn into the Room where we were, and desired him to tell us what he had said to him, I said that affair ought to be carefully Enquired into, for those things are easier prevented by being crushed in the Bud, than suppressed when they come to any heighth, all that was done that night was, that the Provost desired Mr Lyn to trace his Information of that Matter as far as he could, that if it cou'd be learned in what manner the Mob was intended or from what Quarter it was to come, measures might be taken to prevent it   On the Tuesday Evening between six and seven, I went into the Council Chamber, where the Provost & sevl Members of the Council were met, I asked the Provost if Mr Lyn had recovered any further account or made any discovery, of what he told him on Saturday, he answered Mr Lyn was just gone out of the Chamber & that he had reported to him that he had made all the Enquiry he could & could not discover there was any ground for the Report but they told me, they intended to meet early the next morning to have all their Guard under Arms, & to settle the best methods they could to prevent the Rising of a Mob, in case any such thing was attempted

Did the Magistrates give any Order on the Tuesday night for doubling the Guard on the Wednesday?—Not that I know of.

Do you know whether Mr Lyn proposed to the Magistrates the sending Capt Porteous to the Castle for better security of his person?—After Mr Lyn came into the Company and told us of the Report that he had heard, In the course of the conversation, some one, but I cannot say whether it was Mr Lyn, said, Might not he be removed to the Castle, and then they might be free of all apprehensions of Danger, & some one of the Company answered that he doubted whether that could be done, without authority from the Queen Guardian & Council   This passed upon Saturday at the Provost's House as I think, but I cannot be positive because I think I have heard that Proposition talked of oftener than once

Do you remember who was in Company?—I have told already

Do you know any instance when the Magistrates have desired the assistance of the Troops from the Castle?—No I never knew any, never heard of any

Do you think that if it had been asked it would have been granted? —I believe not because the Day after I spoke to the Major of the Castle in the Street, & he told me that he had all his Company drawn out and formed, in case we could have procured a Warrant from the General for them   I asked him whether he would have allowed them to have marched upon the Authority of the Magistrates, and he said, I am no such fool as to March my men out of the Garrison without a sufficient Authority   This brings to my Remembrance that the General while I was with him, asked me whether there was any access to the Castle without going thro' the Town, and proposed to send an Orderly Serjt thither, but I told him there was no access to the Castle but thro' the Town

Had you any Conversation with any other person Except Mr Lyn about a Surmise that a Mob would happen, or did you believe that a Mob would happen?—I heard of that Report before I reached Edinburgh, I heard it in July upon the Road, a few days after the sentence was pronounced, I likewise heard it from several other persons, but I never heard any man of Discretion that look'd upon it as a thing in the least probable   I remember a few days before the thing happened, one Mr George Gordon Brother in Law of Porteous, and one who was very Sollicitous & Anxious to have a Reprieve for him, told me laughing, you have no doubt heard the

Appendix XII.

Story, that the Mob are to hang poor Porteous, I wish we had nothing else to fear   For my own part I had not the least suspicion of it, till they were up

He Withdrew

VIII —Examination of General Moyle

(B M. Add MS 33,049, f 80)

General Moyle was called in and asked,

Had you any orders or directions from the Commander in Chief of his Majesties Forces in Scotland, how you were to Act, when you should be required to assist the Civil Magistrates?—In the year 1733 after General Wade came from the Highlands, he gave me a Verbal Order to give no parties to the Civil Magistrate unless they were requested in writing, giving the reasons why they required it, I had likewise directions to keep their Letters for my Justification in case of Accidents, but if any Justice of Peace or Civil Magistrate applyed to me and offered to go at the Head of the Troops, I had then orders to give them parties when they desired it they giving Directions how the Soldiers should act   I have likewise a Letter from the General in which I have Orders to the same purpose

Then Genl Wade's Letter to him was read

In what manner did the Civil Magistrates usually apply to you, when they wanted the Assistance of the Forces?—Always by Letter, I have two in my hand

Then the said two Letters, one from Lord Justice Clarke, the other from the Lord Provost of Edinburgh, were read

What passed between you and Mr Lindesay?—On Tuesday, fourteen minutes before Eleven a Clock at night, Mr Lindesay came to my house and told me, there was a Great Mob in the City to the number of three or four thousand, that they had seized the City Gates, as also the Arms of the City Guard, and told me he had got out at a Wicket and gave six pence to the person to let him out, and believed by this time that his house was pulled down   I told him I had heard the Report of a Mob before and upon his not producing a Letter from the Provost, I told him my hands were tyed up, I could not take upon me to Order the King's Forces to break open the Gates of the City without an Order from the Civil Magistrate, he did not acquaint me that he was a Justice of the Peace or a Magistrate, if he had I would have asked him to have headed the King's Troops, & I would have given them orders to march, If he would have gone with them, and given them Authority, I would have ordered them to have broke open the Gates

Would you have given Orders to the Troops, if Mr Lindesay had brought you a Written Order from the Lord Provost or any of the Magistrates?—I never refused them when so applyed for, or I would have given orders to the Troops if a Civil Magistrate would have gone with them, or if a Written Order had been brought from the Provost empowering me to break open the Gates   Finding there was no Letter come nor any Magistrate, I asked Mr Lindesay, if Ld Justice Clarke was in Town, Lord Royston or Lord Newhall, he told me Lord Justice Clarke was not in Town, Lord Royston was not in Town, Lord Newhall was but not to be come at, Upon which I

Captain Porteous.

desired Mr Lindesay to write to the Lord Justice Clark in my name, to desire that he would send me an Order, for forceing open the Gates of the Town Mr Lindesay accordingly did write a letter which my servant carried to the Lord Justice Clarke he gallowped all the way thither, but was detained above an hour before he got an Answer, so that the Letter did not come 'till long after Porteous was murdered, It was above two hours from the Writing of the Letter 'till the time the Servant Returned

Did you receive any Order from the Lord Justice Clarke or any Lord of Justiciary for the Troops to march at the Execution of Wilson?—No, I thought the Ld Provost's Letter was sufficient, because consistent with the Orders I received from General Wade.

How came you then to insist upon writing to Ld Justice Clarke?—I had no other method of proceeding then The only thing left was to write him because the Gates were shut, had not Mr. Lindesay told me that Lord Newhall could not be come at, I would have applyed to him because he was nearer, by which perhaps we might have had an Order time enough to have saved the poor Man's Life After finding the Letter did not come in any time, I mounted my Horse and went up to the Regiment, where I remained, waiting for an Answer from Lord Justice Clarke or an Order from the Provost, or one of the Bailiffs, and had the Lord Provost sent me an Order then, I would immediately have ordered the Troops to March, or had a Bailiff come, I would have done the same I waited there a considerable time and until I heard the Man was Murdered

Did Mr Lindesay tell you whether Lord Newhall was in Town or not?—He did not tell me whether he was in Town or out of Town, but only told me, Ld Newhall was not to be come at

Had you any Doubt, that Mr Lindesay did not come from the Magistrates, or did you desire him to give it under his hand, that he did come from the Magistrates?—I did not desire him to give it under his hand, I had a good deal of reason to believe he did not come from the Magistrates because he produced no order from them

Did you ask Mr Lindesay whether he could get a Letter from the Lord Provost or any of the Magistrates before he sent that Letter to the Lord Justice Clarke?—I did not propose it to him, nor did he offer any such thing, he was afraid of being murdered, if he went back to the Town

If Mr Lindesay had given it under his hand, that he did come with a Verbal Order from the Magistrates, could you upon that have ordered your Troops to march?—No, my Lords, it was inconsistent with the Orders I had received

Had you any Information of this Tumult before it happened and when?—I had been ill a long time and seldom went up to the Town, some Gentlemen told me that there was such a Report in Town, That there was a Mob intended to hang Porteous, on Saturday Capn Gumley told me there was such a Report as he was going to dine with Lord Justice Clarke, and I think I saw the Capn the next day and he told me that Ld Justice Clarke told him that they had examined into that Report and that it was without Ground

Did you attempt to send a Message to the Lord Provost by scaling the Wall or otherwise, after you found Mr Lindesay had brought no Letter and whether that was practicable?—I did not, it was more practicable for them to send to me, than for me to send to them

Did you upon the information you had, send any Information to the Magistrates, offering at the same time your Assistance with the Military Force, and if you did not was it because you did not credit that report?—I sent no Message

Did you Credit that Report?—I did not credit it, because my Ld Justice Clarke said it was without ground

Appendix XII.

Had you at any time any Conversation with Lord Justice Clarke about this affair?—On Wednesday morning the day after the Murder, Ld Justice Clarke called at my house as he came from his country house, I then asked him how far I could have been Justified, had I, without an Order forced open the Gates of the City, he told me that if I had I must have answered for the Consequences that might have ensued if I had given those orders

> Then a paragraph out of a Letter from Genl Moyle to the Duke of Newcastle Dated Edinburgh Sepr ye 23rd 1736 was read as follows

When I have the honr of seeing you I shall be able to convince your Grace it was not by any neglect of mine, the poor man lost his life   Had the Lord Provost given me as early notice as he got himself from a Relation of his own, I could with ease have prevented what happened without the Effusion of Blood, but it was a conceited affair that the poor man should dye, to prevent the Resentment of the Mob's falling on a certain person

Upon what foundation did you make use of such Expressions?—Had he sent me that notice and given me leave to have taken possession of the Netherbow Port that led to the Cannon Gate, I should have had a Communication both to the Prison and to the Castle, and I would have lost no time for I would have ordered the Cannongate Guard that consisted of an Officer, Serjt Corporal, Drum and thirty private men to have marched directly and taken possession of it

Do you know when the Lord Provost got that Notice which you mention in your Letter, & what it was?—The Notice I meant was the Letter or Message which was sent to the Lord Provost by his niece

Do you know at what time in the Evening that Message was sent to the Provost?—I was informed it was between eight and nine of the Clock on Tuesday Evening

Who is that Certain Person you hint at in your Letter?—The Lord Provost

What reason have you to think it was a Concerted affair?—Because it was so much talked of and no care taken to prevent it

Had you at any time any conversation with the Writer of the Edinburgh Newspaper relating to Porteous's affair, & what that Conversation was?—The News writer told me he had prepared a Paragraph to Incert in the *Caledonian Mercury*, that I was at the Head of the Troops in the Cannongate waiting for an Order from the Civil Power, but he was threatened to be sent to Prison if he incerted it, so he was obliged to strike it out

Did he tell you by whom he was threatened to be sent to Prison?—To the best of my Remembrance he said either by the Magistrates or Ld Justice Clarke, I cannot say which, or whether both

What is the News Writers Name?—His name is Ruddiman, he writes the *Caledonian Mercury*

> Then a paragraph out of the *Caledonian Mercury* was read

Why do you think the Resentment of the Mob would have fallen upon the Ld Provost?—Because if Porteous had been pardoned it might have appeared that he had received Orders, at the time of the Execution of Wilson, which might have brought the Resentment of the Mob upon the Provost

Do you know of any of the persons that were concerned in this murder that were known to the Magistrates, and that they were suffered to escape?—I know nothing of it

Captain Porteous.

Had you any order from the Lord Provost or any of the Magistrates, between the Hours of twelve and four o'clock on Wednesday morning?—I had none at all

Do you think it was practicable for the Provost to have sent any Message during that time?—I cannot tell he was the best Judge whether he could or no

> Then a Paragraph out of a Letter from Genl Moyle to the Duke of Newcastle dated Edinburgh Sept 18th 1736 was Read as follows

If any of the Criminals are discovered and apprehended, I wish there was Law to try them out of their own Country for fear a Jury should show them more mercy than they deserve here

Please to let the House know what were your Reasons for making that Proposition?—It was my Opinion, that is all

> Then part of a Paragraph out of a Letter from Genl Moyle to the Duke of Newcastle dated Edinburgh Sep 9th 1736 was read as follows

I cannot but mention to your Grace that this is the third Prisoner within the Memory of Man that has been taken out of a Toll Booth here, and barbarously murdered by the Mob

Please to Instance the two other persons you mention in that Letter?—Capn Green was one, and the other I forget the name of, I heard it in Scotland

He Withdrew

[Endorsed]   Examination of Mr Lindesay and Major Genl Moyle
March 18th 1736-7

IX.—Examination of Colonel Duroure

(B M Add MS 33,049, f 87)

Martis 22 Martij 1736

Colonel Duroure was Called in and asked,

Had you any Conversation with Mr Baird relating to the Provost's writing to Genl Moyle and his requesting a Letter from the Provost, and what do you know of that affair?—Mr Baird told me that when the Mob had surrounded the Prison, he was in Company with the Magistrates, and that after Mr Lindesay was gone to General Moyle, he expressed his Concern for the reflections this affair would bring upon the Town, if the assistance of the Troops did not come in time, before the Mob had seized upon Porteous, He then told the Provost that he feared Mr Lindesay would not obtain the assistance of the Troops for want of an Order in Writing, and told him, if you will give it me now, I will hasten away with it, in the best manner I can Upon which the Provost said, there is no occasion, but you may go and say, it is my Request that the Troops make all possible hast   Then he run as fast as he could down to the Netherbow, found the Gate locked, and nobody there but the Keeper from whom the Mob had taken the Keys, he turned to the left hand in a Wind close to the City Wall   got thro' into a Garden, level with the top of the City

Appendix XII.

Wall, got a rope tyed to a tree & let himself down in the Leith Wind ran up the Cannongate & met with Mr Lindesay without the Troops, which surprized him much, and he said, for God's sake, how came you not to have the Troops with you? Mr Lindesay answered, I came from the General, I have done all that could be done & an Express is gone to Lord Justice Clarke to obtain a Warrant, Upon which Mr Baird returned the same way he came & by the help of a Cart, which stood near the place he came down, he helped himself up again Mr Baird further told me that Bailiff Colquhon had twice proposed that night to send for assistance from the Castle

Are there not several places thro' which the Ld Provost could have sent a Messenger, besides that by which Mr Baird passed?—To my knowledge, I do not know those places, but I have been told that there are several houses, thro' which a Messenger might have gone in the same manner Mr. Baird did

He was directed to Withdraw

X —Examination of Major Pool

(B M. Add M S 33,049, f 88)

Then Major Pool was Call'd in and asked,

Were you at any time sent by General Moyle to the Lord Provost, upon occasion of Wilson's Execution?—Yes, that Day and the preceding day

What was your Message and what passed thereupon between you and the Provost?—The day before the Execution of Wilson, General Moyle sent to me in the afternoon, & told me he had received a Letter from the Lord Provost by Capt Porteous, desiring a Detachment from our Regiment to assist at the Execution of Wilson the day following, General Moyle also told me he had refused it, unless the Provost would give an order under his hand writing to indemnify the men, if any accidents should happen, I went from General Moyle into the City and met Capt Porteous a little above the Guard, I went to him and ask'd him, what message he had from the Lord Provost, in answer to General Moyle's Message, He told me the Provost would not indemnify the men, Then I told him we should have no hand in the Affair, they would have it all to themselves, General Moyle the next morning sent the Orderly Serjeant to me, about seven of the Clock in the morning, desiring I would come immediately to him, which I accordingly did He told me, he had altered his mind, for he thought it would be a service to the Government to have so notorious a fellow, as Wilson was executed, upon which, says he, Do you go up to the Lord Provost, & let him know that I have ordered him 150 Men, two Captains & four Subalterns, & a Captain of 50 Men in Reserve in Case of need, I went immediately up into the City, I called at the Guard to inquire where the Lord Provost lived, One of the Soldiers told me, somewhere near the West Port, I desired that Soldier to go to the Lord Provost to know where I might wait upon him. & I would stay at Ross's Coffee House, till he came back, The Messenger came very soon back, and the Provost immediately met me there, we went into a Closet at the Corner of Ross's Coffee house & there I acquainted him with General Moyle's Order, that he had ordered 150 Men, & that this number was to attend at his own time & place; He told me, that he desired they might be drawn up in the Lawn Market, about two of the Clock, But just as he was telling me this, a person came into the room to us (it was the Town Treasurer) and told the Lord Provost, that if the Military came into the City, it would give great

301

Captain Porteous.

Offence Upon which the Lord Provost immediately told me that he would not have us in the City, I desired to know of his Lordship, where he would please to have us? He told me, we might be drawn up at the usual Parade, I told his Lordship, either to have us, where we could be of service, or else not to give us the trouble of being under Arms, then he immediately told me, he would have us, where he formerly ordered us, As I was going to take leave of him, I begg'd the favour of his Lordship, that he would not see the King's Troops insulted & abused, as they commonly are by the Mob in that country; He told me he would take care of that, for he would order their own People, meaning Captain Porteous and his Guard, to be all loaded with sluggs (the Treasurer was by at the same time) and in case there was any disturbance, they should also have his orders, to turn out a few of the men out of their ranks and fire at their legs, and if they did not disperse, then he would give his Orders to Our Detachment, This very same Order I delivered to Captain Hickman who commanded the Party

Did you hear the Provost give these Orders to Captain Porteous, or any other Orders?—No, my Lords, I did not

Had you any Conversation with the Provost after the Execution of Wilson?—Yes, I had, a few days after the Execution of Wilson, I met the Provost at the Cross of Edinburgh & after the usual Compliments, I told him I was very sorry for the accident that happened the day I had the pleasure of seeing him last, upon which he told me, that he supposed Captain Porteous had been disappointed of some of his whores, which had put him out of humour to make him act as he did, I told his Lordship I thought it was very severe, to say so shocking a thing of a person, whom I thought he once had a great regard for especially in his circumstances, I told him that some of the Magistrates had owned to some of our Gentlemen that sup'd with them that night, that his piece was found loaded & had not been fired, But he told me then, that they had since found out the person, who had clean'd his piece, I then told him, that provided he did fire, it was not without his Orders; he immediately made answer to me, that he gave those Orders, but he never gave them to Porteous; Besides My Lord, said I, you use this man exceedingly ill in my humble opinion, in Confining of him in a Dungeon, and stopping his pay for I thought it was a very singular instance for a Gentleman to have his pay stop'd, before he was found guilty of the Fact

Do you know how Captain Porteous was used, when he was in Prison?—No, my Lords, I cannot say, The Comon report was, that he was used very ill, and he was represented in a Starving Condition, in so much that we made a Collection for him in our Regiment

Did you give any Information relating to Porteous before you left Edinburgh, what was the purport of that Information, and to whom did you give it?—I had a letter from Captain Porteous out of Prison, desiring my assistance at his Tryal; I sent an answer by one of our Gentlemen that used to visit him pritty frequently, that if my Evidence would be of any service to him I certainly would do it, Upon which I waited on Mr Grahme, who was his Advocate & told him what I had to say, upon which he told me he believed my Evidence would be of Service to him, then, Sr says I, tho' I have leave to go to England I will stay till the Tryal is over, but says he, I can inform you better in a day or two, when I have spoke to the Lord Advocat, I accordingly waited upon him a day or two after, according to his own appointment he then told me, that he had acquainted the Lord Advocate, with what I could say, and he would take it down in writing and would admit as Evidence at the Tryal, upon which he told me I need not stay a day longer, but prosecute my journey for England.

302

Appendix XII.

What was the Substance of what you told Mr Grahme, you could give in Evidence at the Tryal?—I told him that the Lord Provost told me, he would order all his men to be loaded with Sluggs, & in case of any disturbance, he should have his orders to turn out a few of his men out of their Ranks and fire at the legs of the Mob and if they did not disperse upon that he then would give his Orders to the Party he had from General Sabine's Regiment

Did any Conversation pass between you & Mr Grahme relating to the Tryal of Captain Porteous, and what was that conversation?—I cannot say that I had much conversation with him relating to the Tryal, and it is so long ago, that I cannot charge my Memory with what did pass I know that Mr Grahme thought his case hard, and that the Magistrates were very severe upon him

Was the Information you gave Mr Grahame upon Oath?—All the information I gave to Mr Grahame was in Conversation, & not so much as reduced into writing; I was never asked to make an Oath

Was you at Edinburgh at the time of the Tryal of Captain Porteous?—No, my Lords

He was directed to Withdraw.

XI —Examination of General Wade

(B M Add M S 33,049, f 91)

Then it was proposed to call in Lieutt -General Wade , and three Questions were agreed by the Committee to be ask'd him; and the General being called in accordingly, an Extract of his letter to the Duke of Newcastle dated Edinburgh, 4th Novemb 1736 was read at the Table, as follows, viz —

I send your Grace inclosed a List of the Persons, who have been sent presoners to the Castle of Edinburgh, for the Murther of Captain Porteous , These have been committed since the arrival of Lord Ilay, for before I do not find there was any Enquiry made after them by the Magistrates, who, by the best information I have been able to procure not only permitted the Murther to be comitted (which they might easily have prevented) but suffered all who were conscious of their Guilt, to make their Escapes, and I fear it will be difficult to find a Jury who will not acquit those who are now Prisoners

And then the General was asked

Question 1 —Why did you believe that the Magistrates permitted the Murther of Captain Porteous, and what reasons had you to believe they might have easily prevented it?—I must premise to your Lordships, that I was not then at Edinburgh, & what I shall now advance is the best Information I was able to procure from the English Gentlemen that were there, as well as from the Gentlemen who are Inhabitants of North Britain Captain Porteous was condemned as I am informed upon the 20th July last, which sentence was to be put in Execution upon the 8th Septemb following; In this Interval of time a Petition was promoted & handed about by persons who thought Captain Porteous innocent the reason they gave for it was, that they did not believe, that either he fired his piece himself or Ordered any of his Guard so to do, they thought his sentence was a severe one, considering he was employed by the Magistrates, to defend & protect the Execution of the Law, and to prevent a notorious

303

Captain Porteous.

Offender from being rescued from the hands of Justice by an Outrageous Populace, This Petition my Lords, I was informed was so ill taken by the People, that it was immediately spread abroad in all parts of the Town, that if that Petition should take place and procure his pardon, he should notwithstanding be hang'd upon the day he was sentenced to dye by the Court of Justiciary This Report was not only spread about the Town but in all the country round about, to induce those who were willing to have a hand in this Execrable Murther that they might be prepared to come in and give their Assistance, But her Majesty being graciously pleased, out of her great goodness & mercy, to grant a Reprieve before this Petition was delivered it arrived at Edinburgh about a week before the time appointed for his Execution From the Arrival of ye reprieve to the day appointed for the Execution, the clamours of the People increased and they grew Outragious and it was publicly talked of from that time, that he would certainly be hang'd by the Mob, upon the day he was sentenced to dye, without the least regard to her Majesty's reprieve, and I was informed that it was neither prudent nor safe for any man publickly to justify or vindicate her Majesty's Mercy & Clemency My Lords I was likewise informed that these reports of this intended Murther were so Publick, that it was the topick of all Conversation for a week before it was Committed, both at Taverns, Coffee houses, Tea tables and even at the Market Cross of Edinburgh, It had spread likewise to Glascow Sterling, Perth and was talked of at Carlisle & at Berwick, for some days before, & even at London the day after it was Committed My Lords there were persons as I was informed that went from house to house, where there was a number of Apprentices and Journeymen, acquainting them that Porteous was to be hanged upon the Tuesday following and desiring them to be ready to assist on that day I was likewise told that women's habits on the Tuesday morning were publickly carried about the streets, in Order to disguise the Ringleaders of the Rioters As to the Particular that I have mentioned of People going from Door to Door some days before the Murther was committed, it is not only from hearsay but I have it under the hand of the Sollicitor General, It is a paper he delivered into my hands the 17th of December the day before I left Edinburgh, It mentions one James Maxwell to have been a person who went to an house to acquaint the Journeymen & Apprentices with it

> Then a Paragraph out of the said Paper, Intitled Memorial concerning the Murther of Captain Porteous, was read as follows, viz —

> There is Evidence also against one Robt Anderson, Journeyman & servant to Colin Alison, and against Thomas Linnen and James Maxwell, both servants also to the said Colin Alison who all seem to have been deeply concerned in the Matter Anderson is one of those who put the Rope about Porteous's neck, Linnen also seems to have been very active, and Maxwell (which is pretty remarkable) is proven to have come to a shop upon the Fryday before and charged Journeymen and Apprentices there, to attend in the Parliament Close on Tuesday night to assist to hang Captain Porteous These three did early abscond, and tho' Warrants had been issued out against them and all endeavours used to apprehend them, could not be found

This is the Information I had as to the first part of the Question It seems to me if this Information is true that the Magistrates of Edinburgh were the only persons within fourty miles of Edinburgh. who were ignorant of this intended Barbarity As to the latter part

Appendix XII.

of the Question, My Lords, I never heard that they did anything to prevent it, but by sending a Message, not a Magistrate, to General Moyle, and that after the Gates were seized and the Town Guard disarmed by the Rioters, they likewise made an Excursion from the Tavern for a few minutes when the Mob had surrounded the Prison, but returned to the Tavern without reading or attempting to read the Proclamation Now, my Lords, I shall proceed to acquaint your Lordships, what in my Opinion they might have done to prevent it, Had they sent the Prisoner to the Castle or to the Tolbooth of the Cannongate, where there is a constant Guard kept of an Officer and thirty men, and sometimes of a Captain and fifty, he would then have been secure. Had they sent to the Commander of the Forces desiring him to place a Guard at the Gate of the City that leads to the Cannongate, the Communication with the Regular Troops would have been preserved and consequently the mischief might have been prevented; Had they placed but a Serjeant and ten men within the Tolbooth of Edinburgh, where the Prisoner was kept, it was sufficient to have defended it against double the number that was said to be there Nay after the City [gates] were shut, and the Town Guard disarmed by the Mob, had they sent a Magistrate to the Castle of Edinburgh which is not above a furlong or thereabouts distant from the Prison I am induced to believe they would have been succoured from thence by Major Robertson who then commanded in the Castle My reasons for saying this are, that upon my arrival at Edinburgh, when I saw Major Roberton, I ask'd him if he could not have given any assistance in preventing this inhuman Murther of Captain Porteous   He told me, Yes, he could, if he had been required by a Magistrate, and proceeded as near as I can remember in the words following Sr between 9 & 10 of the Clock on the Tuesday night the riot happened, I had occasion to send a Letter to the Post house directed for the Earl of Orkney, My Servant, as he was obliged to pass near the Prison in his way to the Post house, was stop'd by a Guard of armed men with Muskets and Lochaber Axes in their hands, and asked what he did that way & whither he was going, he told them he was going to carry a Letter to the Post house, directed to Lord Orkney, one of them cryed, let me see the Letter and looked on it by the light of a Link, he said to another that stood by him, this Letter is directed for Lord Orkney, it cannot concern the business we are about, but however do you two (pointing to two of his Associates) go along with him to the Post house, and see that he deliver the Letter in there, and tell him that when he returns to the Castle, he go by the high Street & not this way, otherwise it will be the worse for him, When the servant was returned to the Castle, he acquainted Major Roberton of what he had seen and heard, that the Mob had invested the Prison in Order to seize upon Porteous and to hang him. Upon which he immediately beat to arms, and of 100 Men of which the Castle Company consists, he chose out 50 of the most resolute of them and immediately marched them to the lower Gate of the Castle and sent to the Storekeeper to send him a basket of hand Granades ready loaded and primed, as the best Instruments to disperse a Mob, he said he continued there till two of the Clock in the morning, in expectation of having his assistance required by the Civil Magistrate, & had the Mortification to hear from the Works of the Castle the hammers striking against the Prison Gates, and to see the fire that was set to it to burn it down, But no Civil Magistrate during the time he waited there ever requir'd his assistance I was informed that they were at least an hour and an half breaking in the Prison before they got Porteous into their possession, when succours might have march'd to the Assistance of the Magistrates from the lower gate of the Castle to the Prison in 5 or 6 minutes time This is all I have to answer to the first question; your Lordships are the best Judges

Captain Porteous.

whether the Magistrates permitted it to be done or could have prevented it

Do you know whether it has been usual to Commit Prisoners to the Castle of Edinburgh?—Prisoners of State have been often sent to the Castle and upon some Occasions those who cannot properly be called Prisoners of State, There's a late Instance of persons that were accused of debauching the Kings troops into the Service of his Prussian Majesty, and they were committed to the Castle of Edinburgh, and I never knew or ever heard of any person that was sent for better security to the Castle of Edinburgh by Order of any of the Lords of Justiciary, or any other person that had power to commit prisoners that was ever refused to be received by the Officers commanding in the Castle

How came you to know that it was known in London, the day after the Murther was committed?—After I had received her Majesty's Command to go to Scotland, in the three days I continued at London, I was told by an Officer who was my aid de Camp at that time, that he was told a pretty extraordinary Story, which he had from a Tradesman, which I sometimes employed, But having very little time on my hands to enquire into Tales of that kind, I deferr'd it till my return from Scotland, and then I sent for this Tradesman, who is of North Britain, I asked him pray what was that Story you told my Aid de Camp concerning the Murther of Porteous? Says he, upon Tuesday the 7th of Septembr last a Country man of mine came to my house, recommended to a lodger, and being distressed for want of a bed, I told him for one night he might make use of a bed that was at the back part of my shop, The next morning I went to him to ask him how he liked his lodging and what news there was from Edinburgh? he said the man answered him, that all the news that he could tell him was that Porteous was hanged last night, How do you know that, says the Landlord? I am sure of it says he But you dont know, replies the Landlord, that the Queen has sent a reprieve for Porteous 10 or 12 days ago, 'Tis all one for that, replies the man you will find he was hang'd last night, which some time after to his great surprize he found to be true

Are you of opinion that if the Magistrates of Edinburgh, had sent in a proper way to Major Roberton (who commanded in the Castle) for his assistance, he could have justified his sending such assistance, without an Order from General Moyle?—Yes, he could, General Moyle has no power in the Castle of Edinburgh, unless it was I delegate to him, No General Officer but the Governors and Lieutenant Governors of the Castle in Scotland (except myself) have any power over the Castle, unless it is what proceeds from the Board of Ordnance in relation to the Artillery and Stores

Is there no other Prison under the Jurisdiction of the Magistrates, where (in your opinion) the prisoner might have been kept in safety from the Mob?—Yes, my Lords I take the Cannongate Tolbooth to be under the Power of the Magistrates of Edinburgh, where undoubtedly the Prisoner would have been safe, because there is a constant Guard of the Troops kept there

Question 2—Why did you say the Magistrates suffered all those who were conscious of their Guilt to make their Escapes?—I could not forbear being of that opinion for the reasons following, I was informed it was a very clear Moonlight night that any persons face might be known, from one side of the Street to the other, And I never heard that they ever sent any of their under Officers or Emissaries to mix among this great Crowd of People to inform them who were the most active in the Murther; I never heard that there was any care taken by the Magistrates, the morning after the Murther was committed,

306

Appendix XII.

when they might have had the assistance of the Regular Troops, to secure the Gates of the City till a strickt Examination was made, for I was informed by Gentlemen of unquestioned Credit and reputation that those that came in from the Country to assist in this inhuman Murther, returned by the several roads that lead to and from the Town, in Clusters, triumphing, valueing themselves upon what they had done Another reason is that I never heard that any of the Criminals were taken up, or any way secured by the Magistrates of Edinburgh till the arrival of the Justice General, who, as I am informed, by his own Authority, Committed all those who were ever secured for this Riot & Murther As a further Argument, I must beg leave to have recourse to the Memorial, which I mentioned before, that was delivered to me by the Sollicitor General In which even after the arrival of the Justice General it appears that the Magistrates gave little or no assistance in apprehending those who were supposed to be guilty of this Outrage, and I desire a paragraph out of the said Memorial may be read

Then the said paragraph was read and is as follows

When the Sollicitor arrived here, he perceived the whole Inhabitants under a Consternation, he had no materials furnished him , Nay the inhabitants were so much afraid of being imputed Informers, that very few People had so much as the Courage to speak with him on the Streets, However having received her Majesty's Orders by a Letter from the Duke of Newcastle he resolved to set about the matter in earnest, and entred upon an Inquiry, groping in the dark, had no assistance from the Magistrates worth mentioning, but called witness after witness in the privatest manner before him in his own House, and for six weeks time from morning to Evening, went on in the Enquiry without taking the least diversion or hunting his thoughts to any other business

Do you know what time passed before Warrants were issued to take up these notorious Offenders?—I have said that it was after the arrival of the Justice General, which I take to be a month after the Murther was committed

Question 3 —What reasons had you to think it would be difficult to find a Jury who would not acquit those who were prisoners?—The same reason that induced yo Lordships in the year 1716 to pass a Law for trying the Rebels that were taken after the memorable Victory of Sherriff Muir, in the Courts of Justice in this part of the United Kingdom & not in Scotland

If formerly the commanding Officer had Orders to march his men on a Verbal Order from the Magistrates , How came you to alter those Orders?—I do not know that ever there were such standing Orders, but only given on certain Emergencies ; I do not know that the Officers Commanding in any Quarter are under a necessity from any Law or the King's Order, to interfere in any thing but for the Service of the Revenue, unless they have express Order for so doing , But, my Lords, I must explain to your Lordships the reason that induced me to give Orders (or rather Advice indeed) to Genl Moyle how he should act when the Civil Magistrate required his assistance in the year 1733, upon my return from the Highlands in Scotland, which was the first year of Genl Moyle's service in that part of the Kingdom, I told him that all the troops in their several quarters, as also all the Guards, had Orders to assist the Officers of the Customs & Excise, when ever they were required so to do by such officers ; but I told him, it was possible they might have application for sending of Troops for the

Captain Porteous.

establishment of a Minister, for putting the Decrees of the Courts of Justice in Execution, or on other Occasions, in which I thought the Military ought in no wise to be concerned unless in the outmost Extremity, and under the Direction of a Civil Magistrate, That if such parties were required, I advised him to take it under the hands of the Civil Magistrates, who should so require his Assistance But if the Emergency was such that there was no time to write a Letter that he should let the Troops march provided a Civil Magistrate marched with them and gave them authority how they should act The reason why I advised Genl Moyle to require a Letter or other written Order from the Magistrates, who should require the assistance of the Troops was, from what had happened on a former Occasion as this, I think it was in the year 1720 (I had it from an Officer of the Regiment) An Officer of Col Montague's Regiment was quartered at Dundee with a Company of Foot under his Command, There was a great demand that year for Corn for the Baltick and other foreign Countries, and the populace, who on such Occasions use all their Endeavours to prevent the Exportation of it, came to the number of 7 or 800 to Dundee, rifled the house of the Factor, who had the Embarkation of the Corn and threatened to set fire to the ships in the Harbour which were loaden with Corn In this extremity the Magistrates of the Town came to the Officer who commanded the Company, begged his Assistance and told him otherwise they should be all ruined and undone for that the Mob were going to set fire to the ships in the Harbour, The Officer told them he was ready to give them all the assistance he could but that his endeavours would prove ineffectual in dispersing so large a Mob, unless they would authorise him to fire upon them in case they refused to separate without proceeding to such extremity, They told him they would authorize him to fire if they refused to separate, upon Notice given them that he would fire upon them, Upon this the Officer marched with his company to the Key, where he saw the Mob endeavouring to get aboard the Ships, in order to burn them, he called to them several times to disperse, or he would fire upon them according to the Directions he had received from the Magistrates, They made him no Answer but by a Peal of Stones which wounded several of his men; upon which he advanced four men before the rest, & ordered them to fire, which they did and wounded some of the Mob, They pursued the Officer & his men with Stones and other weapons they had with them, & in his retreat he fired two or three shot and then returned to the Town house, from whence he had marched and drew up his men to defend himself from the Mob who pursued him, By this time further succours of the regular Troops came from Perth and the Mob thought fit to disperse, without doing any further mischief, The next day the Magistrates came to the Officer who commanded this Company & told him he had caused a great deal of Bloodshed & they hoped he would be able to answer for the mischief he had done; The Officer reply'd, that what he had done was by their own Order, Did not you give me Orders to fire in case the Mob did not disperse? The Magistrates answered, We did give you Orders to fire but we did not give you Orders to fire sharp, which in Scotland signifies fireing with Ball This and some other Instances were my reasons for giving my advice to General Moyle. to take it under the hand writing of such Magistrates, as should require the assistance of the Troops I am not insensible that every subject in Great Britain, whether an Officer Soldier or of any other Denomination is personally obliged to assist the Civil Magistrate, when he requires him so to do, But I never cou'd be prevailed upon to be of Opinion, that it is in the power of a Civil Magistrate (in which number a Constable may be included) to order an Officer to assemble a

Appendix XIII.

party of men upon the Parade, which is a thing done in great forme, and according to the Roll of Duty, For if that were admitted of, a petty Constable might Order the Army to assemble and march to such place as he thought fit

Was the Officer that commanded at Dundee brought to a Trial for killing those persons?—The Magistrates were preparing Evidence against him, as I was informed, but the Officer wrote a letter to Brigadier Preston who then commanded the Troops in Scotland stating to him his case and all the Circumstances of it, and the Brigadier thought proper to advise the Magistrates to drop all further prosecution, which advice they thought fit to take

He was directed to withdraw

[Endorsed]   Coll Durourie's
              Major Poole's &
              Gen Wade's
              Examinations

March 22, 1736-7

APPENDIX XIII.

COPIES OF ORIGINAL LETTERS, &c , IN THE BRITISH MUSEUM AND PUBLIC RECORD OFFICE, HITHERTO UNPUBLISHED, RELATIVE TO THE PORTEOUS MOB

I — General Wade to General Moyle

(Hardwicke MSS. B M Add MS 35,875, f 290)

London March 13th 1734 5

Sir,

[Refers to a Petition which had been brought into the Commons the day before, & the Debate on it]   I was glad to find during the whole debate there were no reflections on your Conduct in this affair, which if there had I was ready to defend   However I think it a proper precaution That if any partys are demanded of you, to assist the Civil Magistrate (Unless it be to assist the Officers of his Majesty's Revenue, or to appease some sudden Tumult where Bloodshed or Mischief must be immediately prevented) you take it under the hand of the Lord of the Session or the Judge or Chief Magistrate (who requires your Assistance) by Letter or otherwise specifying the reasons of such demand and that the same cannot be put in Execution but by the assistance of the Military   This will make them more cautious in demanding or desiring the Assistances of the Forces, and be a security both to you and the Officers who command such partys, for being answerable for the Consequences, etc etc

1 am, Sir, your
most humble Servt
GEORGE WADE.

Captain Porteous.

(Hardwicke MSS B M Add MS. 35,875, f 292)

Sir,
I am sorry to give you this Trouble, if it were not a case of Necessity The footmen have got themselves drunk, and Attempted to break open the Doors and some of the Gentlemen endeavouring to restrain them they have had the insolence to beat and wound some of them & I am sorry to Acquaint you that your Son who was forward to interpose in defence of the Ladys has got a slight wound, but he has been taken care of, This makes it necessary that you'd please forthwith march down from the Cannongate what men can be got ready with Orders to quiet the Mobb and Secure and Apprehend such persons as they meet with in a Tumulteres Manner, the Mob have threatn'd to set fire to the Doors I am
Sir,
Your Most obedt humble Servant
ANDR FLETCHER

Abbay of Holyroodhouse
Saturday morning   To the honb Brigadeer Moyle

(Hardwicke MSS B M Add MS 35,875, f 294)

Hond Sir
The Sentence of Death pronounced by the high Court of Justiciary being to be put in Execution to Morrow upon Andrew Wilson Prisoner in Edinburgh Tolbooth and there being some Surmises that there will be a Mob who Intend to rescue and Carry him off, I therefore would beg you would be pleas'd to give Orders that two of the Company of the Cannongate Guard should be in readiness to Assist to disperse the Mob in case of need   please favour me with your Answer
I am Sir,
Your most obedt humble Servt
ALEXR WILSON, provost

Edinbr 13 April
1736

To His Excellency Major Generall Moyle, Commander in Chief of his Majesty's forces in North Brittain

---

(State Papers, Scotland (George II), vol XXIII No 4)

My Lord Duke,
At the desire of persons of Quality & distinction I have taken the Liberty of troubling your Grace with the inclosed petition to her Majesty in favour of John Porteous now under sentence of Death, together wt a petition from himself to the Queen & it is their request your Grace may be pleased to present them to her Majesty as soon

Appendix XIII.

as may be convenient because the 8 of Sept is ye day fixed for the
Execution

At the same time I thought it my Duty to send yr Grace the
Inditement wt a Copy of the prooff or Depositions of the witnesses
I have the honour upon all occasions to be with the utmost Respect,

My Lord
your Graces most
Obedient & most humble
Servant   ANDR FLETCHER

Edr 25 Aug 1736

V —Lord Milton to Patrick Lindsay

(Hardwicke MSS B M Add MS 35,875, f 288)

Sir,

I am just now awaked at your Unluckly News   I am sorry
the Magistrates have had so bad intelligence else all this might easily
been prevented, what is now to be done it is impossible for me at
this distance to Judge when every minute may Change the face of
affairs and possibly by this Time all may be over, at the same time
I suppose upon your Application the General will think it reasonable
to endeavour to save the Magistrates and Town from the Power of
the Mob, it will be proper you go along with them & get Constables
to read the Proclamation in Case they have shut all the Gates, while
the Regiment is beating to Arms in the Canongate some Companys
might try to get in by the Foot of the Castle but as you know the
Pass you can better judge how far it is Advisable, To me it seems the
Way to get into the Town with the least harm   I am sir
Your humble Servt
ANDR FLETCHER

Brunst Wednesday one
in the Morning
I have sent a Servt to
know how matters are

To Patrick Lindesay
Esqr

VI —Lord Milton to Duke of Newcastle

(State Papers, Scotland (George II), vol xxiii No 4)

My Lord Duke

The Mob in Edinburgh having last night in contempt of the
Authority of the Crown, as well as in Defiance of the Laws of the
Land, barbarously murdered Captain John Porteous, I thought it
my Duty without loss of time to transmit to your Grace a short
Narrative of that unheard of cruel action, as far as I have yet been
able to discover

The Mob are now so insolent & the Town Guard so dispirited &
in such Contempt, that I find it would be in vain for the Magistrates
upon their own Authority to attempt to enquire after & seize the
Authors or Actors of this Barbarity, & at the same time considering
what ill blood it might occasion to bring in the Military into the
City contrary to their Privileges, till I receive farther Directions,
I have prevailed with General Moyle to double his Guard in the
Cannon Gate, & to send fifty Men to the Castle of Edinburgh to be

Captain Porteous.

daily relieved by the same number marching thro' the City to be in Readiness, in case of necessity & the Magistrates are to chain back the Gates at the Netherbow so as it cannot be shut, for both which there are Precedents, whereby there will be an open communication from both ends of the City to the Military

Your Grace's Directions in this & all other matters shall always be acknowledged as an honour done to &ca

AND FLETCHER

General Moyle tells me that General Barrel's Regiment of Foot is at Newcastle in their way to Scotland & begs they may have Orders to march here soon, which I submit to your Grace if it may not be proper

Edinburgh 8th Sept 1736

VII —*Narrative referred to*

Friday, the 3d Day of September the Lords of Justiciary served an order upon the Magistrates, intimating a Reprieve for John Porteous, for six weeks

On Saturday, the 4th, there was a surmise that a mob intended to set fire to the Prison on Wednesday night, the 8th of September, if Porteous was not executed that day pursuant to his Sentence This was carefully inquired into by the Magistrates, but they could not discover any foundation for the report

On Tuesday the 7th, about a quarter before ten at night, the magistrates had notice, that a few Boys had seized the Drum of the suburb of West Port, and beat it in the Grassmarket, Within the city; About six minutes before ten they sent to the captain of the Guard, to have his Guard immediately under arms, but a few minutes before the Clock struck ten, a mob suddenly rushed in upon and surprised the Guard and at once drove them from the Guard-Room and seized all their arms being 90 Firelocks in number, besides several Lochaber axes, and distributed them among themselves, and almost at the same time made themselves master of all the Gates of the City

The Lord Provost and Magistrates hereupon immediately dispatched Patrick Lindesay, Esq late Provost of Edinburgh, to General Moyle; This gentleman, who was well known to the General, finding the Netherbow Port shut, and in Possession of the Mob, made shift to get out at the Potter Row Port, and went thro' the Park, and got to the General's House at Abbeyhill, a quarter before eleven

The General, having notice before of the mob at the Nether Bow, had ordered all the men in the Cannongate and Westport to be under arms, and upon Provost Lindesay's application, likewise ordered up the three Companyes from Leith, to join those in Cannongate but in regard that all the Gates were locked up and barricaded by the mob, refused to allow any man to march without a Warrant from the Lord Justice-Clerk, or a Lord Justiciary, who happened then to be all out of town

Immediately after the Mob had seized the Guard, they attacked the jayl, and the magistrates with several of the members of Council and Deacons of Crafts, attempted to disperse them, but the Mob threw stones so violently at them, and threatened to fire, they having furnished themselves with shot by breaking open the shop of one Alexander Dunning, wherewith they had loaded the pieces they had

312

Appendix XIII.

seized in the Guard and having wounded several of those who attended the Lord Provost and Magistrates with Stones, Lochaber axes, and Butts of muskets, obliged them to retire

The mob finding themselves absolutely masters immediately set fire to the Prison Gate, and in about an hour it was so much consumed by the fire that the mob beat it to pieces, and rushed into the Prison, seized the Turnkeys within, and forced them to open every Ward in the Prison dismissed all the Prisoners, and then laid hold of Captain Porteous, dragged him down stairs, and hurried him up the Lawn Market street, down the West Bow to the Grass-market, where they broke open a Shop, and took out a Coil of Ropes, and tyed one end of it about his neck, and threw the other over a Dyer's Tree hard by the Common Place of Execution, and pulled him up and hanged him about a quarter before twelve o'clock at night, several attempts were made to take down the Body, but the Mob beat every one who made such a Proposal, till about Daybreak a few Members of the Council and some neighbours got the Body taken down, and laid it in the Grey Friar's church

---

VIII —General Moyle to Duke of Newcastle

(State Papers, Scotland (George II), vol xxii. No. 48)

My Lord,

I think it my duty to acquaint your grace with what happen'd here last Tewsday night, about a quarter of an hour after ten, being then in my bed, Colonel Pears, who commands lieutenant-general Sabin's Regiment in the Cannongate, came and told me he heard there was a great disturbance in the citty, on which I imediately ordered him to assemble the six companyes quartered here, and to parade them near the guard in the Cannongate and to send for the three Companyes from Leith, which was done with as much Expedition as possible, for some of the companyes are quartered a great distance from the Cannongate I dressed myselfe as soon as possible, in order to join the Regiment I was scarce dressed when Mr Lindesay came to me, and told me there was a great mob in the citty It then wanted but fourteen minutes of eleven, he assured me they had got possession of the citty gates, and that with much difficulty he got out at a small wicket, and was obliged to come round by the King's Park He made no demand of a guard to assist them, but I told him I had ordered the Regiment to be under arms, but that I could not force any of the Town gates, or give orders for attacking the mob, without legal authority from the Lord Justice-Clerk or some other of the Lords of the Justiciary, for it was from one of them I had received all orders relating to the military, since I came into the country I then asked Mr Lindesay if Lord Justice-Clerk or any other of the Lords of the Justiciary were in Town His answer was, that neither the Justice-Clerk or Lord Royston was in town, but Lord Newhall was but there was no getting to him, on which, knowing the Justice Clerk lived but two miles and a half of the Town, I desired Mr Lindesay to write imediately to him for his directions, what he would have the Troops do, and sent the letter by my own servant, who galloped all the way My Lord being in bed, he got no answer from him till near one of the clock The latter was directed to Mr Lindesay, so I never saw the answer, and long before it came, the poor man was hanged by the mob. By what I since hear he was executed before Mr Lindesay came to my house, for they got him out of prison a little after ten It was a great oversight that the poor man was not put

Captain Porteous.

into the castle as soon as his reprieve came for him, that being the only place to secure him from the rage of the mob This unheard-of barbarity had been concerting several days, and I am surprised the magistrates were not more upon their guard The town soldiers, instead of resisting, delivered their arms to the mob The turnkey of the prison owned he had a hint given him in the morning that the prison would be attempted to be brak open that night, and that he acquainted the Gaoler of it, and desired him to make it known to the Lord Provost, that care might be taken to prevent it The magistrates were drinking together in the parliament-close when the mob first assembled, but did not take care to read the proclimation, which was a very great neglect in them On their suspecting the mob would rise that night, the care of the port next to the Cannongate ought to have been immediately put under the guard of the King's forces and then the communication between the citty and suburbs would have been kept open I have to add, that had the troops forced their way into the town by demolishing one of the gates, without a legal authority, your Grace would soon have had a terrible complaint from the magistrates The regiment here are much fatigued, having layn two nights on their arms I can't but mention to your Grace that this is the third prisoner within the memory of man that has been taken out of a Talbooth here, and barbarously murdered by the mob They charge me with procuring Porteous's reprieve, and threaten to murder me in my bed, or set fire to my house but I despise them all I don't hear that any of the criminals are yet apprehended, tho well known by many of the inhabitants of the town

        I am,
           My Lord with great respect Your Grace
              Most obedient humble sert
                    JOHN MOYLE

Edinburgh, Sept the 9th
        1736

IX —Copy of a Letter from Edinburgh concerning the Murder of Captain Porteous

(State Papers Scotland (George II), vol xxiii No 4)

                  Edinburgh Sept 11th 1736

Agreable to my last, I perform my Promise of writing to you this post to give you farther particulars of the villainy of the Raskally and Rebellious Mob of this place in their cruel treatment of the late unhappy Capt Porteous

About nine on Tuesday night last the Rabble met & imediately secured the Gates of the City, placing strong bodies at each Gate, this point being gained they sent a detachment to the City Guard & demanded their arms which were delivered to them without any opposition, thus being secure from any disturbance they might probably expect from us, there being no intercourse between the City and Cannongate, & we in no condition to afford any succour except we had orders from the Magistrates —In this secure situation they went to the Talbooth or principal Goal, & attempted to break the door open but the Gate being strong could not force it, on which they had recourse to a stratagem more successfull, which was to procure two Barrells of Pitch or Tarr which with some other fewell they presently burnt down the Gate, the Goal Keeper then on their demand gave them the Keys and they opened the poor Captains appartment, who surrendered himself to their mercy humbly imploring it, which they

Appendix XIII.

with much contempt and Ill Language refus'd calling him all the murdering Rascalls &c, &c and took him to the Grass Market but in his way he lost one of his shoes which they would not suffer him to put on

They broke open a shop & got a coil of Rope and tyed one end about his neck and the other end over a Dyerstree ⌐¬ He humbly implored time to make a short Prayer which they refus'd, and on lifting up his hands, one of them struck him over the arm with a Lochaber Axe & broke his arm, and hung him up and after he had hung about 4 minutes they let him down in order to augment his terrors and increase his Tortures, at the same time cutting him over the head & burning his foot that had the shoe off, with a Torch, thus ¹ they used him in this barbarous manner three times, so that he was near Expiring when they hung him up the last time   The Tragedy being ended they all dispersed it being then within a quarter of twelve at night & left him hanging where he continued till five next morning   Tis beyond all doubt that the Magistrates connived at this Murder, for they had intimation of the design of the Rabble the Sunday before, & gave the Troops no notice of it in order to secure the Peace, and consequently the poor man's blood, I had forgot to tell you that the villians had the Impudence to have a Watch Word, which was *Hanover*—speaking on all occasions very Disrespectfully of the Queen who granted the Reprieve, and at every intervall of letting him down from the Tree cryed (Insulting Porteous) where is your reprieve, shew it us & we'll save you, & then with insulting curses hung him up again

Genl Moyle who is Genl and Commander in Chief has sent dispatches to London to know the Queens Instructions on this head, in the meantime has caused us to keep under arms and has sent for forces from neighbouring places, a Regt of Dragoons being arrived

I have not been in bed these four nights—all is quiet & eleven taken up and all acquitted but two who are in close confinement near our main Guard

Thus have I ended a barbarous relation & am certain it will give you as much concern in the persual as it does me in the writing   I am &c

P S —The Town I believe would now be glad to be at quiet, their favourite Point being gained, but if severe Reprisals are not made, Lord have mercy upon me !

Your &c

X —*Lord Milton to Duke of Newcastle*

(State Papers, Scotland (George II), vol xviii No 4)

My Lord Duke,

Yesternight I had the honour of your Grace's letter of the 12th instant   And in obedience to her majesty's commands, this morning I met with the magistrates of this city to consult the proper measures for restoring and preserving the peace of the city, and for discovering the authors and actors of the late wicked and audacious proceedings Besides the precautions I had the honour to acquaint your Grace by my last had been taken for maintaining the peace of the city, By order of the Magistrates and Common Council, two Companies of the Trained Bands, consisting of about 200 Burgesses and Inhabitants, have kept guard every night, attended by one of the magistrates, and are to do so while there remains any suspicion of disturbance, and they are all furnished with Firelocks and bayonets from the City's

Captain Porteous.

Armory   As the soldiers of the City Guard are so intimidated that they are unfit for service, which evidently contributed to the insolence of the mobb, an order is made by the magistrates to dismiss them, and inlist able bodied men fit for the service   They were generally old decayed tradesmen or day labourers and if a method could be fallen on to supply this guard at once with well disciplined men from the Regiments of Foot in Scotland, I humbly think it would contribute greatly to strengthen the hands of the magistrates in maintaining the peace of the City   The present Guard consists of three serjeants, three corporals, and about eighty private men   There has been no disturbance since the 7th, nor do I apprehend any till such time as some of the guilty come to be apprehended, and then we must be upon our best guard.

As this outrage was committed not by an ordinary sort of mob guided by sudden rage, but by a well contrived scheme, executed by a cool resolute Gang, taking evidently to themselves authority over the Mobb, and restraining them from every folly but the wickedness they had determined to perpetrate, to which they kept them close at work, there is great reason to believe that some of that abandoned gang of smugglers had a chief hand in all this   One of the first things they were observed to do was to liberate two smugglers then in prison, and all this being done in the night time, though some moon light, it was not easy for bystanders to know persons in the least disguised   Some of the magistrates and I have spoke with several persons who were eye-witnesses to most of the tragical scenes, and yet did not know one of the actors, though they spoke to some of them   I have got some hints of some of the principal actors, but doubt much of getting evidence against them, except from such as if they were not actors were at least abettors, and they will never speak out, I am afraid, unless they be assured of their pardon, and also some encouragement of living elsewhere, in case, as they all dread, they could not live here, if they make any discovery   As there is an end of government, if such practices be suffered to escape punishment, and as it is of the greatest consequence to discover the contrivars of this barbarity, all methods are set agoing to make the discovery, of which I shall from time to time take the liberty to acquaint your grace

I have in obedience to her Majesty's commands, sent an express to the Lord Advocate to come immediately to Edinburgh   I had formerly wrote to the solicitor-general, and have his answer that he is to be here to-morrow   May I beg your grace to assure her Majesty that I shall, with dutiful zeal, endeavour to obey her commands, by doing all that lies in my power to preserve in the most effectual manner the peace of the city of Edinburgh

I have the honour
etc
ANDR FLETCHER

Edinburgh, 16th Sept
1736

XI —Two Letters from General Moyle to Duke of Newcastle

(State Papers, Scotland (George II.), vol xxii Nos 50 & 52

Edinburgh, Sept 18th 1736

My Lord
I was honoured with your Graces letter of the 12th and when application is made by the civil magistrates of the City of Edinburgh the Forces under my command shall assist them, they have not yet

Appendix XIII.

made any application, nor can I hear that any of the murdering villains are yet apprehended, tho known to so many

I hope your Grace will give timely directions to the Lord Provost and the rest of the Magistrates, that when they have taken any of the criminals that they should be confined in the Castle & not in the Talbooth, from whence they will certainly make their escapes some way or other, for they will not want for assistance, the generality of the people approving to much the conduct of the murderes

The common people are very poor and a handsome reward would tempt them to discover the Ring leaders of this barbarous murder

If any of the criminals are discovered & apprehended I wish there was a law to try them out of their own country for fear a jury should shew them more mercy then they deserve here

I dont expect the first devision of Majr General Barretts Regiment will be here till tewsday or wensday next, quarters are provided for them

I sent for two Troops of the Kings own Regiment of dragoons from Haddington to be assisting to the Civil Majistrates in apprehending the Rioters who they pretended lived in the country, but finding no use made of them and forrage excessive dear I sent them back again

If the Civil power will but do their part in detecting these murderes I will ingage they shan't want assistance of the military, who seem very sanguine to be imployed in that service

A company or two in the Castle would be very necessary, but for want of bedding I can't place any there, the Board of Ordinance should be applyed to, to send some down and the sooner the better, for the company now in the Castle are most of them old and invalides from the marching regiments

What further commands your Grace shall please to send me shall punctually be obeyed by

My Lord
your Graces most obliged and
obedient humble sert
JOHN MOYLE

Edinburgh Sepr 23d 1736

My Lord

I had the honour of both your Graces letters by the Messenger and shall not fail to obey the orders you have sent me

At the desire of Ld Justice Clerk and the Solicitor Genl I have sent two companys of Majr Genl Barretts Regt to Dalkeith to be assisting to the Civil Magistrates in the apprehending some of the criminals concerned in the late barbarous murder

I have likewise sent two companys of the same Regt into the Castle to reinforce the Garrison, and as the left port of the City is now left open both night & day I can in halfe an hours time order in two companys more that are quartered very near the Castle

I dont yet hear that any of the offenders are taken up, when they are, I hope they will be so wise as to put the prisoners into the Castle

The two Regiments of Dragoons I have ordered as near Edinburgh as I could get quarters for them, one squadron of the Kings Own Regt are to lye at Haddington & the other at Preston, Preston Pans & adjacent places, the Civil power shall not want the assistance of the Military when applyed to

When I have the honour of seeing you I shall be able to convince your Grace it was not by any neglect of mine the poor man lost his life, had the Ld Provost given me as early notice as he got himselfe from a Relation of his own, I could with ease have prevented what

Captain Porteous.

happened without the Effusion of blood, but it was a concerted affair that the poor man should dye, to prevent the resentment of the mobs falling on a certain person

On Mr Wade's arrival here I hope I shall have Her Majesty's leave to return into the south for the Recovery of my health, haveing been a long time ill

I am with great Respect

My Lord

your Graces

Most obliged and obedient

humble servt

JOHN MOYLE

P S

I must acquaint your Grace that the major commands Majr Genl Barretts Regt lost no time in marching from Newcastle & Durham to this place

---

XII —Lord Provost Wilson to Duke of Newcastle

(State Papers Scotland (George II), vol xxiii No 4)

My Lord

I have the honour of your Grace's Letter by one of his Majesties messengers, in relation to the most inhumane barbarous and wicked murder, that was committed in this city on the 7th Instant This abomination both astonished & greatly afflicted me & the other magistrates, & I take the liberty to assure your Grace, That as far as the surprise & the uncommon circumstances that attended it, did allow of, The Magistrates did exert themselves to have quelled the mobb & to prevent the mischievous consequences that ensued; but it was got to so great a height before we had any notice of it that our endeavours were vain

The moment that we knew our guard was surprized we dispatched Mr Lindsay our present Member of Parliament, who is well known to the General to acquaint him of our situation; But the City gates having been secured by the multitude, the communication betwixt us and the King's forces in the Canongate was cutt of whereby our application proved fruitless

It grieved us exceedingly that such barbarity should have been committed & so flagrant an insult should have been offered to the authority of the best of Sovereignes & to the laws of the country

The Magistrates & Common Council of the City gave immediate orders to discharge those of the Guard who so shamefully allow'd themselves to be surprized, & to levy new men of service in their room They also delivered two hundred stand of arms out of the City's magazine, to be used by our traind bands; who have constantly kept guard since that time; & to preserve the communication with his Majesty's troops, the great gate leading to the Canongate where they are quartered, is taken away and I can assure your Grace with great truth, that nothing has been wanting on the part of the Magistrates to discover the Ringleaders & abettors of this unparalell'd act of Insolence & barbarity, Our discoverys are carried on with the utmost secrecy, least the guilty should escape, and I humbly beg leave to refer your Grace to his Majesty's Solicitor, for the Account of the progress already made, and I can assure your Grace that the Magistrates will with the greatest care & zeal contribute their utmost endeavours to discover & effectually to secure all those who shall

Appendix XIII.

appear to have had any concern in this audacious & most detestable crime

I beg leave to acknowledge with great thankfulness Her Majesty's great goodness & care of the peace of the City, by giving proper directions to the Commanding Officer of his Majesty's forces in this country, to give assistance to the Civil magistrates for the future in preserving the public peace & in suppressing all insurrections or other unlawfull assemblys without loss of time   This cannot fail to be of great service in keeping turbulent spirits from any further attempts to ruffle the tranquility of his Majesty's most just & wise administration, and I beg leave to assure your Grace, that the Magistrates of this City are firmly determined to do every thing in their power for the support of his Majesty's government, upon which our own & the nations happiness entirely depends   And that I have the honour to be with great truth & Esteem

May it please your Grace
Your Graces
most obedient
& most humble Servant
ALEXR. WILSON, Provost

Edinburgh 22d Sept
1736

———

XIII —Lord Milton to Duke of Newcastle

(State Papers, Scotland (George II), vol xxiii No 4)

My Lord

The Messenger arrived on Tuesday night wt the letters from your Grace wch were all delivered yt night except the letter for the Ld Advocate who is not yet come from the North

The Directions her Majesty has been pleased to give to the Ld Provost of Edr, to the Ld Advocate & Sollicitor Generall & to the commanding officers of his Majestys Forces here will I am convinced effectually secure ye peace of the City for the Future, & I am hopefull will be of the greatest use for apprehending & bringing to Justice ye Authors Ringleaders & Abettors of the late barbarous murther & Outrage

There remains one thing usual to be done in such cases, a proclamation with rewards for discovering and wch if it be thought proper, some care will be necessary in wording it, as well as prudence in useing it, because with us none can be received a witness who by the Event of the Tryal can gain or loose, and a single witness is no proof   When ye Ld Advocate comes I shall state ye case to him & the Sollicitor Genll yt yr opinion may be transmitted to yr Grace, & disputes at the Tryal avoided

Her Majesty's Commands shall be obeyed in confining to the Castle of Edr all such persons as shall be committed on this account, where they certainly may be detained with safety   At the same time I humbly beg leave to submit to her Majesty's further consideration, whether as the door of the common prison wch is the County Jayle, is new repaired and wch if necessary may be further fortifyed, be not the proper place of commitment, & that the sending the prisoners to the Castle, may not have the appearance of too great weakness in the Government & too much apprehension of the Mobb & may tend to lead the Mobb to fancy themselves more considerable than they are, when by the orders given & precautions taken we are not in the least apprehensive from ye Mobb

Captain Porteous.

I hope I need not trouble yr Grace again to assure her Majesty that as it is my Duty so it is my great ambition in all cases & in particular in yt (where her Majesty has honoured me wt her repeated Commands) to do my out most endeavour to give due obedience

As it was necessary an effectual communication should be secured betwixt his Majesty's Forces in ye Castle & in the Cannongate the Gate of ye City wch leads that way was at first (as I had the honour to acquaint yr Grace) chained back & to prevent any possibility of accidents one of the sides of ye Gate was on Monday last taken away, on pretence it stood in need of repairs, I choosed this should be done by Degrees & in the easyest way because the populace fancy some of yr priviledges are wrapt up in their Gates

The Sollicitor Generall came to Edr on Saturday and all hands have been at work to make discoveries in wch some progress has been made, being informed that some of ye principall acters came from the conntrey I have sent proper persons in disguise to try to get into ye secret This day I prevailed with one of the Mobb after promising him pardon &ca to discover some of the aiders and Abbettors, wch I hope will lead us into a full discovery of that mystery of Iniquity, of wch I shall from time to time take the Liberty to inform yr Grace I have the honour to be with the outmost Respect,

May it please yr Grace, your Lops most faithful & most obedient servant   AND FLETCHER

Edenburgh 23d Sept
    1736

XIV —Charles Erskine (Solicitor General) to Duke of Newcastle

(State Papers, Scotland (George II), vol xxiii No 4)

Edinburgh, 25th Sept 1736

My Lord
        I am honoured with your Grace's letter of the 17th Current, signifying Her Majesty's pleasure that I should use my outmost endeavours for the discovering, apprehending & effectual prosecution of the Authors, & all others, who shall appear to have been concerned in the inhumane, & Cruel Murder & Outrage, committed by the Mob of the City of Edinr on the 7th instant

Since I came to this place, with great attention I pursued every light offered, to discover the authors and Actors of these most dangerous & detestable Crimes, and one would naturally think it should not be hard to come at the knowledge of these Impudent Monsters, who in open defiance of Laws and humanity, committed, and from Wantonness lengthened out their wickedness, in the face of so many spectators, Yet the disguise in which they had put themselves, the pannick that seizd the innocent, & the Unwillingness in some, ariseing partly from fear of the Mob, to discover what they know, has hitherto obstructed in a great measure the success of our Endeavours, However some discoverys are made and greater seem to be in view We were unwilling to begin the apprehending such against whom we have Informations, untill we saw the event of a furder enquiry, now cairrying on, because I am persuaded that so soon as any warrant is out, it must Start the whole Gang,

I shall be extremely sorry, for the sake of His Majesty's Laws & Authority, for the sake of the Countrey, and of Mankind, if so flagrant offenders go unpunished, And permit me to assure your Grace, that in obedience to Her Majesty's commands, I shall continue with the greatest care, & application to use all endeavours, for bringing them

Appendix XIII.

to a speedy and exemplary punishment, and on this & every other occasion exert myself to promote with Zeal and Attention His Majesty's Service Lord Justice Clerk detain'd the Messenger, waiting His Majesty's Advocates Arrival in this place, but finding that was uncertain, His Lordship did not incline to keep the Messenger too long We are at present in perfect quiet, & have been so ever since I came to town, and after the prudent orders signify'd by your Grace, I hope there is no danger to the publick peace of the City, As often as any thing material occurs, I shall take the liberty to acquaint Your Grace, And with the most perfect truth, and the greatest respect,

I am,
My Lord
Your Grace's most faithfull and
most obedient humble servant
CH. ARESKINE

XV —*Duncan Forbes (Lord Advocate) to Duke of Newcastle*

(State Papers, Scotland (George II), vol xxiii No 4)

My Lord
Late last night I received your Grace's Commands of the 17th of September at this place, where I have been now for some time Upon my first hearing of the unexampled Insolence of the Edinburgh Mob, I intended to have repaired immediately thither, tho' the state of my health was not very good, But having soon received Information, that the peace and Government of the town was restored, and recollecting that nothing was to be done, but to make the strictest Inquiry after the Authors & principal Actors in that daring Insult which Mr Solicitor general was actually examining into, I put off my journey for a few days But now observing from the letter I had the honour to receive from your Grace, that her Majesty is justly solicitous, that this dangerous mischief be searched to the bottom, and the Authors, if discovered, prosecuted with the utmost severity of the Law, I shall without loss of time proceed to Edinburgh, and with the utmost Zeal and attention obey the commands I received I am with very great respect

My Lord Duke
Your Grace's most obedient &
most humble servant
DUN FORBES

Culloden near Inverness
Oct · 1st 1736

XVI —*Sir Robert Walpole to Horace Walpole*

(From Coxe's " Memoirs of the Life and Administration of Sir Robert Walpole ")

London, September 20th—October 1st, 1736

Dear Brother,
You will have received by the last post, from the Duke of Newcastle, an account of the horrible outrage committed last week at Edinburgh. The letter from Lord Justice-Clerk, and the narration that came with it are all the accounts that have come as yet to the

Captain Porteous.

hands of the government, by which you will observe, that the magistrates had not then received any information or made, or attempted to make, the least discovery of any of the authors or ringleaders of this barbarous murder It appears, by some private letters, that the whole villiany was begun and perpetrated in two hours, and that the mob dispersed of themselves as soon as their work was done, and flung down and left all the arms that they had seized in the guard-room, in the Grassmarket, the place of their vile execution, so that all things seem, at present, as quiet at Edinburgh as if nothing had happened

This leaves nothing to be done immediately, but to use all possible means to discover the criminals, and to take effectual care, if they are discovered that they may be secured and brought to condign punishment For the first purpose, the most peremptory orders to the magistrates, attended with ample rewards and encouragements, must be given, and a sufficient force placed in the castle and suburbs of the city, with proper and necessary orders to defend and assist the civil power in putting the laws in execution, if any discoveries can be made, and convictions obtained upon them

But here lie my greatest apprehensions, that we have, as yet, no prospect of coming at either, altho' it is impossible but the chief agents must be known to great numbers of people But so great a panick seized them at the time, and such a terror seems to me to continue upon them, that I very much fear it will be difficult to persuade them to do any thing that may expose them again to the same ill consequences I speak this as my own private observations; notwithstanding which, I think nothing must be omitted that can possibly be done to make examples of such an unheard-of attempt

Lord Islay goes for Scotland this week, and I think is determined to exert himself to the utmost upon this occasion The queen's orders are likewise sent to general Wade to repair immediately to Scotland, to countenance and assist the government in their further proceedings

---

XVII —Earl of Ilay to Duke of Newcastle

(State Papers, Scotland (George II), vol xxiii No 4)

My Lord Duke
I came hither last night & have spent all this in looking into the State of the intelligence already procured of the criminals & finding that some have absconded, that the news of the Proclamation alarmed them greatly, I thought no time was to be lost in endeavouring to seize such as we have information against, & therefore immediately signed warrants against seven of them, & the Justice Clerk has signed warrants against three more, We shall attempt to execute them to morrow morning all at once, by several civil officers, each of which is to have some soldiers to assist, I cannot pretend to forsee what success we shall have but I have endeavoured to take all the precautions that the nature of the thing, & the various circumstances attending this case, do admit of, I shall trouble your Grace again by next post, or if any thing extraordinary happen to morrow, I will send an Express
I am My Lord Duke with the greatest
Respect, Your Graces
most obedient
& most humble
Servant,
ILAY

Edinburg Octob. 5th 1736

322

Appendix XIII.

XVIII —Horace Walpole to Sir Robert Walpole

(From Coxe's " Life of Sir Robert Walpole ")

Gohide, October 6, 1736.

Dear Brother,

I received your letter of September — on the 3d instant, N S by Over the messenger, and have laid it before the King, who was extremely surprised and concerned not only at the horrible outrage committed by the populace at Edinburgh, but at their being able to act in so barbarous a manner with so much ease, in open defiance of all law and government, without the least interruption on the part of the magistrates But his majesty hopes, that now the necessary orders are given, to support the civil authority in discovering the chief authors and abettors of this notorious violence, the unwillingness, or panick fear that affected the civil officers before, will be turned into alacrity and zeal for putting the laws in execution, and bringing some of the murderers to condign punishment, and therefore, the King was extremely pleased with Lord Ilay's resolution to go immediately himself to Scotland, to exert his zeal for the service of the government on this occasion

---

XIX —Two Letters from Lord Ilay to Duke of Newcastle

(State Papers, Scotland (George II), vol xxiii No 4)

My Lord Duke

There are four persons committed to the Castle, & we have A fifth in custody for farther examination, I am in hopes to have some more of them seized to morrow, which has been delayed by their often not lying at home, there was some little grumbling among the Mob who gathered together upon the seizing the criminals, such as saying to one another, we will not suffer our fellow Citizens to be thus dragged away, but upon the first beat of the Drum that attended the party which marched up the street in order to conduct them to the Castle, all was entirely quiet

The Sollicitor Mr Areskin will go to the Castle to morrow to try if he can bring any of them to confess. It is incredible how much every body here is affraid of appearing as evidences, the mob having industriously spread rumours that all were to be murdered that acted against them, those who are taken are shopkeepers, or servants, but I am fully satisfied that there was a few in womens Cloathes or other disguises who had the conduct of the whole This murder has quite drown'd all discourse about the Election, I dont hear the least news about it, & I believe those I have the misfortune to differ with, will hardly think it worth their while to attend

I am my Lord with the greatest Respect

Your Graces
most obedient & most humble
Servant
ILAY.

Edinburgh
Oct 7th 1736

Captain Porteous.

My Lord Duke,

There has nothing hapned remarkable since I troubled your Grace last, except the Countess of Weems, whose footman I had ordered to be taken up, went out of town with him to Haddington, & I have sent A proper person to catch him there   The Advocate & Sollicitor sit together three hours every morning to examine persons Concerning the murder, they daily seem to get some farther light into it, by comparing the several examinations they take, but all the evidence they are yet masters of relate only to the inferiour actors & I think its morally impossible but that the authors of the conspiracy are persons of more distinction than those I have taken up, or have signed warrants against, There is a Master Carpenter here who pretends great innocence, & as yet we have no manner of evidence against him, but had no less than four of his Workmen in the insurrection, & active, He was examined by the Advocate & Sollicitor to day to very little effect, he is A great favourite of one of the Magistrates whom I suspect of somewhat more than neglect This enquiry will of necessity take up A long time, & it seems to be of the last importance to begin the first tryal with one against whom there is the strongest evidence, for we have already reason to suspect that the Criminals are preparing evidence after the manner of Wreathock, as appears by a Petition one of them sent to me to be bailed   I have great difficulty to prevent disputes arising between General Moyle & Mr Lindsay, I have begged of them both to consider that the duty of the Kings servants & the friends of the Government is to assist one another in detecting & bringing to Justice the Criminals instead of wrangling about facts which are altogether immaterial in that respect   I shall desire the Advocate & Sollicitor to draw up before I leave this place, a state of all the Information they have & the evidence they have to support it, that the King's servants may be the better able to give them their directions   The late Election of Magistrates here (at Michaelmas last) has succeeded better than I could have expected, considering the present disposition of the lower sort of people

I am my Lord with the greatest truth & respect

> Your Graces
> most obedient
> & most humble servant,
>
> ILAY

Edinburgh. Oct 15
1736

XX —*Lord Ilay to Sir Robert Walpole*

(From Coxe's " Life of Sir Robert Walpole ")

Edinburgh, Oct. 16

Sir,

I have not writ to you since I came here, because I almost every post gave the duke of Newcastle an account of any thing that occurred, and there remained nothing to trouble you with that could deserve your attention   It is a great concern to me to find it so difficult hitherto to make discoveries of the murderers   I am sure there is all the pains taken in it that is possible and I never before had the pleasure to see all the king's servants here act so uniformly together in the discharge of their duty   On the other side, the secret patrons of the mob seem to be as busy in preparing false evidence to acquit the criminals as we all can be to bring them to justice   They

Appendix XIII.

that are in prison have already in their mouths the names of persons who, they say, will swear to their innocence, that is, their accomplices in the murder will easily perjure themselves to save their friends The most shocking circumstance is, that it plainly appears the high flyers of our Scotch church have made this infamous murder a point of conscience   One of the actors went straight away to a country church, where the Sacrement was given a vast croud of people, as the fashion is here, and there boasted of what he had done   All the lower rank of the people who have distinguished themselves by pretences to a superior sanctity, speak of this murder as the hand of God doing justice, and my endeavours to punish murderers are called grievous persecutions   I have conversed with several of the parsons, and I observe that none of those who are of the high party will call any crime the mob can commit by its proper name   Their manner of talking, were it universal, would extirpate religion out of the world for the good of human society, and indeed I could hardly have given credit to the public reports of the temper of these saints, if I had not myself been witness of it, and been admonished by one of them to have regard to the divine attribute of mercy (in English) to protect the rebels and murderers

Under these and other difficulties, particularly the dread all the common people are in of being murdered if they make discoveries, the inquiry goes slowly on   but I cannot but hope that by degrees this matter will come to light   I have had great difficulty to prevent mischief between general Moyle and Mr Lindesay   Moyle says that Lindesay was drunk, and never asked his assistance   Lindesay says that he told him he came from the magistrates to ask his assistance   I have, as far as it was in my power, enjoined silence upon this subject, or any other of the like nature   The behaviour of the magistrates are certainly worse than can well be imagined, and some of them, I have reason to suspect, were wilfully neglectful, and at the late elections at Michaelmas endeavoured to do all the mischief they could   I spoke to several of the present magistrates the other day, and told them that if they could not or would not show the people of England that the peace of the city of Edinburgh can be maintained, and such vile criminals be detected and brought to justice, I was apprehensive that the parliament would apply remedies very disagreeable to them, and upon such an occasion as this, none of their friends would be able to protect them   They promised me to show such a spirit as to clear them of all imputation of want of zeal in the support of the laws   There shall be an experiment made in two days A proposal shall be made to them by one of their members, to make an order of their town council for the examination of every merchant and every tradesman in the city concerning the apprentices and servants they had on the day of the tumult, and who have absconded since, this will be of use many ways in the further progress of the affair

Mr Wade and I have had some discourses about the forces, and we both agree that this is the best opportunity that could have happened for continuing for the future a strong garrison in the castle of Edinburgh; and we are proposing to make use of an order of the treasury for repairing the offices belonging to the royal palace, towards building stables for 50 or 60 dragoons, to be kept always there   The smuggling bill has had a very good effect here, a ship has been seized merely for want of hands to run the goods ashore as usual, the country people being afraid of the penalties, and are jealous of one another, for fear of the rewards taking place   The gin bill is universally liked here, and will save this country £50,000 a year   And as brandy was the staple commodity in smuggling here, the effect of the act has appeared several ways already.

Captain Porteous.

XXI —Lord Ilay to Duke of Newcastle

(State Papers, Scotland (George II), vol xxii. No 56)

My Lord Duke

I send your Grace inclosed the Edenburgh news paper wherein there is An account published by the friends of the Duke of Hamilton treating their Refusal to admit the Guard which General Wade sent, as a victory   Mr Wade tells me that three days before they had promised him to make no dispute

The footman of the Countess of Weems is taken & seems by the account given of him to have been very active in the murder   I have sent proper persons to-day 18 miles out of the town to Falkirk in Sterlingshire in hopes of seizing a person who walked behind Capt Porteous all the way with a hatchet in his hand in order as it is thought to kill him in case they had been attacked

One of the Kings Chaplains being the other day to preach at the giving the sacrament (which they do here while the Communicants are sitting round a very long table which holds great numbers) I sent to him to desire that he would use some proper expressions upon the late murder of Capt Porteous   He accordingly did it, by warning all sorts of impenitent sinners & (amongst the rest) the murderers of Captain Porteous, the effect of it was that above a hundred, as I am told withdrew & did not receive but the minister who immediately preached next gave many hints of his being of another opinion Tantum Religio potuit !

One of the criminals who is gone to England was formerly a Dragoon in Brigadier Campbells Regiment   I will get an exact description of him which may be of use, for they tell me here that he will certainly list under another name in some Regiment in England

The Magistrates are putting in Execution their Order, which I sent your Grace a copy of & promise to do any thing that is necessary for the publick service   I am my Lord with the greatest truth & Respect,

Your Graces
most obedient
& most humble servant
ILAY

Edinburgh, Octob 30
1736

XXII —General Wade to Duke of Newcastle

(State Papers, Scotland (George II), vol xxii No 58)

Edinburgh Novembr ye 4th 1736

My Lord,

I have this morning received the honour of your Graces Commands with her Majesty's Warrant for placing a Guard at the Pallace of Holly Rood house, which was readily complyed with by the persons who are intrusted with the care of the said Pallace, and a Guard of an Officer and 24 men are ordered to mount there tomorrow Morning, I send your Grace enclosed a List of the persons who have been sent Prisoners to the Castle of Edinburgh for the murder of Capt Porteous, these have been committed since the arivall of Lord Ilay, for before I do not find there was any enquiry made after them by the Magistrates who by the best Information I have been able to procure not only permitted the Murder to be committed (which they might easily

Appendix XIII.

have prevented) but suffered all who were conscious of their guilt to make their escapes, & I fear it will be difficult to find a Jury who will not aquitt those who are now Prisoners   I am
My Lord,

Your Graces most humble and
most obedient servant
GEORGE WADE

XXIII —List referred to

A List of the Persons Committed Prisoners in the Castle of Edinburgh on Accot of the Mob and Tumult on the 7th Sepr last, and the particular Crimes charg'd upon them in the Warrants of Commitment, with the dates of the said respective Warrants, and by whom Signed, Viz

Persons Names, &c	Particular Crimes charged upon them in the Warrants	Date of the Warrants	By whom signed
William Stirling servant to James Stirling Shopkeeper.	Charged to be among the Mob arm'd with a Lochaber Axe or other Mortal weapon, & encouraging them, and carrying them on from the Netherbow Port when seized, to the Tolbooth, and place where they hanged Capt Porteous	5th Octobr 1736	By the Right Honble the Earl of Ilay Lord Justice General
James Braidwood Shopkeeper in Edinburgh	Was in the Evening of 7th Sepr while the mob was attempting to break open the prison door, standing near the same, and among the mob, giving directions to the person who was beating at the prison door with a forehammer, how to open the same more effectnaly, and was otherwise aiding and assisting in the said Mob	5th Octobr 1736	By Do
William Stoddart Blacksmith.	Charged with being in the Mob and aiding and assisting at breaking open the Tolbooth door with a Forehammer	5th Octobr 1736	By Do
Peter Trail Wright	After the Mob had Seized and possest themselves of the Netherbow port, and by force taken the keys from the keeper, did Lock the said Gate and was otherways aiding and assisting in the Tumult and Mob	5th Octob 1736	By Do

327

Captain Porteous.

Persons Names, &c	Particular Crimes charged upon them in the Warrants	Date of the Warrants	By whom signed
John Birney Assistant to Wm Waddell Coachman	Charged wth having been in ye Mob and to have gone along with them in the Land Mercat, arm'd with a Gun, when after burning and breaking open the Tolbooth door they were draging Capt Porteous to the Grass Mercat where they hang'd him	21st Octob 1736	By the Right Honble the Earl of Ilay Lord Justice General.
William McLauchlan servant to the Countess of Weemyss	Was armed with a Lochaber Axe Gun or some other Mortall weapon and stood as part of the Guard planted by the Rioters, between the head of the Locken-booths, and the shops of the other side of the street to stop all persons from passing into the Lawn Mercat, except such as declared themselves friendly to the Rioters	8th Octob 1736	By Do.

Note —The first mentioned William Sterling was admitted to Bail the 23d October, By Order of the Right Honble the Earl of Ilay Justice General, Signify'd to me by Charles Areskine Esqr His Majesties Solicitor   Jo Robertson

XXIV —Five Letters from Charles Erskine (Solicitor-General) concerning the reading of the Act by the Scots Ministers.

(State Papers, Scotland (George II), vol xxiii Nos 9, 11, and 4)

Dumfries 5th Aug 1737

Sir
    I take the liberty by this to acquaint you that after having made the strongest push against me, the Enemys to the administration finding no view of success gave it up and yesterday I was unanimously re-elected for the Countie All things appear quiet here at present, and from what I hear, I believe the great body of the Clergy in this Countrey are to read the Act which has taken up their heads for some time past only they dont seem willing to do it between the Lecture and preaching, but before the blessing is pronounced, for very odd and Metaphisical reasons I intend to go in a few days to Edinburgh to see how matters are going on there, and with candor and great esteem, I am Sr
               your most faithfull humble
                servant
                  Ch Areskine

Edinbr 13th Aug 1737

Sir,
    In my last from Dumfries I acquainted you with the success of my Election, and herewith I send inclosed the return, as the safest

Appendix XIII.

way to transmit it, I hope you'l pardon the liberty I take and order it to be put into Mr Crawford the Messenger his hands, or in some other way cause it to be lodged in the proper office —Many of the clergy have not given obedience to the Act of Parliament, which at present is the subject of discourse here, by which they have incurr'd the disability to sit and vote in Church Judicatorys I have some ground to believe many of them are to comply on the first Sunday of Sepber who offended for the first time, but the motions of our Churchmen on this and several other occasions have been so excentrick that it is not easy to calculate them In the further progress of this affair, I shall endeavour to have ane exact state of it to lay before my superiors for their directions With candor and the greatest esteem, I am, Sir,

your most faithful humble servant

CH ARESKINE

Edin 13th Aug 1737

My Lord,

The letter herewith inclosed, containing ane address to His Majesty from the Commission of the late General Assembly was put into my hands to be transmitted to your Grace

On Sunday the general and exact obedience to the direction of the Law concerning the Infamous Murderers of Captain Porteous I wish't for, was not paid by the Clergy, a great many did not read it, I have ground to hope it may be more universaly obey'd on the first Sunday of September, I shall endeavour to inform myself of their behaviour, and lay the state of it before your Grace, for your directions, which I shall obey, having the honour to be with most perfect truth and the greatest respect,

My Lord

Your Grace's most faithful

and most obedient humble

servant

CH ARESKINE

Edinr 1 September, 1737

My Lord,

In a former letter I took the liberty to mention to your Grace, that exact obedience had not been pay'd by the Clergy to the Act for bringing to Justice the Murderers of Capt Porteous After a carefull examination of the best informations in this place, I do believe above one half read the Act, in some way or other, generally upon their entrance into the pulpit, when the meeting was full, some deserted their Congregations upon diverse pretences, others took no manner of notice of it Many pamphlets have been published upon this occasion for and against reading of the Act, two of them Scandalous, and seditious beyond measure The most abominable of the two had disappear'd before I return'd from my Election I have used all possible dilligence to discover the vile authors, and shall not ommitt doing all in my power to bring them to Justice, if happily I can come at the knowlege of them I hope the number of readers on Sunday next shall be much greater, & when I can have certain Accounts, I shall lay a more particular state of that matter before your Grace In the mean time, I have the honour to be with most perfect truth, and the greatest respect,

My Lord

Your Grace's most faithfull &

most obedient humble servant

CH ARESKINE

Captain Porteous.

Edinr 5th November 1737

My Lord
    In a former letter I took the Liberty to mention to your Grace the state of Our Clergy with regard to the reading the Act of Parliament for bringing to Justice the Murderers of Capt Porteous, and then undertook to inform myself in the best manner I could think of, of what the numbers were of the Readers, and of those who had given no obedience to the Law, As I had early transmitted Copies of the Act, to the several Sheriffs, to be delivred to the parish Ministers within their Jurisdiction, I wrote a second time to them to report to me their dilligence, and at the same time inform me as far as they had access to know, how the numbers Stood of the Readers, and those who had not read within their bounds I have had returns from the Greatest part of them, and from them and the best accounts I can have from other hands, I may venture to say, that not above two thirds have read the Act in any shape, the rest have intirely omitted it   I have done my outmost to prevail with the Ministers with whom I had any Intercourse, to give that obedience to the Law, which is incumbent on them as well as other subjects, but tho the prosecutions against the offenders, are directed to be brought in the name of His Majesty's Advocate. seeing so great a body of the Established Church seems to have fallen under the penaltys of the Law, and that there are so many remaining Sundays in which this Act ought still to be read by them, I judged it improper for me, to take upon me, the determination of the time and number of prosecutions against the offenders, appearing to me to be a subject of a delicate consideration ; and therefore chose as the best for his Majesty's service which I shall ever with zeal persue, to submit it to your Grace's more discerning Eyes, and shall to the best of my understanding with fidelity & the greatest care, follow such orders as your Grace shall be pleas'd to give me having the honour to be with the greatest respect and the most perfect truth,
      My Lord
        Your Grace's most faithfull most
          obedient & most humble servant
                CH ARESKINE

APPENDIX XIV

ACT TO DISABLE PROVOST WILSON AND FINE THE CITY OF EDINBURGH

Anno Decimo

GEORGII II REGIS

An Act to disable Alexander Wilson Esquire, from taking, holding, or enjoying any Office or Place of Magistracy in the City of EDINBURGH, or elsewhere, in Great Britain, and for imposing a Fine upon the Corporation of the said City

amble WHEREAS upon Tuesday the Seventh Day of September, in the Year of our Lord One thousand seven hundred and thirty six, there was a most seditious and outragious Riot in the City of Edinburgh, in that Part of Great Britain called Scotland, notoriously concerted

Appendix XIV.

and carried on by great numbers of wicked, disorderly and blood-thirsty Persons, who did, with open Force and Violence, seize the Arms of the City Guard, possess themselves of the City Gates, and, by setting fire to, and breaking open the Door of the Tolbooth of the said City, did unlawfully and audaciously rescue and set at large several Criminals therein confined   And whereas Captain John Porteous, then a Prisoner there under Sentence of Death, but graciously reprieved by the Queen's most Excellent Majesty, as Guardian of the Realm, was, by the said Rioters, in a cruel Manner, dragged from the said Prison, and most barbarously hanged by the Neck, and murdered, in manifest Violation of the Publick Peace, in Defiance and Subversion of legal Government, in high Contempt of our Sovereign Lord the King and his Laws, and to the most presumptuous and unparallelled Obstruction of the Royal Mercy   And whereas for some time before the committing of the said Murther and Riot, it was commonly reported in the said City of Edinburgh, that some such attrocious Fact would be attempted, which, by proper Care in the Magistrates, Citizens, and Inhabitants of the said City, might have been prevented, notwithstanding which, Alexander Wilson Esquire, then and now Provost of the said City, and then actually resident in the said City, and fully apprized of the said wicked Design, did not take any Precautions to prevent the said Murther and Riot, nor use the proper nor necessary Means to suppress the same, or to preserve the Peace of the said City, or after the Perpetration of the said Fact to discover, apprehend, or secure the Authors, or Abettors thereof, in manifest Violation of the Trust and Duty of his Office of chief Magistrate of the said City, nor were any Means or Endeavours used by the Citizens or Inhabitants of the said City, to prevent or suppress the said notorious Riot, or to hinder the said inhuman and barbarous Murther, or to discover the Persons concerned therein, in order to bring them to Justice   Now, in order to express the highest Detestation and Abhorrence of the said Murther and Riot, and to the End that the said enormous Misbehaviours and Neglects of Duty, herein before mentioned may not go unpunished, and that other Persons may not presume, through hopes of Impunity, to be guilty of the like for the future, be it enacted by the King's most Excellent Majesty, by and with the Advice and Consent of the Lords Spiritual and Temporal, and Commons, in this present Parliament assembled, and by the Authority of the same, That the said Alexander Wilson *The Provost* be, and he is hereby, from and immediately after the passing of this *disabled from* Act, disabled, and made incapable to have, hold, exercise, or enjoy *holding any* the said Office of Provost of the said City of Edinburgh ; and that he *office of* the said Alexander Wilson be, and he is hereby for ever hereafter *Magistracy* disabled and rendered incapable, to have, hold, exercise, or enjoy any Office or Place of Magistracy in the said City of Edinburgh, or elsewhere, in Great Britain

And it is further enacted by the Authority aforesaid, That a new *A new* Provost be immediately chosen in the Room of the said Alexander *Provost to be* Wilson, in the same Manner as if the said Alexander Wilson was *chosen* naturally dead

And be it further enacted by the Authority aforesaid, That the Cor- *Fine on the* poration of the said City of Edinburgh, do forfeit the Sum of Two *Corporation* thousand Pounds Sterling, to be paid out of their Common Good, to His Majesty, by the Magistrates and Town-Council of the said City, which said Sum of Two thousand Pounds, shall be applied to and for the sole Use and Benefit of the Widow of the said deceased Captain John Porteous.

331

Captain Porteous.

APPENDIX XV

ACT FOR BRINGING TO JUSTICE THE MURDERERS OF CAPTAIN PORTEOUS.

Anno Decimo

GEORGII II REGIS

An ACT for the more effectually bringing to Justice any Persons concerned in the barbarous Murther of Captain John Porteous, and punishing such as shall knowingly conceal any of the Offenders

Preamble WHEREAS upon Tuesday the Seventh of September, in the Year of Our Lord One thousand seven hundred and thirty six, great Numbers of wicked, desperate, and blood-thirsty Persons, of most detestable Principles, unlawfully assembled within the City of Edinburgh, in that Part of Great Britain called Scotland, with open Force and Violence seized the Arms of the City Guard, possessed themselves of the City Gates, broke open the Door of the Tolbooth of the said City, and laid violent Hands upon Captain John Porteous then a Prisoner there under Sentence of Death, but graciously reprieved by the Queen's most Excellent Majesty as Guardian of the Realm, and having in a cruel Manner dragged him from the said Prison, hanged him by the Neck, and barbarously murdered him, in manifest Violation of the Publick Peace, in Defiance and Subversion of legal Government, in high Contempt of our Sovereign Lord the King, and his Laws and to the most presumptuous and unparallelled Obstruction of the Royal Mercy And whereas many of the wicked and desperate Persons acting, aiding, and assisting in committing the said Outrages, Riot, and barbarous Murther, have absconded and fled, to avoid their being brought to Justice And whereas upon Discoveries already made, Criminal Letters under the Seal of the Court of Justiciary in that Part of Great Britain called Scotland, have been raised and executed against several of the said Persons, and, upon further Discovery, the like Process may be issued out of the said Court against others who have likewise withdrawn themselves, be it therefore enacted by the King's most Excellent Majesty, by and with the Consent of the Lords,

Fugitives not surrendering themselves to suffer Death Spiritual and Temporal, and Commons, in this present Parliament assembled and by the Authority of the same, That if any Person or Persons, against whom (for any of the Offences aforesaid) Criminal Letters issuing out of the said Court of Justiciary have been, or hereafter may be raised and executed shall, in due Course of Law, be declared Fugitive, on or before the first Day of May, in the Year One thousand seven hundred and thirty eight, for not appearing to abide his or their legal Trial, and shall not render him or themselves to One or more of the Judges of the said Court of Justiciary, within the Space of Twelve Kalendar Months, from and after the Day of pronouncing the respective Sentence or Sentences of Fugitation against them, such Person or Persons shall stand attainted of Felony, to all Intents and Purposes, and shall suffer and incur Pains of Death, and Confiscation of Moveables

Upon their surrendry to be committed to safe Custody, &c. Provided always, That if any Person or Persons against whom such Sentence of Fugitation shall be pronounced as aforesaid, shall surrender him or themselves within the said Twelve Months after such Sentence of Fugitation shall be pronounced, then, and in such Case, the Judge or Judges of the said Court of Justiciary shall, and they

332

Appendix XV.

are hereby impowered, authorized, and required to issue his or their Warrant or Warrants for committing such Person or Persons to safe Custody, there to remain until they are discharged by due Course of Law; and thereof to give Notice immediately to one of His Majesty's principal Secretaries of State, and to His Majesty's Advocate for Scotland for the Time being, or his Deputy

And it be further enacted by the Authority aforesaid, That all and every Person and Persons in that Part of Great Britain called Scotland, who, after the Times appointed for the Surrender of the Persons declared Fugitive as aforesaid, are expired, shall conceal, aid, abet, or succour them, or any of them, who shall not have rendered themselves in Manner aforesaid knowing him or them to be declared Fugitive, being thereof lawfully convicted, shall be punished with the Pains of Death, and Confiscation of Moveables

Persons concealing them to suffer Death.

And to the End that this Act may be the better notified, and that none may pretend Ignorance thereof be it further enacted by the Authority aforesaid, That this Act shall be read in every Parish Church throughout that part of Great Britain called Scotland, on the first Sunday or Lord's Day in every Month for one whole Year, from the first day of August, in the Year One thousand seven hundred and thirty seven, by the Minister of the Parish, or such Minister as shall preach in such Parish Church, respectively, on such Sunday or Lord's Day in the Morning, immediately after the Sermon, and in case such Minister shall neglect to read this Act, as is hereby directed, he shall for the first Offence be declared incapable of sitting or voting in any Church Judicature, and for the second Offence be declared incapable of taking, holding, or enjoying any Ecclesiastical Benefice in that Part of Great Britain called Scotland, and that the said Offenders may be prosecuted by summary Complaint to the Court of Session, or by Process before any Court of Justiciary at the Instance of His Majesty's Advocate

This Act to be read first Sunday of every Month in the Churches of Scotland

And for the more effectual discovering, apprehending and bringing to Justice any Person or Persons concerned in the said Riot and barbarous Murther, be it further enacted by the Authority aforesaid, That if any Person or Persons concerned in the said outrageous Riot and Murther, shall, before the first Day of February next, discover and apprehend, or cause to be apprehended, any other Person or Persons who hath or have been guilty of the said Offences, so as the Person or Persons so discovered, shall be convicted of the said Riot and Murther, every such Person or Persons making such Discovery, shall be freed and discharged from all Prosecution had or to be had concerning the same

Clause in favour of Impeachers.

And as a further Encouragement to such discovering, apprehending, and convicting of any of the said Offenders, be it further enacted by the Authority aforesaid That any Person or Persons who shall before the said first Day of February next, discover and apprehend, or cause to be apprehended, any of the Persons concerned in the said Riot and Murther, or they be convicted thereof, shall have and receive for every Person so discovered, apprehended, and convicted, the Sum of Two hundred Pounds Sterling, to be paid out of any of His Majesty's Revenues

Reward for Informers

Provided always, and it is hereby further enacted, That the Person or Persons making such Discovery, and intitled to such Reward as aforesaid, shall not thereby be disabled to be a Witness against the Person or Persons upon whose Conviction or Convictions such Reward shall be become due, any Law, Usage, or Determination to the contrary thereof in any wise notwithstanding

who may be Witnesses

Captain Porteous.

Biographical Notes

I — The Judges

ANDREW FLETCHER of Milton, Lord Justice-Clerk (1692-1766), son of Henry Fletcher of Saltoun and Margaret, daughter of Sir David Carnegy of Pittarow, and nephew to Fletcher of Saltoun, the famous patriot, was born in 1692 Having been educated for the bar, he was admitted an advocate on 26th February, 1717, and in the year 1724, when only thirty-two years of age, succeeded the celebrated Sir John Lauder of Fountainhall as an Ordinary Lord, taking his seat on 4th June, of that year, by the title of Lord Milton On the 22nd of June, 1726, he was appointed a Lord of Justiciary, in place of James Hamilton of Pencaitland, who resigned, and the following year was named by patent dated 7th July, one of the Commissioners for improving the fisheries and manufactures of Scotland On the resignation of James Erskine of Grange (q v), Lord Milton was constituted Lord Justice-Clerk, and took his seat on 21st June, 1735, and on the 10th of November 1746, he was appointed principal Keeper of the Signet He resigned his office as Lord Justice-Clerk in 1748 but retained his appointments as Keeper of the Signet and judge of the Court of Session till his death, which took place at his country seat Brunstane House, near Joppa, Midlothian, on 15th December, 1766, in the seventy-fifth year of his age When he resigned the office of Justice-Clerk, he also retained the charge of superintending elections, which he considered his masterpiece

As Lord Justice-Clerk Milton presided at the trial of Captain Porteous in 1736, and in May of the following year was examined at the bar of the House of Lords with reference to the inquiry into the Porteous Riot During the Rising of 1745, his lordship was much admired for the mild and judicious manner with which he conducted himself in the exercise of his authority as Lord Justice-Clerk at that unhappy period He abstained as much as possible from harsh or violent measures, when such were not absolutely necessary Indeed, many informations, which he suspected to have been sent by over-officious or malignant persons, were found in his repositories after his death unopened Lord Milton was the friend and coadjutor of Lord Ilay, afterwards Duke of Argyll (q v), who had long the entire direction of Scottish affairs, and from the knowledge which he possessed of the laws, customs, and temper of Scotland, proved a successful auxiliary to that statesman, and a good friend to his country, in pointing out such individuals as he judged to be best qualified to fill vacancies in the Church, and to hold the important office of Sheriff "There was hardly a county or burgh in the kingdom where he was not acquainted with all the friends and opponents of the Administration, and with the characters and views of the leading men on both sides of which knowledge he made proper use If some of his instruments were not always what they ought to have been, they were at least perfectly equal to the task assigned them ; for no Minister ever employed so few weak men. It will readily be admitted that a great deal of the business done by him was by no means well suited to the station of a judge, who ought to be of no party, and is not entitled to shelter himself under the excuse of State necessity " (*Ochtertyre MSS* 1 89). At the same time he did his best to promote the welfare of Scotland

Appendix XVI.

in improving its trade, manufacture, and agriculture, and also took
an active part in the abolition of the heritable jurisdictions   A
number of Lord Milton's letters relating to affairs in Scotland will be
found in the appendix to Home's *History of the Rebellion in the year
1745* (1802)   Dr Carlyle says of him—"Lord Milton was a
man of great ability in business, a man of good sense and of excellent
talents for managing men , and though his conversation was on a
limited scale, because his knowledge was very much so, yet being
possessed of indefeasible power at that time in Scotland, and keeping
an excellent table, his defects were overlooked and he was held to be
as agreeable as he was able " (*Autobiography*, p 260)   " In point
of fashion and accomplishment," says Ramsay, " he was a modern
man compared with his brothers Grange and Dun, who trod in the
steps of their fathers   He wrote and spoke like a man of sense and
knowledge, who attended more to substance than to show   His
mother wit and penetration would have enabled him to have made
a great figure on the bench, had the variety and weight of his other
business not engrossed his attention   His opinions, though not laboured
or profound, were generally much to the point, and expressed in plain,
perspicuous language   Before his demise, in 1766, Lord Milton was
so much enfeebled in mind and body that he diverted himself with
children's playthings, which must have been a humbling sight "
(*Ochtertyre MSS* i 90)
    The large and handsome mansion in the Canongate eastwards from
Moray House, known as Milton House, was erected by Fletcher as
his town residence, in what was formerly the garden of Lord Rox-
burghe's house   The mansion survived until 1890, when it was
demolished to make way for a school   " The old mansion which thus
formed the scene of Court levees, where Hanoverian and Jacobite
candidates for Royal favour elbowed one another in the chase, still
retains unequivocal marks of its former grandeur, notwithstanding
the many strange tenants who have since occupied it   The drawing-
room to the south, the windows of which command a beautiful view
of Salisbury Crags and St Leonard's Hill, has its walls very taste-
fully decorated with a series of designs of landscapes and allegorical
figures   There are various grotesque figures interspersed among the
ornamental borders which have the appearance of being copies from
some illuminated manuscript of the fourteenth century   They represent a cardinal, a monk, a priest, and other churchmen, painted with
great spirit and extreme drollery of attitude and expression   They
so entirely differ from the general character of the composition that
their insertion may be conjectured to have originated in a whim of
Lord Milton " (Wilson's *Memorials*, ii 104)

    Sir James Mackenzie of Royston, Bart , Lord Royston (1670-1744),
third son of Sir George Mackenzie, first Earl of Cromarty was born
in 1670, and succeeded to the estate of Royston in virtue of an entail
executed by his father in 1688   He became an advocate on the 19th
of November, 1698, and soon attained to eminence in his profession
He was created a baronet on 8th February, 1704, and, on the resignation of his uncle, Roderick Mackenzie, Lord Prestonhall, was appointed
his successor, and took his seat on the 7th of June, 1710, as Lord
Royston , and, on the 27th of July following, was also constituted a
Lord of Justiciary.   There is a copy of Mackenzie's *Criminal Law* in
the Advocates' Library, containing copious notes in the handwriting
of Lord Royston
    Lord Royston married Elizabeth, youngest daughter of the celebrated
Sir George Mackenzie of Rosehaugh and widow of Sir Archibald
Cockburn of Langton   He was involved in a lawsuit for his father-

335

Captain Porteous.

in-law's property with the Earl of Bute, who had married another daughter of Sir George Mackenzie's, in which, however, he was not successful   He died at Edinburgh on the 9th of November, 1744, aged seventy-three

Lord Royston is said to have been "a person of vast learning, honour, and probity, impartial in judgment, justly ranked among the first judges, in criminal causes, of the age, and in private life a most polite, friendly, agreeable, facetious and affable gentleman " (*Doug Peer* 1 398)   His lordship's Edinburgh residence was the lower flat of Bailie Macmoran's house in Riddle's Close, Lawnmarket   "Here, therefore, we may presume, his witty and eccentric daughter, Anne, was born and brought up   This lady, who married Sir William Dick of Prestonfield, carried her humorous pranks to an excess scarcely conceivable in our more decorous days, sallying out occasionally in search of adventure, like some of the maids of honour of Charles the Second's Court dressed in male costume, with her maid for a squire, and outvying them in the extravagance of her proceedings   She seems indeed to have possessed more wit than discretion   Some of her poetical lampoons were privately printed by the late Charles Kirkpatrick Sharpe in a rare though well-known little volume, entitled 'A Ballad Book,' and furnish curious specimens of the notions of delicacy at the period " (Wilson's *Memorials*, 1. 219).

DAVID ERSKINE of Dun, Lord Dun (1670-1758), son of David Erskine of Dun, near Montrose, was born in 1670   He studied at the University of St Andrews, and afterwards completed his academical course at the University of Paris   He came to the Scottish bar on the 19th of November, 1698, and soon attained to eminence in his profession as an advocate   He represented the county of Forfar at the Convention of Estates in 1689, and in the Parliaments of 1690, 1691, 1693, 1695 and 1696, and opposed the Union   He succeeded the Earl of Lauderdale as an Ordinary Lord and took his seat on the 1st of November 1710, and on the 13th of April, 1714, was also appointed a Lord of Justiciary in place of John Murray of Bowhill   Owing to failing health he resigned his Justiciary gown in the year 1744, and also his office as an Ordinary Lord in 1753, without asking a pension, to which he was well entitled, and he was by no means rich   He died on the 26th of May, 1758, in the eighty-fifth year of his age   His lordship held the somewhat unusual view that when a judge could not constantly do his duty he ought to retire, which he did when he found himself unable to ride the Circuit, in those days literally performed on horseback   Lord Dun published a work entitled, *Friendly and Familiar Advices, Adapted to the various Stations and Conditions of Life and the Natural Relations to be observed among them* (Edinburgh, 1754)   Dr Robert Wallace, minister of Moffat, in his work on Passive Obedience, is opposed to what Lord Dun has said on that subject, but characterises his lordship as "a venerable old man, of very great experience, and greatly distinguished for piety "   Ramsay records of Lord Dun, "If not a first-rate lawyer, he had sufficient learning to make him a useful judge   As he spared no pains in discharging the duties of his laborious office, so he was accounted a man of honour and integrity, both on and off the bench   The pedantry of his talk and the starchiness of his manners made him the subject of ridicule among people who had neither his worth nor innocence of heart and life   He was likewise overrun with prejudice, which sometimes warps the judgment of able, well-intentioned men " (*Ochtertyre MSS* 1 85)   Lord Dun was a strong Episcopalian, and his Toryism approached very near Jacobitism, and for a number of years his lordship hardly ever voted on the side of the Crown, even when the decision was well-nigh unanimous

Appendix XVI.

SIR WALTER PRINGLE of Newhall, Lord Newhall (1664-1736), second son of Sir Robert Pringle, first Baronet of Stichel, by a daughter of Sir John Hope, Lord Craighall, was born in 1664, and was admitted an advocate on 10th December 1687. He practised at the bar thirty-one years, and during that period displayed great abilities and knowledge of his profession His promotion to the bench was long delayed, and he was passed over in the interest of others, his inferiors in attainments On the death of Sir Gilbert Elliot of Minto, the father of his colleague, the second Lord Minto (q v), he was elevated to the bench, and took his seat as Lord Newhall on the 6th June, 1718, was at the same time, appointed a Lord of Justiciary, and, according to Playfair, also created a knight bachelor. He held his office with great reputation, and was highly esteemed and respected both as a judge and as a gentleman, and at his death, which took place on the 14th of December, 1736, a tribute of honour was paid to his remains which had never been conferred on any of the Ordinary Judges of the Court, his funeral having been attended by his brethren in their robes of office The Faculty of Advocates met on this occasion to consider the propriety of also attending it in a body, when a eulogium on his lordship's character, written by Sir Robert Dundas of Arniston, at that time Dean of Faculty, was ordered to be engrossed in their minutes, expressive of the high esteem in which he had been held by that learned body The following is an excerpt therefrom —" His ability, candour, and careful discharge of the duties of his former employment, added to his moral character, had celebrated his name; he was marked out by the universal suffrage and voice of the subjects as a person whose knowledge and integrity would render their lives and properties secure in his hands, and, as such, was nominated by their gracious Sovereign to execute so high a trust. The faculty do acknowledge, with gratitude and honour to his memory, that his after conduct gave no disappointment to so great expectations. His integrity proved a shining ornament to his learning and knowledge; and these with his other distinguishing qualities of steadiness and unbiassed resolution, enabled him to apply his principle of integrity to useful practice, and to do justice not by accident, but because he knew it to be so And if at any time human frailty and an over-jealousy of himself led him into smaller mistakes, yet the virtuous principles from which he acted, even in those cases, and the extensive habit of justice he had acquired, overshadowed these lesser failings, and gave a becoming lustre to the whole course of his judgments "

The following poetical epitaph on Lord Newhall is from the pen of William Hamilton of Bangour, the poet, whose wife was a niece of his lordship :—

> Its haughty column let ambition raise,
> And guilty greatness load with venal praise,
> This monument, for nobler use design'd,
> Speaks to the heart, and rises for mankind,
> If worth begets its likeness or its love,
> Love what you feel, and be what you approve,
> Studious of life, learn life's each sacred end,
> Hence form the judge, the husband, father, friend
> Here wealth of greatness found no partial grace,
> The poor looked fearless in oppression's face;
> One plain, good meaning through his judgment ran,
> And if he erred, alas! he erred as man
> If, then, unconscious of so fair a fame,
> You read, without a wish to be the same,
> Yet read—perhaps some vice you may resign,
> Be even a momentary virtue thine,
> Here on thy breast Heaven works its first essay,
> Think on this man, and pass unblamed one day

Captain Porteous.

SIR GILBERT ELLIOT of Minto, Baronet, Lord Justice-Clerk (1693-1766), only son of Sir Gilbert Elliot Lord Minto, one of the Senators of the College of Justice, and Jane Carre, daughter of Sir Andrew Carre of Cavers, was born in 1693, and was admitted an advocate on 26th July, 1715. On his father's death in 1718 he succeeded him as second baronet. He was elected M P for Roxburghshire in 1722, and represented that county till 1726. He was elevated to the bench on the death of Sir Francis Grant of Cullen, and took his seat on 4th June, 1726. Following his father's example he assumed the judicial title of Lord Minto. On the 13th September, 1733, he was nominated a Lord of Justiciary in place of Sir William Calderwood of Polton and succeeded Charles Erskine of Tinwald (q v), as Lord Justice-Clerk on 3rd May, 1763. He retained both offices till his death which took place at Minto on the 16th of April, 1766, in his seventy-fourth year, having sat on the bench for the long period of forty-four years.

Lord Minto, though a most accomplished man and an excellent musician, was not specially eminent as a judge. He is said to have first introduced the German flute to Scotland; and he was a member of an Edinburgh "committee of taste for the improvement of the town". He was a staunch Hanoverian, and it is recorded that during the rising of 1745, some of the Highland army on the march into England, appeared before his house. His daughter Jean, authoress of "The Flowers of the Forest," hospitably entertained the unwelcome visitors, while her father fled and concealed himself among the brushwood, where he remained until the refreshed rebels had amicably departed. Ramsay says of him—"Lord Minto falls to be mentioned among the amateurs and early promoters of polite literature in this country. For many years he was one of the *literati* to whose opinion much deference was paid by the authors of new works in verse and prose. Though too lazy, or too busy, to write anything himself, he was looked upon as a very judicious critic, whose taste might be relied on as likely to anticipate that of the public. Perhaps he was better acquainted with *belles lettres* than with the quiddities of the feudal or municipal law. Yet his sound, masculine understanding and long experience in business, joined to his dignified manners, procured him the character of an upright, useful judge, whose opinions were well digested and delivered in gentlemanly language" (*Ochtertyre MSS* i 81). Lord Minto presided, as Lord Justice-Clerk in 1765, at the trial of the notorious Katharine Nairn who with her brother-in-law, was sentenced to death for the murder of her husband, but subsequently made a romantic escape from the Tolbooth and escaped to the Continent.

Minto resided when in Edinburgh at Minto House, the handsome and spacious mansion of his family, situated on the north side of Argyle Square, "forty-five feet square, on the slope down towards the Cowgate, surrounded by trees and recessed back with a pillared carriage entrance, ninety feet from the line of the street". The square disappeared on the formation of Chambers Street.

II —The Counsel for the Prosecution

DUNCAN FORBES of Culloden, Lord President (1685-1747) second son of Duncan Forbes of Culloden, and Mary Innes, daughter of the Laird of Innes, was born on 10th November, 1685, and, with his elder brother John, received the rudiments of his education at the grammar school of Inverness, where the brothers, according to his first biographer, were notorious for their convivial prowess. Delicate

Appendix XVI.

health, however, compelled greater temperance in his later life. The same writer states that, on the occasion of his mother's funeral, Forbes and the other mourners were so influenced by their potations as to proceed to the burial place, leaving the body behind   He lost his father in 1704, and, being the younger son, the landed property fell to his brother as his father's immediate successor   His own inclination led him to be a soldier, but, by the advice of his friends, he is said to have embarked his small patrimony in some mercantile speculations which, having proved unsuccessful, caused him to relinquish any idea of venturing farther in commerce, and to direct his attention to a profession of which he was afterwards destined to become so bright an ornament   With these views he repaired to Edinburgh and commenced his legal studies in the office of John Spottiswood, author of a volume of Styles of Writs   In March 1705 Forbes was present at the remarkable trial of Captain Thomas Green, for piracy, and the impression made upon his mind by the execution of a man subsequently proved to be innocent, appears many years later, from his reference to that case in his speech on the Porteous Riot Bill   Soon after the affair of Captain Green, in accordance with the usual practice of law students of his day   Forbes went to study Roman Law at the University of Leyden, where he remained nearly two years, and, having assiduously devoted himself to his studies, attained to great proficiency as a civilian   He returned to Scotland in 1707, and shortly thereafter married Mary, daughter of Hugh Rose, twelfth Baron of Kilravock   Forbes was admitted an advocate on 26th July, 1709, and shortly after his admission was appointed Sheriff of Midlothian   He obtained this appointment through the interest of John, second Duke of Argyll ($q\ v$), from whose family he received many marks of esteem and friendship   The Duke's brother, the Earl of Ilay, afterwards third Duke of Argyll ($q\ v$), also took a great interest in his career, and his influence did much to forward the success of the young lawyer in promoting his practice at the bar   He was afterwards entrusted by the Duke with the management of his estates during his absence, but declined taking any salary for his services, although the Duke offered him £600 a year for same   He was induced by friendship alone to undertake these labours, which were continued even after he had risen to the first legal position of the kingdom   He had therefore to trust to his profession for the means of his immediate expenses, but his talents and industry were such as to procure him a handsome competency for this purpose, as in a comparatively short time he received very extensive employment both in the Court of Session and also before the House of Lords. The Rising of 1715 formed an important epoch in his life, and the valuable services rendered to Government by his brother and himself during that unhappy period, in raising forces in their support, was rewarded by the office of Advocate-depute   It was some time, however, before he would accept of this office, but, urged by his friends, and particularly by Lord Ilay, he finally entered upon his duty on 12th March, 1716   His reluctance proceeded from the general belief that the office was to be filled for the purpose of assisting in the prosecution of the prisoners in Carlisle, and Forbes regarded the act of sending the accused out of Scotland for trial as highly unjust   He was not however, called upon to prosecute, and he even contributed largely, by himself and his friends, to their pecuniary necessities   He also wrote a remarkable letter to Sir Robert Walpole, strongly protesting against severity being used to the prisoners (*Culloden Papers*, pp 61-5)   His humanity in this instance was maintained by some to his being secretly and at heart a Jacobite, but his subsequent conduct proved to all parties that he had to his utmost done his duty with honour to his Sovereign and country

Captain Porteous.

In 1722 Forbes contested the Inverness district of burghs against Alexander Gordon of Aidoch The latter was returned, but, upon a petition to the House of Commons, Forbes was declared duly elected " Here, as well as at the bar, he was distinguished for the splendour of his eloquence and soundness of judgment, which procured him the countenance of his Sovereign, and the approbation, gratitude, and confidence of his constituents " He was appointed Lord Advocate on the resignation of his coeval and rival, Robert Dundas of Arniston, on 29th May, 1725, and, in that office, " shone conspicuously for impartiality, candour, and moderation, and it has been remarked that comparatively few prosecutions took place during the long period he held it, it being a maxim with this worthy man, ' better twenty guilty persons should escape than one inoffensive man should suffer '" The salary attached to the office of Lord Advocate at time of his appointment was not more than £500 or £600 a year, although the office of Secretary of State for Scotland was suspended during the years 1725-31, and finally abolished in 1746, the correspondence regarding all civil matters devolved upon him, which he sustained in a manner worthy of his enlightened understanding and sound patriotism

Forbes took an active part in suppressing the riots in Glasgow in 1725 occasioned by the malt tax, and received warm thanks from Walpole for settling the strike of Edinburgh brewers, provoked by the same Act He espoused the cause of the infamous Colonel Francis Charteris, on his trial in 1732, who bequeathed to him a legacy of £1000 and the life-rent of his mansion house of Stoneyhill, near Musselburgh, of which Forbes was tenant (Burton's *Life*, pp 309, 310) In 1728 he was engaged as Lord Advocate in the prosecution of James Carnegie of Finhaven, for the murder of Lord Strathmore, when, after a long trial, the prisoner was acquitted

Forbes succeeded to the estate of Culloden on the death of his brother in 1735 The affair of the Porteous Mob, in 1736, engrossed his attention in his official capacity when in conjunction with the Solicitor-General, Charles Erskine, he endeavoured to bring to justice the perpetrators of that outrage In the subsequent debates in Parliament upon the Bill for punishing the Provost and city of Edinburgh, Forbes took a spirited and active part, and the opposition of himself and his friends effected the mitigation of its most objectionable clauses Notwithstanding his thus opposing the Government while acting as chief law officer for the Crown, on the death of Sir Hew Dalrymple of North Berwick, who had sat on the bench for forty years, Forbes was appointed President of the Court of Session, and took his seat on the 21st of June, 1737, when the Faculty of Advocates waited on him with an address, testifying their great satisfaction at his advancement and thanking him for the prudent, wise, and judicious discharge of the trust reposed in him

He immediately set about reforming many abuses that had long lessened the dignity of the Court or retarded business Writing to Lord Hardwicke, then Lord Chancellor, on 29th February, 1740 he was able to say, " When the term ended this day, no cause ripe for judgment remained undetermined, none that, within the rules of the Court could possibly have been decided, was laid over to the next term a circumstance which has not happened in any man's memory, and of which the mob are very fond " (*Culloden Papers*, 157). " He became a terror to evil-doers of every grade, and the rising manufacturing and trading interests of the country, looked down upon and discouraged by the feudal aristocracy could trust to his strong arm for legal protection—a far greater service than the fostering encouragement which he sought to extend to them in other shapes Thus the middle classes were taught to rely on the supreme Court as a protection from the evils of the hereditary jurisdictions " (Burton's *Life*,

Appendix XVI.

pp 361-2) "He was the friend and patron of every lawyer of promising parts, and he had a sort of intuition into character that enabled him to appreciate their merits Nothing could exceed his courtesy to them while pleading before him, behaving towards them like an indulgent parent who knew how to preserve his dignity and authority Nothing could offend him but petulance or want of principle, for which he thought no parts could compensate" (*Ochtertyre MSS.* 1 50).

Previous to the first breaking out of the Rising in 1745, Forbes applied all his powers to stifle it in its birth, and 'it is well known that his firm but temperate conduct his extensive influence with his countrymen, and his patriotic exertions, even to the sacrifice of his private fortune, were the main instruments of its suppression, and that, had his enlightened counsels been attended to and his provident precautions adopted, the seeds of rebellion had, in all probability, never sprung to light and the country had been spared the misery which it actually endured. It is needless, and perhaps might be invidious, to enter into the reasons why the eminent services of this great and good man were treated, on the part of the Government, with a neglect, ingratitude, and injustice which leave a stain upon the annals of the times" (Tytler's *Life of Kames,* 1 34) Forbes protested in vain against the vindictive and savage cruelties of the Duke of Cumberland, who characteristically referred to him as "that old woman who talked to me about humanity" (Burton's *Life,* p 382) The labours and anxieties of this trying time appear to have broken his health He died at Edinburgh on 10th December 1747 and Lord Elchies in noticing this event in his notebook, remarks—"Very much and most justly regretted, for he had many valuable qualities that procured him general esteem, both in his private life and in his public office as a judge And as before his time I never saw that office supplied either with so much dignity or so much to the satisfaction of the country as while he enjoyed it, which was little more than ten years, so do I not expect ever to see it so well supplied again" (Elchies' *Notes, voce* Jurisdiction, No 14)

Forbes was one of the great golfers of his day, and a famous figure upon the Links of Leith He was so keen a golfer as to play on Leith sands when the links were covered with snow Thomas Mathison in his poem, *The Golf* (Edinburgh, 1743), thus refers to him—

> *Yea, here great Forbes, patron of the just,*
> *The dread of villains, and the good man's trust,*
> *When spent with toils in serving human kind,*
> *His body recreates and unbends his mind*

CHARLES ERSKINE of Tinwald, Lord Justice-Clerk (1680-1763), third son of Sir Charles Erskine or Areskine of Alva, baronet, and Christian, daughter of Sir James Dundas of Arniston, and great-grandson of John Erskine, Earl of Mar, was born in 1680 It is supposed that he was at first educated with a view to the Church At the age of twenty he was a candidate for the office of one of the four Regents in the University of Edinburgh, and, after a comparative trial with several competitors, obtained that appointment, 26th November, 1700 He resigned that office on the 17th October, 1707, and presented to the Town Council a commission appointing him professor of public law The Council protested against the institution of this new professorship as being a misapplication of the £300 per annum given to the University by King William, this opposition, however, was of no avail, and he was appointed on the 7th November that same year This was an office requiring considerable ability and an extensive acquaintance with science and literature, and the reputation he gained as a public speaker probably induced him to study the law with a view

Captain Porteous.

of becoming an advocate   He accordingly presented himself for admission, and was received a member of the Faculty of Advocates on 14th July, 1711   In 1714 he was appointed Advocate-depute for the western circuit   He was chosen representative to Parliament for the county of Dumfries in April, 1722, having purchased the estate of Tinwald, in Dumfriesshire. He was nominated Solicitor-General on 29th May, 1725, on which occasion his Majesty addressed a letter to the Lords, dated 2nd June following, in these terms—" We, being pleased to shew a farther mark of our Royal favour, it is our will and pleasure that a seat be placed for him within the bar of your Court, where, and from whence, he may be at liberty to plead causes in your presence " This privilege had hitherto belonged to the Lord Advocate alone, and its extension to the Solicitor-General has continued from that date

He was re-chosen for the county of Dumfries in 1727, and again in 1734, at which period he was also returned for that district of burghs, but preferred the county   In 1736 he appeared for the Crown in the prosecution of Captain Porteous, and, along with the Lord Advocate, conducted the inquiry, exhaustive but fruitless, into the affair of Porteous's murder   He was constituted Lord Advocate, 20th January, 1737, on the appointment of Duncan Forbes of Culloden as Lord President (q v), and in 1741 returned to Parliament for the Wick district of burghs   On the death of Sir James Mackenzie of Royston (q v) Erskine was elevated to the bench, and took his seat as Lord Tinwald on 23rd November, 1744 at the same time succeeding him as a Lord of Justiciary   On the resignation of Andrew Fletcher of Milton (q v), he was appointed Lord Justice-Clerk on 15th June, 1748   " In all these departments he discharged his duty with honour and integrity As a lawyer he was esteemed an able civilian, he spoke with ease and gracefulness, and in a dialect which was purer than that of most of his contemporaries   As a judge his demeanour was grave and decorous, and accompanied with a gentleness and suavity of manners that were extremely ingratiating " (Tytler's *Memoirs of Lord Kames* (1814), 1 53-5) He died at Edinburgh on 5th April, 1763   " If he had not Forbes's impassioned glow of sentiment," says Ramsay of Erskine, while at the bar, " or Dundas's quickness and fire, he was, nevertheless, a very powerful and successful pleader His language was long considered as a pattern of elegance and perspicuity   And, as his sentences had the appearance of being carefully culled, and marshalled in proper order, so they were uttered with such suavity, and in such winning manner, that he often extorted the assent of those that heard him to his propositions " (*Ochtertyre MSS* 1   101-2) " I was much pleased with his manner of speaking on the bench, where, in point of dignity, elegance, and decency he had but one single equal (Lord Alemoor) He delivered his opinion with so much gravity and grace and appeared so thoroughly acquainted with the law and the fact, that he was always heard with reverence and the deepest attention, though he sometimes spoke long   And, as he avoided all extraneous matter in his speeches, it seemed to be his great object not to commit himself rashly on any subject " (*Ibid* 1 103)

HUGH FORBES, advocate (died 1760) was a son of Colonel John Forbes of Pittencrieff, near Dunfermline, Fifeshire   He was admitted a member of the Faculty of Advocates on 6th January, 1728, and was appointed counsel to H R H the Prince of Wales, in 1739   Forbes acted as agent for the Royal burghs from 1742, and in the following year was nominated one of the principal Clerks of Session   He also received the appointment of procurator-fiscal of the Court of Admiralty in 1756   He died in 1760

Appendix XVI.

PATRICK HALDANE of Bearcrofts, advocate (died in 1769), son of the Laird of Gleneagles, was admitted a member of the Faculty of Advocates on 15th January, 1715   He was a representative of the old barons of Gleneagles, in Perthshire, who occupied a prominent place in Scottish history   "Being a younger son, he was bred to the law," says Ramsay, "and from the pregnancy of his parts, very sanguine were the expectations of his friends   I cannot assign the reason why he was so late putting on the gown, or say how he was previously employed, but not long after he was elected member of Parliament for the Cupar district of burghs, and took his seat soon after the suppression of the Rebellion of 1715   There, it was alleged, he made speeches which made him odious and unpopular for the greatest part' of his life   He was accused of saying that he hoped to make a fortune out of the ruins of his country " (*Ochtertyre MSS* ii 479)   Haldane was appointed one of the Commissioners for disposing of the forfeited estates of the Scottish nobility and gentry concerned in the late Rising, an ungracious office for a Scotsman at best.   The exuberant zeal with which he discharged his unpatriotic duties, while it increased the hatred of the Jacobites disgusted also the more moderate supporters of the Government   When the Commission's agreeable labours terminated, Haldane's services were rewarded by the Crown with the appointment as judge of the Court of Session, on the death of Sir John Lauder, Lord Fountainhall, on 20th September, 1722   The Faculty of Advocates, led by Duncan Forbes of Culloden, resolved to oppose this appointment, and presented a petition to the Court setting forth that Haldane could not be a judge, in respect he had not been a practising lawyer for five years, in terms of law.   The Court found by a majority that he could not be admitted but, on an appeal by Lord Advocate Dundas, this judgment was reversed by the House of Lords on 4th February, 1723   "This reversal," says Burton, "was treated by the Court of Session in a temper approaching to fierceness   They believed they could exclude Haldane on grounds not covered by the reversed decision, and opened an inquiry into his personal and political character, in the expectation, it would seem, of damaging his reputation for loyalty to the Hanoverian dynasty " (*History*, vii 352)   In 1724 however, a change took place in the Ministry, Haldane's nomination was cancelled, and the appointment given to Andrew Fletcher of Milton (*q v*), who took his seat on 4th June of that year   The peculiar circumstances of this case occasioned the passing of an Act of Parliament in 1723, abolishing the veto of the judges of the Court of Session, but leaving them the privilege of subjecting the Crown's nominee to an examination, and reporting it they found him disqualified, the Crown retaining the absolute right of appointment   The opportunity was taken of abolishing the Extraordinary Lords of Session these having also voted against Haldane   The circumstances of Haldane's case were, however, unique, and the point has not again arisen   "There are few instances of more general odium against any man, he being execrated by Whigs and Tories, Episcopalians and Presbyterians ' (*Ochtertyre MSS* ii 482)   Haldane died in 1769.

HEW DALRYMPLE MURRAY KYNNYNMOND, advocate (died 1741), was admitted a member of the Faculty of Advocates on 22nd February, 1718   He added to his original name of Hew Dalrymple that of Murray Kynnynmond when he succeeded, in the month of March, 1736, to what remained of the estate of the ancient family of Kynnynmond, as well as to the separate property of Melgund, in Forfarshire, under an entail executed by his brother-uterine, Sir Alexander Murray, Bart   dated the 13th September, 1710   His mother, Janet Rochead, daughter of Sir James Rochead of Inverleith, was twice married, first

Captain Porteous.

to Alexander Murray of Melgund, by whom she had one son, Sir Alexander, the entailer; and, second to Sir David Dalrymple of Hailes, Bart, by whom she had Sir James, his successor, and Hew, who succeeded to the Kynnynmond and Melgund estates, and died on 23rd December, 1741 In the notice of his demise inserted in the *Caledonian Mercury*, he is described as "a most friendly and humane gentleman, and eminently distinguished for his knowledge in the law and eloquence at the bar" He married Isobella Somervell, one of the daughters of Hugh Somervell of Innerteil, W S, and had issue, one daughter, Agnes, who, by her marriage with Gilbert, afterwards Sir Gilbert Elliot Bart, carried the Kynnynmond estates to the Minto family. Hew Dalrymple Murray Kynnynmond died considerably in debt, and the produce of the sale of his town house, books, and furniture was insufficient to satisfy the demands of his creditors His daughter had various law suits with them, the Session papers in which are preserved in Lord Elchies' Collection, vol 18, 1742-1749 (*The Court of Session Garland*, 1888, pp 230-1)

Kynnynmond was the author of the humorous *Complaint of the pollysyllable "Otherwise," against Mr. John Horne, Advocate* (*ibid* pp 230-3), in a note to which Maidment remarks—"In the copy from which this article is printed there is written, 'This was done by Mr Hew Dalrymple, Advocate, afterwards Hew Murray Kynnynmond of Kynnynmond, the prettiest gentleman of the whole faculty in his time'"

SIR JAMES ELPHINSTON of Logie, Baronet, advocate (died 1739), was a son of Sir John Elphinston of Logie, Aberdeenshire, who was also an advocate He was admitted a member of the Faculty of Advocates on 20th January, 1728 He died in April, 1739

III —*The Counsel for the Defence*

JAMES GRAHAM of Easdale, Lord Easdale (1695-1750), second son of John Graham of Dougalston, was born in 1695, and passed as an advocate on 9th February, 1723 He succeeded, at the promotion of Robert Dundas of Arniston, to a seat on the bench, and was received by the title of Lord Easdale on the 3rd of June, 1749 His career as a judge was of very short duration, Graham having died at Edinburgh on the 15th of August, 1750, in the fifty-fourth year of his age Dr Carlyle of Inveresk remarks of him—"There was a Mr James Graham, advocate, living here at this time, a man of distinguished parts and great business He was raised to the bench in 1749, and died in 1751 [sic] He had one daughter, Mrs. Baron Mure He was an open, friendly man, and gave me every sort of countenance both as his minister and friend, and was a man of great public spirit He was liable in a great degree to a nervous disorder, which oppressed him with low spirits He knew when he was going to fall ill, and, as it sometimes confined him for three months, he sent back his fees to the agents, who all of them waited till he recovered, and applied to him again. He was Dougalstone's brother, and a very powerful barrister" (*Autobiography*, p 211)

HENRY HOME of Kames, Lord Kames (1696-1782), son of George Home of Kames, in the county of Berwick, by a daughter of Mr Walkinshaw of Barrowfield, was born in 1696 He was educated at home, and in 1712 was indentured to an Edinburgh Writer to the Signet After an interview with Sir Hew Dalrymple, then Lord President, he determined to read for the bar, and passed advocate on

Appendix XVI.

19th January, 1724   At first he was not successful, but from the publication of his *Remarkable Decisions of the Court of Session, from 1716 to 1728*, his professional progress was assured   On the death of Patrick Campbell of Monzie, he was elevated to the bench, and took his seat by the title of Lord Kames on 6th February, 1752; and, on the promotion of Sir Gilbert Elliot of Minto as Lord Justice-Clerk (*q v*) was also appointed a Lord of Justiciary on 15th April, 1763   Lord Kames sat on the bench for over thirty years, exercising his judicial functions, in spite of increasing infirmities, until within a few days of his death   "As a judge, his opinions and decrees were dictated by an acute understanding, an ardent feeling of justice, and a perfect acquaintance with the jurisprudence of his country, which, notwithstanding the variety of pursuits in which his comprehensive mind had alternately found exercise, had always been his principal study, and the favourite object of his researches" (Tytler's *Memoirs*, 1 208).   The following is an excerpt from a letter from Lord Deskford (Earl of Finlater) to Lord Kames upon his elevation to the bench —"I have several letters, saying that the country is greatly obliged to the Ministry for giving them so good a judge   It has been remarked that without intervals of darkness we should not be sensible of the benefit of light, and that were it not for the bad weather with which we are frequently visited, we should not have so sensible a pleasure in the serenity of a fine day   If administration were always to do what they ought, people would say they only do their duty, but, like sagacious politicians, they often do wrong, to make us receive it as a favour when they sometimes do right" (Tytler's *Memoirs*, 1 152)   As a judge in the criminal Court, Lord Woodhouselee observes— "He has been censured by some for severity as a criminal judge, but he had no other severity than that which arises in a warm and ingenuous mind from the abhorrence of vice, from the hatred of crimes, and the zeal for their suppression" (*ibid* 11 2)   Lord Kames was one of the judges in the famous trial of Katharine Nairn and Patrick Ogilvie, in 1765, and upon that occasion introduced the practice, of charging the jury at the conclusion of the speech for the defence, a custom since then universal, but till then unknown   Alexander Lockhart (*q v.*), in stating a plea in arrest of judgment, cited an Act of the third session of the second Parliament of Charles II, article 10, "That, in all criminal pursuits the defender, or his advocates, be always the last speaker, except in case of treason and rebellion against the King", and proceeded to argue "That this statute notwithstanding, after the advocates for the pannels had concluded their speeches to the jury, and nothing remained, by the forms of Court, but to inclose that jury for the purpose of returning their verdict, one of the judges [Lord Kames] did address himself to the jury in a speech concerning this trial, and the credibility of particular witnesses, whereby the pannels were deprived of a legal and most material privilege, viz, the impression that must be left by the last pleader upon the minds of the jury in their behalf"   This objection, however, was overruled, together with divers others, even more singular to modern ideas, regarding the conduct of the jury in "dispersing, and drinking liquors, in what quantity and of what quality they please in private and while removed from the inspection of the Court," and also conversing in private with the Crown witnesses during the course of the trial

Ramsay records of Kames that "he did more to promote the interests of philosophy and *belles lettres* in Scotland than all the men of law had done for a century before" (*Ochtertyre MSS* 1 179)   "He was universally esteemed a man of great talents and taste, who thought and acted for himself   In fact, the ardour and industry with which he promoted the cultivation and improvement of polite literature and

345

Captain Porteous.

the useful arts in Scotland was almost apostolical   There were, indeed, few departments of literature or science in which he did not take an active concern " (*ibid* 1 195)   A complete catalogue of his lordship's numerous works will be found in *Kay's Portraits* (1877, vol 1, pp 15-16)

Among his lordship's many peculiarities, the quaintest was his notorious predilection for a certain epithet, unhearable by ears polite, which he freely employed on all occasions, and even upon the bench, where, certainly, it must have seemed incongruous   This singularity is noted by James Boswell in his diverting poem, *The Court of Session Garland* (1888, p 65)—

> *Alemoor the judgment as illegal blames,*
> *'Tis equity, you bitch, replies my Lord Kames,*
> *This cause, cries Hailes, to judge I can't pretend,*
> *For justice, I see, wants an e at the end*

Kames attended his judicial duties almost to the close of his existence, and at his last appearance, when the Court rose for the Christmas vacation, 1782, he took a separate and affectionate farewell of each of his learned brothers   On reaching the door, however, he turned round, and, bestowing a last look on his sorrowing brethren, made his exit, exclaiming, " Fare ye a' weel, ye bitches ! "   He survived that period only about eight days, and died on the 27th of December 1782, in the eighty-seventh year of his age   Lord Kames resided in the then fashionable New Street, occupying a self-contained house at the head of the street, facing the Canongate on the east side

ALEXANDER LOCKHART of Covington, Lord Covington (1699-1782), son of George Lockhart of Carnwath, and Lady Euphemia Montgomery, daughter of the Earl of Eglinton, and grandson of Sir George Lockhart, President of the Court of Session, one of the greatest lawyers in an age of great lawyers, was born in 1699. Lockhart passed as an advocate on 20th January, 1722   It is said that after being called to the bar he was so fond of pleasure and play that his friends gave him up as lost. To diminish their hopes, he married a beautiful woman for love, without a fortune, which made them to be called " the handsome beggars "   Much to his credit, however, soon after taking that step, he began to give close application to business, which was the only thing wanting to ensure him success   He obtained an extensive practice at the bar and, with his friend, Ferguson of Pitfour, made a very distinguished figure at the trials of several of the unfortunate prisoners at Carlisle, after the Rising of 1745, acting as voluntary counsel in their behalf. The honourable office of Dean of the Faculty of Advocates was conferred on him by the unanimous suffrages of his brethren, on the 15th June, 1764, which he held till his elevation to the bench   After practising as an advocate for upwards of half a century, he was appointed successor to Alexander Fraser of Strichen, and took his seat by the title of Lord Covington, on the 10th March, 1775, and died on the 10th November, 1782, in the eighty-second year of his age   Lord Newton, when an advocate, continued to wear the gown of Lockhart, Lord Covington, till it was in tatters, and at last had a new one made, with a fragment of the neck of the original sewed into it, whereby he could still make it his boast that he wore " Covington's gown "   In that amusing *jeu d'esprit*, *The Court of Session Garland* (1888, p 65), Boswell thus commemorates Lockhart's forensic ability.—

> *The answer by Lockhart himself it was wrote,*
> *And in it no argument or fact was forgot;*
> *He is the lawyer that from no cause will flinch,*
> *And on this occasion divided the bench.*

Appendix XVI.

" When I began to attend the Parliament House in 1753," says Ramsay, " this gentleman was in the zenith of his fame   In every cause of consequence people flocked to hear him plead but his *forte* seemed to lie in demolishing or underpropping character by means of a train of circumstances nicely arranged   It was alleged, however, that his zeal for his clients made him sometimes lose sight of candour and good nature   He not only spoke with more fire than most of his brother advocates, but frequently accompanied his perorations with tears, and that sometimes in cases where there seemed little room for the pathetic   But, though he had vast business in the Court of Session, it was in addressing juries in the Courts of Justiciary and Exchequor that his eloquence was most powerful and formidable   For a number of years he stood constantly opposed to the Crown lawyers in every great trial, and the ablest of them scrupled not to confess his abilities and resources   He never failed to shine exceedingly in a very long trial, when defending criminals whose case appeared to be desperate   Mr Crosbie told me soon after that in the trial of the Ogilvies, which lasted 48 hours, Lockhart stood the fatigue better than the youngest of them   He took down every deposition with his own hands, but no short ones, when he went out to take a little air   In answering Lord Advocate Millar, who was perfectly worn out, he displayed such powers of eloquence and ingenuity as astonished everybody   To save the life of his unhappy client he gave up, with great art, her character , but contended there was no legal proof of her *guilt*, though enough to damn her fame " (*Ochtertyre MSS* 1 133-4)

The trial referred to is that of Katharine Nairn and Patrick Ogilvie, in 1765, one of the most interesting and remarkable in the criminal annals of Scotland   This lady, who was a daughter of Sir Thomas Nairn of Dunsinnan, Baronet, had married in her nineteenth year, Thomas Ogilvie of Eastmiln, Forfarshire, a gentleman of more than double her age   The marriage took place on 30th January, 1765, on 6th June the husband died with mysterious suddenness, and on 5th August his wife and young brother, Patrick, were indicted for murdering him by poison, and also for having carried on a criminous intrigue together   Lockhart conducted the lady's defence, while the celebrated Andrew Crosbie—the prototype of Scott's " Counsellor Pleydell " in *Guy Mannering*—appeared for Lieutenant Ogilvie   Both pannels were found guilty, and the lieutenant, protesting his innocence to the last, was executed in the Grassmarket on 13th November   In the case of Katharine, sentence was delayed in consequence of her alleged pregnancy, and on 15th March, 1766, a fortnight after her accouchement, she escaped from the Tolbooth, disguised in the garments of the midwife who attended her, to the house in the Parliament Stairs belonging to her uncle, Sir William Nairn, advocate, afterwards Lord Dunsinnan, whose clerk accompanied her to Dover from whence she reached the Continent in safety   Her subsequent career like that of Madeleine Smith, is " wrop' in mystery "   In one account she is said to have gone to America, where she married, and died at an advanced age, surrounded by a numerous family, while another states that she retired to a French convent and ended her days in the odour of sanctity

JAMES LESLIE of Milndeans, advocate (died 1761), was the fourth son of John eighth Earl of Rothes   He was admitted a member of the Faculty of Advocates on 2nd July, 1726   He was subsequently nominated Commissary of Edinburgh, and received the appointment of Sheriff-Depute of Fife in 1748   He also held the post of Solicitor of Exchequer, which office he resigned in 1757   Leslie died on 24th September, 1761

Captain Porteous.

JAMES HOLBURNE, younger of Menstrie, advocate (died 1758), was the eldest son of Sir James Holburne of Menstrie, Clackmannanshire, first Baronet, and a brother of Admiral Francis Holburne (1704-1771). He was admitted a member of the Faculty of Advocates on 20th February, 1714. Holburne held the office of Examiner in Exchequer He died at Penicuik, Midlothian, on 26th July, 1758

IV —Other Persons

JOHN CAMPBELL, Duke of Argyll and Duke of Greenwich (1678-1743), eldest son of Archibald, tenth Earl, afterwards first Duke of Argyll, and of Lady Elisabeth Talmash, was born on 10th October, 1678 He met with a miraculous preservation on the day his grandfather was beheaded, 30th June, 1685 having fallen from a window three stories high, in Lethington House, the seat of his grandmother, in the county of Haddington, without having received any material injury. He was destined for a military career, and in 1694 William of Orange gave him the command of a regiment of foot He succeeded his father as second Duke of Argyll in 1703, and also as one of the Extraordinary Lords of Session, on the 20th of June, 1705, which office he resigned to his brother, the Earl of Ilay (q v), in 1708 In 1705 he was nominated Lord High Commissioner to the Scottish Parliament, which he opened on 25th June with a speech strongly in favour of the Union with England, and mainly through his influence the Act was passed, on 1st September, for a treaty with England to that effect For his services in promoting the Union he was, on his return to London, created Baron Chatham and Earl of Greenwich It may be justly remarked of his lordship that there are few who have signalised themselves more, either in the field or the Cabinet, and he fully realised what a contemporary said of him—" His family will not lose in his person the great figure they have made for so many ages in that kingdom (Scotland) having all the free spirit and good sense natural to the family Few of his years have a better understanding or a more manly behaviour He hath seen most of the Courts of Europe, is very handsome in appearance, fair complexioned, about twenty-five years old " (Mackay's *Secret Memoirs*, p 189) He commanded under Marlborough at the battles of Ramilies (1706), Oudenarde (1708), and Malplaquet (1709) After the peace of Utrecht, in 1712, he was appointed Commander-in-Chief of the Forces in Scotland and Governor of Edinburgh Castle He opposed the imposition of the Malt Tax on Scotland, and became a strong supporter of the motion, in June, 1713 for the dissolution of the Union He was entrusted with the task of crushing the Jacobite rising of 1715, and commanded at the battle of Sheriffmuir and his great services in that connection were later recognised by his being advanced to the dignity of Duke of Greenwich In his subsequent political career, it is admitted even by his opponents that " what he aimed and designed, he owned and promoted above board, being altogether free of the least share of dissimulation, and his word so sacred that one might assuredly depend on it " (*Lockhart Papers*, ii 10) His defence of the city of Edinburgh in 1737, in connection with the affair of the Porteous mob did much to strengthen his reputation in Scotland Scott says of him—" This nobleman was very dear to his countrymen, who were justly proud of his military and political talents, and grateful for the ready zeal with which he asserted the rights of his native country " (*Heart of Midlothian*, Note xv)

After a most active and eventful life, both in the State and in the camp, his Grace died at Sudbrook, in Surrey, on 4th October, 1743,

Appendix XVI.

in the sixty-fifth year of his age, and was succeeded by his brother,
Lord Ilay A brief but eloquent description is given of him by Pope,
in the following couplet.—

Argyll, the State's whole thunder born to wield,
And shake alike the senate and the field

For an account of Argyll's brilliant career, see Robert Campbell's
*Life of the Most Illustrious Prince, John, Duke of Argyll and
Greenwich,* 1745

ARCHIBALD CAMPBELL, Earl of Ilay, afterwards third Duke of
Argyll (1682-1761), second son of Archibald, tenth Earl, and first Duke
of Argyll, and of Lady Elisabeth Talmash, was born at Ham, in
Surrey, in June, 1682   He was educated at Eton till he was seventeen
years of age, when he was sent to the University of Glasgow   Intending
to make the law his profession, he went to Utrecht, where he attained
to considerable proficiency in the study of the civil law, but upon his
father being elevated to the dukedom, he changed his mind, and chose
a military life   Entering the army, he served under Marlborough,
and was appointed colonel of the 30th regiment of foot, and governor
of Dumbarton Castle   Deeming himself better fitted for a statesman
than a soldier, he quitted the army, and assiduously applied himself
to the study of political knowledge   In 1705 he was constituted Lord
High Treasurer of Scotland, and, in the following year, named one
of the Commissioners for the Union, and, on the 19th of October the
same year, was created Earl and Viscount of Ilay, &c   After the
conclusion of the treaty, he was chosen one of the sixteen peers of
Scotland, and sat in Parliament till his death
   At the resignation of his brother, John, second Duke of Argyll (q v),
he was appointed an Extraordinary Lord of Session, and took his seat
on 1st June, 1708, and, on the resignation of the Earl of Cromarty in
1710, he was constituted Lord Justice-General of Scotland, and was
also called to the Privy Council   On the accession of George the First,
he was nominated Lord Clerk-Register of Scotland   When the Rising
broke out in 1715, his lordship again betook himself to arms, and
was present at the battle of Sheriffmuir, where he received two wounds
During the riots in Scotland on account of the Malt Tax, he was
despatched, with full powers, by the Government to Edinburgh, where,
by his spirit and zeal he soon put an end to the combinations formed
at that period   After the execution of Captain Porteous by the mob,
he was sent to Edinburgh by Sir Robert Walpole to adopt measures
for bringing the offenders to justice   He gained the entire confidence
of Walpole, who committed the affairs of Scotland entirely to his
charge, which he managed with such great ability and prudence as to
gain him the appellation of King of Scotland   Lord Ilay succeeded
his brother as Duke of Argyll in 1743   Of his practical sagacity he
gave proof of the highest kind after the Jacobite Rising of 1745,
when he recommended, as a means of pacifying the Highlands, the
formation of the Highland regiments, thus affording scope for the
warlike propensities of the clans in the loyal service of the Crown
His action in presiding as Lord Justice-General at the trial   in
September, 1752, of James Stewart of the Glen, for the murder of
Colin Campbell of Glenure, was a grave judicial scandal, and his
conduct on that occasion has left an indelible stain upon his memory
In his later years he rebuilt the castle of Inveraray, and possessed a
very valuable library, said to be one of the finest private collections
in Great Britain   He died at London on 15th April, 1761 in the
seventy-ninth year of his age   An interesting account of a visit paid
by Dr Carlyle to the Duke at Inveraray, in 1758, is given in his
Autobiography, pp 378 *et seq*

Captain Porteous.

JAMES ERSKINE of Grange, Lord Justice-Clerk (1679-1754), second son of Charles, tenth Earl of Mar and of Lady Mary Maule, eldest daughter of George, second Earl of Panmure, was born in 1679, and was admitted an advocate on 28th July, 1705 His advancement was very rapid, for in less than two years after his admission, he was elevated to the bench, having been appointed successor to Sir Archibald Hope of Rankeillor, on 18th October, 1706 He took his seat, with the title of Lord Grange, on 18th March, 1707, was nominated a Lord of Justiciary in place of Lord Crossrig on 6th June the same year, and, on 27th July, 1710, succeeded Adam Cockburn of Ormiston as Lord Justice-Clerk   Though professing rigid piety, strict Presbyterian principles, and loyalty to the Hanoverian succession, he kept up a connection, as close as it was obscure with the opposite party and especially with his brother, the Earl of Mar He was intimate with and much esteemed by Wodrow, who reckons him "among the greatest men in his time, and would fain hope the calumnies cast on him are very groundless," a pious aspiration which receives no countenance from history

Lord Grange entered deeply and darkly into the politics of his day, and perhaps, deeming the bench too confined a station for his intriguing abilities, and having, at the same time, a wish to join with the opposition to Walpole's administration, to whom he had contracted a violent aversion, he, by intrigue and hypocrisy, secured his election to represent the Stirling district of burghs in Parliament Sir Robert Walpole was the means of getting the statute of 1734, incapacitating judges from being members of Parliament, passed into law, chiefly with a view of excluding Lord Grange from the House of Commons Grange, however, was bent on his purpose, and, in order to qualify himself, resigned his offices in the Courts of Session and Justiciary, and joined the opposition against Walpole He was unable to unseat that veteran statesman, and was, consequently, disappointed in being made Secretary of State for Scotland, to which he had also looked forward With Dundas of Arniston, he was one of the principal advisers of the peers of the Opposition in 1734, and in 1736 he, being learned in dæmonologia, with books on which subject his library was filled, vehemently opposed the abolition of the statutes against witchcraft, known as "The Witches Bill" Walpole is said to have declared that from that moment he had nothing to fear from him He also took an active part in opposing the Porteous Riot Bill

Grange again appeared in the Court as an advocate, but in a short time relinquished his practice and retired from the bar He died at London on 20th January, 1754, in the seventy-fifth year of his age, and, it is recorded, in poverty and obscurity Grange was married to Rachael Chiesley, daughter of John Chiesley of Dalry, who murdered Lord President Lockhart in the High Street of Edinburgh in 1689, for deciding that he was bound to support his wife A curious account of the abduction and confinement of Lady Grange in the Western Isles, by her husband and his unscrupulous accomplice Lord Lovat, for political reasons, will be found in the *Edinburgh Magazine*, 1817, i 333-339 See also, for this extraordinary story, Hill Burton's *Life of Simon, Lord Lovat*, 1847, pp 187-192, and *Autobiography of the Reverend Dr Alexander Carlyle*, 1861 pp 7-16

Grange kept a diary, since edited and published by Maidment, entitled *Diary of a Senator of the College of Justice, 1717-1718* (Edinburgh, 1843)   The following is an interesting extract —" I have reason to thank God that I was put out from the office of Justice-Clerk, for, besides many reasons from the times and my own circumstances, and other reasons from myself, this one is sufficient—that I

Appendix XVI.

have thereby so much more time to employ about God and religion If I consider how very much more I have since I was neither concerned in the Court of Justiciary, nor in the politics, how can I answer for the little advances I have made in the knowledge of religion? If, while I have that leisure I be enabled through grace to improve it for that end, I need not grudge the want of the £400 sterling yearly, for this is worth all the world, and God can provide for my family in his own good time and way "

His character exhibits a curious combination of cant, superstition, and licentiousness "Lord Grange," says Chambers, "was one of those singular men who contrive to cherish and act out the most intense religious convictions, to appear as zealous leaders in church judicatories, and stand as shining lights before the world, while yet tainted with the most atrocious secret vices" (*Domestic Annals of Scotland*, iii 579)

PATRICK LINDSAY, Lord Provost of Edinburgh and member of Parliament for that city (died 1753), was a cadet of the family of Lindsay of Kirkforthar, Fifeshire His grandfather was a joiner in St Andrews, and his father, Patrick Lindsay, was Rector of the Grammar School there Lindsay served as an officer with Sir Robert Riche's regiment in Spain, until, in 1713, he returned to Scotland after the Peace of Utrecht. Having settled in Edinburgh, where he established himself in business as an upholsterer, he entered the Town Council, and was appointed Bailie in 1721, Senior Magistrate in 1724, and Dean of Guild in 1726-7 In 1728 his shop was broken into by thieves, who murdered his apprentice (*Private Letters, chiefly to Robert Wodrow*, 1694-1732, pp 64-5, 1829) In 1729 30 he acted as Lord Provost of Edinburgh, an office which he again occupied in 1733-4, and in the latter year he was elected member of Parliament for the city, which he continued to represent until 1741 On retiring from his Parliamentary duties, he was appointed by the Duke of Atholl Governor of the Isle of Man, and held that post till shortly before his death

On the night of the Porteous Mob, 7th September, 1736, Lindsay was despatched by the magistrates with a verbal message for aid to General Moyle, commanding the Welsh Fusiliers, stationed in the Canongate, in which embassy he was unsuccessful Later, Lindsay was one of the witnesses in the House of Lords enquiry into the circumstances of the riot, and took a prominent part in opposing in the Commons the Bill of Pains and Penalties directed against Provost Wilson and the city of Edinburgh

Lindsay was thrice married By his first wife, a daughter of David Montier, merchant in Edinburgh, he had three sons and two daughters; by his second, Janet, daughter of James Murray of Polton, and his third, Catherine Lindsay, daughter of William, fifteenth Earl of Crawfurd, he had no issue

Lindsay was the author of a pamphlet entitled *The Interest of Scotland, considered with regard to Its Police in employing of the Poor, Its Agriculture, Its Trade, Its Manufactures, and Fisheries* Edinburgh, 1733 He died in the Canongate on 20th February, 1753.

Captain Porteous.

Bibliography.

I Contemporary Tracts

1 The Last | Speech | And | Dying Words | Of | Andrew
Wilson, | Who was execute in the Grass-market of Edinburgh, on
the 14th Day of | April 1736 for the Crime of Robbery | Edin-
burgh, | Printed and Sold in the middle of Forrester's | Wynd
Folio, Broadsheet

2. Edin 15. April 1736. | A List of the Persons that were killed
and wounded in the Grass-market of | Edinburgh, on the 14 April
1736, after the Execution of Andrew Wilson
Quarto, Broadsheet

3 Sept 13, 1736 | A Full | Account | Of the Proceedings of
the Mobb that happened in | Edinburgh the 7th Instant, and the
Way and Man- | ner of their hanging Captain John Porteous
Quarto, Broadsheet, printed on both sides

4. The | Trial | Of | Capt John Porteous, | Before The | High
Criminal Court, | Or | Lords of Justiciary, | In | Scotland |
[*Ornament*] | London | Printed for T. Cooper, at the Globe in
Pater- | noster Row   MDCCXXXVI | (Price Sixpence)
8vo pp 48, consisting of title, verso blank , (1) Indictment, (2)
Interlocutor on Relevancy, (3) Assize, (4) Pannel's Judicial Confession, (5) Depositions of Witnesses, (6) Verdict, (7) Sentence,
pp 3-45 ; p [46] blank , p [47], containing the following
Publisher's Note —"In a few Days will be published, The Information for his Majesty's Advocate, for his Highness's Interest,
against Captain Porteous , and also the Information in behalf of
Porteous, in Answer thereto   Being the Pleadings on both sides.
Together with the Petition which was presented to Her Majesty,
in behalf of Porteous, for a Pardon   With a full and particular
Account of the Method taken by the Mob in executing him, more
authentic than any yet published , several very material Circumstances being omitted in the former Accounts   (This, with the
Trial now published, will give the Publick all the Satisfaction
they can expect, in this surprizing Affair)"; p [48] blank

5. The | Information | For | His Majesty's Advocate, for His |
Highness's Interest , | Against | Captain Porteous , | And Also |
The Information in be- | half of Porteous, in answer thereto |
Being the Pleadings on both Sides | Together with the Petition

Appendix XVII.

which was | presented to Her Majesty, in be- | half of Porteous, for a Pardon | With a full and particular Account of the Me- | thod taken by the Mob in executing him, more | authentic than any yet published | [*Ornament*] | London | Printed for T Cooper, at the Globe in Pater- | noster Row. MDCCXXXVI | (Price One Shilling)

8vo pp 69.

Has a Note at end —" [This, with the Trial just published, will give the Publick all the Satisfaction they can expect, in this surprizing Affair]"

6 The | Genuine Tryal | Of | Capt John Porteous, | Before The | High Criminal Court, | Or The | Lords of Justiciary, | In | Scotland, | For | Firing his own Piece, and ordering the Men under his Command to | fire amongst the Spectators, at the Execution of Andrew Wil- | son, in the Grass-Market of Edinburgh, the 14th of April, 1736 | By which six Persons were kill'd, viz, Charles Husband, Archibald | Ballantyne, John Anderson, Alexander Macneil, Margaret Gordon, | and Henry Graham | And eleven Persons dangerously wounded, viz., Margaret Arthur, | Jane Peat, David Wallace, James Philp, David Kidd, Patrick | Spalding, James Lyle, Alexander Wallace, John Miller, David | Ogilvie, and James Nivan. | Containing | 1 The Libel or Indict- ment of his Majesty's Solicitor General against Porteous. 2 Interlocutor, or Judgment of the said Lords on the 6th July, 1736, upon it 3 The Names of the Assize or Petit-Jury 4. The Prisoner's judicial Confession 5. The Information for his Majesty's Advocate, for his Highness's Interest, against Captain Porteous, on July 12th, 1736 6 The Information of the Council, or Advocates for the said Captain Porteous, on the 13th July, 1736. N B —These contain the curious and learned Pleadings of Council of both sides, according to the Civil, Muni- cipal, and Common Law of all Nations in such Cases 7 The particular Depositions and Examinations of twenty-six Witnesses, adduced upon the 19th of July, 1736, by his Majesty's Advocate or Attorney-General, for proving the Libel 8 The Depositions and Examinations of the sixteen Witnesses adduc'd by the Council for the Prisoner 9. Verdict return'd by the aforesaid Jury, the 20th July, 1736. 10 The Sentence pronounc'd by the Lords upon the Jury's returning this Verdict 11 The Petition of Captain Porteous presented to her Majesty Queen Caroline, Guardian of these Realms, for Mercy 12 A full and true Account of the Mobb's executing him the 7th of September, 1736 More Authentick than any yet publish'd | The Second Edition | London | Printed for T Cooper, at the Globe, in Pater-Noster Row | MDCCXXXVI (Price 1 s 6 d)

8vo. pp. 46, and 70, consisting of title, verso blank, Indict- ment, &c (reprinted from No. 4), pp 3-45, p [46] blank;

Captain Porteous.

Informations, &c (No 5, with the title and note at end omitted), pp [1]-69 , p [70] blank   The Contents on the title-page are in two columns of twenty and twenty-one lines respectively

In a bookseller's catalogue issued in 1897 there appeared Tryal before the Lords of Justiciary   *Stamford, F   Howgrave.* 1736.   No copy of this has been seen

7. The | Trial | of | Capt John Porteous, | Before The | High Criminal Court, | Or | Lords of Justiciary, | In | Scotland , | For | Wounding and Killing several Per- | sons at a late Execution of a Criminal, in the | Grass-Market at Edinburgh, by Firing and order- | ing his Men to Fire on the Spectators | Newcastle upon Tyne | Printed and Sold by John White. Sold also | by the Booksellers of Newcastle and Durham | (Price Three-Pence)
8vo pp 32
A reprint of No 4

8. The | Tinklarian Doctor's | Twenty-first Epistle, | Which contains three new Lights, | concerning Captain *Porteous*, two | of these great Lights was written | in his Life-time, the other after his Death | Written in the 66 Year of his Age | I dedicate this wonderful Epistle to their | Majesty's, both to the King and to the | Queen, I know their Majesty's will under- | stand it, because their Majesty's gave me | two Guineas for my Light, before their | Majesty's was set on the Throne   *Long | may their Majesty's live   and well may their Majesty's prosper,* is the Prayer of | William Mitchell. | Printed in the Year 1736
8vo pp 12

9 Act of the Town-council of Edinburgh, appointing the | Apprentices and Servants of the Freemen of said City, who have deserted their Service at, or | since the 7th September 1736, to return thereto in a limited Time. | At Edinburgh the nineteenth Day of January One thousand seven hundred and thirty-seven Years
Folio, Broadsheet

10 Authentick Extract | Of The | Proceedings | In The | Trial | Of | Capt John Porteous, | Laid | Before the House by the Duke of | Newcastle, March the 3d, 1736 [ie Old Style.] | London | Printed by John Baskett, Printer to the King's | Most Excellent Majesty   1737
Folio, pp. 68
The official record of the trial, printed by order of Parliament from the Books of Adjournal of the High Court of Justiciary at Edinburgh, 25th March, 1737

11 Act of the Town-Council of Edinburgh, settling | and determining the Places at which the Merchants and Craftsmen
354

Appendix XVII.

are to | assemble themselves, on the Appearance of any Mob or Disorder.

Folio, Broadsheet

Dated at Edinburgh, 3rd August, 1737.

12 Edinburgh, 31st August, 1737 | Act of Council | Against | Throwing Stones, &c., at the Execution of | Criminals.

Folio, Broadsheet

13 The | Life and Death | Of | Captain John Porteous; | Containing | The following curious Particulars, never before Printed, viz | I. His Birth, Education, and Adventures in his Youth | II His Behaviour when in Flanders | III His Conduct, while Captain of the Town-Guard of Edin- | burgh | IV Some remarkable Circumstances, which preceded his | Murder | V His personal and moral Character | VI An impartial and full Account (not to be met with else- | where) of the Debates in P——t upon the | Two Bills relating to his Murder, with the Charac- | ters of the Principal Speakers, and of the late Lord Pro- | vost of Edinburgh | VII. Remarks on the present Dispositions of the People and | Clergy of Scotland | To which is added | A Letter containing some further Remarks | [*Quotation*] | Edinburgh · Printed and sold by J Wilford, behind | the Chapter-House, in St Paul's Church-Yard, and by the | Booksellers in Town and Country, MDCCXXXVII | (Price One Shilling)

8vo pp. 48. consisting of title, verso blank, Six unnumbered leaves, and Text, pp [3]-48. The imprint is correctly given

One copy noted has a second title-page, presumably cancelled, as follows :—The | Life and Death | Of | Captain John Porteous, | With an Account of the | Debates in Parliament | Upon The | Two Bills | Concerning his Murder, | Also many curious Particulars relating to the | said Murder, never before published | [*Quotations*] | [*Ornament*] | Printed in the Year MDCCXXXVII.

14. The | Life and Death | Of | Captain John Porteous, | With an Account of the | Two Bills, | As they were reasoned in both | Houses of Parliament, | And The | Speeches of the Great Men | on both Sides concerning them | [*Quotations*] | [*Ornament*] | Printed in the Year MDCCXXXVII

8vo pp 96

A reprint of No 13, with additional particulars of the proceedings in Parliament anent the Edinburgh Bills

15 [Acts] Anno Regni | Georgii II. | Regis | Magnæ Britanniæ, Franciæ, & Hiberniæ, Decimo | At the Parliament begun and holden at Westminster, | the Fourteenth Day of January, Anno Dom 1734. | In the Eighth Year of the Reign of our Sovereign | Lord George the Second, by the Grace of | God, of Great Britain, France, and Ireland, King, | Defender of the Faith, &c | And

355

Captain Porteous.

from thence continued by several Prorogations to the First | Day of February, 1736, being the Third Session of this present | Parliament. | [*Royal Arms*] | London, | Printed by John Baskett, Printer to the King's most | Excellent Majesty 1737.

Folio, pp. 10 (577-586), consisting of Title, verso blank , *An Act to disable Alexander Wilson Esquire* . pp 579-80, second title, as above, verso blank , *An Act for the more effectual bringing to Justice* . pp 583-6

Printed in Black Letter   From the Acts of Parliament

16 [Acts | For | Disabling Alexander Wilson Esq , from | being Lord Provost of Edinburgh | And | for bringing to Justice the Murderers | of Captain John Porteous]   Anno Regni | Georgii II..... (as in No 15) | Edinburgh, | Printed by James Blair and John Nairn, His Majesty's Prin- | ters, and Sold at their Printing-House at the Foot of Craig's | Closs   MDCXXXXVII [*sic*]

8vo pp 7, and 9   Second title   Anno Regni Georgii II   . MDCCXXXVII

A reprint of No. 15

17 [Act | For | Bringing to Justice the Murderers of | Captain John Porteous] | Anno Regni | Georgii II.   (as in No 15) | Edinburgh, | Printed by James Blair and John Nairn, His Majesty's Printers, and | sold in their Printing-house at the Foot of Craig's Closs   MDCCXXXVII.

8vo pp 9

Reprinted from No 15.

18 Reasons | Against The | Bill | Before The | House of Lords, | (For Disabling the Lord Provost of the City | of Edin-burgh, to hold any Office of Ma- | gistracy, and for Fining the said City in | £ 2000 Sterling) | Chiefly with regard to the said City and Citizens. | [*Ornament*] | London | Printed by S. Osborn, and Sold by the Book- | sellers of London and Westminster   1737 (Price Six-pence)

8vo. pp 22

By James Erskine of Grange

19. A | Memorial | For The | People of Scotland, | Or | Some brief Animadversions on the In- | famous Act | Of The | British Parliament , | Unjustly imposed on the Ministers and | People in this Land, on the seventh of | August 1737 | With a brief account of the Life of John | Porteous | [*Ornament*] | Dublin, Printed in the Year 1737

8vo pp 16

20 A | Letter | Published in the Weekly Paper, | Called | The Old Whig, | Concerning the Bill, intituled, | An Act to disable Alexander Wilson, Esq; | from taking, holding or enjoying any

Appendix XVII.

Office or | Place of Magistracy in the City of Edinburgh, or | else-where in Great Britain, and for imprisoning | the said Alexander Wilson, and for abolish- | ing the Guard kept up in the said City, called the | Town Guard and for taking away the Gates of | the Nether-Bow Port of the said City, and keep- | ing open the same | [*Ornament*] | Edinburgh | Printed in the Year MDCCXXXVII. | (Price One Penny.)

8vo pp. 8

21. A Second Letter   [As in No 20]
8vo pp 7

22. A Third Letter . [As in No 20.]
8vo pp. 7

23. A Fourth Letter . . [As in No. 20.]
8vo pp 7

24 A Surprising | Conversation | Of A | Highlander | Who has the | Second-Sight, | And some others, | With an Indian Bramin, | About | Captain John Porteous. | The | Speeches of the honourable Members of | the House of Commons, for and against | the Two Bills, before they were turn'd into | an Act | With The | Addition of many curious Things, where the | Reader may observe the Fate of many a Family | in Scotland | . Terent. [*Quotation*] | [*Ornament*] | Printed in the Year MDCCXXXVII.

8vo pp 94

25 Queries | Offered to the Publick, by a Well-wisher of | the present Constitution in Church and | State
8vo pp 7 Title heading No imprint By Joseph Brodie, Painter, Edinburgh.

26 Answers to the | Queries, &c , | By a sincere Well-wisher of the Pro- | testant Interest, and Clergy of | this Kingdom.
8vo. pp 20 Title heading No imprint. By Patrick Lindsay, M.P

27. A Few | Observations | Upon | A Pamphlet, intituled, Answers to the | Queries, &c , and published Saturday 6th | August 1737
8vo pp 7 Title heading No imprint By Joseph Brodie.

28 A | Letter | To The | Learned Author of the Queries, | Being | A Detection of several Errors and Heresies, | contain'd in a Pamphlet, entituled, An- | swers to the Queries | Milton's Paradise Lost [*Quotation*] | Edinburgh, Printed in the Year 1737
8vo. pp 43
By Patrick Lindsay

Captain Porteous.

29 The | Letter | To The Learned | Author of the Queries, |
Unmasked | Presented to the Review of the Author. | Le
Repos, an Epistle to the Publick   [*Quotation*] | Edinburgh, |
Printed in the Year MDCCXXXVII
    8vo pp 34
    By Robert Wallace, minister of New Greyfriars Church.

30 The | Clergy's Plea | of | Conscience | considered, | In an
Address to the Author of a Pamphlet, | intitled, | The Letter to
the learn'd Author of the | Queries unmasked | By the Author
of that Letter | *Tuantum Relligio potuit suadere Malorum* |
[*Ornament*] | *Quam honesta voluntate miseri errant* | Edinburgh,
Printed in the Year 1737
    8vo pp 64   With a plate

31. A | Letter | from | a Minister in the Country, | to | One
in the City | 3 John, Ver 12, Demetrius hath good Report of
all | Men, and of the Truth itself | [K—— 12th October, 1737] |
[*Ornament*] | Printed in the Year MDCCXXXVII
    8vo pp 1-16
    The only copy available for collation, that in the British
Museum, is imperfect, wanting all after p 16

32 A | Letter | From A | Layman in the Country, | To, &c |
Concerning the Act of Parliament, | for bringing to Justice the
Murderers of | Captain John Porteous | . Tit. 3 Ch 1 Ver.
[*Quoted*] | [*Ornament*] | Printed in the Year MDCCXXXVII
    8vo pp 36
    By Alexander Webster, minister of the Tolbooth Kirk

33 The | Lawfulness | And | Necessity | Of | Ministers their
reading the | Act of Parliament, | For bringing to Justice the
Murderers of Cap- | tain John Porteous | [Matth x 10   1 Cor
x 15   Tit iii 1   Deut. xxi 18-21. *quoted*] | Edinburgh |
Printed and sold at most Booksellers Shops in Town, 1737.
    8vo pp 49
    By George Logan, minister of Trinity College Kirk

34 A | Letter | From A | Gentleman at Edinburgh, | To A |
Minister in the Country, | Containing | An Account of the Sub-
stance | of the late Conferences of Ministers at | Edinburgh,
concerning the Act of Parli- | ament for bringing to Justice the
Mur- | derers of Captain John Porteous | [*Ornament*] | Edin-
burgh | Printed . and sold by most Booksellers in Town   1737
    8vo pp 40.
    By William Grant, Advocate, afterwards Lord Prestongrange.

35 A | Letter | To The | Author of a Pamphlet, | Intituled, |
The Lawfulness and Necessity of Min- | isters their reading the
Act of Parlia- | ment for bringing to Justice the Mur- | derers of |

Appendix XVII.

Captain John Porteous | [Rom xiv 5, 10, 22 *quoted*] | [*Ornament*] | Edinburgh, | Printed and Sold by most Booksellers in Town | MDCCXXXVII

8vo pp 35.

By George Wishart, Minister of the Tron Kirk

36 A | Defence | Of The | Layman's Letter, | In | Answer | To The | Lawfulness and Necessity, &c | With | Some Observations upon a Let- | ter from a Gentleman at Edin- | burgh to a Minister in the Country | . Rom xiv 22 [*Quotation*] | [*Ornament*] | Edinburgh | Printed, and sold by most Booksellers in Town 1737.

8vo. pp 60

By Alexander Webster.

37 An | Answer | To A | Letter to the Author of | The Lawful-ness and Necessity, &c | And To The | Defence of the Layman's | Letter, in Answer to the said Author , | In A | Letter | To The | Authors of these Pamphlets | [Job vi 25 Prov. xxiv. 21-22 Rom xiii 1 *quoted*] | Edinburgh | Printed, and sold at most Booksellers Shops in Town. | (MDCCXXXVII)

8vo pp 64

By George Logan

38 Reasons | Why | Several Ministers | Of The | Church of Scotland | Did not read the Act of Parliament | relating to the Murderers of Ca- | ptain Porteous; Directed to the Au- | thor of the Reasons for reading | the said Act | [*Ornament*] | Edin-burgh, | Printed in the Year MDCCXXXVII.

8vo pp 8

By John Willamson Minister of Inveresk.

39 A | Letter | From A | Gentleman in the North, | To A | Minister, who has not intimated the Act | of Parliament, for the more effectual | bringing to Justice the Murderers of Captain | John Porteous | Occasioned | By two Pamphlets lately published , | The one enti- | tuled, A Letter from a Layman, &c The other, | Queries offered to the Publick. &c. | 1 Pet ii 17 [*Quotation*] | *Nec Tamen Consumebatur.* | Motto of the Ch. of Scot | Hoadly Ser. on Acts xii 22, 25 [*Quotation.*] | Printed in the Year, MDCCXXXVII

8vo pp 24

40 A | Conference | Between A | Modern Malcontent, | And A | Revolution Whig, | Concerning the Act for bringing | to Justice the Murderers of | Capt John Porteous, | And the present Disputes thereon | [*Ornament*] | Edinburgh, | Printed in the Year, MDCCXXXVII

8vo pp 35

Captain Porteous.

41. Some | Considerations | Concerning the | Difficulties | About Reading the | Act of Parliament | For bringing to Justice the Murderers of | Captain John Porteous | Search the Scriptures. John v 39 | [*Ornament.*] | Printed in the Year MDCCXXXVII | (Price Four Pence)

8vo pp. 39

42 Remarks | On The | Pamphlets lately published, | on Occasion of the late Act of | Parliament, for bringing to Ju- | stice the Murderers of Captain | John Porteous

8vo pp. 10

Refers to —(1) Queries offered to the Publick, &c (2) An untimely Birth, called Answers to the Queries (3) Observations on the Answers to the Queries, &c (4) A Letter from a Layman in the Country to &c (5) The Lawfulness and Necessity of Ministers, &c (6) A Letter to the Author of the Lawfulness, &c. (7) A Defence of the Laymans Letter, &c (8) A Clish Ma-claver Conference between a modern Malcontent, &c (9) Some Considerations concerning the Difficulties, &c (10) A Letter from a Gentleman at Edinburgh, &c (11) A Letter from a Gentleman in the North to &c. (12) A Letter to the learned Author of the Queries, &c. (13) The Letter to the learned Author of the Queries unmask'd (14) An Answer to the Letter to the Author of the Lawfulness, &c. (15) A silly Thing of an Address to the Clergy (16) A weak and wicked Memorial (17) Jenny Geddes, a scurrilous Ballad (18) The Flight of the timorous Clergyman to I——l——d. (19) The undetermin'd Clergyman's Journey on the first Sabbath of September to ——Well, which was at that Time impregnate with salutary Particles (20) The uncollegiate Clergyman's Lamentation (21) The North Country Clergyman's Apology for reading the Act, &c (22) The Conclusion, a poem

Prefixed to the Remarks is the following Advertisement.— " Lately published, and to be sold in most Booksellers Shops in Town, the following Pamphlets writ on Occasion of the *Act of Parliament, for the more effectual bringing to Justice the Murderers of Captain John Porteous,* whose Death brings to Mind the following Lines made on Cardinal Beaton's, and applied by an Historian of our own Time, to the Murder of Archbishop Sharp

> As for this Cardinal, I grant,
> He was a Man we might well want,
>   God will forgive it soon .
> But of a Truth the Sooth to say,
> Altho' the Loun be well away,
>   The fact was foully done "

A copy of this Pamphlet in the possession of Mr. William Cowan, Edinburgh, contains marginal notes in a contemporary hand of the author's names of the various tracts enumerated above, vizt —(1) Mr Joseph Brodie, Painter (2) Patrick Lindsay,

Appendix XVII.

Esq, late Provost of Edinburgh and Member of Parliament   (3)
Mr Joseph Brodie.   (4) Mr Alex Webster, Minr of the Tolbooth
Kirk, Edinburgh   (5) Mr Geo Logan, Minr. of the College
Kirk, Edinburgh   (6) Mr Geo Wishart.   (7) Mr Alex.
Webster.   (10) Mr Wm Grant, Solicitor, afterwards Ld
Prestongrange.   (12) Provost Lindsay   (14) Mr Geo. Logan
(15) R Freebairn   (18) Mr Pat. Cuming, Minr Old Kirk,
Edinr   (19) Mr Kinloch, Minr New Kirk, Edinburgh
(20) Mr. John Glen, Minr Haddo's hole Kirk, Edinr

43 Scribimus Indocti Doctique Poemata passim —Le Repos
An Epistle to the Publick.
  8vo. pp. 8
  Title heading   No title page.
  This poem contains the following note   " Pills in Prose—This
"refers to a scurrilous Piece lately published, called A Pill for
"the Clergy   A weak and wicked Memorial, &c.   An untimely
"Birth, called Answers to the Queries.   A silly Thing of An
"Address to the Clergy   The Necessity and Lawfulness, or a
"voluminous Performance full of Blunders in Law, Precedents
"misapplied, and Remarks foreign to the Purpose   An Exhortation
"to the Ministers, &c, and such like Productions, that have more
"Words than Sense "

44 Memoirs | Of The | Times, | In | A Letter to a Friend in |
the Country | Containing | An Account of, and Reflections on |
some late Remarkable Occurrences, such as, | The Tumult at
Edinburgh, the Present Disposi-| tion of the Inhabitants of
North Britain ; the | Consequences of putting in Execution the
Act for | Restraining the Sale of Spirituous Liquors, the |
Proceedings of Baron Neuhoff, with a View | of the Island of
Corsica, Conjectures on the | Designs of Spain, and the Prospect
of a General | Peace, Heads of Political Debates, Account of |
Dramatick Entertainments, Characters of New | Books, News
Papers, &c | Nec Laedere, nec Adulari | London | Printed for
Anne Dod, at the Peacock without | Temple-Bar | MDCCXXXVII |
Price One Shilling)
  8vo pp iv +56, and Postcript consisting of four unnumbered
leaves

45 The | Year of Wonders | Being A | Literal and Poetical
Translation | Of An Old | Latin Prophecy, | Found near Merlin's
Cave | By S——n D——k | Virg Eclog, Æneid [Quota-
tion] | [Ornament] London | Printed and Sold by J Johnson,
and the Booksellers of London | and Westminster   MDCCXXXVII.
  Quarto, pp 6
  Contains the following reference to the Porteous Mob —

  When from the North loud Discontents do blow,
  And Justice hangs Men up we know not how.

Captain Porteous.

46. A | Letter | Concerning the | Ministers in Scotland, | Their | Reading and Not Reading | The | Act for bringing to Justice those | Concerned in the Murder of | Capt Porteous | Which Act was passed in June 1737 | [*Ornament*] | London, | Printed for T Cooper, at the Globe in Pater- | Noster-Row, MDCCXXXVIII.

8vo pp 28   Half-title —A | Letter | Concerning the | Reading and Not Reading | the Act for bringing to Justice those | concerned in the Murder of | Capt Porteous | (Price Six-Pence)

47 A Letter to a Member of the | Town Council of Edinburgh
Folio, Broadsheet
A poem consisting of thirty-eight lines, beginning—

> *You know, dear Friend, and doubtless do lament*
> *The Town's Misfortune in the late Event.*

48 A Poem, occasioned by the Death of the Persons un- | fortunately killed and wounded in the Grass-Market | of Edinburgh, April 14, 1736   after the Execution of | Andrew Wilson | *Salus Populi suprema Lex*
Folio, Broadsheet
A poem consisting of six stanzas of 9, 8, 6, 12, 14 and 10 lines each, beginning—

> *Shall Innocence by fatal Rashness bleed,*
> *And shall the Muse unconscious view the Deed ?*

49 Captain Porteous's | Ghost, | Giving | An Account how he was dragged from the | Tolbooth of Edinburgh by the outragious Mob, and | hung up by the Neck like a Dog on a Dyster's | Tree instead of a Gallows, and how he was after- | wards raised out of his Grave, and made his Ap- | pearance at the Parliament of Great Britain, and | after various Debates and Consultations of both | Houses, how he was dismist to the Church of Scot- | land, with Orders to be received a Brother, and in- | vested with Holy Orders   Together with the va- | rious Debates and Reasonings of the Clergy at his | Arrival   In fine, how he was actually invested, and | received the Right Hand of Fellowship, and how | for some time he hath performed his sacred Fun- | ction , With many other pleasant Jests relating | thereunto , All in Elegiack Verse | [*Quotation*] | [*Ornament*] | Edinburgh | Printed in the year MDCCXXXVIII

8vo. pp. 16.

50 The | Examinations | Of The | Four Baillies | Of | Edinburgh, | For the Year 1737. | Before the House of Lords, | In The | Enquiry into the Murder | Of | Captn Porteous | [*Ornament*] | Edinburgh, | Printed in the Year MDCCXXXVIII

8vo. pp 36

362

Appendix XVII.

51 Copy | of the | Paper | called | Porteous's Roll, | Which was sent to the Ministers of Scotland, | to be read from the Pulpit of each of their | Churches, immediately before Public Wor- | ship, upon the first Sabbath of each Month, | for a whole Year | Which occasioned much Division and Dissension | in the Church of Scotland | Printed in the Year MDCCLXXVI

8vo. pp 8

52 Account of the cruel | Massacre | Committed by | John Porteous, | Captain of the City Guard of Edinburgh. | at the execution of Andrew Wilson | Merchant, upon the 14th of April, 1736 | Together with | The terrible execution of Captain John Por- | teous, on the 7th of September, 1736, in | the Gras-Market of Edinburgh, on a Sign | -post, about twelve o'clock at night. | [*Ornament*] | Printed in the year 1789

8vo. pp. 8

II. CONTEMPORARY NEWSPAPERS AND MAGAZINES

The Caledonian Mercury for 1736 and 1737

The Edinburgh Evening Courant for 1736 and 1737

The Gentleman's Magazine, Vol VI 1736.
Pp 230, 351, 422, 486, 514-522, 549-550, 618, 681

The London Magazine, Vol V 1736
Pp 217, 399, 458, 498-511, 520, 579.

The Gentleman's Magazine, Vol VII. 1737.
Pp 186-7. 251,296-8, 346-353, 363-4, 373-408, 448, 457-469, 514, 537 541, 605-610, 645-651, 701, 709-712, 803-830

The London Magazine, Vol VI 1737
Pp. 219, 254-6, 286-300, 302 4, 334-5, 548, 715-757.

III LATER AUTHORITIES

The Life of the Most Illustrious Prince John, Duke of Argyle and Greenwich, by Robert Campbell. London, 1745
Pp 304-320.

The History of Edinburgh from its Foundation to the Present Time, by William Maitland   Edinburgh, 1753
Pp 123-124.

Captain Porteous.

The Newgate Calendar, or Malefactors Bloody Register [etc] London, *n d* [1773]
    Vol III. 22-34

Arguments and Decisions in Remarkable Cases Before the High Court of Justiciary, and other Supreme Courts in Scotland, by John Maclaurin of Dreghorn   Edinburgh, 1774
    Pp, xxiv.-xxvi, 82-84, 633-645

The History of Edinburgh from the Earliest Accounts to the Present Time, by Hugo Arnot   Edinburgh, 1788
    Pp 205-210

Memoirs of the Life and Administration of Sir Robert Walpole, by William Coxe   London, 1798.
    Vol I 493-497, Vol. III. 360-369

The Beauties of Scotland, by Robert Forsyth   Edinburgh, 1805
    Vol I 233-237

A Treatise on Various Branches of the Criminal Law of Scotland, by James Burnett   Edinburgh, 1811
    Pp 5, 73 *n*

Cobbett's Parliamentary History of England   London, 1811.
    Vol. IX 1271-1311; Vol X. 187-319.

A Complete Collection of State Trials, compiled by T. B. Howell London, 1813
    Vol. XVII 923-1003

Criminal Trials, illustrative of the Tale entitled "The Heart of Mid-Lothian," published from the Original Record   Edinburgh, 1818

Commentaries on the Law of Scotland respecting Crimes, by David Hume   Edinburgh. 1819
    Vol I. 54, 204-208, 264, 418, 423, 518

Illustrations of the Author of Waverley, being Notices and Anecdotes of Real Characters, Scenes, and Incidents, supposed to be described in his Works   By Robert Chambers. Edinburgh, 1825.
    Pp 133-143

Celebrated Trials and Remarkable Cases of Criminal Jurisprudence, from the earliest records to the year 1825   London, 1825
    Vol IV. 261-277

Appendix XVII.

Traditions of Edinburgh, by Robert Chambers   Edinburgh, 1825
Vol I 142   Also edition 1869, pp. 65, 201.

A Series of Sketches of the Existing Localities alluded to in the Waverley Novels, etched from Original Drawings by James Skene of Rubislaw   Edinburgh, 1829
Pp 77-96

Tales of a Grandfather, being Stories taken from Scottish History, by Sir Walter Scott   Edinburgh, 1830.
Third Series, Vol II 156-180

The Heart of Mid-Lothian (Tales of My Landlord, Second Series), by Sir Walter Scott   Edinburgh, 1831
Waverley Novels, Vols XI and XII , with the Author's Notes

The Waverley Anecdotes, illustrative of the Incidents, Characters, and Scenery described in the Novels and Romances of Sir Walter Scott, Bart   London, 1833
Vol. II. 368-405.

Miscellany of the Maitland Club, consisting of Original Papers and Other Documents Illustrative of the History and Literature of Scotland   Edinburgh, 1840
Vol II Part 1 51-74

Lives of Simon, Lord Lovat and Duncan Forbes of Culloden, by John Hill Burton   London, 1847.
Pp 349-356.

Memorials of Edinburgh In the Olden Time, by Daniel Wilson   Edinburgh, 1848.
Vol I 109, 194-196, 211 , Vol II 209, 214

Autobiography of the Rev. Dr Alexander Carlyle, Minister of Inveresk, containing Memorials of the Men and Events of his Time   Edinburgh, 1861.
Pp 33-42

Domestic Annals of Scotland from the Revolution to the Rebellion of 1745, by Robert Chambers   Edinburgh, 1861
Vol III 566, 594-597, 600-601.

The History of Scotland, from Agricola's Invasion to the Extinction of the Last Jacobite Insurrection, by John Hill Burton   Edinburgh, 1873.
Vol VIII 359-367.

Captain Porteous.

A Series of Original Portraits and Caricature Etchings, by John Kay Edinburgh, 1877.
Vol I 19, Vol II 123, 186

Reminiscences of Old Edinburgh, by Sir Daniel Wilson   Edinburgh, 1878
Vol. I 234-235, Vol II. 79-91.

The Lord Advocates of Scotland from the close of the Fifteenth Century to the passing of the Reform Bill, by George W. T. Omond Edinburgh, 1883
Vol. I 350-355

Cassell's Old and New Edinburgh its History, its People, and its Places, by James Grant London, n d [1884]
Vol I. 4, 123, 128-131, 178, 218, 319, Vol. II. 231-232, Vol. III 84, 262-263

Etchings illustrative of Scottish Character and Scenery, by Walter Geikie (Sir Thomas Dick Lauder's Edition) Edinburgh, 1885.
Pp. 14-15

The True Story of the Porteous Riots, by A H Millar Dundee, *People's Journal*, June 11—August 13, 1887

The Porteous Riot, by George W. T. Omond *The Scottish Review*, July, 1892.
Vol. XX 52-67

The Heart of Mid-Lothian, Border Edition, edited by Andrew Lang. London, 1893
Vol I., Editor's Introduction and Notes.

The Social Life of Scotland in the Eighteenth Century, by Henry Grey Graham London, 1900
Vol II 102-103

A History of Scotland from the Roman Occupation, by Andrew Lang Edinburgh, 1907
Vol IV 304, 428-434

History of Scotland, by P Hume Brown Cambridge, 1909.
Vol III 218-227.

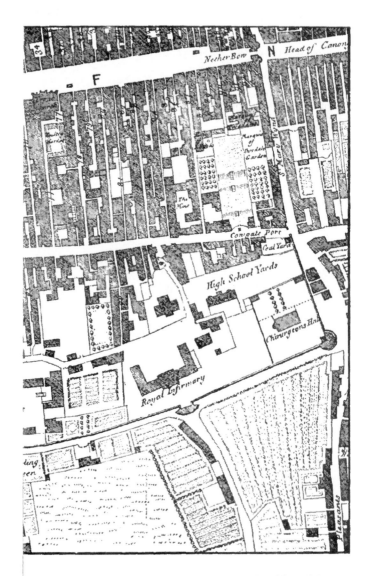

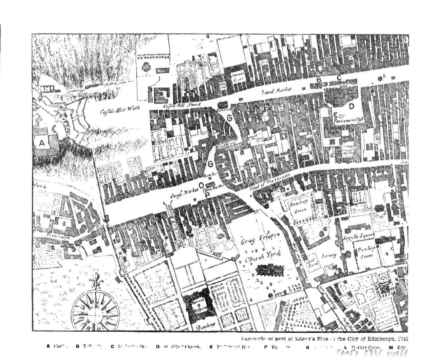

Facsimile of part of Edgar's Plan of the City of Edinburgh, 1742

A Castle, B ..., C Lawnmarket, D St Giles' Church, E Parliament House, F ..., G ..., L Market Cross, M City

NOTABLE SCOTTISH TRIALS

Messrs. William Hodge & Co have arranged for the publication of a series of volumes under the above title, the object of which is to present a full and authentic record of the more notable Trials that have a place in the annals of our Scottish jurisprudence. Of many of these Trials the details are at the present time not readily accessible, being either confined to the pages of official reports or buried in the files of the daily press, and it is intended to issue in a uniform series such a narrative of our more important *causes célèbres* as shall prove not only of interest to the general reader, but also of utility to those concerned, professionally or otherwise, with the study and application of the legal principles involved in the various cases to be dealt with

To each Trial a separate volume will be assigned; and, where verbatim evidence is available, it will be reproduced in full, special care being taken to ensure accuracy of detail

The series is founded upon careful research into every available source of information, and, so far as permissible, the opportunity has been taken of consulting with and acquiring reliable information from gentlemen who may have been authoritatively associated with any of the Trials in contemplation

"A remarkable series "—*Glasgow Herald*

" . Altogether a most interesting and welcome series these 'Notable Scottish Trials.' "—*Law Journal.*

"Messrs William Hodge & Co are doing distinct service not only to the legal profession, but also to the general public by the publication of 'Notable Scottish Trials' "—*Dundee Courier*

" The series of 'Notable Scottish Trials' which has just been initiated with a volume dealing with the trial of Madeleine Smith forms an enterprise on which the publishers are to be heartily congratulated "—*Glasgow Evening Times*

" Messrs William Hodge & Co. are doing good public service in issuing a series of volumes dealing with 'Notable Scottish Trials ' Since many of those trials took place a new generation has arisen, to whom most of the persons tried are mere names, and the series promised by Messrs Hodge & Co will necessarily take the form of educative works of considerable historic value."—*The Scotsman*

" While abounding in the dramatic interest of the 'higher crime,' they are edited with all the completeness and accuracy and attention to the legal issues involved of reports intended for lawyers, and there is no class of reading more useful for students of law than the study of the laws of evidence as they appear in practice during such trials At the same time for the general reader they have the intense fascination of revelation of the darker side of human nature "—*Saturday Review.*

Notable Scottish Trials—*continued*

THE TRIAL OF MADELEINE SMITH   Edited by A DUNCAN SMITH, F S A (Scot), Advocate   Dedicated to Lord Young. Fully illustrated.   Demy 8vo, 400 pp   Price 5s.   1905.

" If all subsequent volumes are as full of interest as the present, their publication should be an assured success "—*Daily News*.

" This full record of the trial, while as ' good as a novel' for many lay readers, has also a deeper meaning for the student of law or of humanity "—*Aberdeen Free Press*.

" The volume has been admirably got up, and the type is beautifully clear."—*Edinburgh Dispatch*

" An excellent production—figuring up the various characters in the drama, and portraying in graphic style the whole tragical romance "—*Glasgow Citizen*

" As a record of one of the most remarkable criminal trials of modern times, the book will be found of supreme interest."—*The Scotsman*

" The publishers are to be congratulated on their selection of Mr. Duncan Smith as the editor of the present number   He brings to his task a delightful freshness, and unfolds the romantic tale in a truly romantic manner   . .   It is only when we come to the appendices that the real importance of Mr. Smith's report is apparent. Those show an amount of research unequalled in any report of the trial yet issued
    It is not too much to say that, if the succeeding volumes maintain the high standard of work which marks the present number, the series should have a ready and abundant market "—*Glasgow Herald*

THE TRIAL OF THE CITY OF GLASGOW BANK DIRECTORS   Edited by WILLIAM WALLACE, Advocate, Sheriff-Substitute, Campbeltown, Joint Author of " Banking Law "   Fully illustrated from contemporary photographs   Demy 8vo, 500 pp   Price 5s   1905

" A work of permanent value "—*The Bailie*.

" The volume is very full and complete "—*Dundee Advertiser*

" It will prove most interesting reading to all commercial men, and especially to those engaged in the business of banking "—*Dundee Courier*

" The reader will find it worth while to peruse the whole extraordinary tale The volume is of absorbing interest all through "—*Evening Times*.

" The evidence on both sides is given verbatim, and the entire work of editing has been exceedingly well done by Mr. William Wallace   There are some excellent portraits "—*Glasgow Citizen*.

" Mr Wallace, the editor, has discharged his duty admirably, and his skilful guidance is exceedingly helpful and valuable   The introductory chapter is a singularly lucid and effective piece of writing "—*Aberdeen Daily Journal*

Notable Scottish Trials—*continued*

THE TRIAL OF DR. PRITCHARD.   Edited by WILLIAM ROUGHEAD,
W S , Edinburgh.   Dedicated to the late Sheriff Brand, Ayr.   Fully
illustrated   Demy 8vo, 346 pp   Price 5s.   1906.

"   The narrative is most interesting, and one which lawyers and laymen
alike will read with fixed attention "—*Law Times*

"   .   . Mr. Roughead's highly interesting book."—*Lancet*

"   One of the most absorbing of a remarkable series "—*Glasgow Herald*

"   This carefully prepared report has real historic value "—*Sheffield Daily
Telegraph*

"   . The record of the trial in the present volume is the most complete and
accurate that has yet appeared "—*Westminster Gazette*

"   .   . The volume, which forms one of the 'Notable Scottish Trials' series, is
the best of its kind we have yet seen "—*Lloyd's Weekly News*

"   This book, which Mr Roughead has edited with a skill and completeness worthy of the highest praise, is a record of great interest to every student of
criminology."—*Scottish Review*

"A volume which is of outstanding interest not only to lawyers and medical men,
but to the general public as well, for the revelation of human nature which it
contains "—*Glasgow Weekly News.*

THE TRIAL OF EUGÈNE MARIE CHANTRELLE   Edited by A.
DUNCAN SMITH, F S.A (Scot).   Dedicated to Sir Henry D Little-
john, M D , LL D   Demy 8vo, 250 pp.   Price 5s   1906

"The book is a thoroughly well-edited chapbook."—*Daily News*

"Apart from its undoubted interest as a tragic story, the book is valuable as a
judicial record "—*Glasgow News.*

"Apart from its interest for lawyers and medical men, the book possesses a strong
fascination for the general reader   It is full of human tragedy "—*Dundee Courier*

"Mr. Duncan Smith may be congratulated on the able manner in which he has
executed his task "—*Law Times.*

"It is an interesting case from the point of view of either the lawyer, the medical
man, the student of crime, or the man in the street."—*Solicitors' Journal.*

"The trial is edited for lawyers and doctors, and not as a mere popular newspaper
report, by Mr. Smith with all the thoroughness which distinguishes the series."—
Saturday Review

2 A

Notable Scottish Trials—*continued*

THE TRIAL OF DEACON BRODIE   Edited by WILLIAM ROUGHEAD,
W S, Edinburgh.   Dedicated to the Honourable Lord Dundas.
Fully illustrated   Demy 8vo, 280 pp   Price 5s   1907.

" The work forms a valuable addition to the series of ' Notable Scottish Trials ' "
—*The Scotsman*

"This volume admirably edited by Mr Roughead.   .   The editor has contributed a very full and well-handled introduction "—*The Daily News*

"The volume is edited by Mr Wm Roughead, whose introduction, giving a
succinct account of the Deacon's career, is a thoroughly capable piece of work "—
The Tribune

" This biography .   more interesting than many novels."—*The Daily
Telegraph*

" This latest volume of the admirable series of ' Notable Scottish Trials ' at present
being published in Glasgow by Messrs William Hodge & Company—the ' Trial of
Deacon Brodie '—is, from all points of view, one of the most interesting and
valuable "—*Glasgow Evening Times.*

"The full report of the trial is here given, and the book is illustrated with a
number of portraits of judges, counsel, and prisoners, which, together with an admir
able introduction, make a work of considerable interest "—*Law Magazine.*

THE TRIAL OF JAMES STEWART (The Appin Murder)   Edited
by DAVID N MACKAY, Writer, Glasgow.   Dedicated to Alexander Campbell Fraser   Fully illustrated.   Demy 8vo, 386 pp
Price 5s   1907

" In compiling this addition to an important and valuable series of criminal trials,
Mr Mackay has shown singular assiduity and industry   He has ransacked the
records and chronicles of the time with care and diligence   His introductory summing up of the case is lucid, judicious, and complete, grasping the facts with a firm
and sure hand, and exposing the hollowness of the theories of the prosecution with
convincing force "—*The Scotsman*

"The volume deserves a permanent place in one's library not only because of its
deep human interest, but by reason of its political and literary association "—
Aberdeen Free Press.

" Mr D N Mackay has done his work well, and it will doubtless give rise to fresh
controversies and be the mine from which new theories will be dug "—*The Tribune*

" In certain respects this is the most interesting of the series yet to hand
The editor of this fascinating volume is Mr. D N Mackay, who has discharged his
task with much ability   To all fond of the mysterious the narrative before
us should make very good reading." —*Law Times*

"Too much praise can scarcely be given to the admirably comprehensive introduction provided by Mr David N Mackay, in which many different points are
elucidated and the reader's path rendered smooth and clear.   .   .   A well-
equipped and most important book "—*Evening Times*

Notable Scottish Trials—*continued*

THE TRIAL OF A. J MONSON   Edited by J. W. MORE, B A
(Oxon), Advocate, Edinburgh   Dedicated to the Lord Justice-
Clerk   Fully illustrated.   Demy 8vo, 480 pp   Price 5s   1908

"Mr More has done his work of editor well, and he contributes a brief but well-written introduction covering the facts of the whole case. . . . This book gives an accurate account of the most famous Scottish trial of this generation "—*Edinburgh Evening News*

"The volume is got up with the same scrupulous care that has been bestowed on the others of the series, and is illustrated in a manner which greatly assists the reader in following the evidence."—*Evening Dispatch.*

"The publishers have been fortunate in securing the services of Mr More as editor He has done his work well   .   Everything has been done to make this report accurate and full "—*Scotsman*

THE DOUGLAS CAUSE.   Edited by A FRANCIS STEUART, Advocate,
Edinburgh   Dedicated to the Honourable Lord Guthrie.   Fully
illustrated   Demy 8vo, 247 pp   Price 5s   1909

"Out of the mass of materials at his command, the editor has woven a narrative of surpassing interest which will appeal to the layman as strongly as to the lawyer."
—*Scotsman*

THE TRIAL OF CAPTAIN PORTEOUS   Edited by WILLIAM ROUGHEAD,
W S, Edinburgh.   Dedicated to the Honourable Lord Ardwall
Fully illustrated   Demy 8vo   Price 5s.   1909

The following volumes are in preparation and will shortly be published :—

THE TRIAL OF LORD LOVAT.   Edited by DAVID N. MACKAY,
Writer, Glasgow

THE TRIAL OF OSCAR SLATER.   Edited by WILLIAM ROUGHEAD,
W S., Edinburgh.

Particulars of other volumes will be duly announced

WM. HODGE & CO., EDINBURGH AND GLASGOW

PRINTED BY
WILLIAM HODGE AND COMPANY
GLASGOW AND EDINBURGH
1909

Ingram Content Group UK Ltd.
Milton Keynes UK
UKHW022321050623
422929UK00005B/477

9 781019 220948